THE MEAT COOKBOOK

NICHOLA FLETCHER

Recipes by Christopher Trotter, Elena Rosemond-Hoerr, Rachel Green

LONDON, NEW YORK,
MUNICH, MELBOURNE, and DELHI

DK UK
Senior Editors Bob Bridle, Vanessa Daubney
Senior Art Editors Lucy Parissi, Sara Robin
Editorial Assistant Elizabeth Clinton
Managing Editor Dawn Henderson
Managing Art Editor Christine Keilty
Senior Jacket Creative Nicola Powling
Pre-Production Producer Raymond Williams
Senior Producers Oliver Jeffreys, Jen Scothern
Art Director Peter Luff
Publisher Peggy Vance

DK US
US Editors Rebecca Warren, Christy Lusiak
US Senior Editor Margaret Parrish
Consultant Kate Ramos

DK INDIA
Senior Art Editor Balwant Singh
Project Editor Neha Samuel
Editor Manasvi Vohra
Art Editor Anjan Dey
Assistant Editor Arjun Pereira
Assistant Art Editor Pallavi Kapur
Managing Editor Alicia Ingty
Managing Art Editor Navidita Thapa
Pre-Production Manager Sunil Sharma
Senior DTP Designer Tarun Sharma
DTP Designers Anurag Trivedi, Satish Chandra Gaur

NOTE: Every effort has been made to include sustainable foods in this book. Food sustainability is, however, a shifting landscape. We encourage readers to keep up to date on the subject so they are equipped to make their own ethical choices.

WARNING: Take care when using knives and saws and when handling animal carcasses and heavy sections of meat. Neither the author nor the publisher can accept responsibility for accidents that may result from following instructions in this book.

First American Edition, 2014
Published in the United States by DK Publishing
4th floor, 345 Hudson Street, New York, New York 10014

14 15 16 17 18   10 9 8 7 6 5 4 3 2 1
001—192992—September/2014

Published in Great Britain by Dorling Kindersley Limited.

A catalog record for this book is available
from the Library of Congress.

ISBN 978-1-4654-2287-3

Color reproduction by Alta Image
Printed and bound in China by South China Printing Co. Ltd.

Discover more at **www.dk.com**

CONTENTS

FOREWORD

Meat, as we all know, was at one time just something you bought at the supermarket. It came in white Styrofoam containers, tightly bound by plastic wrap and identified with industrial black ink. These "pork chops" or "chicken thighs boneless," or, most mysterious of all, "ground beef," were the mainstay of nearly all our diets, and we were, generally speaking, happy about it.

But then something changed. Over the last few years, increasing numbers of people began asking themselves some simple questions. What am I eating? Where does this meat come from? What is the best way to cook it? *The Meat Cookbook* answers these questions and more—as well as containing a multitude of delicious recipes. Nichola Fletcher, its accomplished author, has been both a farmer and a historian, an expert on meat (game, in particular), and a guide for home cooks looking to do more with meat than just unwrap it.

That's a big task. Meat isn't just something you cook, even if it is from small farms, cruelty- and hormone-free, and naturally raised. Really, it isn't even "meat"; it is other animals, in part or whole. Animals have bodies not that different from our own, with muscles and bones, organs and nerves. Taking those bodies apart—which is what butchering essentially consists of—isn't simple. Despite the traditional, seemingly straightforward diagrams that show, with dotted lines, just where every steak and roast can be found on a carcass, the reality of eating animals requires care and patience and skill. And, once the butchering is finished, so does cooking them.

This is all a way of saying that there is more to cooking meat than just seasoning it and heating it. The conscientious modern meat-eater wants to know where the animal came from, how it lived, what it ate, and how it was cut and aged. These things matter. Regardless of how it is cooked or cut, meat goes into our own bodies; in a very real way, it's part of us.

It's also something that binds nearly all peoples together. *The Meat Cookbook* includes not just recipes for many of the meat "classics," but also a broad survey of the way other peoples cook meat. American fried chicken and burgers, Polish bigos, Mexican mole shredded beef, Thai beef salad, blanquette de veau, Greek lamb stew, and so many other dishes, drawn from diverse food cultures, are all here, as are the essentials of how to butcher, age, cure, slice, choose, and chop meat. Even more important, readers can learn the essentials of what meat is: the animals it comes from, how these animals ought to be raised and fed, and everything else a conscientious cook needs to know about meat. Nichola Fletcher has written a comprehensive book you can feast on.

JOSH OZERSKY

MEAT
KNOW-HOW

MEAT MATTERS

MEAT—SUCH A MOUTHWATERING WORD. FOR MANY PEOPLE, A MEAL IS NOT A REAL MEAL IF THERE IS NO MEAT. MOST EMERGING COUNTRIES WANT TO EAT MORE OF IT. CONSUMPTION HAS NEVER BEEN SO HIGH. BUT IT CAN ALSO BE EMOTIVE—THERE ARE MANY REASONS WHY SOME PEOPLE CHOOSE NOT TO EAT MEAT. SO SHOULD WE EAT IT OR NOT? PERHAPS THE ANSWER IS "BOTH." WE CAN EAT MEAT AND ENJOY IT WHERE WE FEEL COMFORTABLE ABOUT THE WAY IT IS PRODUCED, BUT WE SHOULD PROBABLY AVOID IT WHERE WE DON'T.

Critics often say that feeding grain and oil seeds to animals is not a sustainable way to produce food. People should eat the grain themselves. There is some truth in that argument, but it applies mainly to intensively farmed meat such as feedlot cattle (see p142) and intensive pig and poultry production. These systems rely on crops to produce meat quickly and at a price to satisfy the world's demand for cheap meat. Hens are the most efficient converters of grain into food, followed by pigs, cattle, and sheep.

GRASS-FED MEAT

Many areas of the world, however, cannot grow crops sustainably. Think of arid scrub or cold countries; mountains or forest regions. Grasses grow most efficiently in these places. Humans can't digest grass, so the most sensible thing to do is to allow animals to turn it into nutritious meat, which they do admirably.

And then there are wild animals—lots of them. This is meat at its most natural. Yet there are so few hunters nowadays that some populations are out of control. Pigeons raid crops; wild boar dig up vineyards; roe deer nibble young trees; elk lumber across roads into vehicles—they have become pests and have sometimes started to destroy their own environment. Are rabbits eating your vegetable garden? Why not eat the rabbit and enjoy the flavor of the wild combined with your carrots.

THE GRAIN DRAIN

Crops like wheat, barley, soy, oil seeds, beans, and peas are crops that humans can eat. But these same crops are used to make animal feed (known as "concentrates"). Our planet needs its forests desperately, so to cut them down to grow crops creates ecological problems, no matter who eats the crop. To cut them down to feed livestock is certainly questionable in the long-term. So what an animal or bird has been fed on is ethically important, too.

MEAT AND NUTRITION

Meat is a good source of protein, iron, and other nutrients and vitamins, but we are all warned not to eat too much animal fat as this can lead to obesity and heart problems.

Given the environmental problems of feeding animals on grain, it is interesting, but perhaps not surprising, to discover that ruminants (grazing animals such as cows, sheep, deer, and goats)—which munch their way slowly through a natural diet of grasses and vegetation instead of being stuffed with concentrates—are nutritionally far better for us. It is concentrated, high-energy diets that change meat from having "good" fat to having "bad" fat.

THE MEAT TO EAT

Pigs and poultry are more problematic. They have been reared for centuries in people's backyards on a varied diet of scraps and whatever else they can forage in the fields and woodlands. Some are still raised like that for private consumption. But apart from slow-grown Iberian pigs living on acorns, commercial production almost always relies on concentrated feed. The best systems combine concentrates with an outdoor life. So free-range hens and geese that can scratch around or graze grass and outdoor pigs that can wallow in mud and root around for insects produce the best quality meat.

However, the vast majority of pigs and poultry are contained in buildings. They rarely experience the outside world, and are fed not only on concentrates, but in many countries the animals are on antibiotics and growth promoters as well. Intensive feedlot cattle are also given these and other medications. They make meat cheaper. But how sensible is it to use antibiotics in food production? Do we really want to feed our children on meat produced with growth promoters?

PROVIDING CONDITIONS THAT ARE CLOSEST TO AN ANIMAL'S NATURAL HABITAT AND BEHAVIOR IS THE BEST HUSBANDRY A FARMER CAN OFFER HIS STOCK.

IT'S IN THE BREEDING

All over the world animals have adapted to cope with local conditions and to make remarkably good use of available food. Goats thrive in near-desert conditions and climb trees to nibble thorns and leaves. To survive long, arctic winters, reindeer lay down 6in (15cm) of fat in the short summer. Island sheep survive on salt grass and seaweed washed up by winter storms. In dry climates, cattle developed fatty humps to tide them over lean periods. In addition, different breeds have been carefully selected over hundreds of years to produce something extra that farmers want. In the past, domestic animals were selected to produce lots of fat. Nowadays, the reverse is true. Sheep are bred to produce more than one lamb. Some beef breeds now have an extra leg muscle. Pigs and poultry are bred to survive, and even be content, under the most intensive conditions. It is worth noting, however, that most animal diseases are the result of animals being bred for a special characteristic.

HAPPY MEAT

In many countries, consumer pressure has led to a vast improvement in animal welfare, although in other countries they fare much worse. Research into animal behavior helps farmers understand how their livestock can live contented lives and how they can be transported and slaughtered more humanely. This is in everyone's interest because contented animals are more profitable.

Good animal welfare is the art of balance. Too much stress (excitement) produces fear; too little brings boredom with its own problems. Overcrowding is bad for any animal but equally most are happiest living together in flocks or herds. Too much food is just as bad as too little, and for an animal to experience extreme heat or cold can be as bad as not being able to experience any weather at all. Above all, providing conditions that are closest to an animal's habitat and natural behavior is the best husbandry a farmer can offer his stock.

QUALITY NOT QUANTITY

We should feel comfortable about the meat we eat because we have chosen it carefully, thought about how it was produced, and not wasted any. It was only in the 20th century, when people started to eat such large amounts of meat, that obesity became a major problem. So perhaps many of us would lead healthier lives if we chose our meat more carefully, but ate a little less. Perhaps our natural world would be a better place if less meat was raised intensively.

ASK THE BUTCHER

GOOD QUALITY MEAT COMES FROM A VARIETY OF SOURCES. HOWEVER, AS POOR QUALITY MEAT CAN COME FROM THESE SAME SOURCES IT IS IMPORTANT TO FIND A SUPPLIER THAT YOU TRUST, WHERE YOU CAN ASK QUESTIONS AND RECEIVE HONEST ANSWERS.

SHOPPING AROUND

• **Supermarkets** In the West, the majority of meat is bought in supermarkets. These giant conglomerates are highly aware of the need for customer trust and some are proactive in working with their suppliers to ensure good quality at low prices. But where costs are cut and supply chains are complicated, unpleasant practices can, and do, creep in.

• **Markets and farmers' markets** It is tempting to assume that when food is purchased in the open air from a cheery vendor, it will be of superior quality. Usually it will, especially where producers sell their own meat and poultry. But some vendors simply sell on anonymous mass market meat. Even producers selling their own meat may have sausages manufactured for them by a central plant that uses many additives. But increasing numbers of enthusiastic producer– manufacturers are usually found at these specialty local markets and they are well worth seeking out.

• **Butchers' shops** The best ones are family businesses rather than chains. Some have been in the same family for generations and have built up a reputation and a clientèle prepared to pay for excellence. They know where their meat comes from and are likely to have facilities for dry-aging it. They will be able to obtain even the most obscure cut for you (though you may need to order it in advance).

• **Online** As with all online shopping, a good website can disguise a low-grade business. But direct selling with overnight courier deliveries has made it possible for countless excellent small businesses to become viable. The many media guides will direct you to good sources.

DRY-AGING MEAT Cold air circulating around the carcass allows the meat to mature without creating harmful molds. Harmless molds often occur but they are trimmed off.

ASKING THE RIGHT QUESTIONS

The different methods of meat production are described on pp10–11 and will help you decide what to seek out and ask for when buying meat. Almost always, meat that is produced sustainably and under good welfare conditions will be the most expensive. Here are some other key questions to ask when buying meat.

WHERE DOES YOUR MEAT COME FROM?

Local meat is of better quality where the butcher can visit the producer and build up a trusting relationship. But in areas where the land is unsuitable for free-range and grazing animals, local might mean very intensive, so the best meat may be brought in from some distance away, even imported. Provided that it is suitably transported and stored, the quality should not be compromised. However, the further away the source is, the more difficult it is to be really certain of how it was produced.

HOW IS YOUR MEAT MATURED?

Some meat tastes better if it is matured for a period; this practice is more traditional in cold climates. Beef and game meats are usually matured; domestic poultry, lamb, and pork are not. There are two main ways of aging meat:

• **Dry-aging or hanging** This produces the best results. The carcass (or a section of the carcass) is hung in cold, airy conditions so that it slightly dries out and also produces enzymes that tenderize the meat. This concentrates and improves the flavor. Dry-aged meat is usually darker.

• **Wet-aging** Meat (usually boneless) is packed into strong, vacuum bags and all the air is removed. The meat then matures for several weeks and becomes more tender. However, the improvement in flavor gained by dry-aging is not achieved using this method.

WHICH BREEDS ARE YOUR BEEF, LAMB, AND PORK—AND WHAT SPECIES IS THE GAME?

Commercial breeds are selected to produce a particular trait. Sometimes this improves quality, but often the reverse is true. Traditional heritage breeds are still reared, but they tend to be local specialties. Although more expensive, they are worth seeking out because their producers tend to take special care of these rare animals and their meat. Game animals and birds are different species, not different breeds. A good butcher should know which he is selling.

WHAT ARE YOUR MEAT PRODUCTS MADE OF?

A vast array of meat products (such as burgers, meatballs, hot dogs, sausages, and bologna) are made from ground offcuts unsuitable for other forms of cooking. These make efficient use of the whole carcass. However, most commercial products contain additives that help them last longer, or alter their flavor, color, and texture. Very cheap products often contain mechanically recovered meat (MRM) that is usually marked on the label. Most of these products are easy, quick, and cheaper to make at home and will taste much better when freshly made, so consider buying ground meat rather than made-up products.

WHAT DOES THE BEST MEAT LOOK LIKE, AND HOW SHOULD IT SMELL?

• **Color** Each meat has its own natural color, but exercise, green vegetables or grass, the presence of iron, and dry-aging makes it darker. Oxidized meat becomes a dull brown. Vacuum-packed meat can darken or appear iridescent in the pack but reverts to its natural color once opened.
• **Smell** Fresh meat should have a faint, sweet smell, however it is packed. Sometimes, though, vacuum-packed meat that has been stored for some time smells strong when taken out of the package. Leave it in the open air for about an hour and the smell should disappear. If it doesn't, discard it. Game that has been hung will also have a stronger smell.

WHICH CUTS ARE BEST?

It is tempting to stay with a few "best" cuts that are familiar, but all carcasses produce a range of flavors and textures. Prime (ie, expensive) cuts come from the loin and top of the legs. Shoulders and the lower parts of the legs contain more collagen so need longer cooking. Very often, cheaper cuts have the most interesting flavor and texture.

AGED MEAT Dry-aged meat is deep red but not brown; a dark band around the outside indicates partly aged meat. Brown meat has been oxidized.

NON-AGED MEAT Many people think that bright red meat is better. In fact, it has far less flavor than well matured meat.

HOW MUCH SHOULD I BUY?

Eating smaller portions of meat is part of a healthy diet. Although some people enjoy much larger portion sizes, a guideline for main portions is:

• **Boneless meat:** 5–6oz (140–175g).
• **Meat on the bone:** 9–12oz (250–350g).
• **Whole domestic poultry or game birds:** 12oz–1lb (350–450g).
• **Poultry and game bird bone-in cuts:** 9–12oz (250–350g).

Reduce portion sizes for children and older people, or where a meal has many courses.

A CUT ABOVE

THE ENJOYMENT OF MEAT IS MADE UP OF SEVERAL ELEMENTS, INCLUDING TENDERNESS, FLAVOR, SUCCULENCE, AND JUICINESS. PERSONAL PREFERENCE IS ALSO A FACTOR—ONE PERSON'S OVERCOOKED IS ANOTHER'S UNDERCOOKED; ONE PERSON'S CHEWY IS ANOTHER'S DELIGHTFUL TEXTURE; AND A SUBTLE AND DELICATE FLAVOR COULD EQUALLY BE REGARDED AS TASTELESS.

TENDERNESS

Tender meat is the aim of every cook and many aspects of meat can affect its tenderness:

• The age of the animal is important; young animals are always more tender. Old ones have thicker sinew and gristle as well. However, a good butcher can greatly improve the meat of older animals such as mutton or wild deer by trimming off these parts.

• Dry-aging and vacuum-maturing meat (see pp12–13) makes it tender, as does keeping meat in any liquid that excludes the air. So storing meat in oil or in a non-acid marinade will tenderize it.

• Mechanical ways of tenderizing meat, such as beating, grinding, or cutting it across the grain, can shorten the meat fibers to make it feel more tender.

• Some fruit, such as pineapple and papaya, contain enzymes that will break down meat fibers and are used in marinades. Artificial tenderizers contain similar enzymes. Alternatively, Chinese cooks cover tough cuts of meat in a mixture of baking soda, sugar, wine, and flour to tenderize them.

• Using the right cooking method for each cut will make sure it becomes tender. Overcooking roasts and steaks makes them tough, while undercooking stews doesn't allow time for the meat to become tender.

FLAVOR

Good flavor is the second great aim of the cook, whether it needs enhancing or toning down, and it can be achieved by a combination of many things.

The flavor of any fat will be affected by what the animal eats because fats readily pick up flavor, good or bad. So free-ranging and wild animals normally have more interesting

IN THE PINK Juicy meat has a high water content and, since blood is made mainly of water, this is why pink meat can never be dry.

meat. Animals wandering over fields, salt marshes, or heather hills will all pick up nuances of flavor from their varied diet. However, very lean meats such as venison are less affected by diet. On the down side, stress at slaughter, or bruising beforehand, can leave a bitter or sour taste. Intensively raised pigs are especially prone to stress.

Dry-aging or hanging improves the flavor of many domestic and game meats, whereas meat kept in a vacuum pack for too long will have a sour taste.

Perfectly raised and prepared meat needs little enhancement and its flavor is often best enjoyed in its simplest form. But in the kitchen, other ingredients add flavors. Sometimes they disguise an overpowering taste, but usually they enhance flavor. Spices and herbs as well as vegetables, fruits, and liquids all add complexity of flavor.

SUCCULENCE

This is the slippery texture that makes meat so pleasant to eat; it is usually associated with fat. Although fat is nowadays regarded as a mixed blessing, it transforms the texture as well as flavor, especially if the meat has some intermuscular fat and is well marbled.

Fat on the surface of meat keeps the outside moist, and where it is present within the meat, it melts away during the cooking to keep the interior moist too. When meat is lean, cooking it past the pink stage by any method will make it dry unless something is added to keep it succulent. This could be fat, introduced by larding or barding (see p232), or it could be ground fat included in sausages, burgers, and pies. A creamy sauce can also make any dry meat feel succulent.

Succulence can be added without using unwanted fat, too. The silky texture of slowly cooked shin, and other cuts with a lot of collagen, make meat feel succulent. Likewise, vegetables that cook down to a slippery texture not only add flavor but also succulence. An alternative for lean meat is to simmer it and then, when it is cooked, plunge it into a mixture of vegetable oil, herbs, and spices until cool. The oil counteracts any dry texture well.

JUICINESS

Juicy meat has a high water content. This is why pink and red meat is more moist than well-done meat—it is impossible for pink meat to be dry. If there is no fat, meat will feel unpleasantly dry if cooked past the pink stage. As mentioned above, cooking meat

VERY LEAN MEAT
Meats such as venison and bison have little or no visible fat, either within the muscle meat itself or between the blocks of muscle.

LEAN MEAT
This steak has a chunk of fat between the muscles but there is hardly any within the muscle meat.

MARBLED MEAT
This steak has specks of fat evenly distributed within the muscles as well as a generous amount between the muscles.

gently in a liquid and then keeping it immersed until cold will help meat retain moisture and prevent it from drying out.

A HEALTHY DIET

Humans have been eating meat for more than a million years as it contains many beneficial nutrients. Protein is an obvious one, but red meat offers one of the most easily available sources of iron (most Western women are iron deficient). The darker the meat, the more iron it contains, so game meats are especially good.

A healthy diet should not contain too much fat. This is a simple message, but although it is harmful to eat too much saturated fat, some fatty acids (such as Omega-3) are essential for building the brain and repairing our bodies.

For the maximum health benefit, choose meat from wild animals or meat from grass-fed cattle and sheep, or meat from pigs and poultry that live a truly free-range existence.

ASSESSING FAT CONTENT

Fat is distributed throughout the carcass, some species having more than others. The animal's diet will also affect how much fat there is. There are three main types of fat:
• **External fat** This accumulates just under the skin and is thickest along the back and rump of the animal. It is reasonably hard fat and it is easy to trim off any excess. Unless you want more, leave a maximum of ¾in (2cm) of fat to cover a large roast and ¼in (5mm) around small cuts, steaks, and chops.
• **Intermuscular fat** This appears between the individual muscles and is most prevalent in cuts from the shoulder and fore ribs. A good butcher will trim most of it off but pockets of fat will remain.
• **Intramuscular fat or marbling** When animals are in peak condition, small specks of fat become distributed throughout the muscles of the meat. This lubricates it as it cooks and makes the meat feel succulent.

CLEAVER

LARGE
CHEF'S
KNIFE

MEDIUM
BONING
KNIFE

PARING
KNIFE

STAY SHARP

The dos and don'ts of keeping
your knives sharp:

- **Do** store knives on a knife
  rack—either a magnetic or
  slot type.
- **Do** protect sharp tips by
  keeping a cork on them.
- **Do** chop onto a wooden or
  food-grade plastic board.
- **Don't** chop onto hard surfaces
  such as ceramic, slate, stone,
  or steel.

KNIFE STORIES

A CHEF'S FAVORITE KNIFE IS A PERSONAL MATTER. SOME PREFER HEAVY KNIVES; OTHERS FIND LIGHT ONES SUIT THEM BETTER. ONE THING, HOWEVER, IS CERTAIN— THE SECRET TO SUCCESSFUL MEAT PREPARATION IS KEEPING YOUR KNIVES SHARP.

TYPES OF KNIFE
- **Cleaver** Some people prefer to use a cleaver for all kitchen tasks; others never use one at all. Most Chinese cooks use nothing else.
- **Large chef's knife** Use for slicing large pieces of meat and for carving boneless roasts. Use long stroking cuts rather than a sawing motion to produce the neatest slices.
- **Medium boning knife** The thin curved blade allows the knife to be manipulated around bones without damaging the meat.
- **Paring knife** This is invaluable for many tasks, such as boning out poultry or chopping small items.

BLADE MATERIALS
Knife blades are made from many materials, but the most common are:
- **Carbon steel and damasked steel** These are the easiest to sharpen but rust unless oiled. They are unsuitable for dishwashers.
- **Stainless steel** The most common material, it keeps its edge but takes longer to sharpen. Different alloys and ways of tempering them can produce very light, thin blades.
- **Ceramic knives** Although they are very sharp, ceramic knives are expensive, fragile, and need special sharpeners.

ADDITIONAL EQUIPMENT
Equipment lists can seem daunting, but each piece is designed for a particular job and many people enjoy collecting these specialty tools. Not everything listed below is essential and many can be used for more than one function.
- **Meat thermometer** Apart from good knives, this is the most important tool for the meat cook (see p29 for more information).
- **Oven thermometer** Useful for checking the temperature of the oven as very few— especially older ones—actually operate at the marked temperature.
- **Cutting boards** Wooden boards used to be thought of as unsanitary, but now they are regarded as better than plastic (which is harder to clean thoroughly when scored by knives) as wood contains natural antibacterial properties.
- **Tongs** Invaluable for turning roasts and steaks when browning them, tongs prevent fat from being splashed onto the hand. Use long-handled tongs for barbecue grills.
- **Gravy skimmer** This pitcher with a low spout efficiently separates meat juices from fat.
- **Kitchen/Carving fork** Use to lift or turn poultry and large roasts in the oven and to hold meat while slicing. The guard prevents the knife from slipping onto your hand while carving toward you.
- **Poultry shears or strong scissors** Use for cutting through thin bones, usually poultry. Good quality, strong general-purpose scissors may also be used.
- **Trussing needle** A very long, very strong needle that can be threaded with string to truss or tie meat.

POTS AND PANS FOR THE MEAT COOK
- **Stock pot** Stock bones occupy a surprisingly large space, so a stock pot needs to be large (3½–4½ gallons/15–20 liters) and have a lid.
- **Extra large colander or sieve** Use to strain stock into a large bowl or pan. A cheesecloth is useful to strain out fine debris.
- **Cast-iron lidded casseroles** These allow an even distribution of heat. Meat and vegetables can be browned in them before adding liquid and either simmering or oven cooking.
- **Frying pans** Use a large pan for browning many small pieces of meat without overcrowding them. Medium and smaller pans are good for cooking steaks or small pieces of meat. Buy pans with the heaviest base possible for the best heat distribution because thin bases can warp.
- **Wok** Good for stir-frying, woks can be used over gas or charcoal. Electric attachments and stand-alone woks are also available.
- **Deep-fat fryer with basket** Buy one large enough for your needs as deep-fried food must not be crowded or it will absorb the oil.
- **Roasting pans or dishes with racks** Several sizes are useful, including a small dish for two-person roasts. The rack allows excess fat to drain off the meat.
- **Electric slow cooker** These use very little energy to slow-cook meat and are ideal for busy people because they can be left to cook all day.

SHARPENING KNIVES
Blunt knives squeeze the juice out of meat, and can make cutting through skin and sinews hard. There are several ways to sharpen knives:

USING A SHARPENING STEEL
Method 1 Hold the steel vertically with its point on a wooden board or folded cloth. Keeping the angle of the knife consistently at about 10–20 degrees, stroke it down either side of the steel to sharpen both edges.
Method 2 Hold the steel in one hand and the knife in the other. Stroke the knife down alternating sides of the steel toward your hand, keeping the angle consistent at all times.

USING DRAW-THROUGH HAND SHARPENERS
Steel blades inside the device sharpen the knife as it is drawn between them. Handheld and electric (below) versions are available. Press the knife firmly downward and draw it through the device to sharpen it. Remember to tilt the end as you draw the knife through, to make sure the tip is sharpened.

THE RAW DEAL

PROCESSING MEAT HAS MANY FUNCTIONS. SLICING AND CHOPPING MEAT ALTERS ITS TEXTURE SO THAT IT CAN EVEN BE EATEN RAW. GRINDING ALSO MAKES USE OF OFFCUTS TO MAKE A VARIETY OF TRADITIONAL PREPARATIONS.

SLICING, CHOPPING, GRINDING, AND PROCESSING MEAT

- **Slice meat across the grain** to make it feel more tender, or to prevent it from distorting during cooking.
- **Slice meat with the grain** for stir-fry strips so that they don't break apart when cooked.
- **Chop large pieces of meat** before grinding or processing, or into even-sized pieces for frying and grilling so that they cook evenly.
- **Grind meat that is too tough** to cook whole (breaking it into tiny pieces makes it feel more tender), to help it cook quicker, and for terrines, sausages, raised pies, and burgers.
- **Process or pound meat** using a food processor, blender, or mortar and pestle to make a paste for a smooth pâté, stuffing, or quenelles.

HAND-CHOPPING GROUND MEAT

Finely chopping meat by hand produces meat that is far juicier than meat ground with a grinder, which can squeeze out moisture. This method is ideal for making gourmet burgers and steak tartare. Aim to chop the meat as close to the cooking and serving time as possible for a fresher tasting dish. You will need a heavy cutting board and two matched heavy knives, which must be exceedingly sharp:

GOURMET BURGERS These are made from good quality hand-chopped meat with its own natural fat for flavor and succulence. Little else apart from chopped onion is needed.

1 Trim off every scrap of gristle, fat, and sinew from the meat.
2 Cut the meat into ½in (1cm) cubes and spread it out across the cutting board in a single layer.
3 Using a motion rather like beating two drumsticks, use the weight of the knives to chop the meat with an easy rhythm.
4 From time to time, scrape the meat back to the center of the board to ensure even chopping. Continue until the desired fineness is achieved.

MAKING CARPACCIO

Typically made from very thin slices of beef tenderloin cut about ⅛in (2mm) thick, carpaccio can be sliced from raw meat or the outside can be quickly seared first. Partially freezing the meat first makes it easier to cut very thin slices. If the slices are too thick, flatten them by beating them between sheets of plastic wrap.

MAKING GROUND MEAT PRODUCTS

Meatballs, burgers, patties, satays, and koftes all use a ground meat mixture. Most meat contains enough of its own natural fat, but lean meats may need extra fat to keep the meat moist.

As a healthier alternative to adding fat to lean ground meat, add finely chopped vegetables instead. Onions, eggplant, bell peppers, or mushrooms—softened in a very small amount of oil—all work well. Serving ground meat products with a sauce will also help to make them feel more moist when you eat them.

Burger purists use hand-chopped meat (see above) mixed with only salt, pepper, and sometimes a little chopped onion. These burgers can be cooked pink. Most, however, are made from meat and a variety of vegetables, herbs, and spices added to taste. Patties are a flatter version of burgers.

FORMING BURGERS BY HAND

1 Divide the meat into equal portions. Squeeze each one tightly to form a firm ball.
2 Lightly press each ball to flatten the sides. Press harder to make patties.

FORMING BURGERS WITH A BURGER PRESS

1 Line the press with waxed paper or cellophane disks.
2 Fill with meat and press into shape.

FORMING MEATBALLS

Use rubber gloves or wet your hands to prevent the meat from sticking to your fingers:
1 Divide the meat into equal amounts. Make reduced-fat meatballs very small so there is a large surface to be coated with sauce. This makes them seem less dry.
2 Squeeze each portion together firmly and roll it into a ball between your fingertips.
3 Roll the meatballs in flour just before you cook them.

MAKING SATAYS AND KOFTES

Spicy flavored ground meat is pressed onto sticks before being grilled or fried. Miniature versions with a dipping sauce make good canapés:
1 Soak wooden sticks in water to prevent the meat from turning on the stick and to allow even cooking—this also prevents the sticks from burning.
2 Press the meat firmly onto the sticks.

COOKING GROUND MEAT

Ground meat has a higher risk of contamination due to its large proportion of outer surface. Unless you have prepared your own meat and are confident that it has not been contaminated, all these ground meat products should be cooked until the internal temperature reaches 165°F (75°C).

BEEF CARPACCIO The essence of carpaccio is its ultra-thin slices, which make it seem lusciously tender. Scrupulously clean utensils are needed if meat is to be eaten raw.

GLAZING MEAT A good way of introducing different flavors is to glaze meat. Mustard and honey can help spices and herbs to stick to the meat as it cooks.

MEAT KNOW-HOW UNDER THE SKIN

UNDER THE SKIN

USING HERBS, SPICES, AND FLAVORED LIQUIDS WILL TRANSFORM NOT ONLY THE FLAVOR OF MEAT, BUT SOMETIMES ITS TEXTURE AS WELL. DIFFERENT FLAVOR PAIRINGS COMPLEMENT DIFFERENT MEATS—SEE PP32–33 FOR SUGGESTIONS.

SPICE AND HERB RUBS

Rubbing spices and herbs onto the surface of meat, or under the skin of poultry, introduces new flavors. Adding salt or oil helps to draw the flavors into the meat. Leave the rub for several hours before cooking to intensify the flavors.

UNDER-THE-SKIN RUBS FOR POULTRY

• Try making a pocket in a small fillet of meat or poultry, then stuff with herbs and spices mixed with butter or oil into the pocket. Secure with string or a toothpick.
• Lift the skin off the breast meat of a bird and slash the meat underneath. Mix herbs and spices with butter and smear this mixture into the meat. Replace the skin.

HERB CRUSTS

These can be as simple as pressing herbs onto the oiled surface of meat, or using a thicker crust made of herbs and grains bound with egg to add flavor and a crunchy texture. Once you have prepared the crust mixture, press it on firmly so it does not crumble off the meat during cooking. If the crust is thick, allow a little extra cooking time. Note that covering meat with a herb crust will prevent it from browning.

MARINATING MEAT

Marinades flavor meat without preserving it. Acid liquids (such as vinegar, wine, and citrus juice) dry out meat. Oily marinades absorb spice, vegetable, and herb flavors and transmit them to the meat. Depending on its size (a roast or small pieces), marinate the meat for 1–5 hours before cooking.
1 Mix together the marinade ingredients and heat if instructed. If heated, allow to cool before proceeding.
2 Immerse the meat in the marinade. For awkward-shaped pieces of meat, use a strong plastic bag to hold the meat and draw up liquid around it.

SALTING AND CURING MEAT

Using salt to cure meat is an ancient technique. It is simple, because just salt, flavored with spices, is used to draw out some of the meat's moisture, but it is also complicated because only trial and error will produce the effect you want to achieve. Experiment, and keep notes of all your weights and timings.

TYPES OF SALT

Curing salt prevents bacteria forming and maintains the meat's red color.
• **Pickling or kosher salt** A fine salt that dissolves quickly, but does not contain iodine or anti-caking agents that can turn brine cloudy. Good for brine-curing.
• **Coarse salt** Free of iodine or anti-caking agents, it is cheaper but takes a little longer to dissolve. Good for dry-salting.
• **Curing salt or Prague powder no. 1** Often colored pink, this contains sodium nitrite that helps to preserve meat and keeps it red.
• **Dry-curing salt or Prague powder no. 2** Similar to Prague powder no. 1, but contains sodium nitrate as well. Highly recommended for home dry-salting in place of saltpeter.

HOW LONG DOES IT TAKE?

Meat that is to be fully preserved will need longer to cure than meat that will be cooked afterward. The thinner the meat, the more quickly it will cure.
• **Pork belly** Dry-salt or brine for one week to make bacon.
• **Whole pork leg** Dry-salt for 4–6 weeks to make ham ready to cook. After salting it can take 6–12 months to fully dry.
• **Rolled beef brisket** Brine for approximately one week to make salt beef ready to cook (see p150). If salted for longer, soak the meat for 12–24 hours before cooking.

DOS AND DON'TS

• Never use old-fashioned saltpeter, which contains potassium. Use modern curing salt.
• Never use metal dishes for salt cures; they will corrode.
• Boneless meat preserves better than meat on the bone.
• Lightly cured meat has an enhanced flavor but will not be preserved; it must be cooked.
• Due to the risk of food poisoning, do not attempt to preserve poultry. It should always be cooked after being cured.

DRY-SALTING MEAT

Use salt for small pieces, or two parts salt to one part sugar for larger roasts. Add spices if wished. Allow approximately 3lb 3oz (1.5kg) salt mix plus 1oz (30g) dry-curing salt for every 6½lb (3kg) meat. Work in a cool place.

Dry-cured meat is ready when it has lost about 30 percent of its weight, but test it for taste and give it longer if needed.

Adding sugar or honey to the salt prevents the meat from becoming hard. If the meat is very hard after curing, soak it before cooking.

BRINE-CURING MEAT

A more gentle way of curing than salting, the brine can be made of water, wine, hard cider, or other liquids, plus spices and herbs to add flavor. The strength of brines varies, but start with 8¾ pints (5 liters) of liquid for every 2¼lb (1kg) of salt. Add 1oz (30g) of curing salt for a full cure.

Brine meat for 8–12 hours if it is to be cooked or smoked, or for at least one week if being fully cured.

CURING SALT

SMOKING HOT

HOT-SMOKING YOUR OWN MEAT OPENS UP A WHOLE WORLD OF FUN AND THERE ARE AS MANY DIFFERENT WAYS OF SMOKING AS THERE ARE TYPES OF SMOKER. HOT-SMOKING INVOLVES BUILDING A FIRE AND DAMPING IT DOWN WITH MOISTENED WOOD TO PRODUCE SMOKE, WHICH FLAVORS THE MEAT WHILE IT GENTLY COOKS. THE MEAT IS USUALLY FIRST MARINATED OR RUBBED WITH SPICES, AND THEN GLAZES ARE BRUSHED ON DURING THE SMOKING PROCESS TO GIVE A RICH, STICKY CRUST.

IN HOT-SMOKING, the meat should be much farther away from the open fire than when grilling, as it needs to cook for several hours. To make sure the meat does not cook too quickly, build the fire on one side of the grill and place the meat on a rack on the opposite side, then close the lid. Charcoal separators make sure the fire remains in place.

WHAT EQUIPMENT DO I NEED?

The Internet is bursting with suggestions, which range from instructions for building a pit in the ground, or a brick grill, to a professional smoker costing well over $1,500. They will all produce good results. Manufacturers will provide detailed instructions on how to use each one. Three of the most popular types of smoker include:
- **Charcoal kettle grill or bullet smoker** An economical smoker, this type can be used with briquettes or wood charcoal as well as more specialty woods. It can be powered by gas or electricity.
- **Electric wood pellet grill** An electric spark ignites flavored wood pellets that trickle down an auger to the fire. The pellets will have the correct amount of moisture and the temperature can be regulated.
- **Ceramic grill** This uses a very small amount of charcoal in a little firebox. The meat will need spraying with liquid as there is no room for a pan of water.

YOU WILL ALSO NEED:
- **Chimney starter** For lighting the grill, but also for replenishing ready-ignited fuel so the temperature does not drop.

CHARCOAL SMOKING A charcoal and wood mixture is added to the fire; this is dampened to make moist, steamy smoke.

- **Grill thermometer** For measuring the temperature in the grill as the food smokes. The ideal temperature for hot-smoking is 225–250°F (110–120°C)
- **Meat thermometer** For checking if the meat is cooked.
- **Brushes** For applying glazes to the meat as it cooks. Long-handled paintbrushes or cotton mops can be used.
- **Plastic spray diffuser** For spraying the meat while it cooks.
- **Tongs** For turning the meat (preferable to using a fork, which pierces the meat).
- **Insulated gloves** Recommended for protecting your hands and wrists from spitting fat.

WHICH WOOD SHOULD I USE?

You can use any type of wood provided it has not been treated with chemicals. Small logs, chunks of wood, woodchips, shavings, and sawdust are all suitable. Wood pellets are made from compressed sawdust. Unless you are experienced at hot-smoking, it is best to start with a charcoal fire, then add a mixture of charcoal and your chosen wood so the smoke is not too intense and bitter.
- **Pine and mesquite** These woods give the strongest, most resinous smoke.
- **Oak, pecan, walnut, and hickory** These give a deep, richly flavored smoke.
- **Alder, maple, and vine** These woods give a subtle light to medium smoke.
- **Fruit woods** These give a sweet, aromatic smoke.

HOT-SMOKING IN THE OVEN

This is a simple way of hot-smoking without the need for specialty equipment. The meat benefits from being marinated in oil and herbs first, and should be browned before being smoked. Try this with a piece of meat about 2in (4cm) thick. Preheat the oven to 450°F (230°C):

1 Cover the base of a flat-bottomed roasting pan with ½in (1cm) of smoker's sawdust. Add flavorings, such as herbs or fruit tea, and cover with foil. Pierce holes in the foil.
2 Put the meat on top of the foil and cover with a lid or additional foil. Place the pan over high heat until it starts to produce smoke, then cook in the oven for 6 minutes.
3 Remove from the oven and allow it to cool under the foil. When cold, wrap in plastic wrap and refrigerate. Slice thinly and serve with spiced fruit jelly.

HOT-SMOKING A CHICKEN

Use a sweet, mild wood to smoke chicken and sit a pan of hot water beside the meat to make steam. Prepare the chicken by splitting it in half, then brine or marinate (see p21) it for 5 hours using some fruit juice in the liquid. Then rinse, and pat it dry:

1 Lift the breast skin and rub spices, herbs, and butter into the meat.
2 Light the smoker and bring it to 250°F (120°C). Place the chicken halves skin-side up on a rack, well away from the fire with the thighs closest to the heat, and close the lid.
3 Keep checking the temperature and the smoke. Every hour, brush or spray the skin with a flavored liquid. Make sure it does not get too hot and burn.
4 The chicken will take about 4 hours and is cooked when the internal temperature of the thigh meat reaches 165°F (75°C).
5 Once cooked, shred all the meat, mixing all the spices and the glaze from the skin into the meat, and then serve.

SLOWLY DOES IT

LOW TEMPERATURES, LIQUIDS, AND LONG COOKING TIMES ENSURE THAT MEAT STAYS MOIST AS IT COOKS ALL THE WAY THROUGH. SLOW-COOKING IS PERFECT FOR CHEAPER CUTS OF MEAT THAT MAY BE TOUGH OR SINEWY; THEY COST BARELY HALF AS MUCH AS PRIME CUTS. THESE DISHES LEND THEMSELVES TO "GETTING AHEAD," SINCE THE FLAVORS IMPROVE WITH TIME.

BROWNING THE MEAT

Most slow-cooking methods start off by browning the meat. Although it is not essential, it always adds lots of extra flavor and color to the dish.

Make sure the meat is completely dry so that it browns quickly. If meat takes too long to brown, it becomes tough.

Cook the pieces in small batches, making sure they have plenty of space so the outside browns very quickly. If crowded they will release water, which makes them boil rather than brown.

DEGLAZE THE PAN

The frying pan will accumulate a lot of caramelized bits during the browning process. Add a little water to dissolve them and add this delicious browning to your dish, otherwise it may burn onto the pan and taste bitter.

COOKING METHODS

• **Stewing** Small pieces or slices of meat are browned, covered with liquid and cooked in a lidded dish in the oven or on the stovetop. Where there is plenty of gravy, dumplings can be cooked in the stew once the meat is cooked. Electric slow-cookers use very little electricity and can be left to cook all day.

• **Braising** Cuts or roasts are cooked to well-done in a covered dish in a slow oven. Braising uses less liquid than in a stew but the steam produced keeps the meat moist. Fatty cuts cook really well this way; very lean pieces benefit from larding. This method is especially good for poultry pieces or slices of pork and lamb shoulder, which cook in about an hour.

• **Pot roasting and slow roasting** Prime cuts can be cooked pink; tougher cuts are cooked to well-done. Place the meat in a deep tray

BEEFY DISH A deep, rich gravy surrounding meltingly tender pieces of beef; this is the epitome of the perfect stew.

or dish with some vegetables, if desired. Pot roasts usually have some liquid, too. The meat is browned first at a high temperature, then loosely covered and cooked slowly for several hours at around 275°F (140°C).

• **Simmering and poaching** The meat is not browned, so no extra fat is used. A roast or whole bird is completely immersed in liquid (usually water) that is brought slowly to a boil. The temperature is immediately reduced to very low heat so that the water is barely bubbling. Cool the meat in its liquid before straining it off to prevent it from drying out. Reduce the stock and use it to make a sauce for the meat. Simmering is especially good for meat on the bone as the stock is rich and silky.

• **Steaming** Thin strips or small pieces of very tender meat can be cooked in a steamer for very low-fat dishes. Care must be taken to cook the meat enough but at the same time not to toughen it by overcooking. A meat thermometer shows when it is just cooked. The cooked meat is quite bland so benefits from added flavorings. See also sous vide and steam "roasting" on p29.

Ground meat preparations, such as covered terrines, are placed in a dish of water (known as a double boiler) and cooked in the oven—the water ensures that the meat is cooked gently and evenly throughout.

• **Pressure cooking** Meat is prepared in the same way as for stewing or braising, but when the lid and pressure cap are put on and the temperature raised, the pressure in the pan cooks the meat extremely quickly, so this is a very economical way of cooking meat. Make sure the pan is cooled before opening the pressurized lid.

• **Slow barbecue** Perfect for cooking meat slowly so it falls off the bone; it can also be shredded. The process is the same as for hot-smoking (see p22), except that damp wood is not used since no smoke is required.

TASTE AND TEXTURE

• Never try to speed up slow-cooked dishes (except when pressure cooking); if they get too hot, the moisture is squeezed out of the meat, leaving it tough and dry.

• Only dust meat in flour if you want a flour-thickened gravy. Make sure the meat is almost dry and use only a very light dusting or the gravy will be too thick.

• Don't use flour if other starchy ingredients, such as potatoes, are included in the dish.

• If there is flour in the dish, don't cook it on top of the stove as it will stick to the bottom of the pan. Cook it in the oven.

• If a broth is too watery at the end, strain off the meat, reduce the broth, and return it to the meat. Don't boil the meat in the broth or it will fall to pieces.

• Adding vegetables improves the texture and flavor; they are especially helpful for dishes containing lean meat, and also make the dish go further, which reduces the cost.

• Chopped bacon adds flavor to a stew.

• Although herbs and spices are cooked with the meat, only add salt near the end of cooking otherwise the dish could be too salty.

EXCESS FAT

If a stew produces too much fat during cooking, skim off any excess from the top with a spoon or ladle. Start at the center of the dish and depress the spoon, but do not let any liquid enter it. Using a circular spiral motion, move the spoon to the edge of the dish where the fat will have accumulated. Allow the fat to trickle into the spoon and remove it. Repeat the procedure until you have removed as much excess fat as possible.

FAST AND FURIOUS

PAN-FRYING AND GRILLING MEAT IS AN EXCITING METHOD OF COOKING THAT REQUIRES SKILL TO MAKE SURE THE MEAT DOESN'T OVERCOOK. A COMBINATION OF FIERCE HEAT FOLLOWED BY GENTLE RESTING PRODUCES THE BEST RESULTS.

IN GRILLING OR PAN-FRYING MEAT, the aim is to produce a brown, flavorsome outer surface with moist flesh inside. Many cuts of meat can be cooked this way, as well as burgers, sausages, kebabs, and satays.

For rare and medium-rare meat, prime cuts are usually recommended, although many of the cheaper cuts can also be used. For those who like their meat cooked to well-done, only the prime cuts will stay tender enough.

How well cooked the meat should be is a matter of personal preference, although poultry and ground meat products should be cooked until the juices run clear with an internal temperature of 165°F (75°C). In some countries, the same applies to pork (see the cooking charts on pp40–45).

Ideally, meat should be brought to room temperature before cooking so there is less contrast between the outside and inside temperatures during cooking. In reality, most meat is cooked straight from the fridge and needs a little extra time to cook.

PERFECTLY PINK

Some people like meat with a cooked band surrounding an undercooked center. Others prefer the color to be uniformly distributed so the juices and flavors are distributed throughout the meat. To do this requires three stages, especially if it is more than ¾in (2cm) thick. For pieces under ½in (1cm) thick, just follow steps 1 and 3.

1 Brown the outside of the meat as quickly and thoroughly as possible—2 minutes per side is the minimum for a steak.

2 Lower the heat and partially cook the meat.

3 Rest the meat in a warm place for 2 minutes for every ½in (1cm) of thickness to finish its cooking and distribute the juices.

ON THE HEAT When cooking meat on the barbecue grill, make sure there is a warm place to one side of the heat to rest thick steaks or roasts.

SEARING OR BROWNING MEAT

Grilling or pan-frying at a high temperature caramelizes the surface of meat and gives it its delicious flavor. Heavy-bottomed frying pans produce the best results. Thin pans overheat easily and often warp, which causes uneven browning.

Apply a thin layer of pure lard, beef dripping, or oil that can be heated to high temperatures—such as grapeseed, canola, or peanut. Heat the pan until it starts to smoke. Lay the meat in it and do not touch it for a minute or two. Then check the meat and when it is well browned, turn it over. If you turn the meat before it is really brown, some liquid will be pushed out and the meat will boil, not brown.

SHALLOW FRYING AND GRILL PANS

Use a heavy frying pan, or a ridged cast-iron grill pan, which uses less fat and produces a striped effect on the meat. Brown the meat as above, using butter if wished, then reduce the heat. Turn the meat a few more times until cooked. Large pieces of meat need more fat to cook than thin ones.

STIR FRYING AND SAUTÉING

Use a wok or deep-sided frying pan over high heat. Slice everything thinly beforehand, so it cooks evenly. The meat is put in first, then any vegetables, moving the food around quickly all the time. Liquid is added at the end. The whole process takes only minutes and the food is served at once.

CHARCOAL AND BARBECUE GRILLING

This is usually done outside, although indoor artificial charcoal grills are available. Wait until the coals have subsided to a gray ash before cooking. If possible, have a cooler area to rest large pieces of meat after grilling. Very fatty cuts can cause flames to flare up so turn them frequently to avoid a burned coating.

DEEP-FAT FRYING

Large, uneven pieces of meat that do not sit easily in a flat frying pan, or are coated in

BROWNING MEAT If using butter to cook, wait until it stops foaming before placing steaks into the frying pan. This helps the meat to brown more quickly.

batter, can be cooked in a deep-fat fryer. Half fill the pan with oil or fat and heat it to 350–375°F (180–190°C). If the oil is not hot enough, it gets absorbed into the food.

BROILING IN THE OVEN

Meat is placed under a fierce heat that cooks it from above. Good for reduced fat cooking as only a spray of oil is needed to brown the meat. Best for thicker pieces of meat as anything thinner than ¾in (2cm) is easily overcooked.

TANDOOR OVEN

A heavy, cylindrical clay oven built to retain and reflect the fierce heat from a charcoal fire. Meat is covered in a marinade or paste, threaded on metal skewers, and lowered into the oven; it cooks very quickly and keeps the meat juicy.

DOUBLE-SIDED GRILLS

These grill on both sides at once under a closed lid. Surplus fat drains into a tray. Fatty meats cook well but lean meats steam rather than grill and don't brown.

ROASTING MEAT

A PERFECTLY ROASTED PIECE OF MEAT TURNS ANY MEAL INTO AN OCCASION, WHETHER IT IS A HUGE CELEBRATION ROAST, A MEDIUM-SIZED FAMILY ONE, OR A TINY ROAST FOR TWO PEOPLE. UNDERSTANDING WHAT HAPPENS TO THE MEAT WHILE IT COOKS GIVES YOU GREATER CONTROL.

CHOOSING THE RIGHT CUT

Roasts are good on or off the bone, although bone-in cuts look very impressive. When cooking roasts to well-done, bones lubricate the meat. In rare cuts, however, they are less important. Bone-in cuts (with the exception of loin cuts) contain several different muscles, some of which cook at different times and whose grain lies in different directions. This can make carving more awkward.

The best roasting cuts come from the middle part of an animal (ribs, saddle, and loin), or the hind leg, although tender lamb and veal shoulders make excellent, more informal roasts. Tougher cuts can be slow-roasted successfully.

If the meat is marbled with fat, it will stay succulent from rare to well done; very lean meat, such as most game, is not successful roasted to well-done. Very small cuts (less than 2in/5cm thick) are more like a thick steak (see pp174–5).

OVEN ROASTING: THE THREE STAGES

1 Brown the meat. This is what makes roasted meat taste so good. Extra small roasts and birds will not be roasted for long enough to brown the outside so should be browned all over in a frying pan first (see p27) and then only given 5–10 minutes in the hot oven. For larger cuts, start them off for 20–30 minutes in a hot oven at 425°F (220°C) for convection ovens and 450°F (230°C) for standard ovens. Very large roasts, such as turkey and goose, will need 45–50 minutes to brown and may need to be turned around in the oven midway.
2 Partly cook it. The oven is then turned down to 350°F (180°C) to nearly (but not quite) cook the meat. This is where a meat thermometer is invaluable because the number of variables (temperature of the meat when

PERFECTLY COOKED This roast has been rested, so the juices in the meat are evenly distributed, making it moist all the way to the edge.

it started, its thickness and fat cover, oven variations, and degree of doneness required) make it impossible to give exact timings. The meat must come out of the oven when it is 5–8°F (3–5°C) below the desired finished temperature to avoid it overcooking. For dark game meats, taking the meat out 16°F (10°C) below is even better.

3 Rest the meat. This crucial stage completes the cooking and makes the meat more tender. It also distributes the juices evenly because the heat continues toward the center of the meat while the less-cooked juices in the center are drawn back to the edge. This is the secret to perfectly roasted meat. All you need to do is keep the meat warm—it must not be cooked any more. The ideal temperature is 175°F (80°C). A plate-warming drawer is perfect, otherwise put the roast over a stove or a warm radiator. Cover it with foil and a thick cloth to keep in the heat. Make sure the roast does not get cold. The meat thermometer should show the temperature rising until the meat is cooked to your liking.

SPIT ROASTING

This is how all meat used to be roasted and gives arguably the best results of all. Browning, cooking, and resting is combined in one process. The meat is slowly turned in front of a hot fire, held in a cage, or on a metal skewer. Spit roasts work best when the meat has a good covering of fat, so lean meat should be barded (see p232). A drip tray catches the fat and juices. Some ovens have electric spits—use a meat thermometer to check how it cooks.

LOW TEMPERATURE "ROASTING"

This slow method cuts out the second stage of roasting. Meat is cooked rare but there is no danger of overcooking if a meal is delayed slightly. Brown the roast all over, in a pan or a hot oven. Open the oven door afterward and fan out the intense heat. Then cook it very slowly at a temperature of 175–200°F (80–100°C) for several hours. A thin cut—less than 2in (5cm) thick—will cook in about an hour. Large roasts take 2–3 hours or more; use a meat thermometer to show how it is cooking. This method is not suitable for domestic poultry.

SOUS VIDE AND STEAM "ROASTING"

Meat is sealed into a vacuum pack (sous vide) that is immersed in a bath of water kept at a tightly controlled temperature. The process is slow but utterly reliable, although not everyone likes such uniformity of cooking. Steam cooking is similar but the meat cooks in moist steam rather than a water bath. The meat is quickly browned before serving to improve flavor and appearance.

PIT COOKING

This is popular in the Pacific Rim, especially New Zealand. A fire is lit in a sizeable pit containing large stones. The meat and other food is prepared beforehand and packed into a metal basket. This is placed onto the hot stones and immediately covered in wet matting or leaves to produce steam. It is then covered with earth and left to cook for about three hours using the heat stored in the pit.

MEAT THERMOMETERS

A meat thermometer is the best piece of equipment for successful roasting. It is more reliable than any cooking chart because it tells you exactly what stage your meat has reached, whatever its size, weight, or shape, and however inaccurate your oven controls might be. Never submerge any part other than the metal probe in water. Clean it carefully, and use a disinfectant wipe before storing. Avoid touching any bones in the meat, as this distorts the reading. There are two main types:

Clock dial thermometer: These are made of metal and sometimes silicone, and are robust and cheap to buy, with no batteries to run out. They use markers or colors to indicate the doneness of the meat and are easy to read at a glance. Insert the probe into the thickest part of the meat, ideally into the surface facing the oven window so that it can be read without having to move the meat. Leave it in the roast throughout the cooking and resting time.

Digital probe thermometer: The sharp tip makes it easy to probe the thickest part of the meat and quickly read the temperature from time to time. This type can also be used while frying to check the temperature of steak, poultry breasts, and burgers. Longer handled versions with folding probes are also available; these are ideal for the barbecue.

FINISHED INTERNAL TEMPERATURE OF MEAT AFTER RESTING
(Take-out-of-the-oven temperature should be 5–8°F/3–5°C below this.)

BEEF, VENISON, LAMB, GOAT

Blue	120°F (50°C)
Rare	55°C (130°F)
Medium	140°F (60°C)
Well done	150°F (65°C) (not recommended for dark-fleshed game)

PORK

Medium	160°F (70°C)
Well done	165°F (75°C)

DOMESTIC POULTRY

165°F (75°C)

GETTING SAUCY

HOWEVER PERFECTLY COOKED IT IS, ADDING A SAUCE TO DRY-COOKED (ROASTED OR GRILLED) MEAT MAKES IT FAR MORE ENJOYABLE. SOME SAUCES TAKE TIME TO PREPARE SO MAKE THEM IN ADVANCE TO PREVENT THE MEAT FROM OVERCOOKING WHILE WAITING FOR THE SAUCE TO COOK.

MAKING STOCK

Keeping small tubs of reduced stock in your freezer makes cooking any kind of sauce simple. Stock that is not reduced makes a good base for soup. Every time you have spare bones, wrap and freeze them until you have enough to make stock. Or buy some from the butcher. Use a mixture of meaty bones and scraps (for flavor) and bones with cartilage (for texture).

1 Brush the bones with oil and roast them until they are really brown. Don't let them burn though, or the stock will taste bitter.

2 Pack the bones tightly into a large pan with vegetables, if desired, and completely cover with water. Bring to a boil and reduce to a low simmer, or place in an oven heated to 325°F (160°C). Poultry bones should not be allowed to boil, however, or the stock will become cloudy.

3 After 2–3 hours, strain the stock through a fine sieve or cheesecloth. When it is completely cold, skim off any fat.

4 Return the stock to the clean pan. Add wine, if desired. Boil until it has reduced to between one half and one third of its original volume. This will concentrate the flavor.

5 Cool and pour into small tubs or ice cube trays and freeze for later use.

MAKING JUS

These clear sauces, made by boiling off the meat juices after cooking, work best where there is plenty of flavorsome caramelized browning left in the pan or roasting tray. Add concentrated jellied stock for a savory, syrupy texture, or a little fruit jelly for a sweet, syrupy texture.

THICKENING SAUCES

A variety of textures can be added to a dish by adding a thickened sauce. Creamy sauces, for example, are good for well-done meat.

ADDING FLOUR

• Add a few teaspoons of flour to the roasting pan, stir to absorb the juices, then add liquid gradually and let it cook.

• Make a thin white sauce using flour with stock or milk, and add to the roasting pan. This is good for large amounts of gravy.

• Make *beurre manié* ("kneaded butter") by mashing together 2 tablespoons each of butter and flour. Whisk small amounts into a thin sauce and simmer for 10–15 minutes.

ADDING EGG, CREAM, AND BUTTER

• Whisk butter and lemon juice into egg yolks in a water bath. Then add complementary herbs.

• Use heavy cream to thicken sauces. It can be safely boiled and will readily absorb flavors.

• Whisk small pieces of butter into a thin jus over low heat just before serving.

ADDING VEGETABLES AND FRUIT

Cook vegetables or fruit until soft, then rub them through a sieve or blend to a purée. Add this to the roasting pan or sauce.

CREAMY SAUCE Poultry breasts such as pheasant, chicken, or guinea fowl, can feel quite dry when cooked through, so they benefit from a creamy sauce.

EMERGENCY FLAVORS

Sometimes a sauce or gravy lacks taste and needs something—fast—to make it interesting. Decide which flavor pairings will go with your meat (see pp32–3), start by adding small amounts, and don't add too many. Tiny amounts of stock cube can also be used.

Acid flavors: orange, lemon and lime juice, wine, wine vinegar, yogurt.
Sweet, fruity flavors: fruit jellies, fruit juices, honey, brown sugar, hard cider, spirits.
Rich, savory flavors: soy sauce, tea, mustard, coffee, cocoa powder, curry paste.

BÉARNAISE SAUCE

Makes ³/₄ cup

Prep: 10 mins   **Cook:** 5 mins

INGREDIENTS

2 small shallots, finely chopped

1 tbsp chopped tarragon

2 tbsp white wine vinegar

2 tbsp white wine

1 tsp peppercorns, crushed

3 egg yolks

13 tbsp unsalted butter, softened and cubed

salt and freshly ground black pepper

1 tbsp lemon juice

1 Put the shallots, tarragon, vinegar, wine, and peppercorns in a heavy nonmetallic saucepan and boil for 2 minutes, or until reduced by at least half. Strain through a sieve, and set aside to cool.

2 Put the egg yolks and 1 tbsp water in a heatproof bowl, set over a pan of barely simmering water. The bowl must not touch the water. Whisk in the cooled liquid, then whisk in the butter, one cube at a time, until it has melted and combined. Season to taste with salt, pepper, and lemon juice.

BLUE CHEESE DRESSING

Makes 1 cup

Prep: 10 mins

INGREDIENTS

³/₄ cup sour cream

3¹/₂oz (100g) Roquefort cheese, crumbled

1 garlic clove

1 tsp Dijon mustard

1 tbsp white wine vinegar

1 tbsp finely snipped chives

salt and freshly ground black pepper

1 Place the sour cream, cheese, garlic, mustard, white wine vinegar, and 3 tbsp of water in a food processor, and blend until smooth. Transfer the mixture to a bowl, and stir in the chives. Season to taste with salt and pepper.

2 Pour into a serving bowl and chill until ready to serve.
(This dressing can be made 3 days in advance and kept in the refrigerator.)

HOLLANDAISE SAUCE

Makes ³/₄ cup

Prep: 10 mins   **Cook:** 5 mins

INGREDIENTS

1 tbsp white wine vinegar

juice of 1/2 lemon

3 large egg yolks

salt and ground white pepper

12 tbsp butter

1 Put the vinegar and lemon juice in a small saucepan. Bring to a boil and remove from the heat.

2 Meanwhile, place the egg yolks in a food processor or blender, season with a little salt and pepper, and blend for 1 minute. With the motor running, slowly add the lemon juice and vinegar mixture.

3 Put the butter in the same pan and leave over low heat until melted. When it begins to foam, remove from the heat. With the food processor running, gradually add the butter to form a thick sauce. Serve immediately.

CRANBERRY SAUCE

Makes 1¹/₄ cups

Prep: 5 mins
Cook: 15 mins

INGREDIENTS

9oz (250g) fresh or frozen cranberries

1 small shallot, finely chopped

¹/₃ cup light brown sugar

zest and juice of 1 orange

4 tbsp red wine or port

1 Put the cranberries in a sauce pan with the shallot, sugar, orange zest and juice, and red wine. Bring to a boil, stirring, until the sugar is dissolved.

2 Simmer gently for 10–12 minutes, or until the cranberries are beginning to break up.

3 Leave to cool, then transfer to a serving dish or storage jar.
(This sauce can be kept refrigerated for up to 1 week.)

BÉARNAISE SAUCE

HOLLANDAISE SAUCE

BLUE CHEESE DRESSING

CRANBERRY SAUCE

FLAVOR PAIRINGS

A whole world of ingredients is now available to the cook. Although some are common partners to all meat, others go particularly well with certain meats. Sometimes it is the flavor combinations that excite us, sometimes a texture complements the meat. Here is a brief guide to get you started.

POULTRY

With their delicate flavor, turkey, chicken, and Cornish game hens make a good background for a variety of flavors. Duck and goose benefit from stronger flavors that counteract the flavorsome layer of fat.

- Cardamom
- Paprika
- Ginger
- Citrus fruit
- Yogurt
- White wine
- Cherries
- Miso

PORK

With its slightly fungal overtones, combined with its fat, pork can absorb complex and powerful flavors. Where fat is trimmed off, it is more delicate and some poultry flavors apply.

- Capers
- Soy sauce
- Oyster sauce
- Cloves
- Hard cider
- Sage
- Nutmeg
- Leeks
- Apples

VEAL

Being such a pale and delicately flavored meat, veal is traditionally paired with delicate seasonings, although occasionally a small amount of something piquant accentuates its subtle flavor.

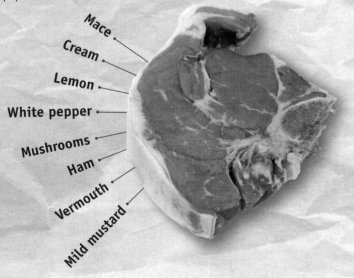

- Mace
- Cream
- Lemon
- White pepper
- Mushrooms
- Ham
- Vermouth
- Mild mustard

BEEF

One of the most robustly flavored of meats, beef delights in powerful flavors, but use these sparingly. If the beef is very lean, use slippery textures to keep it from feeling dry.

- Black pepper
- Tarragon
- Chile
- Cilantro
- Horseradish
- Red wine
- Truffles
- Mustard

LAMB AND YOUNG GOAT

Even though lamb is leaner than mutton, it can still carry an amount of fat, so choose ingredients that cut through this. Young goat is leaner, so pairs with delicate flavors.

- Rosemary
- Oregano
- Eggplant
- Garlic
- Harissa
- Mint
- White wine
- Red currants
- Apricots

MUTTON AND OLD GOAT

Both dark and powerfully flavored, mutton and old goat meat work well with punchy flavors and moist textures. Try also some of the recommendations for dark game.

- Cardamom
- Pearl barley
- Fennel
- Caraway
- Turnip
- Vinegar
- Red currants
- Fresh cilantro
- Cashews
- Olives

LIGHT GAME

From pheasant, partridge, woodcock, and quail to rabbits, light-fleshed game meat has a huge range of complex and delicate flavors that may sometimes be enhanced by hanging.

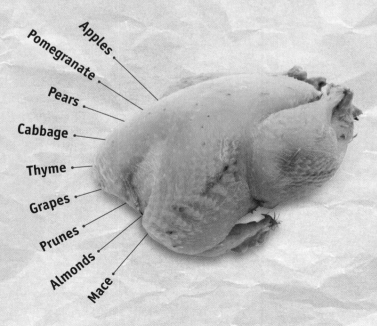

- Apples
- Pomegranate
- Pears
- Cabbage
- Thyme
- Grapes
- Prunes
- Almonds
- Mace

DARK GAME

Hanging dark game meat, such as venison and hare, can make it taste powerful, but when fresh it has a concentrated meaty taste. These meats go well with fruity flavors and succulent textures.

- Cranberries
- Fennel
- Wild mushrooms
- Eggplant
- Ginger
- Juniper
- Whisky
- Chocolate
- Pine nuts
- Red cabbage

MORE FOR LESS

MEAT CAN BE AN EXPENSIVE INGREDIENT AND SHOULD NEVER BE WASTED. OVER THE CENTURIES, THE MANY WAYS OF MAKING A MODEST AMOUNT OF MEAT STRETCH TO FEED A FAMILY HAVE EVOLVED INTO A WHOLE RANGE OF TASTY DISHES.

REDUCING THE COST
- Use the whole beast. Prime cuts are an expensive luxury and are best enjoyed only occasionally. Use cheaper cuts more often.
- Explore the world of ground meat dishes. This is one of the least expensive forms of meat, but makes countless tasty dishes, from meatballs to satays.
- Try cooking some offal (see pp270–87 for recipes). You might be amazed at how delicious and cheap it can be.
- Cook several portions at once and freeze some for another time. This also makes the best use of the oven or stove, and your time.

STARCHY SIDES
Many cuisines have traditional ways of making a small amount of meat feel satisfying. This often involves serving some delicious form of starch either just before the meat or alongside it.

PASTRY
Pastry can transform a small amount of meat into a delicious pie or casserole.
- Dish meat pies are topped with a filling crust of pie dough or flaky pastry.

PASTA SAUCES A creamy sauce coats pasta, such as spaghetti, well and requires only a small quantity of meat.

- Pork pies are completely enclosed in a hearty pastry crust.
- Meat pies can also be covered in a rich lard pastry and steamed in a covered bowl.

DUMPLINGS
Made with flour, fat, baking powder, and seasoning, dumplings are made by forming balls and dropping them into a bubbling stew or broth. Many contain herbs and vegetables.

PASTA AND NOODLES
These filling, starchy sides—made from flour, egg, and water—require only a small amount of meat sauce to taste good.

BATTER
- Yorkshire pudding (popovers) are batter that is oven cooked in very hot fat. Traditionally served with gravy before the meat, it is now usually served with roast beef.
- Spätzle are made from a thick batter forced through holes into boiling water to make small irregular shapes. Sometimes they are fried in butter afterward.

STUFFING
This is a mixture of bread crumbs, seasoned with onions, herbs, and spices, all bound together with egg.
- Small balls of forcemeat can be fried and served with meat dishes.
- Stuffing can be baked in a dish and served alongside poultry or meat.
- Stuffing can be used to stuff birds, either in the cavity or under the skin.

VEGETABLES
Serving a variety of interesting vegetables makes the meat go further.
- Serve them in a sauce to add a creamy texture for fried or roasted meat.
- Scatter lots of fresh herbs or lemon juice on them just before serving.
- Boil root vegetables and add them to a vinaigrette and serve warm with fresh herbs.
- Dip them in batter or egg-and-bread crumbs and fry them as a great contrast to stews.

- Roast root vegetables alongside roasting meat for added color and flavors.
- Add layers of soft vegetables such as canned tomatoes, cooked onions, eggplant, or bell peppers to ground meat dishes to bulk them out and add flavors.

USING LEFTOVER MEAT
There are many ways of turning leftover meat into a delicious second meal.

MAKING RISSOLES
If there is a small amount of cooked meat left over, use it to make rissoles:
1 Chop the leftover meat finely. Then cook and mash some potato, parsnip, or other starchy root vegetable.
2 Stir in the meat along with some fresh herbs and seasoning. Roll in bread crumbs and fry.

MAKING A PIE
After a roasted chicken meal, it is surprising how much meat is left on the bird. This is perfect for making a pie:
1 Remove all the meat from the carcass and mix it with leftover gravy or sauce. If there is not enough gravy, make a white sauce from butter, flour, and milk.
2 Add some vegetables, such as cooked onions and mushrooms.
3 Pour the mixture into a dish, cover with pastry, and serve as a delicious pie. (Alternatively, leftover chunks of roast or stewed meat can be made into pasties.)

MAKING PASTA SAUCE
This is a good option when only a small amount of meat is left over:
1 Chop the meat finely, add any leftover sauce, as well as some cooked onion, garlic, tomatoes, and herbs.
2 Moisten with liquid such as water, stock, wine, or cream, and serve with pasta.

SLOW COOKED Cheaper cuts of meat make delicious meals when slowly cooked. Add lots of vegetables such as onions, leeks, and carrots to make it go further.

FREEZING MEAT

As long as raw meat is wrapped tightly in a thick layer of plastic to exclude the air, it will keep for many months in the freezer. Vacuum-packed meat keeps for years.

- Cooked meat that is frozen in its liquid—such as a stew—will freeze well for several months. Ensure it has cooled before freezing.

- Freeze ground or finely chopped meat products in thin packs so that they defrost quickly and evenly. They will also keep for several months.

Note that the following situations can lead to unpleasant tasting meat, although it will not be harmful:

- Fat eventually changes its flavor and will taste rancid when frozen for too long.

- Cooked products with a high water content—such as terrines and pies—become mushy and wet when frozen for too long.

- If air reaches meat through burst packaging, the surface will become white and dry with freezer burn. This can be cut off.

- Whole poultry is prone to freezer burn in the cavity.

THAWING MEAT

Thaw meat in as cold an environment as possible to avoid the cell walls breaking down and releasing too much moisture.

- If using a microwave to thaw meat, use the lowest possible setting and allow it to stand for a while afterward to avoid moisture loss.

- Thaw large pieces in the fridge so that the outer surface does not become too warm while the interior defrosts.

- A little liquid is always produced so place meat in a dish in the fridge to prevent moisture dripping onto other food.

- Vacuum-packed meat can be quickly and safely thawed in a bowl of cold water. Even a large roast will thaw in about two hours.

CARVING POULTRY

On all poultry, the dark leg and thigh meat is the most succulent. Breast meat is paler and more tender, but can be dry. Remove the wishbone before cooking to make carving the breast easier.

CARVING KNOW-HOW

All meat is easier to carve if it has been rested beforehand. If the meat squeaks as it is being carved, then either it is undercooked, or it has not been rested for long enough.

THE CARVING KNIFE

A carving knife should be thin and flexible but strong enough to cut through joints. Above all, the knife needs to be very sharp to avoid flaking the meat rather than cutting it. A blunt knife will squeeze the juice out of the meat. The carving knife should be long enough to protrude 2in (5cm) either side of the roast to allow large slices to be cut, using a sawing action.

CARVING FORK

A carving fork has a guard to prevent the knife from slipping up the fork when cuts are being made toward the fork. It also has curved prongs so that it can be used to hold the meat in place while being carved.

WHAT TO CARVE ON?

Any meat cooked to well done can be carved on a board that won't blunt the knife. If the roast or bird has a lot of red juices, these will run off a board. In that case, use a warm carving platter that will collect these juices. For informal eating, slow-roasted meat can be carved or pulled off the bone and served in the roasting pan. Pour off any excess fat first, and add a little liquid to dissolve the roasting juices, then carve the meat and allow it to soak up all the juices.

REMOVE STRING AND SKEWERS

Remove any skewers, trussing strings, or elastic bands before carving. If possible, remove any netting, although be aware that sometimes this causes rolled meat to fall apart.

CARVING SMALL BIRDS

Small birds may be served whole, or halved. Or the legs and breasts are removed. This is a little more wasteful, but much easier to eat with a knife and fork.

1 Cut the bird lengthwise along the breast bone. Open out the bird.

2 Using strong scissors or a heavy knife, cut down either side of the backbone to divide the bird in two.

CARVING CHICKEN AND MEDIUM-SIZED BIRDS

All parts of a chicken and domestic duck will be tender. But on some game birds, the legs, and in particular the drumsticks, can be tough and sinewy.

1 Bend the legs outward and remove them at the joint. Serve whole or divide into drumsticks and thighs.

2 Carve the breast into slices, starting at the thicker (neck) end (see Step 5, opposite). Cut off the wings and serve separately if wished.

CARVING A TURKEY OR LARGE GOOSE

Only carve off as much meat as you will need because the rest of the meat will remain moist on the carcass. Serve the meat with stuffing, either from the cavity or from a separate dish.

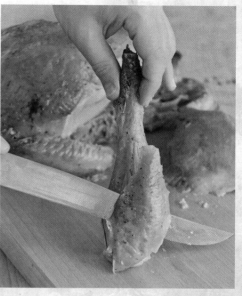

1 Remove the wishbone. To do this, lift up or cut off a small flap of skin from the neck end. Feel for the wishbone with your fingers. Cut around it as closely as possible, then pull it out.

2 Now remove the leg. Pull it outward using a carving fork and then cut through it at the joint.

3 Divide the leg into drumstick and thigh. Then slice off the leg meat parallel to the bone, including the skin if desired.

4 Cut off the wing at the joint, including a little bit of breast meat. Divide it at the joints and carve the meat as above. Alternatively, reserve the wing for stock.

5 Carve the breast into slices, starting at the thicker (neck) end. Place the back of the fork against the meat as you carve it to hold the slices in place.

6 Repeat for the other side of the bird, but this time secure it by sticking the carving fork straight down into the carcass of the side without any meat.

CARVING CUTS OF MEAT

All cuts of meat will feel more tender if carved across the grain of the meat, rather than with the grain. However, very tender cuts, such as loin and fillet, can cope with being cut with the grain. Steaks and tiny cuts may be so thin that to cut across the grain would make the slices too small. They should be cut on the slant to make the slices bigger, but always cut across the grain.

CARVING RIB AND LOIN CUTS

Racks are carved by cutting between the ribs. Beef ribs are usually carved by taking the meat off the bone first. Boneless loin cuts are usually carved across the grain.

1 Run the carving knife down the inside of the ribs, keeping it flat against the bone. Turn the knife outward 90°. Cut the meat off the wing bone or rib.

2 Turn the meat over and remove the fillet, if present, using the same procedure. Cut the meat across the grain into slices.

CARVING SADDLE AND RACK CUTS

If a rack cut has had the chine bone fully removed, then it is simply sliced between the rib bones. If not, carve like a saddle. A young, tender saddle can be carved along the length of the muscles.

1 Place the meat with the fillet/rib side facing downward. Run the knife down one side of the backbone. There is a small bump at the base; make sure the knife goes over it to avoid cutting into the muscle. Turn the knife outward 90° and cut the meat off the wing bone or rib.

2 Cut the meat across the grain into slices. Repeat on the other side, if it's a full saddle. Turn the meat over and remove the fillet(s), if there are any. Slice on the slant, across the grain, and serve each person some loin and some fillet.

CARVING A WHOLE LEG ON THE BONE

A whole leg is much easier to carve if the pelvic bone (or aitch bone) has been removed before cooking.
If it hasn't, ask the butcher to do this, or follow the instuctions on p293.

1 Cut off a thick slice of the meat from the thinner side of the bone so that it sits firmly on its base.

2 With the plump muscle uppermost, start to slice straight across the meat until you hit the bone. Continue to cut slices about ¼in (4mm) thick.

3 Turn the knife and make a horizontal cut along the top of the bone to release the slices.

4 Turn the meat and repeat the exercise. Cut slices on the slant, so that they are not too small.

CARVING A SHOULDER CUT

Carving a shoulder is similar to carving a leg, except for the curious shape of the bladebone.

1 Turn the shoulder skin-side uppermost. Cut all the way down one side of the bladebone. Tilt the knife 90° outward to lift the meat off the flat of the bone.

2 Repeat with the other side. Carve both these muscles across the grain into slices. Turn the cut over and carve the meat off the other side, slightly slanting it to make the slices larger.

COOKING CHARTS—POULTRY AND FEATHERED GAME

CUT	BROIL/GRILL	PAN-FRY/STIR-FRY	ROAST	BRAISE/STEW
NOTES	Internal-temperature reading for all domestic poultry: 165°F (74°C). Use a meat thermometer to check internal temperature. **For Ostrich, see page 45.** **Temperatures** listed are for general cooking, but may vary in recipes.			
CHICKEN AND TURKEY Whole or half chicken, chicken quarter, bone-in chicken breasts, turkey quarters	**Chicken quarter:** Grill on medium heat for 25–30 mins, turning at least twice, or until cooked through. **Half chicken and turkey quarters:** Broil skin-side down at medium heat for 30 mins. Turn, then broil 15–20 mins, until cooked. Brown skin side before serving. Not recommended for whole, bone-in breasts, or whole turkey.	**Chicken quarter:** Grill or fry in deep fat for 20–30 mins, or until cooked through.	**Whole** or **half chicken:** Preheat oven to 350°F (180°C). Roast for 20 mins per 1lb (450g) plus 20 mins, or until juices run clear. **Chicken quarter:** Roast for 30 mins, or until juices run clear. **Turkey:** Slow-roast unstuffed, whole turkey at 325°F (160°C) for 3½–4 hours for 6–9lb (3.5–5.5kg); 4–4½ hours for 12–15lb (5.5–7kg), and 4½–5 hours for 15–20lb (7–9kg). Do not undercook. Rest for 30 mins.	**Whole** or **half chicken:** Brown if desired, then add liquid, plus vegetables if required, and cover. Simmer or stew at 325°F (160°C), for 1–2 hours. **Turkey:** Stew turkey pieces as indicated for chicken, adding 30 mins to cooking time.
Whole leg, thigh, drumstick	Grill or broil whole leg, thigh, and drumstick as indicated for the chicken quarter.	Cook whole leg, thigh, and drumstick as indicated for a quarter. Not recommended for larger pieces of turkey.	Roast whole leg, thigh, and drumstick as indicated for a quarter.	Simmer or stew whole leg as indicated for a whole or half chicken, but for 1 hour. Also suitable for soup. **Turkey:** Stew turkey as indicated for chicken, adding 30 mins to cooking time.
Wing	Grill or broil chicken wings for 20–25 mins, turning at least twice, or until cooked through.	Cook wing as indicated for a quarter. Not recommended for larger pieces of turkey.	Roast wing as indicated for a quarter, but for 20 mins.	Simmer or stew wing as whole or half chicken, but for 1 hour. Also suitable for soup. **Turkey:** Stew turkey as chicken, adding 30 mins to cooking time.
Skinless, boneless breast	Grill or broil skinless, boneless breast for 20–30 mins turning at least twice, or until cooked through.	Cook skinless, boneless breast as for a quarter, but for 10–20 mins, or until cooked through. Not recommended for larger pieces of turkey.	Brush with oil, season, and roast at 400°F for 15–20 minutes, or until cooked through.	Simmer or stew skinless, boneless breast as whole or half chicken, but for 1 hour. **Turkey:** Stew turkey as indicated for chicken, adding 30 mins to cooking time.
Tenders, diced and sliced chicken and turkey	Heat grill or broiler to medium-high. Thread onto skewers and brush with oil. Brown on all sides, then cook for 10–15 mins, or until cooked through. **Turkey:** Broil turkey quarters as indicated for half chicken.	Heat oil in a frying pan over high heat. Brown dice all over, then lower heat and continue cooking for 5–15 mins (3–5 mins for tenders and strips), or until cooked through. Not recommended for larger pieces of turkey.	Not recommended.	Not recommended for tenders or small slices. **Diced and thick slices:** Simmer or stew as indicated for a whole or half chicken, but for 1 hour.
Ground poultry	Heat grill or broiler to medium-high. Press the meat onto skewers or shape into patties; season with salt and pepper. Cook for 10–20 mins, depending on thickness, or until cooked through.	Heat oil in a frying pan over medium heat. Press meat onto skewers or shape into patties; season with salt and pepper. Cook for 10–20 mins, depending on thickness, or until cooked through.	Not recommended.	Brown meat and vegetables, then add liquid and simmer, or cook at 325°F (160°C) for 1–1½ hours.
CORNISH GAME HEN AND SQUAB	Halve or butterfly. Cook for 10–15 mins per side, or until cooked through.	Not recommended.	Roast whole at 425°F (220°C) for 20–30 mins.	Brown the meat all over. Add liquid and cook at 325°F (160°C) for 1–1½ hours, or until tender.
DUCK AND WILD DUCK (e.g., MALLARD)	**Duck:** Broil breast for 2 mins per side, then cook for 8–10 mins with skin side nearest the heat. Rest for 2–3 mins. **Wild duck:** Broil breast 3–5 mins per side until rare or pink, then slice thinly.	**Duck:** Cook breast for 2 mins per side, then cook for 10–12 mins skin-side down. Rest for 2–3 mins. **Wild duck:** Pan-fry breast 3–5 mins per side until rare or pink, then slice thinly.	**Duck:** Roast whole for 30 mins at 425°F (220°C), then reduce to 350°F (180°C) for 1–1½ hours. **Wild duck** (young birds only): Brown by searing, then roast for 30–45 mins at 425°F (220°C). Rest for 5 mins.	**Duck:** Stew as indicated for chicken. Remove excess fat before serving. **Wild duck:** Brown the meat all over. Add liquid and cook at 325°F (160°C) for 2–2½ hours, or until tender.
GOOSE AND WILD GOOSE	**Goose:** Broil breast for 5 mins per side. Cook for 10–15 mins skin-side down. Rest for 5 mins. **Wild goose:** Only broil young wild goose. Serve rare.	**Goose:** Sear breast for 5 mins per side. Cook for 15–20 mins skin-side down. Rest for 5 mins. **Wild goose:** Only broil young wild goose. Serve rare.	**Goose:** Roast whole for 45 mins at 425°F (220°C), then at 350°F (180°C) for 2–2½ hours. **Wild Goose** (young birds only): Roast as above, but for 30 mins at 425°F (220°C), then at 325°F (160°C) for 1–1½ hours.	Stew goose pieces as indicated for chicken but for 1½–2 hours. Remove excess fat before serving.
PHEASANT AND GUINEA FOWL	Broil breast for 7–10 mins per side, or until juices run clear.	Cook breasts for 7–10 mins per side, or until juices run clear.	Roast whole birds at 190°C (375°F) for 40–50 mins, or until juices run clear. Rest for 5–10 mins. Do not overcook.	Brown the meat all over. Add liquid and cook at 325°F (160°C) for 2–2½ hours, or until tender.
GROUSE, PARTRIDGE, SQUAB, QUAIL, SMALL WILD DUCK, WOODCOCK	**Grouse, partridge,** and **squab:** Halve or butterfly. Cook for 10–15 mins per side, or until juices run clear. **Quail, wild duck,** and **woodcock:** As above, but cook for 7–10 mins per side.	**Grouse, partridge,** and **squab:** Cook breast 2–4 mins per side until rare or pink, then slice thinly. **Quail, wild duck,** and **woodcock:** Not recommended.	Only roast young birds. Brown the breasts, then roast at 400°F (200°C) for 20–30 mins (up to 40 for grouse). Rest before serving.	Brown the meat all over. Add liquid and cook at 325°F (160°C) for 2–2½ hours, or until tender.
SNIPE	Using a hot broiler, cook for 10–15 mins, turning twice.	Not recommended.	Roast at 425°F (220°C) for 10–15 mins, then rest for 5 mins.	Brown all over in butter, then simmer for 30–45 mins, or until tender.

PORK

CUT	BROIL/GRILL	PAN-FRY/STIR FRY	ROAST	BRAISE/STEW
NOTES	Internal-temperature reading for well-done pork: 165°F (74°C). Remove from heat and rest when thermometer reads 145°F (63°C). Use a meat thermometer to check internal temperature. **Temperatures** listed are for general cooking, but may vary in recipes. **For timing,** weight is less important than if meat is sliced, diced, or cooked as a roast.			
Boston shoulder (Boston butt roast and blade roast)	Not recommended.	Not recommended.	Not recommended.	Preheat oven to 325°F (160°C). Season meat; brown in hot oil in a Dutch oven. Transfer meat to a plate and drain all but 1 tablespoon of the oil. Return the pan to the stove on medium heat, add chopped onions or garlic (or both), season with salt and pepper, and cook until soft. Add liquid (wine, water, or broth) and scrape the pan to add any brown bits. Add meat, bring to a boil, cover, and put in the oven. Braise until tender enough to shred with a fork.
Picnic shoulder (smoked or fresh hock, picnic roast)	Not recommended.	Not recommended.	Not recommended.	Cook as indicated for the Boston shoulder roast.
Loin (sirloin, Canadian bacon, boneless loin roast, bone-in center loin, tenderloin, loin chop, rib chop, blade chop, baby back ribs, country-style ribs)	**Tenderloin, loin chop, rib chop, blade chop:** Rub with oil; season with salt and pepper. Cook over medium-hot grill or under broiler until browned. Flip and cook to desired doneness, or 150°F (65°C) for medium. **Baby back and country-style ribs:** Brush with barbecue sauce and grill.	**Tenderloin, loin chop, rib chop, blade chop:** Oil, and season with salt and pepper. Over medium-high heat, cook meat in a frying pan until browned. Flip; cook to desired doneness. Stir-fry **tenderloin** strips and vegetables in oil. Dry-fry **Canadian bacon** over low heat.	**Sirloin, boneless loin roast, bone-in center, tenderloin, loin chop, rib chop:** Preheat oven to 450°F (230°C). Coat in oil; season with salt and pepper. Place meat in a roasting pan and roast until golden brown—150°F (65°C) for medium, 165°F (74°C) for well-done.	**Sirloin, boneless loin roast, blade chop, baby back ribs, country-style ribs:** Braise as indicated for the Boston should roasts. If grilling unsmoked **ribs**, they should be braised first.
Side (spareribs, bacon, pork belly)	**Spareribs** can be grilled or broiled over medium heat if they are smoked or have been braised first. Coat with sauce and cook until heated through.	Heat a dry frying pan over medium heat and pan-fry **bacon** slices in a single layer until browned on one side. Flip and continue cooking until crisp.	Preheat oven to 375°F (190°C). Lay slices of **bacon** on a baking sheet in a single layer and roast in the oven, turning occasionally, until crisp.	**Spareribs** and **pork belly:** Braise as indicated for Boston shoulder roasts. If grilling unsmoked **spareribs**, they should be braised first.
Leg (cured or fresh ham)	Thick slices of smoked **ham** can be reheated over a medium grill or under a broiler until browned on both sides and cooked through.	Thick slices of smoked **ham** can be pan-fried as indicated for bacon.	Cook as indicated for the loin cuts.	Cook as indicated for the Boston shoulder cuts.
Ground pork	Form **ground pork** into patties or press on skewers, coat with oil, and season with salt and pepper. Cook as indicated for **loin** cuts until well-done—10-15 minutes, or 165°F (74°C).	**Patties** can be cooked as indicated for loin cuts. **Ground pork** can also be stir-fried in hot oil with vegetables until browned and cooked through.	Not recommended.	Browned **ground pork** can be formed into meatballs and added to a simmering stew with vegetables. Simmer both until cooked through, 1–1½ hours.
Head, cheeks/jowl, neck/collar, shank/knuckle/hock	Not recommended.	Not recommended.	**Head:** Preheat oven to 375°F (190°C). After braising, protect ears with foil and roast for 30–45 mins to color the skin; remove foil for the last 15 mins. Not recommended for other cuts.	**Head:** Brown vegetables, add head and liquid. Simmer, or cook in oven at 300°F (150°C) for 3–3½ hours. **Cheeks/jowl:** Brown with vegetables, add liquid, cover, and simmer, or braise at 375°F (190°C) for 45–60 mins. Braise **neck/collar** as Boston shoulder roasts. **Shank/knuckle/hock:** Simmer for 2–3 hours.
Trotters	After cooking and cooling, split in half, brush with butter, and roll in bread crumbs. Broil for 15–20 mins, or until crisp and golden brown.	Not recommended.	After cooking and cooling, prepare as for broiling. Roast at 400°F (200°C) for 15–20 mins, or until crisp and golden brown.	Simmer gently for 1–2 hours. Then cool, split in half, roll in bread crumbs, and broil or roast.
Sausage links	Cook **sausage links** as indicated for loin cuts until well-done—10-15 minutes or 165°F (74°C).	**Sausage links** can be cooked as indicated for **loin** cuts (sausages do not need to be seasoned first).	**Sausage links** can be cooked as indicated for bacon.	Browned **sausage links** can be added to a stew with vegetables. Simmer both until cooked through, 1–1½ hours.
Suckling pig	Not recommended.	Not recommended.	See Suckling pig technique, p106–07.	Cook as for fillet for 3–4 hours. Then increase heat to 400°F (200°C) and cook uncovered for the last 20–30 mins to crisp the skin.

BEEF

CUT	BROIL/GRILL	PAN-FRY/STIR FRY	ROAST	BRAISE/STEW
NOTES	Internal-temperature readings for beef: rare 140°F (60°C), medium-rare 145°F (63°C), medium 150°F (65°C), and well-done 165°F (74°C). Use a meat thermometer to check internal temperature. **Temperatures** listed are for general cooking, but may vary in recipes. **For timing,** weight is less important than if meat is sliced, diced, or cooked as a roast.			
Shoulder/chuck (chuck pot roast, blade roast, shoulder pot roast, chuck steak, stew meat, flat iron steak)	Rub **chuck steak** or **flat iron steak** with oil and season with salt and pepper. Cook over a medium-hot grill or under the broiler undisturbed until browned. Flip, then cook to the desired doneness, or 115°F–120°F (46°C–49°C) for rare, 125°F–130°F (52°C–54°C) for medium-rare, and 150°F (65°C) for medium-well.	Rub **chuck steak** or **flat iron steak** with oil and season with salt and pepper. Heat a large frying pan over medium-high heat until hot. Place the meat in the pan and cook undisturbed until browned on the first side. Flip, then cook to the desired doneness (see cooking temperatures above). Steaks can also be cut into thin strips and stir-fried in hot oil with vegetables until browned and cooked through.	Preheat oven to 375°F (190°C). Coat **shoulder pot roast** with oil and season with salt and pepper. Place meat in a roasting pan and roast until golden brown and cooked to desired doneness (see cooking temperatures above).	Preheat oven to 325°F (160°C). Generously season **chuck pot roast, blade roast, shoulder pot roast, stew meat** or **flat iron steak** and brown in hot oil in a large Dutch oven. Transfer meat to a plate and drain off all but 1 tablespoon of oil. Return the pan to the stove on medium heat, add chopped onions or garlic (or both), season with salt and pepper, and cook until golden and softened. Add liquid (wine, water, or broth) and scrape the pan to incorporate any browned bits. Add meat, bring to a boil, cover, and transfer to the oven. Braise, covered, until meat is tender and shreds easily with a fork.
Shank/brisket	Not recommended.	Not recommended.	Cook **brisket** as indicated for shoulder pot roast.	Cook **brisket** and **shank** as indicated for shoulder/chuck cuts.
Rib (rib roast, bone-in, rib eye steak, boneless rib eye steak, spareribs)	Cook both **rib eye steaks** as indicated for chuck steak. **Spareribs** can be grilled or broiled over medium heat if they are smoked or have been braised first. Coat with sauce and cook until heated through.	Cook both **rib eye steaks** as indicated for chuck steak.	Preheat oven to 450°F (230°C). Coat **rib roast** or either **rib eye steak** in oil and season with salt and pepper. Place meat in a roasting pan and roast until golden brown and cooked to desired doneness (see cooking temperatures above).	Cook **spareribs** as indicated for shoulder/chuck cuts.
Short loin (T-Bone steak, Delmonico steak, porterhouse steak, tenderloin, shell roast, strip steak, hanger steak)	Cook **steaks** and **tenderloin** as indicated for chuck steak. **Hangar steak** is best if marinated first.	Cook any of the **steaks** and the **tenderloin** as indicated for chuck steak.	Cook **tenderloin** and **shell roast** as indicated for rib roast.	Not recommended
Sirloin (tri-tip, sirloin steak, diced sirloin)	Cook **tri-tip** and **sirloin steak** as indicated for chuck steak. Marinate and thread **diced sirloin** onto skewers for kebabs and cook as indicated for chuck steak.	Cook **sirloin steak** as indicated for chuck steak.	Cook **tri-tip** as indicated for rib roast.	Not recommended.
Plate and flank (skirt steak, flank steak, short ribs)	Marinate **skirt steak** or **flank steak,** then cook as indicated for chuck steak.	Marinate **skirt steak** or **flank steak,** then cook as indicated for chuck steak.	Not recommended.	Cook **short ribs** as indicated for shoulder/chuck cuts.
Round (round steak, rump roast)	Not recommended.	Not recommended.	Cook **round steak** as indicated for rib roast.	Cook **rump roast** as indicated for shoulder/chuck cuts.
Ground beef	Form **ground beef** into patties, coat with oil, and season with salt and pepper. Cook **patties** as indicated for chuck steak.	Cook **patties** as indicated for chuck steak.	Not recommended.	**Ground beef** can be formed into meatballs and added to a simmering stew with vegetables or tomato sauce. Simmer until cooked through.

VEAL

CUT	BROIL/GRILL	PAN-FRY/STIR FRY	ROAST	BRAISE/STEW
NOTES	**Internal-temperature readings for veal:** rare 140°F (60°C), medium-rare 145°F (63°C), medium 150°F (65°C), and well-done 165°F (74C°). Use a meat thermometer to check internal temperature. **Temperatures** listed are for general cooking, but may vary in recipes. **For timing,** weight is less important than if meat is sliced, diced, or cooked as a roast.			
Shoulder (stew meat, boneless shoulder roast)	Not recommended.	Not recommended.	Preheat oven to 375°F (190°C). Coat **boneless shoulder roast** with oil and season with salt and pepper. Place meat in a roasting pan and roast until golden brown and cooked to desired doneness, or until 150°F (65°C) for medium.	Preheat oven to 325°F (160°C). Generously season **stew meat** or **shoulder roast** and brown in hot oil in a large Dutch oven. Transfer meat to a plate and drain off all but 1 tablespoon of the oil. Return the pan to the stove on medium heat, add chopped onions or garlic (or both), season with salt and pepper, and cook until golden and softened. Add liquid (wine, water, or broth) and scrape the pan to incorporate any browned bits. Add meat, bring to a boil, cover and transfer to the oven. Braise, covered until meat is tender and shreds easily with a fork.
Rib (rib chop, rib roast, crown roast)	Rub **rib chop** with oil and season with salt and pepper. Cook over a medium-hot grill or under the broiler undisturbed until well browned. Flip, then cook to desired doneness or 115°F–120°F (46°C–49°C) for rare, 125°F–130°F (52°C–54°C) for medium-rare, 150°F (65°C) for medium-well.	Rub **rib chop** with oil and season with salt and pepper. Heat a large frying pan over medium-high heat until hot. Place the meat in the pan and cook undisturbed until browned on the first side. Flip, then cook to desired doneness (see cooking temperatures above). **Chops** can also be cut into thin strips and stir-fried in hot oil with vegetables until browned and cooked through.	Preheat oven to 450°F (230°C). Coat **rib chop, rib roast,** and **crown roast** in oil and season with salt and pepper. Place meat in a roasting pan and roast until golden brown and cooked to desired doneness (see cooking temperatures above).	Not recommended.
Round (cutlets, boneless rump roast, diced round)	Cook **cutlets** as indicated for rib chop. Marinate and thread **diced round** onto skewers for kebabs and cook as indicated for rib chop.	Cook **cutlets** as indicated for rib chop.	Cook **boneless rump roast** as indicated for boneless shoulder roast.	Cook **boneless rump roast** as indicated for boneless shoulder roast.
Breast/ribs	Not recommended.	Not recommended.	Cook **breast** as indicated for boneless shoulder roast.	Cook **breast** and **ribs** as indicated for boneless shoulder roast.
Shank (osso buco)	Not recommended.	Not recommended.	Not recommended.	Cook **osso buco** as indicated for boneless shoulder roast.
Ground veal	Form **ground veal** into patties, coat with oil and season with salt and pepper. Cook **patties** as indicated for rib chops.	Cook **burgers, kebabs,** etc. in hot oil, lard, or butter for 10–15 mins, or until temperature reaches 165°F (75°C), turning from time to time.	Not recommended.	**Ground veal** can be formed into meatballs and added to a simmering stew with vegetables or tomato sauce. Simmer until cooked through.

LAMB, MUTTON, AND GOAT

CUT	BROIL/GRILL	PAN-FRY/STIR FRY	ROAST	BRAISE/STEW
NOTES	Internal-temperature readings for lamb, mutton, and goat: rare 140°F (60°C), medium 150°F (65°C), and well-done 165°F (74°C). Use a meat thermometer to check internal temperature. **Temperatures** listed are for general cooking, but may vary in recipes. **Timings** will vary according to thickness of the meat.			
LAMB Shoulder (blade chop, arm chop, shoulder roast)	Not recommended.	Not recommended.	Preheat oven to 375°F (190°C). Coat **shoulder roast** with oil and season with salt and pepper. Place meat in a roasting pan and roast until golden brown and cooked to desired doneness, or until 150°F (65°C) for medium.	Preheat oven to 325°F (160°C). Generously season **blade** or **arm chop**, or **shoulder roast** and brown in hot oil in a Dutch oven. Transfer meat to a plate and drain all but 1 tablespoon of the oil. Return the pan to the stove on medium heat, add chopped onions or garlic (or both), season with salt and pepper, and cook until golden and softened. Add liquid (wine, water, or broth) and scrape the pan to incorporate any browned bits. Add meat, bring to a boil, cover and transfer to the oven. Braise, covered, until meat is tender and shreds easily with a fork.
Rib (rack of lamb, rib chop, rib roast)	Rub **rib chop** with oil and season with salt and pepper. Cook over a medium-hot grill or under the broiler undisturbed until well browned. Flip, then cook to desired doneness, or 115°F–120°F (46°C–49°C) for rare, 125°F–130°F (52°C–54°C) for medium-rare, 150°F (65°C) for medium-well.	Rub **rib chop** with oil and season with salt and pepper. Heat a large frying pan over medium-high heat until hot. Place the meat in the pan and cook undisturbed until browned on the first side. Flip, then cook to desired doneness (see cooking temperatures above). Chops can also be cut into thin strips and stir-fried in hot oil with vegetables until browned and cooked through.	Preheat oven to 450°F (230°C). Coat **rack of lamb, rib chop,** or **rib roast** in oil and season with salt and pepper. Place meat in a roasting pan and roast until golden brown and cooked to desired doneness (see cooking temperatures above).	Not recommended.
Loin (loin chop, loin roast)	Cook **loin chop** as indicated for rib chop.	Cook **loin chop** as indicated for rib chop.	Cook **loin roast** as indicated for rack of lamb.	Not recommended.
Sirloin (sirloin roast, sirloin chop)	Not recommended.	Not recommended.	Cook sirloin cuts as indicated for shoulder roast.	Not recommended
Breast and ribs	Not recommended.	Not recommended.	Not recommended.	Cook **breast** and **ribs** as indicated for shoulder roast.
Leg (whole leg roast, shank, boneless leg roast, diced leg)	Marinate and thread **diced leg** onto skewers for kebabs and cook as recommended for rib chop.	Not recommended.	Cook **whole leg roast** and **boneless leg roast** as indicated for shoulder roast.	Cook **leg cuts** as indicated for shoulder roast.
Ground lamb, mutton, and goat	Form **ground lamb** into patties, coat with oil, and season with salt and pepper. Cook **patties** as indicated for rib chops.	Cook **patties** as indicated for rib chops.	Not recommended.	**Ground lamb** can be formed into meatballs and added to a simmering stew with vegetables or tomato sauce. Simmer until cooked through.
MUTTON AND GOAT Leg	Not recommended for old mutton and goat. **Leg chops** and **kebabs:** Cook as lamb chops and kebabs. **Young goat** and **mutton cuts:** Cook as lamb leg.	**Leg chops** and **kebabs:** Heat oil and butter in a frying pan. Cook chops for 3–5 mins per side, according to taste. Cook kebabs for 2–4 mins per side.	**Leg:** Preheat oven to 450°F (230°C). For pink meat, roast for 12 mins per 1lb (450g), then rest for 12 mins per 1lb (450g). For well-done, lower heat to 350°F (180°C) for another 15–20 mins per 1lb (450g), then rest for 5–10 mins.	**Leg chops** and **diced leg:** Brown meat, then add liquid and simmer, or stew in oven at 350°F (180°C), for 1–1½ hours. **Leg:** Brown all over, then add vegetables and liquid, cover, and simmer for 2–3 hours, until tender.
Loin and rib	Broil **loin chops** and **cutlets** as indicated for chops.	Cook **loin chops** and **cutlets** as indicated for rib chops.	Cook as indicated for rack of lamb.	**Loin chops:** Braise and stew as leg chops. **Loin joint:** Preheat oven to 300°F (150°C). Brown all over, add liquid, and cook in oven for 50 mins; reduce heat to 250°F (130°C), baste well, and cook for 45 mins longer.
Forequarter	Not recommended.	Not recommended.	Not recommended.	**Shoulder cuts, neck,** and **flank:** Braise as indicated for lamb shoulder, but for 2–2½ hours. **Diced shoulder:** Braise for 1½–2 hours. **Shank:** Braise or stew as indicated for lamb shoulder, but for 2½–3 hours.

FURRED GAME AND OTHER ANIMALS

CUT	BROIL/GRILL	PAN-FRY/STIR FRY	ROAST	BRAISE/STEW
NOTES	**Internal-temperature readings are:** rare 140°F (60°C), medium 150°F (65°C). Use a meat thermometer to check internal temperature. **Temperatures** listed are for general cooking, but may vary in recipes. **Timings** vary according to thickness.			
VENISON	**Venison steaks, racks, kebabs, and loins** (only from young animals): Preheat broiler or grill to high—450°F (230°C). Rub meat with oil and season with salt and pepper. Cook undisturbed until browned. Flip, then cook to desired doneness, or 115°F-120°F (46°C-49°C) for rare, 125°F-130°F (52°C-54°C) for medium-rare. Do not overcook.	**Venison steaks** and **loins** (only from young animals): Rub meat with oil and season with salt and pepper. Heat a large frying pan over medium-high heat until hot. Place the meat in the pan and cook undisturbed until browned on the first side. Flip, then cook to desired doneness (see cooking temperatures above). Chops can also be cut into thin strips and stir-fried in hot oil with vegetables until browned and cooked through.	**Bone-in** and **boneless venison loin, rack,** and **leg roasts:** Preheat oven to 450°F (230°C). Coat meat in oil and season with salt and pepper. Place meat in a roasting pan and roast until golden brown and cooked to desired doneness (see cooking temperatures above).	**Venison shoulder** and **leg:** Preheat oven to 325°F (160°C). Generously season meat and brown in hot oil in a large Dutch oven. Transfer to a plate and drain off all but 1 tablespoon of oil. Return the pan to the stove on medium heat, add chopped onions or garlic (or both), season with salt and pepper, and cook until softened. Add liquid (wine, water, or broth) and scrape the pan to incorporate browned bits. Add meat, bring to a boil, cover and transfer to the oven. Braise, covered, until meat is tender and shreds easily with a fork—approximately 1½–2 hours for younger animals, 2½–3½ hours for older animals.
OSTRICH	Cook **ostrich steaks** as indicated for venison steaks. Only grill cuts from young animals.	Cook **ostrich steaks** as indicated for venison steaks. Only cook cuts from young animals.	Cook **boneless ostrich breast** and **leg** as indicated for venison steaks. Only roast cuts from young animals.	Cook **boneless ostrich breast** and **leg** as indicated for venison leg roast. Braise for 1½–2 hours for younger animals, 2½–3½ hours for older animals.
BISON/BUFFALO	Cook **bison** and **buffalo leg steak, T-bone, rib eye, tenderloin,** and **sirloin** as indicated for venison steaks.	Cook **bison** and **buffalo leg steak, T-bone, rib eye, tenderloin,** and **sirloin** as indicated for venison steaks.	Cook **bison** and **buffalo loin, sirloin, rump roast,** and **rib eye roast** as indicated for venison leg roast.	Cook **bison** and **buffalo osso buco** and **ribs** as indicated for venison leg roast.
GROUND: All meats.	Preheat broiler to high. Press meat onto skewers or form into patties. Brush with oil and broil, turning occasionally, for 8–10 mins.	Brown meat, then add liquid and simmer for 45 mins–1 hour. Or, form into patties and cook for 3–5 mins per side.	Not recommended.	Brown, then simmer, or braise at 325°F (160°C), for 1–2 hours.
WILD BOAR	Only broil young wild boar. Broil as venison.	Only cook young wild boar. Cook as venison.	Only roast young wild boar. Roast as venison.	Braise wild boar as venison from older deer.
HORSE AND KANGAROO	Broil as venison. Only broil young kangaroo.	Cook as venison. Only cook young kangaroo.	Only roast horse cuts and kangaroo cuts if young, then roast as venison.	Braise as venison.
HARE	Not recommended.	Not recommended.	Hare **tenderloin**. Roast as venison bone-in cuts.	Braise as venison bone-in cuts.
RABBIT AND SQUIRREL	Only broil cuts of domestic rabbit. Marinate in oil, then broil for 15–20 mins on medium heat.	Only cook cuts of domestic rabbit. Marinate in oil, then cook for 15–20 mins on medium heat.	Roast **loin** and **legs** from domestic rabbit; only **tenderloin** from wild rabbit. Brown cuts in a frying pan, then roast at 425°F (220°C) for 5–10 mins. Rest for 5 mins before serving.	Immerse in liquid, then very slowly simmer for 1½–2½ hours, or until tender.
GUINEA PIG	Halve or butterfly, then broil on medium heat for 20–30 mins, until juices run clear.	Halve or butterfly, then cook slowly in a covered pan for 20–30 mins, until juices run clear.	Stuff the cavity, then cover with butter or oil and roast at 400°F (200°C) for 30–40 mins; less if not stuffed.	Immerse in liquid, then very slowly simmer for 1½–2½ hours, or until tender.

RECIPE PLANNERS

SLOW-COOKED

OSSO BUCO
page 287

POT ROAST SMOKED HAM
page 136

CHOLENT
page 92

CAJUN ANDOUILLE GUMBO
page 139

WILD BOAR CURRY
page 239

HUNGARIAN GOULASH
page 113

TAJINE BIL MISHMISH
pages 200–201

BRAISED SHIN OF BEEF IN RED WINE
page 177

VENETIAN DUCK RAGÙ
page 91

BRAISED OXTAIL WITH CLEMENTINE
page 286

PORK WITH CLAMS
page 114

DAUBE OF BEEF WITH PRUNES
page 155

ALSO TRY...

ROASTS

ROAST GROUSE
page 248

HERBY ROAST CHICKEN
page 80

MAPLE AND MUSTARD CRUSTED RIB OF BEEF
page 160

TURDUCKEN
page 83

**SLOW-COOKED PORK SHOULDER
WITH CIDER GRAVY** page 112

**PROSCIUTTO-WRAPPED PORK
TENDERLOIN** page 121

**ROASTED CORNISH GAME HEN WITH
PRESERVED LEMONS** page 95

**SCANDINAVIAN LEG OF MUTTON WITH
HONEY MUSTARD AND ROOTS** page 218

FAISAN NORMANDE
page 245

FIERY BEEF FILLET WITH ROASTED VEG
page 165

PORK BELLY PORCHETTA
page 127

RACK OF LAMB WITH CELERY ROOT GALETTES page 205

FRANGO PIRI PIRI
page 79

BAVARIAN ROAST PORK
page 110

PAN-FRIED

VEAL SCALOPPINI WITH SALSA VERDE
page 179

VEAL SCHNITZEL WITH FRIED EGG, CAPERS, AND PARSLEY page 180

FILLET STEAK WITH BLUE CHEESE SAUCE page 163

BUTTERMILK CHICKEN WITH BISCUITS
page 64

FRIKADELLER
page 109

VENISON STEAK WITH BLACKBERRIES
page 238

ALSO TRY...

- **Southern fried chicken** (page 71)
- **Seared duck breast with a raspberry and cardamom glaze** (page 85)
- **Pork satay with peanut dipping sauce** (page 124)
- **Pork schnitzel with creamy mustard sauce** (page 132)
- **Country ham and eggs with red-eye gravy and grits** (page 136)
- **Spicy beef and pea patties** (page 152)
- **Pan-fried fillet of beef** (page 164)
- **Wasabi beef and bok choy** (page 170)
- **Veal cutlets with peppers** (page 180)
- **Lamb burgers with roasted tomato relish** (page 195)
- **Lamb loin with red bell peppers** (page 203)
- **Venison cutlets with chanterelles** (page 236)
- **Guinea fowl with smoked bacon** (page 253)
- **Breasts of wild duck with sauce bigarade** (page 255)
- **Calf's liver with sage** (page 271)
- **Sautéed liver, onions, and potatoes** (page 272)
- **Venison liver with onions** (page 272)
- **Quick fry venison hearts** (page 274)
- **Chicken liver with marsala** (page 275)

ON THE GRILL

CUBANO
page 137

DRY-RUBBED STEAK WITH CHIMICHURRI SAUCE page 159

LAMB KEBABS WITH YOGURT AND POMEGRANATE page 196

OSTRICH BURGERS
page 257

CAJUN-SPICED CHICKEN
page 74

CLASSIC BURGERS
page 153

MOROCCAN SKEWERED LIVERS AND HEARTS page 272

ALSO TRY

- **Butterflied and grilled turkey** (page 83)
- **Gai Yang** (page 95)
- **Chipotle cinnamon bacon** (page 125)
- **Barbecue ribs** (page 130–1)
- **Flat iron steak with black olive butter** (page 153)
- **Caribbean jerk beef** (page 162)
- **Grilled balsamic steak with beets** (page 164)
- **Ginger, honey, and soy glazed beef sirloin** (page 172)
- **Goan veal kebabs** (page 183)
- **Grilled lamb koftas** (page 194)
- **Lamb fillet basted with anchovy paste** (page 198)
- **Lamb fillet with tomato and basil salad** (page 202)
- **Broiled lamb cutlets and eggplant with red cabbage slaw** (page 206)
- **Barbecued lamb with mint hollandaise** (page 209)
- **Barbecued haunch of venison** (page 236)
- **Ostrich steaks** (page 254)

POULTRY

POULTRY

POULTRY IS ONE OF THE MOST UNIVERSALLY LOVED MEATS. DELICIOUS AND TENDER, IT READILY ABSORBS A RANGE OF FLAVORS. THIS VERSATILITY, COUPLED WITH THE FACT THAT POULTRY IS EASY TO COOK AND RELATIVELY INEXPENSIVE, MEANS THAT IT IS ENJOYED IN EVERY COUNTRY OF THE WORLD.

SUCH POPULARITY MEANS that the demand for poultry of all sorts is enormous. Around the world, the production of chicken alone is approaching 110 million tons per year, and most of this comes from birds raised using a variety of intensive methods of production.

PRODUCTION METHODS

There are many different ways of rearing poultry. The main types of production are described below—although some of these methods merge into others.

• **Domestic free-range** Domestic fowl are free to scratch about outside—sometimes in a yard, sometimes with access to fields and scrubland. With a varied diet and adequate exercise, their flesh has the best flavor and texture of all. Most of these birds are reared for home consumption by their keepers, but a few are sold locally and are well worth seeking out. **Diet:** varied, but often includes concentrated feed or concentrates (see opposite).

• **Commercial free-range** With fresh air and exercise, free-range birds grow slowly. The best systems for rearing chickens provide outdoor space with plenty of vegetation so that the birds can roam about and exhibit natural flock behavior. A building is available for shade, shelter, and for protection at night. **Diet:** concentrates, plus vegetation.

• **Intensive free-range** These free-range birds go outside by day, but under such crowded conditions that, although they benefit from fresh air, their enclosures have little or no vegetation left. In the most intensive systems, large flocks are housed in huge, deep-litter sheds, with their access to outdoor conditions limited to one or two small exit doors that few birds ever find. **Diet:** concentrates.

• **Intensive deep-litter** Thousands of birds live in large, climate-controlled or ventilated sheds with no access to the outside. They are at liberty to walk about

AROUND THE WORLD, THE PRODUCTION OF CHICKEN ALONE IS APPROACHING 110 MILLION TONS PER YEAR—MOST OF WHICH COMES FROM INTENSIVELY RAISED BIRDS.

and have perches to roost on, but conditions are crowded. Ammonia build-up from their droppings can cause the birds to develop health problems and deformities. **Diet:** concentrates.

• **Caged production** Mostly restricted to egg-laying birds (or layers)—although birds bred for meat can be caged, too—these birds cannot fly or perch. Even walking around is difficult. While in some countries such very cramped conditions are outlawed, in other countries they still exist. **Diet:** concentrates.

• **Organic poultry** There are many different organic production marks, although an organic label is likely to indicate low stocking densities under good, free-range conditions with organic feed. Many organic birds are also reared in intensive free-range units. The organic system works on the assumption that a well-managed flock will need little medical treatment, although drug use is still permitted. **Diet:** organic concentrates, plus vegetation.

POULTRY FEED
All species of poultry are omnivores, except for ducks and geese which are predominantly herbivores (vegetarians). Virtually all methods of poultry rearing use concentrated feeds that contain proteins such as soy, grain, fishmeal, or animal protein. They also contain vitamins and the necessary trace elements to keep the birds healthy (see pp12–13 for more about grain production and the seeds used in concentrated feed).

HEALTH AND SAFETY
In many countries, birds are fed growth promoters to speed up production. These can include antibiotics, growth hormones, and arsenic-containing chemicals. Some of these (growth hormones, in particular) are banned in some countries but still used in others.

Because of the risk of Salmonella and E. coli food poisoning from raw and undercooked poultry, it is always recommended that you cook poultry meat

to an internal temperature of at least 165°F (75°C). Always wash equipment that you have used to handle raw poultry thoroughly in hot water. All poultry should be sold and stored properly chilled.

BUYING POULTRY
For poultry to be cheap, compromises have to be made. Production methods (see opposite) will affect the price. It is also common practice in the trade to inject poultry breasts with water, salts, and flavorings to make them cheap and appear plumper. Highly processed products made of reformed poultry, such as nuggets and sausages, often come from old laying hens—the most intensively raised birds—or from ground-up bones, skin, and fat. Few of these facts will appear on packaging. Where good practices are kept, they will be promoted, so always check the label carefully before buying.

SPECIES AND BREEDS
Any poultry show will exhibit hundreds of different breeds, each having been bred for a specific purpose: egg-laying, meat production, dual-purpose, or even for fighting. Most commercial birds are hybrids, fine-tuned to thrive and be productive under very specific conditions.

• **Turkey** Modern turkeys are descended from the small, wild, Mexican turkey. Nowadays, they are industrially reared and far bigger than their ancestors, but there are also a number of premium free-range birds available, such as the bronze turkey, which has a better texture and flavor.

• **Chicken** Domestic chickens evolved from the Indian jungle fowl. Modern commercial chickens are hybrids, not breeds, but domestic chicken-keepers have kept alive many local heritage breeds such as the Dorking or Plymouth Rock. There are several different categories of chicken:

Broilers are about 12 weeks old and are reared for roasting.

Capons are castrated males that are fattened to produce tender, plump breasts.

Boiling fowl are older, often ex-laying hens that need stewing but have an excellent flavor.

Poussin are young chickens sold at 4–6 weeks old, as are Cornish Game Hens, which are slightly larger; despite their name, they are neither game birds nor necessarily female.

• **Duck** Having been domesticated for more than 4,000 years, nowadays most ducks are intensively reared. Most breeds are descended from the wild mallard, with the most common being White Pekin and Aylesbury. The colorful Rouen duck grows more slowly, while the larger, leaner Muscovy is technically of the goose family.

• **Goose** Domestic breeds, such as the Toulouse goose, are descendants of the wild Greylag goose; Asian and African domestic geese are descended from the white Swan Goose. Geese are grass-eaters and rarely housed, so tend to be a seasonal treat. They may be fed on grain for short periods.

POULTRY CUTS

POULTRY MEAT IS ENDLESSLY VERSATILE, with cuts for every dish; marinating adds extra flavor to grilled and roasted meat. Poultry should be plump and firm, without dry patches, tears, or bruising. It should have a clean, fresh smell; if not, discard it because the meat will not be safe to eat.

WING

BREAST

LEG

CHICKEN

Always store chicken at the bottom of the fridge so that it can't drip onto other food. Make sure it is cooked all the way through to the thickest parts.

DRUMSTICK Rarely boned or skinned and less meaty than thighs, drumsticks are popular with children and also as finger food, especially when marinated or coated in a sauce.

SUPREME (SKINLESS) The breast with part of the wing bone attached. Without the skin and nicely trimmed, a supreme makes an elegant cutlet. It can be coated in bread crumbs before frying.

WHOLE WING Made up of three parts. Most of the meat is on the breast end, so the bony tip is often removed. Great for buffalo wings, finger food, or making stock.

BREAST FILLET Skinless breast is the leanest cut. However, the skin can be stuffed to keep the meat moist. Breasts are broiled, steamed, baked, simmered, or stir-fried.

LEG QUARTER This is the whole leg plus a section of the backbone. It is a cheaper cut because of the high bone content. However, it makes tasty stews and can also be broiled and barbecued.

WHOLE CHICKEN Corn-fed chicken has yellow skin and fat; grain-fed chicken is pinker. The breast cooks a little quicker than the legs, so putting stuffing under the skin keeps it moist.

THIGH, SKIN-ON AND BONE-IN Thigh meat is dark and succulent and makes excellent casseroles as well as broiling superbly because the skin crisps nicely, keeping the meat moist. Thighs are also sold skinless and boneless.

DICED CHICKEN Lean and tender, diced chicken is useful for casseroles and kebabs for broiling, while strips and **TENDERS** (the meat under the breast) are best for stir-frying.

TURKEY

Turkey meat is leaner than chicken. The average size of a turkey is 12lb (5.5kg); smaller birds are supplied outside the festive seasons.

WHOLE TURKEY The ultimate festive bird. Make sure it is at room temperature 1 hour before cooking.

BONE-IN TURKEY BREAST The whole bird without legs and back, so easy to cook and to carve.

BONELESS TURKEY ROLL May be breast or leg meat, or a combination. A easy-to-carve cut.

GROUND Lean turkey meat can be used as a beef substitute for healthy eating.

CORNISH GAME HEN

This is a young chicken sold at 4–6 weeks old. Because these birds are immature, there is a high proportion of bone to meat.

WHOLE Tender and succulent, these young birds have little fat, so brush them with oil.

BUTTERFLIED Opened out and butterflied, game hen roasts or broils very quickly and evenly.

GOOSE

The proportion of meat to bone is low, so goose is an expensive treat; however, the light fat is superb for frying and other cooking.

WHOLE GOOSE Prick the fat before cooking so that it drains off. Allow 1½lb (650g) per person.

GOOSE BREAST, SKIN-ON Cook with the skin downward (upward if under a broiler) to keep meat moist.

DUCK

With all duck, the ratio of meat to fat and bone is low, but the meat is very tasty and rich. The fat is also sold separately for cooking.

WHOLE DUCK The fat is delicious, but avoid birds with too much. Allow 1½lb (650g) per person.

WHOLE DUCK LEG Delicious broiled, roasted, or made into confit. Score fat before cooking.

DUCK BREAST, SKIN-ON If the fat layer is very thick, score it before cooking, and fry fat-side down.

DUCK TENDERS These are slices of the main breast muscle and are good for marinatimg and stir-frying.

PRESERVED POULTRY

PRESERVED POULTRY IS LESS COMMON than preserved meat, partly because of the dangers of contamination. However, where ducks and geese are produced in large numbers, a range of preserved products has evolved. Chinese cuisine also uses a number of fully or partly dried poultry products.

GUANGDONG SAUSAGES A salty sweetness characterizes these dried sausages from China, which are made from coarsely chopped duck or chicken. They are air-dried and usually steamed over rice, or sliced and stir-fried.

SAUCISSON SEC DE CANARD From the great duck-producing areas of France, this saucisson sec is well laced with duck fat. The flavor is best when the sausage is sliced paper-thin.

SALAME D'OCA Goose fat, liver, and fatty pork are stuffed into a skin or goose neck to make this Italian sausage. It is then dried and cooked. Soft and mottled pink, it is served with mostarda.

ALHEIRA DE BARROSO-MONTALEGRE A Portuguese sausage originally made by Jewish cooks from any white meat other than pork, alheira can be made from any kind of poultry flavored with garlic. It is lightly smoked.

JAMBON DE CANARD AUX HERBES Thick strips of duck are rolled in herbs, bound with string and then immersed in dry salt until cured into a firm ham. The dark meat has an intense flavor.

CASSOULET A specialty of southwest France, cassoulet is a stew of beans studded with generous pieces of conserved duck or goose. The Toulouse version also includes sausage.

KIEŁBASA TORUNSKA From the medieval town of Torun in eastern Poland, this is a slim sausage, normally made with pork but sometimes with chicken instead. The traditional long loops are hot smoked.

Confit d'Oie
sous la graisse

MILHAC-OIE
EN PÉRIGORD

1 membre
=
2 parts

CONFIT D'OIE Pieces of goose are dry-salted then very slowly cooked in their own fat. This is put into glass jars or cans and sealed to preserve it for many months.

MAGRET DE CANARD SECHÉ AU POIVRE Whole duck breasts are rubbed with cracked black peppercorns, then dry-salted and hung up to dry. The meat has a rich covering of fat on one side.

MAGRET DE CANARD AU FOIE GRAS Duck breasts are stuffed with a core of foie gras, then brined and air-dried. The creamy foie gras contrasts with the dark rich magret. This lightly preserved product has a limited shelf life once sliced open.

MAGRET DE CANARD FUMÉ Similar to the Italian prosciutto below, this French version is smoked after curing, which lends a complementary tartness to the rich duck fat.

PROSCIUTTO D'ANATRA Duck breasts are brined and air-dried until the meat is rich, dark, and powerfully flavored with a succulent layer of fat.

DEBONING A BIRD

Deboned poultry makes eye-catching dishes such as Turducken (see p83). Keep the knife edge tilted toward the bone to avoid cutting the meat. To sever the joints, bend the limb backward until it cracks.

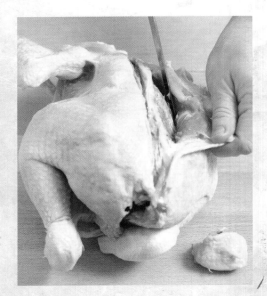

1 Turn the bird breast-side down. Cut off the tail. Then cut the skin along the backbone. Pulling the skin up and away from the carcass, scrape the meat off one side of the flat back part.

2 At the thigh joint, remove the meat around the ball and socket joint to expose it. Scrape off the meat from the thighbone. Sever the drumstick joint at the ball-and-socket joint and at the drumstick joint and remove the thighbone.

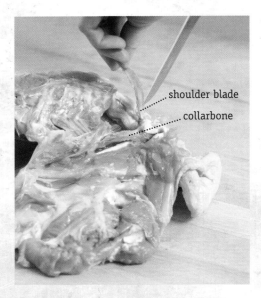

shoulder blade
collarbone

3 Moving up the bird, continue to scrape the meat off the rib cage and around the thin shoulder blade lying over it. This bone, the collarbone, the wing bone and wishbone all converge in one place.

wing bone

4 Sever the shoulder blade and collarbone from the wing bone, leaving the wing attached by the connecting flesh to the rest of the chicken. The wing bone will be removed later.

wishbone

5 Scrape off the meat from around the wishbone, bend it backward and remove it. Now repeat steps 1–5 with the other side of the bird.

6 Scrape the meat off either side of the breastbone. Keeping the knife close to the ridge of the bone, carefully cut off the deboned meat, then remove the skeletal frame.

7 To remove the wing bone, cut off the wing tips. Scrape the meat off the bone inside the wing (accessing it either from the main carcass end, or the wing tip end) and pull out the bone.

8 To remove the remaining drumsticks in the legs, cut around the scaly end of the drumstick skin. Scrape the meat off the drumstick (accessing it as for the wing bone) and pull out the bone. The bird is now completely deboned. Cover and store in the fridge until ready to stuff or use in a recipe.

BUTTERFLYING A BIRD

Butterflying involves flattening a bird (of any size) that is to be cooked on a grill or smoked on a barbecue grill. It avoids the risk of burning thinner parts while leaving thicker parts undercooked.

1 Turn the bird upside down. Using poultry shears, cut along one side of the backbone, then cut along the other side and remove the backbone completely. Open out the bird and turn it over.

2 Flatten the bird by pressing down sharply on the breast with the palms of your hands, making it as evenly flat as possible. Where the muscles are of different thicknesses, slash the plumpest parts to ensure even cooking.

3 Push a skewer diagonally through the drumstick, thigh, lower breast and wing as shown. Repeat with another skewer on the other side and press down again to ensure it is flat. If wished, marinate before cooking.

MATZO BALL SOUP

A simpler version of the traditional Passover dish, the matzo balls are judged to be good if they float in the broth.

 Chicken stock

SERVES 4–6
PREP 10 mins, plus chilling **COOK** 1 hr

FOR THE MATZO BALLS

1 cup matzo meal

¼ cup chicken stock

4 large eggs

1 tsp baking powder

¼ cup vegetable oil

salt and freshly ground black pepper

FOR THE BROTH

7 cups chicken stock

5½oz (150g) carrots, thinly sliced into rounds

2 tbsp chopped dill

1 Mix the matzo meal, chicken stock, eggs, baking powder, vegetable oil, and salt and pepper in a bowl to make a batter. Stir well until fully combined. Cover with plastic wrap and chill for 1 hour.

2 In a medium stock pot, combine the chicken stock, carrots, and dill. Bring to a boil, then reduce the heat to medium-high, and cook for 15 minutes.

3 Take the matzo batter out of the fridge. Using a spoon, form the batter into 6 even-sized balls, about the size of a lime. Drop the balls, one at a time, into the hot soup. Allow them to cook for 2–3 minutes, then use a spoon to flip the balls. Cover the pot, reduce the heat, and simmer for 30–40 minutes, until fully cooked and puffed. Serve hot.

NO PEEKING!

Keep the matzo balls firmly covered as they simmer—lifting the lid to peek inside may cause the matzo balls to fall apart.

TANDOORI CHICKEN SAMOSAS

With roots in Northern India, these spiced meat pastries have been a favorite appetizer across the Middle East for centuries.

THE CUT **Cooked chicken**

SERVES 16–20
PREP 30 mins, plus chilling **COOK** 35 mins

FOR THE DOUGH

1½ cups all-purpose flour, plus extra for dusting

1 tbsp ground turmeric

1 tbsp curry powder

1 tsp salt

¾ cup vegetable fat

1 egg, beaten to glaze

FOR THE FILLING

5½oz (150g) cooked chicken, shredded

10oz (300g) sweet potato, peeled and mashed

1 tbsp tandoori paste

9oz (250g) white onion, finely chopped

1 tbsp ground turmeric

1 tbsp curry powder

1 tbsp garam masala

3 garlic cloves, crushed

3oz package frozen peas

juice of 1 lemon

1 Sift the flour, spices, and salt in a large bowl. Rub in the fat until the texture resembles bread crumbs. Stir 1 cup cold water into the flour mixture, a little at a time, until a loose ball of dough has formed. Wrap in plastic wrap and chill for 1 hour.

2 For the filling, combine all the ingredients in a large bowl. Stir well, making sure the chicken mixes evenly. Preheat the oven to 350°F (180°C) and line a baking sheet with parchment paper.

3 On a lightly floured surface, roll out the pastry as thinly as possible. Use a pastry knife to cut the pastry into 4in (10cm) wide strips. Cut the strips crosswise into 4in (10cm) squares, then in half to make triangles. Place a tablespoon of filling in the center of each, then bring the points of the triangle together, and use your fingers to pinch the sides closed. Repeat until all of the filling and pastry is used.

4 Place the samosas on the baking tray and brush with the beaten egg. Bake the samosas in the oven for 30–35 minutes, or until golden brown. Cool slightly before serving.

CHICKEN JAMBALAYA

A traditional Creole dish from Louisiana, jambalaya combines the summer flavors of peppers, peas, and herbs with a little heat from the cayenne pepper.

THE CUT Chicken thigh and breast

SERVES 4–6
PREP 15–20 mins **COOK** 1 hr 30 mins

2 tbsp olive oil

salt and freshly ground black pepper

6 boneless chicken pieces (thighs and breasts), cut into large chunks

2 tbsp chopped oregano

2 tsp cayenne pepper

1 red onion, finely chopped

3 garlic cloves, finely chopped

1 green bell pepper, seeded and finely chopped

1 red bell pepper, seeded and finely chopped

7oz (200g) thick slices cooked ham, roughly chopped

3 cups hot chicken stock

6oz (175g) easy-cook long-grain rice

5oz (140g) shelled fresh peas

small handful of cilantro, finely chopped (optional)

1 Heat half the oil in a large, heatproof casserole or Dutch oven over medium-high heat. Season the chicken pieces, toss them in the oregano and cayenne pepper, and add to the casserole (in batches, if necessary). Cook for 6–10 minutes, until golden brown. Remove and set aside.

2 Heat the remaining oil in the casserole over medium heat. Add the onion, garlic, and bell peppers and cook for 5–8 minutes, stirring, until soft. Return the chicken to the casserole and stir in the ham. Pour in the stock and bring to a boil. Then reduce to a simmer, season well, partially cover with the lid, and cook gently for about 40 minutes. Check occasionally and add a little hot water if it's drying out.

3 Stir in the rice, turning it so it absorbs all the stock, and cook for about 15 minutes or until the rice is cooked, adding more stock if necessary. Add the peas for the last 5 minutes.

4 Taste and and season, if needed, and stir in the cilantro, if using. Serve with a green salad, plain yogurt, or sour cream.

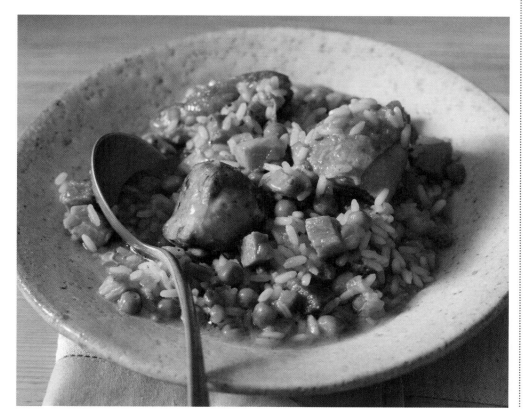

CHICKEN AND PESTO MEATBALLS

Pesto, with its fresh basil and nutty olive oil, adds a complex flavor to these moist meatballs.

THE CUT Ground chicken

SERVES 4
PREP 25 mins **COOK** 45 mins

¾ cup pine nuts

3½oz (100g) basil

3 garlic cloves

1¾oz (50g) freshly grated Parmesan

salt and freshly ground black pepper

5 tbsp olive oil

1lb (450g) ground chicken

1 cup dried bread crumbs

1 egg

1 shallot, finely chopped

1lb (450g) dried penne pasta

1 In a dry frying pan, lightly toast the pine nuts until golden and set aside to cool. In a food processor, combine the basil, garlic, Parmesan, pine nuts, and salt. Pulse to combine. Turn the processor on high and add 4 tablespoons of the oil in a thin drizzle, until a sauce is formed.

2 Preheat the oven to 350°F (180°C). Line a baking sheet with parchment paper. In a large bowl, combine the chicken, bread crumbs, egg, salt and pepper, shallot, and half of the pesto. Stir well to incorporate.

3 Form the chicken mixture into evenly sized balls, approximately 2in (5cm) in diameter. Place on the lined baking sheet. Bake for 30–40 minutes or until the meatballs turn golden.

4 Meanwhile, cook the pasta according to the package instructions. Drain and toss in the remaining pesto along with the remaining oil. Top the pasta with the cooked meatballs and serve hot.

VARIATION

Beef meatballs Make beef meatballs by combining 1lb (450g) ground beef, 2 eggs, 1¾oz (50g) freshly grated Parmesan, 1 cup dried bread crumbs, and 2 teaspoons each of dried oregano, basil, thyme, and rosemary. Season the mixture well, form into evenly sized balls, and bake as above. Serve the meatballs with store-bought chunky tomato sauce.

MARINATED CHICKEN FAJITAS

A classic crowd pleaser, this Tex-Mex dish gets its name from the Mexican term for "little meat strips."

 Chicken breast

SERVES 3–4
PREP 15 mins, plus marinating   **COOK** 15 mins

FOR THE MARINADE

2 tbsp olive oil

1 tbsp lime juice

2 tsp ground cumin

1 tsp smoked paprika, plus extra for the onions

1 tsp dried oregano

1 tsp cayenne pepper or chili powder

salt and freshly ground black pepper

FOR THE FAJITAS

2 large skinless boneless chicken breasts, sliced

2 tbsp sunflower oil

1 red onion, cut into ½in (1cm) slices

1 red bell pepper, cut into ½in (1cm) slices

1 yellow bell pepper, cut into ½in (1cm) slices

8 tortillas

sour cream or plain yogurt, to serve

chile sauce, to serve

guacamole, to serve

classic tomato salsa, to serve

1 Place the chicken in a large bowl. Whisk together the marinade ingredients and pour over the chicken. Cover and chill in the fridge for at least 30 minutes, or up to 4 hours.

2 Preheat the broiler on its highest setting. Broil the chicken slices for 3–5 minutes on each side, until golden and cooked.

3 Meanwhile, heat the sunflower oil in a large frying pan or wok over high heat. Fry the onion and peppers for 5–7 minutes, or until cooked through and colored on the edges. Season with a little salt and pepper and smoked paprika.

4 Warm the tortillas in a microwave or a low oven, according to package instructions. Divide the vegetables and the chicken into 8 equal portions. Place 1 portion of the vegetables on 1 tortilla, top with 1 portion of the chicken, and roll the tortillas to make the fajitas. Serve alongside a choice of sour cream, guacamole, and classic tomato salsa.

BUTTERMILK CHICKEN WITH BISCUITS

This popular Southern dish is a delicious combination of hot, fried chicken and flaky, buttery biscuits.

 Chicken breast

SERVES 4
PREP 30 mins, plus overnight marinating
COOK 35–40 mins

FOR THE CHICKEN

1lb 5oz (600g) skinless boneless chicken breasts

1 cup buttermilk

1 tbsp cayenne pepper, plus 1 tsp for the marinade

3 tsp salt, plus extra for the biscuits

2½ cups fresh bread crumbs

1⅓ cups self-rising flour

2 tsp red pepper flakes

oil, for frying

FOR THE BISCUITS

1½ cups all-purpose flour, plus extra for dusting

½ tsp baking powder

1 tsp baking soda

1 tsp cayenne pepper

6 tbsp vegetable fat

⅔ cup buttermilk

honey, to serve (optional)

1 In a large bowl, combine the chicken breasts with the buttermilk, 1 teaspoon cayenne pepper, and 1 teaspoon salt. Cover with plastic wrap and chill in the fridge overnight.

2 For the biscuits, sift the flour, baking powder, baking soda, cayenne pepper, and a pinch of salt into a large bowl. Rub in the fat until the mixture resembles bread crumbs. Then stir in the buttermilk, a little at a time, until a ball of dough is formed. Preheat the oven to 350°F (180°C).

3 On a lightly floured surface, roll out the pastry to ¼in (5mm) thickness. Fold the pastry in half and roll it out again. Repeat this process 3–4 times, then roll it out to ½in (1cm) thickness. Use a biscuit cutter to cut 4–5in- (10–12cm-) wide biscuits. Transfer them to a baking sheet and bake in the oven for 15 minutes, or until raised and golden brown.

4 Meanwhile, heat the oil in a frying pan to 350°F (180°C). Combine the bread crumbs, ¾ cup flour, 1 teaspoon red pepper flakes, ½ tablespoon cayenne pepper, and ½ teaspoon salt in a bowl. In a second bowl, combine the remaining flour, red pepper flakes, cayenne pepper, and salt.

5 Remove the chicken pieces from the marinade. Dip each piece first in the flour mixture, then in the marinade, and then the bread crumb mixture. Shallow-fry the chicken pieces for 7–8 minutes, flipping them over if necessary, until golden brown and cooked through. Remove with a slotted spoon and drain on a plate lined with paper towels. Serve the chicken and biscuits alongside each other or in the form of a sandwich, with some honey, if preferred.

VARIATION

Turkey sausage biscuits Combine 1lb 5oz (600g) turkey sausage with 1 tablespoon red pepper flakes and 1¾oz (50g) freshly ground Parmesan cheese. Season the mixture with salt and pepper and form into thick burgerlike patties. Chill in the fridge for about 1 hour to help them retain their shape. Coat the patties in the bread crumb and flour mixtures and fry as above. Serve the turkey with the buttermilk biscuits and honey.

PAD THAI

A popular Thai street food, this easy stir-fry is a delicious combination of savory, mildly sour, and sweet flavors.

THE CUT Chicken breast

SERVES 8
PREP 15 mins   **COOK** 15 mins

1¼lb (550g) medium or thick dry rice noodles

3 tbsp sunflower oil

4 large eggs, lightly beaten

1 tsp shrimp paste (optional)

4 hot red chiles, seeded and finely chopped

6 skinless boneless chicken breasts, cut into ¼in (5mm) slices

2 bunches of scallions, finely chopped

splash of Thai fish sauce, such as nam pla

juice of 2 limes

2 tbsp demerara sugar

salt and freshly ground black pepper

2 cups unsalted peanuts

handful of cilantro leaves, finely chopped

lime wedges, to garnish

1 Place the noodles in a large bowl, cover with boiling water, and leave for 8 minutes, or until soft. Then drain and set aside. Heat 1 tablespoon of the oil in a large wok over high heat. Swirl it around the pan, pour in the beaten egg, and tip the pan to spread it around the wok. Cook the egg for about 1 minute, or until it begins to just set, but don't let it set completely. Remove from the wok, chop, and set aside.

2 Add the remaining oil, shrimp paste (if using), and chiles to the wok, and stir to mix. Then add the chicken and stir vigorously for 5 minutes, or until cooked through and no longer pink. Add the scallions, fish sauce, lime juice, and sugar, and toss well. Cook for 1–2 minutes, until the sugar has dissolved, then season well with salt and pepper. Return the egg to the pan.

3 Add the noodles to the pan and toss to coat with the sauce. Then add half the peanuts and half the cilantro and toss again. Transfer to a large, shallow warmed serving bowl. Scatter over the remaining peanuts and cilantro, garnish with lime wedges, and serve hot.

WALDORF CHICKEN SALAD

This contemporary take on a classic dish, with yogurt in the dressing for lightness, is a great way to use up leftover roast chicken.

THE CUT Chicken breast

SERVES 6
PREP 25–30 mins, plus chilling
COOK 25–35 mins

4 celery stalks

1 onion, quartered

1 carrot, quartered

10–12 black peppercorns

1 bouquet garni, made with 5–6 sprigs of flat-leaf parsley, 2–3 sprigs of thyme, and 1 bay leaf

salt and freshly ground black pepper

1lb 10oz (750g) skinless, boneless chicken breasts

1 cup walnuts

1lb 2oz (500g) tart, crisp apples

juice of 1 lemon

⅔ cup plain yogurt

⅔ cup mayonnaise

1 Trim the tops from the celery. Place the trimmings and stalks in a wide saucepan. Add the onions, carrots, peppercorns, and bouquet garni.

Season with salt and bring to a boil. Then reduce the heat to a simmer and cook for 10–15 minutes. Then add the chicken and cook for 10–12 minutes, turning once, until the juices run clear when the meat is pierced at its thickest point.

2 Remove from the heat and leave the chicken to cool in the poaching liquid for 10–15 minutes, then drain on paper towels. Use a fork to shred the chicken into slivers about 2in (5cm) long.

3 Preheat the oven to 350°F (180°C). Spread the walnuts on a baking sheet and bake for 5–8 minutes, until crisp, turning occasionally.

4 Meanwhile, take the celery stalks out of the poaching liquid and slice them. Set aside. Cut the top and bottom ends from the apples. Halve and core them, then dice the flesh. Place in a large bowl, pour the lemon juice over, and toss to coat.

5 Add the chicken, celery, yogurt, mayonnaise, and two-thirds of the walnuts. Season, stir to combine, and chill for 1 hour. Roughly chop the remaining walnuts. Spoon the salad onto 6 plates, sprinkle the chopped nuts on top, and serve.

CHICKEN PARMESAN

Nothing says classic comfort food like Parmesan-breaded chicken, aromatic sauce, and melted mozzarella.

THE CUT Chicken breast

SERVES 4–6
PREP 30 mins **COOK** 1 hr 40 mins

2¼lb (1kg) skinless, boneless chicken breasts

½ cup all-purpose flour

2 tsp garlic powder

1 tsp white pepper

½ cup dried bread crumbs

3½oz (100g) freshly grated Parmesan, plus 1oz (30g) extra for the topping

2 large eggs, beaten with 1–2 tbsp water

3 tbsp olive oil, for frying

7oz (200g) mozzarella cheese, cut into slices

FOR THE SAUCE

1 tbsp olive oil

5½oz (150g) onion, diced

3 garlic cloves, crushed

1¾lb (800g) tomatoes, diced

1 cup chicken stock

1 tbsp rosemary

1 tsp basil

1 tsp dried oregano

1 tsp dried thyme

salt and freshly ground black pepper

1 For the sauce, heat the oil in a large saucepan over medium heat. Add the onion and garlic and cook for 5 minutes, stirring, until caramelized. Add the remaining ingredients, season to taste, and reduce the heat to a simmer. Cook for 45 minutes, stirring occasionally. Taste and season, if necessary.

2 Place the chicken between two pieces of plastic wrap and flatten with a meat tenderizer or rolling pin. Mix the flour, half the seasonings, and 1 teaspoon salt in a shallow dish. Combine the bread crumbs, Parmesan, and remaining seasoning in a second dish. Place the beaten eggs in a small bowl. Heat the oil in a heavy-bottomed pan. Dust the chicken with the flour mixture, dip in the beaten eggs, and coat with the bread crumb mixture. Fry the chicken for 4 minutes on each side.

3 Set the broiler to its highest setting. Transfer the sauce and chicken to a casserole, partially covering the chicken with sauce. Top with both cheeses and broil for 15 minutes, or until the mozzarella is bubbling. Serve hot over pasta.

JAMAICAN JERK CHICKEN

Serve this spicy chicken with mango salsa, Jamaican rice, and peas for a truly Caribbean feast.

THE CUT Chicken drumstick

SERVES 4
PREP 10 mins, plus marinating
COOK 30–40 mins

4 scallions, chopped

1 garlic clove, chopped

¾in (2cm) fresh ginger, finely chopped

1 red chile, seeded and finely chopped, or more to taste

¼ cup sunflower oil

2 tbsp soy sauce

1 tbsp apple cider vinegar

juice and finely grated zest of ½ lime

½ tsp dried thyme

½ tsp ground allspice

¼ tsp ground nutmeg

¼ tsp ground cinnamon

1 tbsp dark brown sugar

salt and freshly ground black pepper

8 skin-on bone-in chicken pieces

1 For the sauce, place all the ingredients except the chicken in a food processor and season well. Pulse to a thick, smooth sauce, scraping down the sides with a spatula during the process. Remove and place in a large bowl.

2 Cut 2 or 3 slashes on each side of the chicken pieces, where the meat is thickest. Add to the sauce, and mix to coat. Cover and marinate in the fridge for at least 2 hours, turning over once halfway through to ensure they are evenly coated.

3 Preheat the grill or broiler to its medium setting. Cook the chicken—30 minutes for drumsticks, 40 minutes for thighs—turning over frequently, and basting with the leftover jerk sauce as it cooks.

4 The meat will separate slightly where it has been slashed, which enables it to cook through and gives a bigger surface area for the sauce. The chicken is cooked through if the juices run clear when the meat is pierced at its thickest point.

CHICKEN ADOBO

This celebrated Filipino dish brings together the saltiness of soy sauce, the tang of vinegar, and the fragrance of bay leaf.

THE CUT Chicken thigh

SERVES 8
PREP 20 mins   **COOK** 1 hr

1 tbsp olive oil
3lb 3oz (1.5kg) skin-on bone-in chicken thighs
1lb 2oz (500g) white onion, sliced into rings
4 garlic cloves, crushed
1 tbsp freshly ground black pepper
1 tbsp arrowroot
½ cup white wine vinegar
½ cup soy sauce
juice of 3 limes
1 bay leaf

1 Heat the oil in a saucepan. Add the chicken and cook for about 5–6 minutes on each side, until well-browned all over. Do this in batches to avoid overcrowding the pan. Remove with a slotted spoon and set aside.

2 Add the onions, garlic, pepper, and arrowroot to the pan. Toss to coat the onions. Then return the chicken to the pan. Pour in the vinegar, soy sauce, and lime juice, and add the bay leaf.

3 Reduce the heat to simmer and cook uncovered for 45 minutes or until the chicken has cooked through. Remove the bay leaf. Serve hot spooned over white rice.

CHICKEN AND DATE EMPANADAS

First mentioned in a 16th-century Catalan cookbook, empanadas have since become popular across the globe. The chipotle paste in this recipe is an American influence.

THE CUT Chicken thigh

MAKES 10–12
PREP 40 mins, plus chilling   **COOK** 1 hr 20 mins

FOR THE PASTRY

1¾ cups all-purpose flour, plus extra for dusting
1 tbsp cayenne pepper
salt
½ cup vegetable fat
14 tbsp butter, chilled and diced
1 large egg, beaten to glaze

FOR THE FILLING

1lb 10oz (750g) skin-on bone-in chicken thighs
2 tbsp olive oil, plus extra for greasing
3½oz (100g) dried dates, finely chopped
½ cup honey
½ tbsp cayenne pepper
½ tbsp chipotle paste
½ tbsp ground cinnamon

1 For the pastry, sift the flour, cayenne pepper, and half a teaspoon of salt into a large bowl. Rub in the fat and butter until the mixture resembles bread crumbs.

2 Preheat the oven to 350°F (180°C). Stir 1 cup water into the flour mixture, a little at a time, until a loose ball of dough has formed. Wrap in plastic wrap and chill for 1 hour.

3 Place the chicken thighs on a baking sheet and drizzle with oil. Roast in the oven for 35–40 minutes or until cooked through. Remove from the oven and let cool. Leave the oven on and lightly grease a baking sheet with oil.

4 Remove the skin and bones from the chicken, lightly shred the meat with a fork, and transfer it to a bowl. Add the dates, honey, and spices to the chicken. Season with salt and stir to combine.

5 On a lightly floured surface, roll out the pastry to a thickness of ¼in (5mm). Use a biscuit cutter to cut 10–12 circles, about 4in (10cm) in diameter. Place 1 tablespoon of the filling in the middle of each circle and fold the pastry over to create a semicircle. Dampen the edges a little and press them together to seal.

6 Place the empanadas on the baking sheet and brush with the beaten egg. Bake for 35–40 minutes or until golden brown. Arrange on a plate and serve hot.

CHICKEN TAJINE

An easy-to-make North African dish, this crowd-pleaser shines with the flavor of the preserved lemon.

THE CUT Chicken thigh

SERVES 4
PREP 10 mins   **COOK** 2 hrs 15 mins

2 tbsp olive oil
3lb 3oz (1.5kg) skin-on bone-in chicken thighs
2 garlic cloves, crushed
10oz (300g) white onions, sliced into thick rings
2 tbsp ground turmeric
2 tbsp curry powder
1 tbsp paprika
1 tbsp mustard powder
1 tbsp ground cinnamon
salt and freshly ground black pepper
3½oz (100g) black olives
1 preserved lemon, sliced
2 cups chicken stock

1 Heat the oil in a tagine, heatproof casserole, or Dutch oven. Add the chicken and cook for about 5–6 minutes on each side, until well-browned all over. Remove with a slotted spoon and set aside.

2 Add the garlic to the pot and sauté for 5 minutes, until browned. Then add the onions and spices and season to taste. Toss to coat the onions. Spread the onions evenly over the bottom of the pot.

3 Place the chicken on top of the onions along with the olives and preserved lemons. Then pour in the stock and bring to a boil.

4 Reduce the heat to simmer, cover, and cook for 2 hours. Check the sauce occasionally, to make sure it does not get too dry or stick to the pot. Add more stock, if necessary. Remove from the heat and serve hot with couscous.

COQ AU VIN

A classic French dish, this makes a comforting winter meal. The alcohol cooks off, leaving only a rich taste.

THE CUT Chicken thigh or drumstick

SERVES 4
PREP 10 mins   **COOK** 1 hr 10 mins

¼ cup olive oil

3½oz (100g) chopped bacon

5½oz (150g) small crimini mushrooms, rinsed, dried, and halved, if necessary

12 small pearl onions or shallots

¼ cup all-purpose flour

salt and freshly ground black pepper

8 skin-on bone-in chicken thighs, drumsticks, or a mixture

¼ cup brandy (optional)

1¼ cups red wine

1¼ cups chicken stock

1 tbsp red currant jelly

bunch of bouquet garni

1 Heat half of the oil in a large, lidded saucepan over medium heat. Cook the bacon, mushrooms, and onions for 5 minutes, until golden brown. Remove from the heat.

2 Heat the remaining oil in a separate pan. Place 1 tablespoon of the flour in a small bowl and season with salt and pepper. Dust the chicken with the flour, shaking off any excess. Fry the chicken for 3–5 minutes, on each side, until golden brown. Do this in batches to avoid overcrowding the pan. Remove from the heat, add the brandy (if using), and ignite with a match to cook off the alcohol.

3 Remove the chicken from the pan and add to the vegetables and bacon. Stir in the remaining flour and cook for 1 minute. Add the wine, stock, red currant jelly, and bouquet garni. Return to the heat and bring to a boil. Then reduce to a simmer, cover, and cook for 40–45 minutes, until cooked through. Remove the bouquet garni and serve hot.

ONE-POT SPANISH CHICKEN WITH RICE

Also known as *arroz con pollo*, this hassle-free recipe is packed with warm spicy flavor and is the perfect one-pot meal.

THE CUT Chicken thigh

SERVES 4–6
PREP 20 mins   **COOK** 1 hr

¼ cup olive oil

1 heaping tbsp all-purpose flour

salt and freshly ground black pepper

2 tsp smoked paprika, plus extra for dusting

8 skinless boneless chicken thighs, cut into bite-size pieces

1 onion, finely chopped

1 red bell pepper, cut into ¾in (2cm) cubes

1 orange bell pepper, cut into ¾in (2cm) cubes

7oz (200g) Spanish-style chorizo, casing removed and cut into 1in (3cm) slices

2 garlic cloves, chopped

½ tsp cayenne pepper (optional)

3 cups chicken stock

3 heaping tbsp chopped flat-leaf parsley

10oz (300g) long-grain or basmati white rice

2½oz (75g) frozen peas

1 tbsp butter

1 Heat 2 tablespoons of the oil in a large, lidded, heavy-based saucepan. Season the flour with salt, pepper, and a little smoked paprika to taste. Dust the chicken evenly with the flour, shaking off any excess. Cook the chicken for 2–3 minutes on each side over medium heat, until golden brown all over. Do this in batches to avoid overcrowding the pan. Set aside and keep warm.

2 Heat the remaining oil in the pan and cook the onion and bell peppers for 3–5 minutes, until softened and turning brown. Add the chorizo and cook for 1–2 minutes, until beginning to turn crisp at the edges. Add the garlic, smoked paprika, and cayenne pepper (if using) and cook for 1 minute, until fragrant.

3 Add the stock and scrape up the meaty residue from the pan. Return the chicken to the pan, add two-thirds of the parsley, and bring to a boil. Reduce to a simmer, cover, and cook for 10 minutes.

4 Add the rice and stir well. Cover and cook over very low heat for about 15 minutes, until the rice has cooked and absorbed most of the liquid. Stir in the peas, butter, and remaining parsley. Remove from the heat and let rest, with the lid on, for 5 minutes. Serve warm.

SOUTHERN FRIED CHICKEN

The trick for keeping this dish crisp, light, and juicy is to maintain the oil at the correct temperature.

 THE CUT Chicken leg and thigh

SERVES 4
PREP 20 mins **COOK** 15 mins

2 cups buttermilk

1 tbsp hot sauce

8 skin-on, bone-in chicken legs and small thighs

1 cup self-rising flour

2 tbsp cornstarch

1 tsp salt

1 tsp garlic powder

1 tsp cayenne pepper

1 tsp paprika

1 tsp black pepper

4 cups peanut or sunflower oil, for frying

1 Whisk together the buttermilk and hot sauce, and season well. Put the chicken pieces into a dish in a single layer and pour the buttermilk over them. Cover the dish in plastic wrap and chill for at least 4 hours, or preferably overnight.

2 When you are ready to cook the chicken, put all the dry ingredients together in a large plastic bag and shake well to combine. Take the chicken pieces out of the buttermilk mixture and shake off any excess. Put the chicken pieces into the bag, one at a time, and shake until they are well covered with the coating. Lay them on a wire rack as you work, and allow them to rest for 30 minutes at room temperature (this will help the coating to stick during frying).

3 In a large, heavy-bottomed saucepan or deep-fat fryer, heat the oil to 375°F (190°C) and carefully lower the chicken pieces into the oil, without overcrowding the pan. Cook for 5–7 minutes on each side (depending on the size of the pieces), turning them over occasionally so that they brown evenly. The temperature of the oil will dip when the chicken is added, and should be maintained at 300–325°F (150–160°C). The chicken is ready if the juices run clear when a skewer is inserted into the thickest part of the meat.

4 Remove the chicken pieces from the pan with a slotted spoon and drain well on paper towels. If you are cooking in more than one batch, keep the fried chicken warm in the oven at 300°F (150°C) while you cook the remaining pieces.

KARAHI CHICKEN

This relatively simple dry curry from North India gets its name from the wok or "karahi" in which it is traditionally prepared.

 THE CUT Chicken thigh

SERVES 4
PREP 15 mins **COOK** 1 hr

1 tsp coriander seeds

2 green chiles, seeded

3 garlic cloves

1 tsp ground turmeric

2 tbsp sunflower oil

salt and freshly ground black pepper

8 skin-on chicken thighs, slashed crosswise

1 onion, roughly chopped

6 tomatoes, roughly chopped

3 cups hot vegetable stock

2in (5cm) piece of fresh ginger, peeled and finely chopped

3–4 green bird's eye chiles

bunch of cilantro leaves, finely chopped

1 Place the coriander seeds, green chiles, garlic, turmeric, and 1 tablespoon of the oil in a food processor and pulse to a paste. Season the chicken and coat with the spice paste, pushing it into the cuts. Heat half the remaining oil in a large heatproof casserole over medium-high heat. Add the chicken and cook for 5–6 minutes on each side or until it begins to color. Remove the chicken from the casserole and set aside.

2 Heat the remaining oil in the casserole over medium heat. Add the onion and cook for 3–4 minutes, until softened. Add the tomatoes and cook for an additional 5–10 minutes, until soft. Pour in the stock and bring to a boil. Reduce to a simmer, stir in the ginger and chiles, and return the chicken to the casserole.

3 Cover and cook gently for 30–40 minutes. Check the sauce occasionally to make sure it does not get too dry or stick to the bottom, adding a little hot water, if necessary. Remove the bird's eye chiles, season to taste as necessary, and stir in the cilantro. Serve with rice or chapatis, and some minted yogurt on the side.

VARIATION

Karahi rabbit Use a whole rabbit, cut into 8 pieces, instead of the chicken thighs. For the spice paste, add 1 teaspoon roasted cumin seeds and 1/4 teaspoon ground cloves to the other spices, then pulse in a food processor. In step 2, add 2 diced red bell peppers with the tomatoes, and cook as above.

BUFFALO CHICKEN WINGS

Hailing from Buffalo, New York, these sweet and spicy chicken wings are easy to prepare and make excellent finger food when served with a salty blue cheese dressing.

THE CUT Chicken wings

SERVES 6
PREP 20–30 mins, plus chilling
COOK 40–50 mins

1 cup all-purpose flour

1¾ cups bread crumbs

1 tsp paprika

½ tsp cayenne pepper

½ tsp salt

2 cups buttermilk

24 bone-in chicken wings

3½ cups peanut or sunflower oil, for frying

FOR THE SAUCE

1 cup hot chili sauce

2 garlic cloves, chopped

2 tbsp honey

8 tbsp butter

FOR THE DRESSING

¼ cup mayonnaise

½ cup sour cream

⅓ cup buttermilk

4oz (115g) blue cheese, crumbled

2 tbsp cider vinegar

MAKE YOUR OWN

Instead of using store-bought buttermilk, you can make it at home by combining 1 tablespoon of lemon juice or vinegar with 1 cup of skim milk. Set aside for 10 minutes before using.

1 Place the flour, bread crumbs, paprika, cayenne pepper, and salt in a large bowl and mix to combine. Place the buttermilk in a separate bowl. Dip the chicken wings in the buttermilk, then toss them in the flour mixture, making sure each one is evenly coated, and shaking off any excess. Chill the coated chicken wings in the fridge for at least 1 hour.

2 Meanwhile, for the sauce, place the hot chili sauce, garlic, honey, and butter in a saucepan over low heat. Let the butter melt, then reduce the heat to a simmer and cook for about 5 minutes. Remove from the heat and keep warm.

3 Heat the oil in a large, heavy-bottomed saucepan or deep-fat fryer to 375°F (190°C). Fry the chicken wings in the oil for 8–10 minutes, or until golden brown all over. Do this in batches of 4–5 wings to avoid overcrowding the pan. Remove the chicken wings from the pan with a slotted spoon and place on a plate.

4 Dip the chicken wings in the sauce mixture. Turn them through the mixture to ensure that they are evenly coated on all sides. Place on a wire rack to cool. For the dressing, place all the ingredients in a food processor and pulse until combined. Serve the dressing in a small bowl along with the chicken wings.

CAJUN-SPICED CHICKEN

This sweet, spicy marinade is delicious and versatile—it can be used in the oven, on the grill, and even under the broiler.

THE CUT Chicken thigh or drumstick

SERVES 4
PREP 10 mins, plus marinating
COOK 40–45 mins

2 tbsp olive oil

2 tsp light brown sugar

2 tsp paprika

½–1 tsp cayenne pepper or chile powder, to taste

1 tsp ground cumin

1 tsp dried thyme

1 tsp ground coriander

salt and freshly ground black pepper

8 bone-in, skin-on chicken thighs or drumsticks

1 Place all the ingredients, except the chicken, in a large bowl and mix to combine.

2 Add the chicken to the marinade and mix to coat. Cover and chill in the fridge for at least 1 hour, or preferably up to 4 hours.

3 Preheat the oven to 400°F (200°C). Arrange the chicken in a roasting pan, spaced well apart and in a single layer.

4 Place the roasting pan in the oven and cook the chicken for 40–45 minutes, turning occasionally, until the chicken is dark golden brown and cooked through. Place on a warm plate and serve with rice or sautéed vegetables.

CHICKEN CACCIATORE

Italian for "hunter-style chicken," this dish is traditionally served with polenta to soak up the juices.

THE CUT Chicken leg

SERVES 4
PREP 20 mins   **COOK** 35–40 mins

3lb 3oz (1.5kg) chicken legs, trimmed

salt and freshly ground black pepper

2 tbsp olive oil

2 garlic cloves, sliced

1 onion, chopped

¾ cup dry white wine

1 celery stalk, chopped

7oz (200g) crimini mushrooms, sliced

1 x 14oz (400g) can chopped tomatoes

⅔ cup chicken stock

1 tbsp tomato paste

2 tsp chopped rosemary

2 tsp chopped sage

8 pitted black olives, halved

1 Season the chicken with salt and pepper. Heat half the oil in a large, heavy-bottomed frying pan. Add the chicken legs and fry until well-browned on all sides. Do this in batches to avoid overcrowding the pan. Remove with a slotted spoon, place on a plate lined with paper towels, and keep hot.

2 Pour the excess fat out of the pan and add the remaining oil. Add the garlic and onion and fry for 3–4 minutes, until soft but not brown. Then add the wine and boil for 1 minute.

3 Add the celery, mushrooms, tomatoes, stock, paste, rosemary, and sage. Stir to mix and reduce the heat to low. Return the chicken to the pan, cover, and cook for 30 minutes, or until the chicken is cooked through.

4 Then add the olives and cook, uncovered, for an additional 5–10 minutes. Remove from the heat and serve hot with soft polenta and a salad of fresh mixed leaves.

CHICKEN TIKKA MASALA

An Indian dish that is loved across the world. The combination of garam masala, tomatoes, cilantro, and cream gives the sauce a sweet and spicy flavor.

THE CUT Whole chicken

SERVES 6
PREP 20 mins   **COOK** 3 hrs

1 chicken, about 4lb (1.8kg)

1¼ cups plain yogurt

2 tbsp ground coriander

1 tbsp salt

FOR THE SAUCE

2 tbsp ghee or clarified butter

2 tbsp garam masala

1 tbsp curry powder

1 tbsp ground turmeric

1 tsp ground cumin

1 tsp cayenne pepper

1 tsp ground ginger

1 tsp ground coriander

4 x 14oz (400g) can diced tomatoes, with juices

1lb 2oz (500g) white onion, diced

4 garlic cloves, crushed

1 cup heavy cream

7oz (200g) chopped cilantro leaves, to garnish

1 Preheat the oven to 350°F (180°C). Coat the chicken with the yogurt. Place it on a baking sheet and sprinkle with the coriander and salt. Transfer to the oven and roast for 1½ hours, or until the internal temperature reaches 165°F (75°C).

2 Meanwhile, combine the ghee and spices in a large saucepan over medium heat. Cook, stirring constantly, for 1–2 minutes, or until the spices and ghee have browned. Stir in the onions and garlic, cover, and cook for 5–7 minutes, until the onions have softened. Then add the tomatoes and juices and bring to a boil. Reduce the heat and simmer for 45 minutes, stirring occasionally.

3 Remove the chicken from the oven and let cool slightly. Remove the skin and bones and, using a fork, lightly shred the meat. Add the shredded chicken into the sauce and stir well. Then add the heavy cream and simmer for an additional 5–7 minutes. Remove from the heat. To serve, garnish with the chopped cilantro and serve hot with basmati rice.

LOCRO DE PAPAS

Variations of this rich and hearty potato soup are found throughout the Andes mountains of South America.

THE CUT Whole chicken

SERVES 6
PREP 15 mins
COOK 1 hr 45 mins—2 hrs 15 mins

3lb 3oz (1.5kg) waxy white potato, such as Yukon Gold, peeled

1 chicken, about 4lb (1.8kg)

6 garlic cloves, crushed

1 tbsp olive oil

1lb 2oz (500g) onion, chopped

2 tsp dried oregano

1 tsp red pepper flakes

1lb 2oz (500g) corn kernels

1 cup whole milk

salt and freshly ground black pepper

7oz (200g) queso fresco or feta cheese

1 Chop 1lb 2oz (500g) of the potatoes in half and set aside. Place the chicken in a large stock pot, add just enough water to cover the meat, and bring to a boil.

2 Add one-third of the garlic and the chopped potatoes to the pan, and reduce the heat to a simmer. Cover and cook for 45 minutes, or until the chicken is cooked through.

3 Remove the chicken, along with the garlic and potatoes from the pot. Discard the skin and bones and use a fork to shred the meat. Return the shredded meat to the pot.

4 Cut the remaining potatoes into cubes. Heat the oil in a frying pan, add the onions and remaining garlic, and sauté for 5–7 minutes. Stir in the potato cubes, oregano, and red pepper flakes, and cook for 3–5 minutes, until they turn brown. Then add the corn, stir well, and remove from the heat.

5 Transfer the potato and corn mixture to the stock pot, stir in the milk, and season. Bring to a boil, then reduce the heat and simmer for 35–40 minutes or until the potatoes are soft. Stir in the queso fresco and cook for another 10 minutes. Remove from the heat, spoon into bowls, and serve hot.

POULE AU POT

Literally meaning "chicken in a pot," this classic French dish served with sauce gribiche, a cold-egg sauce, is a complete meal in itself.

THE CUT Whole chicken

SERVES 4–6
PREP 20 mins **COOK** 1–1½ hrs

1 onion, trimmed

1 clove

1 chicken, about 4½lb (2kg)

salt and freshly ground black pepper

1 bouquet garni

14 cups chicken stock, plus extra if needed

2¼lb (1kg) leeks, trimmed, cut lengthwise, and sliced

13oz (375g) carrots, sliced

13oz (375g) turnips, diced

2oz (60g) vermicelli

FOR THE SAUCE GRIBICHE

2 hard-boiled eggs, shelled

juice of ½ lemon

1 tsp Dijon mustard

2 tbsp dry white wine

1 cup vegetable oil

1 tbsp drained capers, finely chopped

3 gherkins, finely chopped

5–7 sprigs of flat-leaf parsley, finely chopped

small bunch of chives, finely snipped

1 Stud the onion with the clove. Place the chicken in a Dutch oven, season, and add the bouquet garni and onion. Add just enough stock to cover three-quarters of the chicken. Bring to a boil, cover, and simmer for 45 minutes.

2 Wrap the leeks in cheesecloth and tie securely to make a bundle. Repeat with the carrots and turnips in separate cheesecloth. Add to the chicken and pour in more stock to cover. Cover and simmer for 25–30 minutes.

3 For the sauce, separate the hard-boiled yolks from the whites. Cut the whites into strips and chop finely. Sieve the yolks into a bowl using the back of a spoon. Add the lemon juice, mustard, wine, and seasoning and whisk until combined. Gradually pour in the oil, whisking constantly. Add the egg whites, capers, gherkins, and herbs, and whisk to combine.

4 Remove the chicken from the Dutch oven. Carve the chicken, cover the pieces with foil, and keep warm. Remove the vegetables from the broth and keep warm. Strain the broth into a pan and simmer for 10–20 minutes. Skim off the fat and adjust the seasoning. Add the vermicelli and cook according to package instructions.

5 Unwrap the vegetables, discarding the cheesecloth, and add them and the chicken to the broth. Stir; remove from the heat. Serve in bowls with the sauce gribiche in a separate bowl.

TOM KHA GAI

This authentic Thai soup is full of herbs and spices, with the whole chicken making a rich and flavorsome base.

THE CUT Whole chicken

SERVES 6
PREP 10 mins **COOK** 3 hrs

1 chicken, about 4lb (1.8kg)

1 turnip, halved

1in (2.5cm) piece of fresh ginger, peeled

1 tbsp red curry paste

juice of 2 limes

2 tbsp Thai fish sauce

1½oz (40g) galangal or fresh ginger, sliced into rounds

7oz (200g) straw, oyster, or crimini mushrooms, thickly sliced

2 shallots, sliced into rings

3 lemongrass stalks, chopped

2–3 bird's eye chiles, seeded and diced

6 makrut or kaffir lime leaves, finely chopped

2 cups coconut milk

1¾oz (50g) cilantro leaves, chopped

salt and freshly ground black pepper

1 Place the chicken in a large stock pot, cover with water, and bring to a boil. Add the turnip and ginger and reduce the heat. Cover and simmer for 2 hours, or until the chicken is fully cooked.

2 Remove from the heat, take the chicken out of the pot, and discard the turnip and ginger. Discard the skin and bones and lightly shred the meat using a fork. Return the shredded meat to the broth.

3 Add the curry paste, lime juice, fish sauce, galangal, mushrooms, shallots, lemongrass, chiles, and makrut or kaffir lime leaves to the broth and bring to a boil.

4 Reduce the heat to a simmer and stir in the coconut milk. Simmer for 45 minutes, stirring occasionally. Stir in the cilantro and season to taste. Ladle into soup bowls and serve hot.

VARIATION

Shredded chicken and rice soup Cook as above but add 1 cup uncooked rice to the soup for the last 15 minutes of cooking. Serve hot.

POT-ROAST CHICKEN

A simple one-pot meal, this dish makes for a succulent and tender variation to the traditional roast.

CUT Whole chicken

SERVES 4
PREP 10 mins   **COOK** 1 hr 45 mins

2 tbsp olive oil

1 large onion, cut into 8 wedges

1 leek, cut into 1in (3cm) pieces

1 celery stalk, cut into 1in (3cm) pieces

4 carrots, cut into 1in (3cm) pieces

2 garlic cloves, chopped

8 skin-on new potatoes, halved

1 1/2 cups chicken stock

sprig of thyme

1 bay leaf

salt and freshly ground black pepper

1 chicken, about 3lb 3oz (1.5kg)

pat of butter

1 Preheat the oven to 350°F (180°C). Heat the oil in a large, heatproof casserole. Cook the onion, leek, celery, and carrots for 5 minutes until soft and beginning to brown. Stir in the garlic and potatoes and cook for 2 minutes.

2 Add the stock, thyme, and bay leaf, and season to taste. Then cook for an additional 2 minutes and remove the casserole from the heat.

3 Rub the chicken with the butter and season the breast with salt and pepper. Place it on the vegetables. Cover and cook in the oven for 1 hour. If the chicken is too close to the lid of the pan, cover it loosely with parchment paper to prevent it from sticking.

4 Remove the lid, increase the oven temperature to 400°F (200°C), and cook for an additional 30 minutes, or until the breast is golden brown and the sauce has reduced. Remove the herbs before serving.

SESAME CHICKEN SALAD

Bright flavors and fresh vegetables come together in this light and tangy salad.

CUT Whole chicken

SERVES 4
PREP 20 mins   **COOK** 1–1 1/2 hrs, plus chilling

1 chicken, about 2 3/4lb (1.3kg)

1 tbsp salt

3 1/2oz (100g) celery stalks, thinly sliced

3 1/2oz (100g) carrots, peeled and grated

7oz (200g) red cabbage, shredded

3 1/2oz (100g) shallots, thinly sliced

3 garlic cloves, crushed

1 3/4oz (50g) cilantro leaves, chopped

1 3/4oz (50g) scallions, chopped

1 tbsp sesame seeds

juice of 2 limes

FOR THE DRESSING

5 tbsp sesame oil

3 tbsp soy sauce

3 tbsp rice vinegar

1 tbsp red chile paste

1 Preheat the oven to 350°F (180°C). Place the chicken, breast-side up, in a roasting pan and rub with the salt and 2 tablespoons of the oil. Roast for 1–1 1/2 hours, or until the internal temperature reaches 165°F (75°C). Remove from the oven and leave to cool.

2 When the chicken is cool enough to handle, remove the skin and use a fork to lightly shred the meat off the bones. Discard the skin and bones and transfer the shredded chicken to a large bowl.

3 For the dressing, mix all the ingredients and the remaining oil in a small bowl and stir until well combined. Taste and adjust the quantity of the oil and soy sauce if required.

4 Add the celery, carrots, cabbage, shallots, and garlic to the shredded chicken. Add the dressing and toss to coat.

5 Stir in the cilantro, onions, sesame seeds, and lime juice. Cover and chill in the fridge for 1 hour or overnight. Serve at room temperature on its own, in a sandwich, or over a green salad.

CIRCASSIAN CHICKEN SALAD

Smoky paprika flavors blend with a creamy walnut sauce in this dish from the Caucasus mountains.

 Whole chicken

SERVES 6
PREP 15 mins   **COOK** 2 hrs 10 mins

1 chicken, about 4lb (1.8kg)

salt and freshly ground black pepper

3½oz (100g) walnuts

2 slices bread

1lb 2oz (500g) white onions, chopped

4 garlic cloves

1 tsp cayenne pepper

2 tbsp paprika

1¼ cups chicken stock

1 tbsp walnut oil

juice of 1 lemon

3½oz (100g) flat-leaf parsley

1 Place the chicken in a large stock pot, cover with water, and bring to a boil. Add a pinch of salt and reduce the heat to a simmer. Cover and cook for 2 hours.

2 When the chicken is cooked through, remove from the water. Set the cooking liquid aside. Discard the skin and bones from the chicken and lightly shred the meat using a fork. Transfer the shredded chicken to a serving platter and, using a fork, spread it on the platter. Set aside.

3 In a food processor, pulse the walnuts until they are finely chopped. Dip the bread slices in the chicken cooking liquid and add to the food processor, along with the onions, garlic, cayenne pepper, and 1 tablespoon each of paprika and black pepper. Pulse until a thick paste forms. Add the stock to the paste, a little at a time, until it takes on the consistency of a sauce.

4 Pour the sauce over the shredded chicken. In a small pan, heat the oil and the remaining paprika. Cook for 2–3 minutes, stirring frequently, until the paprika is toasted. Pour the paprika oil over the chicken, along with the lemon juice. Garnish with parsley and serve at room temperature or chilled.

FRANGO PIRI PIRI

This spicy grilled chicken is a Portuguese favorite and ideal for long summer afternoons outdoors.

 Whole chicken

SERVES 6
PREP 15 mins, plus 24 hrs marinating
COOK 1 hr 10 mins

10 red chiles

½ cup olive oil, plus 1 tbsp extra

4 garlic cloves

¼ cup red wine vinegar

1 tsp sea salt

1 tsp oregano

1 tsp smoked paprika

1 chicken, about 4lb (1.8kg)

salt and freshly ground black pepper

1 Place the chiles and 1 tablespoon of oil in a small bowl. Toss to coat, then grill for 5–10 minutes over medium-high heat, turning once, until roasted. Remove the stalks.

2 Place the remaining oil, garlic, vinegar, sea salt, oregano, smoked paprika, and the roasted chiles in a food processor and pulse until smooth.

3 Butterfly the chicken using kitchen shears (see p61). Place it in a plastic bag with the chile sauce and marinate for at least 24 hours.

4 Preheat the oven to 400°F (200°C). Remove the chicken from the chile sauce, arrange in a roasting pan, and season well. Roast for 50 minutes to 1 hour, or until the internal temperature of the meat reaches 165°F (75°C).

HERBY ROAST CHICKEN

Herb butter adds incredible flavor to this roast and helps keep the bird moist as it cooks.

 Whole chicken

SERVES 4–6
PREP 10 mins
COOK 1 hr 15 mins – 1 hr 30 mins, plus resting

3 tbsp butter, softened

1 tbsp finely chopped tarragon

1 tbsp finely chopped flat-leaf parsley

1 tbsp chopped thyme

1 garlic clove, crushed

grated zest and juice of ½ lemon

1 chicken, about 3lb 3oz–4½lb (1.5–2kg)

1 tbsp olive oil

salt and freshly ground black pepper

1 Preheat the oven to 450°F (230°C). For the herb butter, place the butter, herbs, garlic, and lemon zest in a large bowl and mash together to combine. Season well with salt and pepper.

2 Place the chicken on a clean work surface. Loosen the skin on the chicken breast and gently separate it from the meat, without tearing the skin, creating a pocket. Spread the herb butter evenly under the skin.

3 Place the chicken in a large roasting pan. Rub the skin with the oil and season. Drizzle with the lemon juice and place the lemon shell in the body cavity.

4 Transfer to the oven and roast for 15 minutes, then reduce the temperature to 350°F (180°C) and roast for another 1–1 hour 20 minutes, or until the juices run clear when the meat is pierced with a knife. Rest for 10 minutes, covered with foil. Serve warm.

BEER CAN CHICKEN

This recipe really spices up a barbecue and is well worth the trouble of balancing a chicken on a beer can.

 Whole chicken

SERVES 6
PREP 20 mins   **COOK** 2 hrs, plus resting

1 chicken, about 4lb (1.8kg)

5 tbsp butter, softened

1 tbsp salt

2 tbsp chopped rosemary

1 x 12fl oz (330ml) can of beer, preferably lager

1 Place the chicken on a clean work surface and brush evenly with the butter. Rub all over with the salt and sprinkle with the rosemary.

2 Preheat the barbecue smoker or oven to 350°F (180°C). Pour out half the beer from the can, then gently wedge the can in the cavity of the chicken so that the chicken is propped up on the can.

3 Place the chicken, sitting upright on the can, onto the grill. Close the lid and cook for 1½–2 hours, or until the internal temperature reaches 165°F (75°C). Check the chicken occasionally to make sure it is still upright. Remove from the grill and let rest and cool slightly. Carve and serve hot.

VARIATION

Herby beer can chicken Sprinkle the chicken with 1 tablespoon of chopped thyme and 2 teaspoons of smoked paprika along with the seasoning in step 1. Cook as above and serve hot.

TURKEY TETRAZZINI

This easy, comforting, and cheesy casserole is the perfect way to enjoy leftover turkey from a big festive meal.

 Cooked turkey

SERVES 8–10
PREP 10 mins   **COOK** 55 mins

1lb 2oz (500g) dried pasta

3 tbsp butter

4 garlic cloves, crushed

1lb 2oz (500g) onion, chopped

3½oz (100g) button mushrooms, sliced

1 cup white wine

2 cups chicken stock

½ cup all-purpose flour

1 cup turkey stock

½ cup heavy cream

1 cup milk

14oz (400g) cooked turkey, shredded

1 tsp ground nutmeg

10oz (300g) Monterey Jack or Cheddar cheese

3½oz (100g) freshly grated Parmesan cheese

8oz (225g) frozen peas

salt and freshly ground black pepper

juice of 1 lemon

1 cup panko bread crumbs

1 Cook the pasta according to package instructions. Strain and set aside. Melt the butter in a large frying pan. Add the garlic and onions and sauté for 5–7 minutes, until the onions are tender. Stir in the mushrooms and cook for 5 more minutes, stirring frequently.

2 Stir in the wine and chicken stock, reduce the heat to a simmer, and let reduce for 10 minutes. Add the flour, stir to incorporate, and pour in the turkey stock a little at a time, whisking into a sauce.

3 Reduce heat to medium-low. Stir in the cream, milk, turkey, nutmeg, and both types of cheese. Season well, mix to incorporate, and simmer for 15–20 minutes. Stir in the pasta and the peas. Preheat the oven to 350°F (180°C).

4 Remove the pan from the heat and stir in the lemon juice. Transfer to a casserole dish and top with the bread crumbs. Bake for 25 minutes or until golden brown and bubbling. Serve hot.

TURDUCKEN

Duck fat bastes the turkey and chicken from the inside, making this dish incredibly moist.

THE CUT Whole turkey, duck, chicken

SERVES 20–25
PREP 2 hrs **COOK** 4–5 hrs, plus resting

1 turkey, about 13lb (6kg)
2 tbsp cayenne pepper
salt and freshly ground black pepper
2 tbsp garlic powder
2 sticks butter, about 9oz in total, cut into cubes
1 duck, about 4½lb (2kg)
1 chicken, about 4lb (1.8kg)

1 Line a large roasting pan with foil. Debone the turkey, leaving the drumsticks and wings bone-in (see p60). Lay it skin-side down on the roasting pan. Generously sprinkle the cayenne pepper, salt, pepper, and garlic powder over the bird. Top with one-quarter of the butter.

2 Debone the duck, removing the wings entirely and removing the bones from the drumsticks (see p60). Lay the duck skin-side down on top of the turkey, centering the bird. Generously sprinkle with the cayenne pepper, salt, pepper, and garlic powder. Top with one-quarter of the butter.

3 Debone the chicken, removing the wings entirely and removing the bones from the drumsticks (see p60). Lay the chicken skin-side down on top of the duck, centering the bird. Generously sprinkle the cayenne pepper, salt, pepper, and garlic powder over the bird. Top with one-quarter of the butter.

4 Fold the turkey onto itself so that it wraps around the two center birds. Using butcher's string sew the turkey up where the backbone was. Take care to make sure that the duck and the chicken stay within the turkey cavity. Preheat the oven to 350°F (180°C).

5 Flip the turkey so the bird is seam-side down on the pan. Top generously with the remaining spices, seasoning, and butter. Bake for 3–4 hours, or until the internal temperature for the chicken reaches 165°F (75°C). The juices should run clear when the turkey thigh is pierced at its thickest point.

6 Remove from the oven and let rest for 30 minutes. Slice across the bird so that each serving contains chicken, duck, and turkey.

TURKEY AND OLIVE QUICHE

A medley of flavors from salty olives, ripe tomatoes, and cinnamon makes this an ideal brunch quiche.

THE CUT Cooked turkey

SERVES 6
PREP 15 mins, plus chilling **COOK** 45 mins

FOR THE PASTRY

1 cup all-purpose flour, plus extra for dusting
1 tsp ground cinnamon
1 tsp salt
¼ cup vegetable fat
½ tbsp butter, chilled and diced, plus extra for greasing
1 egg, beaten to glaze

FOR THE FILLING

6 large eggs
½ cup heavy cream
3 tbsp milk
7oz (200g) cooked turkey, shredded
3½oz (100g) black olives, pitted and halved
3½oz (100g) cherry tomatoes, halved
1¾oz (50g) fresh spinach

1 tsp red pepper flakes
1 tsp ground cinnamon
1 tsp garlic powder

1 For the pastry, place the flour, cinnamon, and salt in a large bowl and mix well. Rub in the fat and butter, until the mixture resembles bread crumbs. Then pour in ⅓ cup water, a little at a time, until a loose ball of dough has formed. Wrap in plastic wrap and chill for 1 hour.

2 Preheat the oven to 350°F (180°C). For the filling, beat the eggs with the cream and milk. Then add the turkey, olives, tomatoes, spinach, red pepper flakes, cinnamon, and garlic powder. Mix to combine.

3 Grease and line a 9in (23cm) loose-bottomed tart pan. On a lightly floured surface, roll the pastry out to a thickness of ¼in (5mm) and use to line the tart pan. Lightly brush the edges of the pastry with the beaten egg. Pour in the filling and spread it evenly into the pastry shell. Bake for 45 minutes or until firm. Serve warm.

BUTTERFLIED AND GRILLED TURKEY

Flattening the bird reduces the cooking time, making turkey a delicious anytime meal.

THE CUT Whole turkey

SERVES 8–10
PREP 30 mins **COOK** 2 hrs, plus resting

1 turkey, about 13lb (6kg)
2 tbsp each salt and freshly ground black pepper
1 tbsp garlic powder
1 tbsp cayenne pepper
16 tbsp butter, softened

1 Butterfly the turkey using kitchen shears or a boning knife (see p61). Place the turkey, breast-side up, in a large roasting pan. Spread it out flat and press down hard along the breast bone with your palm until you feel it snap.

2 Preheat the grill to 375°F (190°C). Place the seasoning and spices in a small bowl and mix to combine. Rub the turkey with the butter and

coat evenly with the spice mix. Place on a large roasting pan and grill for 1½–2 hours or until the internal temperature reaches 165°F (75°C).

4 Remove from the grill and transfer to a large serving plate or tray. Cover with foil and let rest for 30 minutes. Carve and serve hot.

VARIATION

Butterflied and roasted turkey Try cooking the turkey in the oven instead of broiling it. For the spice mix, reduce the cayenne pepper by 1 teaspoon and add 1 teaspoon paprika in its place. Preheat the oven to 375°F (190°C) at the end of step 2. Place the turkey in a large roasting pan and cook in the oven for 2 hours, basting with the juices every 30 minutes. Remove from the oven and let rest for at least 30 minutes. Carve and serve hot.

DEEP-FRIED TURKEY

The perfect Thanksgiving recipe—this whole deep-fried turkey is sure to impress your guests.

 Whole turkey

SERVES 6
PREP 15 mins, plus 2 days marinating
COOK 30 mins, plus resting

1 turkey, about 6½lb (3kg)

peanut oil, for deep frying

FOR THE BRINE

4 lemons, halved

4 whole heads of garlic, unpeeled and halved

⅓ cup salt

3 bay leaves

½ cup brown sugar

1 For the brine, begin two days before you plan to make the dish. Place the turkey in a large stock pot and cover with water. Add the lemons, garlic heads, salt, bay leaves, and sugar. Cover and keep in a cool place for at least two days.

2 Heat the oil in a large deep-fat fryer to 375°F (190°C). Place a colander over a large bowl. Remove the turkey from the brine and place in the colander to drain for about 1 hour.

3 Pat the turkey dry with paper towels. Use a turkey hook or large tongs to slowly lower it into the deep-fat fryer, taking care to avoid splashing the hot oil.

4 Cook the turkey, turning occasionally, for 30 minutes, or until it turns a deep, rich brown and the internal temperature reaches 165°F (75°C). Remove from the oil, place it on a plate, and set aside to rest for at least 1 hour. Carve the turkey and serve warm.

SAFETY FIRST!

Set up the deep-fat fryer outdoors and make sure you follow the instructions on the kit. Keep your arms and feet covered and use gloves while handling the turkey.

TURKEY, MINT, AND ENDIVE WRAPS

Crisp Belgian endive, fresh mint, and creamy yogurt come together in these light and refreshing wraps.

THE CUT Cooked turkey

SERVES 4
PREP 15 mins, plus chilling   **COOK** 45 mins

4oz (200g) cooked turkey, shredded

3½oz (100g) Greek-style yogurt

3½oz (100g) red onions, thinly sliced

3½oz (100g) carrots, grated

1 tsp ground ginger

juice of 1 lemon

salt and freshly ground black pepper

1¾oz (50g) mint, finely chopped

8 Belgian endive leaves

1 In a large bowl, mix the shredded turkey, yogurt, onions, carrots, ginger, lemon juice, and season. Toss until well combined. Chill in the fridge for 30–45 minutes.

2 Arrange the Belgian endive leaves on a platter. Divide the filling into 8 equal portions. Spoon a portion of the filling on top of each of the endive leaves and serve.

SEARED DUCK BREAST WITH A RASPBERRY CARDAMOM GLAZE

The tangy, slightly tart raspberry sauce perfectly complements the rich flavors of the crisp duck breast.

 Duck breast

SERVES 4
PREP 20 mins   **COOK** 20 mins

1lb 5oz (600g) skin-on duck breasts

salt and freshly ground black pepper

FOR THE SAUCE

1 tbsp butter

1 tbsp brown sugar

3½oz (100g) shallots, finely chopped

7oz (200g) fresh raspberries, chopped

1 tsp cardamom seeds, crushed

1 tbsp red wine vinegar

1 Use a sharp knife to score the skin on the duck breasts. Rub the meat generously with salt and pepper.

2 Place the duck skin-side down in a heavy-bottomed frying pan over medium-low heat. Allow the duck fat to render for about 10–12 minutes. Flip and cook for an additional 3–5 minutes. Set aside to rest. Keep warm.

3 Drain off the duck fat. In the same pan, melt the butter. Add the brown sugar and shallots and cook until caramelized.

4 Add the raspberries, cardamom, and vinegar. Cook, stirring frequently, for 5–7 minutes. Transfer the duck to a serving plate and serve topped with the raspberry sauce.

VARIATION

Seared pork chops with blackberry glaze Use pork chops in place of duck breasts, blackberries in place of raspberries, and leave out the cardamom seeds. Cook as above but cook the pork chops for at least 10–15 minutes, until cooked through.

DUCK PÂTÉ

A simple country pâté comes to life with bursts of freshly ground pepper, citrus, and pistachios.

 Duck breast

MAKES about 2lb (900g)
PREP 25 mins, plus chilling   **COOK** 2 hrs

9oz (250g) skinless duck breasts, cut into cubes

4 garlic cloves, crushed

3 tbsp orange liqueur

2¼lb (1kg) pork shoulder, finely chopped

3½oz (100g) bacon, chopped

7oz (200g) chicken liver, chopped

9oz (250g) shallots, chopped

1lb (450g) pork back fat

3 large eggs, beaten

1 tbsp chopped thyme

½ tsp ground cloves

½ tsp ground ginger

1 tsp ground allspice

3½oz (100g) pistachios, shelled

1 tsp sea salt

1 tbsp freshly ground black pepper

1lb (450g) butter

1 Combine the duck breast, garlic, and orange liqueur in a small bowl. Cover and chill for 1 hour. Place the pork, bacon, chicken livers, shallots, and pork back fat in a food processor, in batches if necessary, and pulse to combine. Transfer to a bowl and stir in the eggs, thyme, cloves, ginger, allspice, pistachios, salt and pepper. Add the duck mixture and stir until well combined.

2 Preheat the oven to 325°F (160°C). Melt the butter in a pan, skimming off any foam. Press the meat mixture into a terrine dish, leaving a ½in (1cm) space at the top. Spoon the butter over the meat, covering it completely. Place the terrine in a roasting pan. Boil some water and half-fill the pan with it.

3 Transfer the roasting pan to the oven and bake for 2 hours, or until the internal temperature reaches 145°F (63°C). Remove from the oven and allow to cool completely. Slice and serve over toast or bread. The pâté will keep in the fridge in an airtight container for up to 2 weeks.

DUCK CONFIT

Curing and slow-cooking duck legs in their own fat gives
this dish a rich and buttery taste that is unparalleled.

THE CUT Duck leg

SERVES 6
PREP 15 mins, plus 2 days marinating
COOK 3 hrs, plus chilling

¼ cup coarse sea salt

1 tsp freshly ground black pepper

6 skin-on bone-in duck legs, about 2¾lb (1.3kg)
in total

4 garlic cloves, crushed

3½ cups duck fat

LOW-FAT CONFIT

Sear the duck in its own fat by placing
it skin-side down in a frying pan over
medium heat until one-quarter of
the fat is rendered. Then cover, place
in the oven, and cook as before.

1 Place the salt and pepper in a small bowl and mix to combine. Rub the duck legs thoroughly with the mixture and place in a sealable plastic bag or a bowl into which the legs fit neatly. Seal the bag, or cover the bowl, and chill in the fridge for at least 24 hours and up to 2 days.

2 Preheat the oven to 225°F (110°C). Remove the legs from the salt and wipe them dry to remove the excess salt. Melt the fat in a large heatproof casserole or Dutch oven. Add the legs, skin-side down, and bring to a gentle boil. Cover and cook in the oven for 3 hours or until tender.

3 Remove from the oven and transfer the legs to a deep, lidded, air-tight container. Pour in the fat from the casserole, cover, and chill. Store in the fridge for at least 24 hours, and up to 2 weeks.

4 Remove the legs from the container and scrape away all visible fat. Heat a heavy-bottomed frying pan and cook the legs for 10–12 minutes, until hot and crisp. Serve hot with green beans.

CRISPY DUCK CHAR SIU

Chinese roast duck is tasty, but it is tricky to cook a whole bird. Try this easy version with duck breasts instead.

THE CUT Duck breast

SERVES 4
PREP 5 mins, plus marinating   **COOK** 25 mins

4 skin-on boneless duck breasts

3 garlic cloves, crushed

3 tbsp soy sauce

3 tbsp rice wine

1 tbsp hoisin sauce

2 tbsp honey

2 tsp five-spice powder

salt and freshly ground black pepper

1 Place the duck breasts, skin-side up, on a clean work surface. Use a knife to score the skin in a criss-cross pattern, being careful not to cut down into the meat.

2 Place all the remaining ingredients in a wide, shallow dish and whisk to combine. Add the duck breasts to the marinade and mix to coat the meat. Cover the dish with plastic wrap and leave to marinate for 2–4 hours in the fridge.

3 Preheat the oven to 400°F (200°C). Line a baking sheet with foil. Place the duck, skin-side down, in a frying pan. Cook the breasts over medium heat for about 8 minutes. Remove from the heat.

4 Place the duck breasts, skin-side up, on the baking sheet. Cook in the top of the oven for 10 minutes. Remove and let rest for 5 minutes. Cut the duck breasts into slices on the diagonal and serve with stir-fried noodles or a green salad.

BATCH AND FREEZE

You can cook double this recipe and bag it up in portions for the freezer to produce a near-instant addition to a quick stir-fry anytime.

CASSOULET

This rich dish originating in France is named after the earthenware pot in which it was traditionally cooked.

THE CUT Duck leg

SERVES 6–8
PREP 20 mins   **COOK** 3½ hrs

7oz (200g) pancetta cubes

3 Toulouse sausages, about 7oz (200g) in total

1¾lb (850g) duck legs

salt

1 tbsp olive oil

2 onions, chopped

4 garlic cloves, crushed

7oz (200g) carrots, cut into cubes

1 tbsp chopped thyme

1 tbsp oregano

14oz (400g) tomatoes, diced

1 cup white wine

2 cups chicken stock

14oz (400g) white beans, rinsed, soaked in cold water overnight, and dried

5 tbsp butter, softened

1 cup bread crumbs

1 Place the pancetta, sausages, and duck legs in a large heatproof casserole or Dutch oven and season with a pinch of salt. Cook the meat over medium heat for 10–15 minutes, until well-browned. Remove all the meat with a slotted spoon and set aside. Preheat the oven to 300°F (150°C).

2 Add the oil to the pot, then add the onion and garlic and cook for 5 minutes over medium heat, until the onions are browned. Add carrots, thyme, and oregano, stir well to incorporate, and simmer for 2–3 minutes.

3. Stir in the tomatoes, wine, stock, and beans. Return the meat to the pot, bring to a boil, then remove from the heat. Place the butter and bread crumbs in bowl and mix to combine. Spread the bread crumb mixture evenly over the contents in the pot. Bake, uncovered, in the oven for 3 hours. Serve hot.

VARIATION

Pork cassoulet Use pork loin in place of the duck legs and substitute half the white beans with red kidney beans. Cook as above and serve hot.

THAI RED DUCK CURRY

This hot curry will keep you warm and satisfied. An unexpected ingredient, pineapple, brings vitality to the dish.

 Duck leg

SERVES 4
PREP 15 mins   **COOK** 1 hr 15 mins

2lb (850g) skinless bone-in duck legs

3 tbsp sesame oil

2 tsp salt

1 tsp freshly ground white pepper

1 tsp red pepper flakes

FOR THE SAUCE

14oz (400g) can coconut milk

½ cup Thai red chile paste

10 makrut lime leaves, chopped

3 garlic cloves, crushed

1 tbsp finely chopped fresh ginger

2 tbsp Thai fish sauce

2 tbsp sugar

juice of 1 lime

3½oz (100g) bird's eye chiles, seeded and chopped

3½oz (100g) fresh pineapple, peeled, cored, and cut into cubes

24 cherry tomatoes, whole

handful of basil, chopped

1 Preheat the oven to 325°F (160°C). Place the duck leg and thighs fat-side down in a cast-iron frying pan. Drizzle in the sesame oil and add the salt, white pepper, and red pepper flakes.

2 Roast for 40–45 minutes, or until the internal temperature reaches 165°F (75°C). Remove and let it rest for 10 minutes. Remove and discard the bones, slice the meat, and set aside.

3 Combine 1 cup of the coconut milk and the red chile paste in a saucepan over medium-high heat. Bring to a boil then reduce the heat and simmer for 10 minutes.

4 Add the duck, remaining coconut milk, makrut leaves, garlic, and ginger. Cook for 15 minutes, stirring occasionally.

5 Once the flavors have infused, stir in the fish sauce, sugar, lime juice, bird's eye chiles, and pineapple. Cook for 3–5 minutes, or until the pineapple is tender. Add the tomatoes and basil, stir, and remove from the heat. Serve hot over basmati rice.

CHINESE ROAST DUCK AND PANCAKES

A classic Chinese recipe, this dish is likely to become a favorite with the entire family.

 Duck leg

SERVES 4
PREP 20 mins   **COOK** 1 hr 10 mins

4 duck legs

1 heaping tsp five-spice powder

1 tsp coarse sea salt

freshly ground black pepper

1 cucumber, peeled

2 bunches of scallions

2 x 4oz (110g) package Chinese pancakes

10oz (285g) jar hoisin sauce or plum sauce, to serve

1 Preheat the oven to 325°F (160°C). Prick the skin of the duck legs all over with a fork. Mix the five-spice powder, salt, and a generous grinding of pepper in a small bowl. Rub the spice mix all over the legs.

2 Place the duck legs, skin-side up, on a rack inside a roasting pan and cook in the oven for 45 minutes. Then increase the oven temperature to 425°F (220°C) and cook for an additional 25 minutes, until the skin is crisp and the duck cooked through.

3 Meanwhile, prepare the vegetables. Cut the cucumber in quarters, lengthwise, then use a teaspoon to scoop the seeds from each piece. Cut each long piece into 4 chunks, then cut each chunk lengthwise into thin strips, so that you are left with a pile of thin cucumber batons. Cut the scallions into thin strips.

4 Place the duck on a cutting board and use a sharp knife to gently shred the crisp skin and meat off the bones. Discard the bones, transfer the shredded meat and crisp skin to a plate, and keep warm.

5 Heat the pancakes according to the package instructions. Serve the duck with the vegetables, pancakes, and the hoisin or plum sauce.

VENETIAN DUCK RAGÙ

A Northern Italian specialty featuring a rich meat sauce, the aromatic herbs will ensure you keep coming back for more.

THE CUT Duck leg

SERVES 6
PREP 40 mins   **COOK** 1½ hrs

3lb (1.3kg) skin-on bone-in duck legs

salt and freshly ground black pepper

2 tbsp olive oil

4 garlic cloves, crushed

1lb 2oz (500g) white onion, chopped

3½oz (100g) celery stalk, sliced

7oz (200g) carrots, peeled and sliced

2oz (60g) porcini mushrooms, finely chopped

1 tbsp dried or fresh rosemary

2 x 14oz (400g) can of chopped tomatoes

1 cup duck stock, or chicken stock

1 cup red wine, such as Chianti

1lb 2oz (500g) pappardelle

1 Place the duck legs on a clean work surface and season well with salt and pepper. Heat the oil in a large casserole or Dutch oven. Add the duck legs and cook for 4–5 minutes on both sides until brown.

2 Add garlic and onions to the pan and cook, stirring frequently, for about 10 minutes, or until caramelized. Stir in the celery and carrots and reduce the heat to simmer.

3 Stir in the mushrooms, rosemary, tomatoes, duck stock, and red wine. Return the duck legs to the pan, nestling them in the sauce. Simmer, uncovered, for 1 hour.

4 Remove the duck legs from the sauce and set aside until cool enough to handle. Cook the pappardelle according to package instructions.

5 Remove the skin and use a fork to lightly shred the meat off the bones. Discard the skin and bones. Return the shredded meat to the pan and stir well to incorporate.

6 Strain and plate your pasta, drizzling with a bit of olive oil. Top each dish with a generous portion of the ragù.

ROAST GOOSE

This oven-roasted goose, with crisp skin and tender meat, is the quintessential roast bird for your festive meal.

THE CUT Whole goose

SERVES 6–8
PREP 30 mins
COOK 3 hrs 40 mins, plus resting

2lb (900g) carrots, peeled and sliced

2lb (900g) red potatoes, peeled and quartered

1lb 2oz (500g) white onions, chopped

5 garlic cloves, crushed

3 tbsp olive oil

2 tbsp balsamic vinegar

2 tbsp salt

1 goose, wings clipped and giblets removed, about 12lb (6kg)

8 tbsp butter, softened

freshly ground black pepper

¼ cup chopped rosemary

1 lemon, halved

bunch of thyme

1 Preheat the oven to 375°F (190°C). Place the carrots, potatoes, onions, and garlic in a large roasting pan. Drizzle over the oil and vinegar, sprinkle over half the salt, and toss to coat.

2 Place the goose breast-side up in the roasting pan. Rub generously with the butter and sprinkle over the pepper, rosemary, and remaining salt. Squeeze over the lemon and place the halves in the body cavity, with the thyme.

3 Roast the goose, uncovered, for 45 minutes or until well-browned. Baste the bird with the drippings, cover with foil, and roast for an additional 2½ hours or until the internal temperature reaches 165°F (75°C). Remove from the oven and set aside to rest for 30 minutes. Carve and serve hot with the roasted vegetables.

GOOSE POT PIE

In this delicious and spicy recipe, a light and flaky crust is paired with a hearty and flavorsome goose stew.

THE CUT Cooked goose

SERVES 6
PREP 30 mins, plus chilling
COOK 1½ hrs

1½ cups all-purpose flour, plus extra for dusting

1 tsp chipotle powder

1 tsp salt

5 tbsp vegetable fat

5 tbsp butter, chilled and diced

1 large egg, beaten, to glaze

FOR THE FILLING

2 tbsp butter

1lb 2oz (500g) shallots, sliced

4 garlic cloves, chopped

1lb 2oz (500g) carrots, peeled and sliced

1lb 2oz (500g) peas

1 tbsp chipotle powder or smoked paprika

1 tsp cayenne pepper

1 tsp each salt and freshly ground black pepper

1¾lb (800g) cooked goose, shredded

1 cup chicken stock

1 Sift the flour, chipotle, and salt in a large bowl. Rub in the fat and butter until the mixture resembles bread crumbs. Add 1 cup cold water, a little at a time, until a loose ball of dough has formed. Wrap in plastic wrap and chill for 1 hour.

2 Meanwhile, make the filling. Heat the butter in a large frying pan. Sauté the shallots and garlic until browned. Add in the carrots, peas, spices, and season. Stir in the goose, add the stock, and reduce the heat to simmer. Cook for 30 minutes or until the liquid has reduced. Preheat the oven to 350°F (180°C).

3 On a lightly floured surface, roll out half the pastry to a ¼in (5mm) thick circle. Use it to line a 4 x 2in (10 x 5cm) pie dish and pour in the filling. Roll out the remaining pastry and spread it evenly over the pie. Crimp the edges, cut slits across the top, and brush with the beaten egg. Bake for 45 minutes or until golden brown. Serve warm.

CHOLENT

The perfect slow-cooked Sabbath meal, cholent is allowed to simmer overnight and into the next day.

THE CUT Goose breast

SERVES 6
PREP 10 mins   **COOK** 8–12 hrs

3 tbsp olive oil

1lb 8oz (700g) bone-in beef short ribs

1lb 2oz (500g) skinless boneless goose breast

1lb 2oz (500g) skinless bone-in chicken thighs

1lb 2oz (500g) white potatoes, such as Yukon gold, peeled and quartered

1lb 2oz (500g) onions, thickly chopped

9oz (250g) carrots, peeled and sliced

4 garlic cloves, crushed

3½oz (100g) dried white beans, rinsed, soaked in cold water overnight, and dried

3½oz (100g) kidney beans, rinsed, soaked in cold water overnight, and dried

3½oz (100g) pearl barley

1 tbsp smoked paprika

salt and freshly ground black pepper

5½ cups chicken stock, plus extra if needed

2 tbsp honey

1 Heat the oil in a large casserole or Dutch oven. Add the ribs, goose breast, and chicken thighs and cook for 3–4 minutes on each side, until well-browned. Remove the meat with a slotted spoon and set aside.

2 Add the potatoes, onions, carrots, and garlic and spread them evenly over the bottom of the pot. Return all the meat to the pot, placing it on top of the vegetables. Top with the beans, barley, smoked paprika, and season well.

3 Pour in the stock and the honey. Cover, bring to a boil, and then reduce the heat to simmer. Cook the stew for 8–12 hours, stirring occasionally, and adding in more stock if needed. Remove and discard the bones. Serve hot.

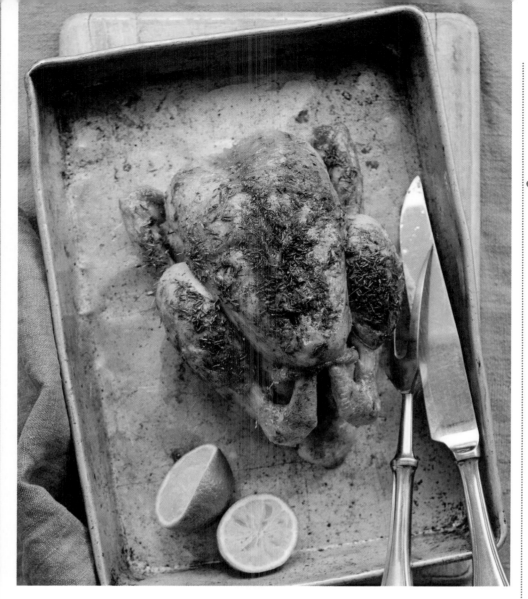

BRAISED CORNISH GAME HEN OVER POLENTA

Polenta provides the ideal base for sweet, stewed tomatoes, spicy chorizo, and red wine braised Cornish game hen.

SERVES 6
PREP 20 mins   **COOK** 2 hrs

3 skin-on Cornish game hens, about 1lb 2oz (500g) each

3½ cups chicken stock

1 cup red wine

1 tbsp ground allspice

1 bay leaf

1 tbsp sea salt, plus 1 tsp extra for the polenta

FOR THE SAUCE

7 tbsp butter

1 whole garlic bulb, finely chopped

7oz (200g) white onions, finely chopped

7oz (200g) crimini mushrooms, stems removed, rinsed, and sliced

3½oz (100g) cherry tomatoes

1 tbsp honey

½ tsp dried red pepper

½ tsp paprika

salt and freshly ground black pepper

FOR THE POLENTA

3½ cups chicken stock

1½ cups polenta

1 cup heavy cream

1 Preheat the oven to 325°F (160°C). Place the Cornish game hens in a heavy stock pot or Dutch oven. Add the stock, wine, allspice, bay leaf, and salt. Cover and cook in the oven for 2 hours, or until the meat falls off the bones.

2 For the sauce, heat the butter in a saucepan over medium-low heat. Add the garlic and onion and cook for 10 minutes, until caramelized. Then add the remaining ingredients, reduce the heat to simmer, and cook for about 20 minutes.

3 For the polenta, boil the stock in a large casserole. Add the remaining ingredients, season with sea salt, and bring to a boil. Reduce the heat, cover, and simmer for 12–15 minutes, stirring occasionally. Remove the hens from the pot and take out the bay leaf. Stir a ladleful of the braising liquid into the polenta and place it in a bowl. Top with the Cornish game hens and pour the sauce over the top.

CARIBBEAN JERK CORNISH GAME HEN

Jerk poussin, with its peppery spice blend and crisp roasted skin, is a favorite among Caribbean nations.

SERVES 4
PREP 10 mins   **COOK** 45 mins, plus resting

2 Cornish game hens, about 1lb 2oz (500g) each

5 tbsp butter, softened

1 tbsp ground allspice

1 tsp dried thyme

½ tsp ground cinnamon

pinch of salt

1 tbsp freshly ground white pepper

½ tsp grated nutmeg

1 tbsp cayenne pepper

juice of 2 limes

1 Preheat the oven to 375°F (190°C). Place the Cornish game hens breast-side up in a small roasting pan and rub evenly with the butter.

2 Place the spices and seasoning in a small bowl, mix well, and sprinkle over the meat. Transfer to the oven and roast for 45 minutes, or until the internal temperature reaches 165°F (75°C).

3 Remove from the oven and drizzle over the lime juice. Cover with foil and let rest for 10–15 minutes before carving. Serve warm with the cooking juices drizzled over the top.

ROAST CORNISH GAME HEN WITH PRESERVED LEMONS

The delicate flavor of the preserved lemons adds an exciting layer of flavor to the classic roasted Cornish game hen.

THECUT Whole Cornish game hen

SERVES 4
PREP 20 mins   **COOK** 45 mins

1 tsp ground cinnamon

2 tsp fine sea salt

1 tsp paprika

1 tsp freshly ground black pepper

1 tsp garlic powder

¼ cup olive oil

2 Cornish game hens, about 1lb 2oz (500g) each

4 preserved lemons, sliced

4 garlic cloves, chopped

1 Preheat the oven to 350°F (180°C). Place the cinnamon, salt, paprika, pepper, garlic powder, and oil in a small bowl. Mix well to combine. Place the hens breast-side up in a roasting pan and rub evenly with the oil and spice mix.

2 Divide half of the lemons and garlic between the cavities of the birds. Arrange the remaining lemons on top of the birds.

3 Place the roasting pan in the oven and roast for 35–40 minutes, or until the skin is crisp and the internal temperature reaches 165°F (75°C). Serve hot with lemon rice or couscous.

GAI YANG

This traditional Thai-spiced grilled poussin dish is served with a sweet chile sauce and fresh cilantro.

THECUT Whole Cornish game hen

SERVES 4
PREP 20 mins   **COOK** 35 mins, plus resting

2 Cornish game hens, about 1lb 2oz (500g) each

1 tbsp finely chopped cilantro stems

1 tbsp light brown sugar

1 lemongrass stalk, finely chopped

1 tbsp ground ginger

1 tsp garlic powder

¼ cup Thai fish sauce

1¾ oz (50g) cilantro leaves, finely chopped

FOR THE SAUCE

4 garlic cloves, crushed

2 red chiles, seeded and finely chopped

¼ cup rice vinegar

1 tsp salt

1 tbsp cornstarch, mixed with a little warm water

1 Butterfly the Cornish game hens using kitchen shears (see p61). Spread them on a plate, breast-side up. Preheat the broiler to medium-low.

2 Mix the cilantro stems, sugar, lemongrass, spices, and the fish sauce in a bowl. Brush the hens with the spice mix and broil, breast-side up, for 30–35 minutes, or until the internal temperature reaches 165°F (75°C).

3 Meanwhile, make the sauce. Place the garlic, chiles, vinegar, ½ cup water, and salt in a saucepan. Simmer for 10–15 minutes or until the chiles and garlic have softened. Whisk in the cornstarch mixture, a little at a time, stirring constantly. Cook the sauce for another 10 minutes, until thickened.

4 Remove the Cornish game hens from the heat and let rest for 10 minutes. Brush with the sweet chile sauce and garnish with cilantro. Serve hot.

PORK

PORK

FROM EAST TO WEST, PIGS PROVIDE HUMANS WITH MEAT AND FAT THAT IS EASY TO PRODUCE. PIGS ARE OMNIVORES, ABLE TO THRIVE ON A WIDE RANGE OF PLANTS AND ANIMALS, AND ARE SKILLED AT SCAVENGING FOR FOOD. FOR CENTURIES, THEY WERE THE ONLY SOURCE OF MEAT FOR MANY PEASANTS.

NOWADAYS, PIGS ARE BIG BUSINESS, with nearly two billion animals being produced each year. Asia produces 65 percent of the world's pigs, with the EU being the second largest producer in the world. Germany, with its thousands of types of sausage, has the highest pig population in the EU, although Denmark boasts three times as many pigs as humans. The United States is the third largest pig producer.

While some people regard pigs as dirty, this is far from the truth. They are intelligent and fastidious animals, but because they have no sweat glands they are prone to heat stress, and their habit of rolling in mud to cool themselves does make them look scruffy. A number of religions forbid the eating of pork, which is something to consider when offering hospitality. Most Jews, Muslims, Rastafarians, and some Hindus do not eat pork, and neither do some Christian sects.

Few people would disagree that the pig's main contribution to our enjoyment of food is the huge range of preserved products (see pp102–5): dried hams, bacon, and cured and smoked sausages of every imaginable shape and size all originated from the need to preserve meat before the invention of refrigeration.

ANIMAL WELFARE
The main welfare considerations in pig farming focus on farrowing (giving birth) and slaughter. In many countries, sows are confined to farrowing crates so they cannot roll over and crush their piglets. Critics argue that pigs are intelligent creatures that are unlikely to squash their offspring when given adequate space to interact with them. Sow crates are banned in the EU and a few US states, but pork is often imported from countries with different welfare laws. Pigs are easily stressed, so careful handling before slaughter is crucial, and some large units slaughter their pigs on site to eliminate transportation. As pigs are omnivores, commercial feed consists of a combination of grains, soybeans, and animal protein.

PRODUCTION METHODS
The following are the main commercial pig production methods:
• **Domestic** Although few pigs are raised for sale this way nowadays, across the world, keeping a backyard pig has been a long-standing tradition and in many countries people still keep a pig or two for home consumption. Sometimes they live in a pigsty, otherwise in a run or paddock. **Diet:** a mixture of household scraps and grain.

BLOOD SAUSAGE, PÂTÉS, TERRINES, AND HEADCHEESE WERE THE DELICIOUS RESULTS OF NOT WISHING TO WASTE A SINGLE SCRAP OF THE ANIMAL.

- **Free-range (outdoor reared)** It is not easy to divide free-range pig production into categories because so many different combinations of systems are used, and there are no legal definitions. Sometimes sows farrow outside in "arcs" (semicircular sheds) and the piglets may live indoors, more or less intensively, after weaning. Sometimes it is the reverse: the sows farrow inside, but the weaners live outside until ready for slaughtering. Outdoor pigs can turn a damp field into a quagmire. Equally, pigs suffer from sunburn, so they need shelters to protect them from both sun and rain.
Diet: concentrates, roots, and vegetation.
- **Intensive** Most pigs are kept intensively. Sows farrow in crates unless the use of these is banned, and the weaned piglets are reared in large, temperature-controlled sheds, either on slats or with straw on the floor. The units are closely monitored to prevent outbreaks of disease, while vitamins and antibiotics are often administered to prevent disease and encourage fast growth.
Diet: concentrates.
- **Organic** Most organic systems insist on outdoor rearing and sow crates are forbidden. Prophylactic drugs, growth promoters, and antibiotics are not permitted. Medication is only permitted to control disease and longer than usual withdrawal times are often required before slaughter. All feed has to be organic.
Diet: organic concentrates, roots, and vegetation.

BREEDS AND CATEGORIES
- **Commercial pigs** are highly specialized hybrids bred to be productive under intensive conditions. American hybrids are based on the Duroc, while Europe uses many Landrace crosses. However, the trend for producing artisanal pork from heritage breeds is growing, and old-fashioned breeds such as the Tamworth or Gloucester Old Spot are raised to produce free-range pork.

DRIED HAMS, BACON, AND CURED AND SMOKED SAUSAGES OF EVERY SHAPE AND SIZE ALL ORIGINATED FROM THE NEED TO PRESERVE MEAT BEFORE THE INVENTION OF REFRIGERATION.

- **Premium pork products**, such as hams or salamis, often rely on traditional pig breeds. In Spain and Portugal, the Black Iberian pig is greatly prized, as is the woolly Mangalica pig from Hungary, which is bred specially for its superb fat. Many European products using heritage pigs are recognized by symbols, such as PDO (Protected Designation of Origin), PGI (Protected Geographical Indication), TSG (Traditional Specialities Guaranteed), and AOC (*Appellation d'Origine Contrôlée*), that acknowledge the importance of these breeds.
- **Suckling pigs** These are 2- to 6-week-old piglets that are fed on their mothers' milk. Some may be older. The skin is a creamy white and the meat a delicate, pale pink.
- **Pork pigs (porkers)** Most pigs are about eight months old and have a covering of fat but are otherwise lean. The meat is pink and the fat is white. In contrast, the flesh of many heritage and outdoor pigs is often much darker, due to their diet and the fact that they are slower grown.
- **Processing pigs (baconers)** These pigs are older and fatter and are used for pork products such as bacon, ham, sausages, and salamis, all of which need a greater proportion of fat to lean meat.

BUYING PORK
Because so much pork is shipped across the world, it is not easy to know how it was produced. Also, there are no legal definitions for "free-range" pork. If the method of production is not mentioned, then it is probably intensively raised, as welfare-friendly production is usually promoted at the point of sale.

Some commercial bacon and ham is cured by injecting it with brine. This reduces the cost but makes the meat wetter. It may exude a milky white liquid when cooked and is difficult to brown. Dry-salted products will not do this. Highly processed, cheap products, such as sausages, that have no recognizable pieces of meat in them could be made from mechanically recovered meat (MRM), which could be from any part of the animal. Sometimes this is marked on the label. Some pig diseases are very contagious, so many countries forbid travelers from importing pork, and pork products such as sausages and salami.

PORK CUTS

MORE THAN ANY OTHER MEAT, PORK is used for sausages, hams, and other cured products. Fresh pork, however, offers tasty dishes at affordable prices; it is one of the cheapest of meats. Good pork is pink, not gray, and outdoor pork is darker than intensively raised pork.

FOREQUARTER   MIDDLE   HINDQUARTER

BELLY AND RIBS

FOREQUARTER CUTS

Pork forequarter cuts have fat running through them so are great for slow-cooking. Spare rib cuts from the neck and ribs are also good for grilling.

SHOULDER (GROUND) This contains fat and is great for meatballs, meat loaf, and Chinese dumplings.

BOSTON BUTT Called "collar" when cured, this bone-in shoulder and neck roast is also sold deboned and tied for easier carving.

BLADE STEAK With a generous marbling of fat, shoulder steaks are perfect for slow baking.

Additional forequarter cuts

- **BONELESS BOSTON BUTT** Many parts of the shoulder are rolled and tied for slow roasting.

- **COUNTRY-STYLE RIBS** These "ribs" are actually the long neck bones. They are cooked in the same way as spare ribs from the flank (see opposite).

- **BLADE ROAST** This neat, well-marbled cut is boneless spare ribs. Cook with or without the skin.

- **PICNIC HAM** This is a bone-in cut from the top of the leg with the hock removed. Simmer or braise.

- **HAM** Often smoked and useful for soup and stock as it has a high gelatin content.

SUCKLING PIG

A whole suckling pig (see pp106–7) makes a spectacular centerpiece and is so tender that, when perfectly cooked, it can be cut with the side of a plate. Make sure your butcher cleans the ears and snout properly.

MIDDLE CUTS

The loin muscle is very lean but the thick layer of fat on the outside can be cut off, if preferred. Be careful not to overcook these cuts because they can dry out.

RACK An elegant-looking cut, especially when French trimmed (above), you should ask your butcher to remove the sharp chine bone.

PORK PORTERHOUSE Cut from the best end of the bone-in loin, these chops have loin on one side (left) and fillet on the other (right).

BONELESS PORK CHOPS From the boneless loin, these can include the outer fat or can be trimmed.

LOIN OR TENDERLOIN The most tender cut of all, a loin will feed 2–3 people and cooks very quickly.

Additional middle cuts

- **BONELESS LOIN** This tender muscle runs the length of the back so can be cut to any length. Steaks can also be cut from it.

- **PORK CHOPS** Sliced from the rack, these are usually one rib thick but can be more.

- **LOIN, BONE-IN SKIN-ON** The skin on this cut provides good crackling but there is often a thick layer of fat underneath.

- **LOIN EYE, TRIMMED** The eye muscle completely trimmed of skin and fat, so a healthy lean cut.

BELLY AND RIB CUTS

These cuts have a large proportion of fat. Whole pieces can be cooked on the barbecue, but it is usually cut into smaller pieces. Bacon is made from the belly.

RACK OF SPARE RIBS Often cooked as a whole piece, individual ribs can be cut to make sticky Chinese spare ribs. Best slow-cooked before being crisped.

BELLY SLICES, BONE-IN These can contain a little cartilage as well as bone, both of which will soften on slow cooking.

Additional belly and rib cuts

- **SHORT-CUT RIBS** A short-cut length of ribs from the rack. Cook as forequarter spare ribs or barbecue.

- **BELLY** A fatty cut, this is delicious when slowly blackened with a sticky sauce. It may be cooked as a whole piece or in slices.

- **ROLLED BELLY** Sometimes stuffed before being rolled and tied, this needs long, slow cooking.

HINDQUARTER CUTS

The hindquarter produces some very lean cuts. Whole legs are used to make traditional cured and dried hams as well as cured ham steaks.

WHOLE LEG A traditional affordable family cut, this is at its best with the skin scored to make crackling. It may also be deboned and rolled into smaller cuts.

LEG STEAK This lean steak is perfect for broiling and stir-frying. It can also be beaten out thinly to make schnitzels. It is best not to cut them too thickly as they may toughen when cooked.

HOCK Called knuckle when cured and smoked, the hock has a high gelatin content that makes it perfect for soup and stock. It can also be enjoyed as a cheap form of ham.

Additional hindquarter cuts

- **RUMP ROAST, BONE-IN** This is a plump, tender and meaty cut that includes a little fillet.

- **ROLLED BONELESS LEG ROAST** Useful for making smaller roasts, the meat cooks evenly.

- **RUMP CHOP** With a distinctive semicircular shape, this is one of the meatiest types of chop.

- **RUMP STEAK** As above but without any bone, this is sometimes also referred to as a chump chop.

BACON AND HAM

BACON IS USUALLY PORK BELLY that has been cured with salt and then sliced. The cure may be dry-salt or brine. Often it is smoked afterward. Ham is usually made from pork legs that are salted and then air dried; many are smoked as well. Dried hams keep well and most are eaten raw.

SPECK Made in the mountainous region between Austria and Italy, this ham is salted with herbs and spices and very slowly smoked and dried.

PANCETTA Pork belly is dry-salted with herbs, spices, and garlic then dried for three months. It is used by cooks around the world to flavor dishes. *Stesa* is flat pancetta, *arrotolata* is rolled up.

LARDO Thick pork back fat is brine-cured with herbs and spices to make this Italian bacon. Its silky texture and deep flavor is enjoyed on toast as an antipasto.

BRITISH AND AMERICAN BACON These are both lightly cured and need to be cooked before eating. Most is made from pork belly (above) but some is made from loin (top). It may be dry-salted or brined, smoked or unsmoked.

LAP YUK Literally translated as "wax meat," this strongly flavored Chinese bacon is made from pork belly marinated in Chinese spices and then slowly dried. It is normally chopped to add flavor to other dishes.

JAMBON DE BAYONNE The salt brine for this ham from Bayonne in southwest France includes wine, which gives it its special flavor and moist texture.

COPPA Also called *capocollo*, this ham is made from pork shoulder or neck so has a high fat content. The meat is marinated and salted, packed into casings, and dried.

JAMÓN The three best Spanish hams are *Serrano*, from the mountains, *Ibérico* (above) from the black Iberian pig and dried for up to three years, and *bellota* from pigs that graze on acorns.

ELENSKI A popular Bulgarian ham that is dry-cured for 40 days then air-dried for many months. When dried in the traditional farmhouse kitchen, it acquires a smoky flavor.

JINHUA HAM With its cream-colored fat and dark red meat, this popular Chinese ham is first dry-salted, then soaked before being dried, to develop its distinctive flavor.

CULATELLO From the Parma region of Italy, this ham is made from pigs that are older and fatter than those used for conventional prosciutto.

PRESUNTO This dry-cured Portuguese ham is similar to Spanish *jamón*. The best presunto is also made with pork from the black Iberian pig.

BLACK FOREST HAM A robustly flavored ham from the Black Forest in Germany. Pork is salted, spiced, and then very slowly cold-smoked over pine. It should be sliced very thinly.

WESTPHALIA HAM This air-dried German ham gets its special flavor from the pigs feeding on acorns in the Westphalian forest. This is enhanced by being smoked over juniper and beech wood.

CURED AND DRIED SAUSAGES

THERE IS A HUGE FAMILY OF PORK SAUSAGES. Some are cured in wine vinegar or curing salts, which gives them a fermented taste. The sausages on these pages have also been dried to preserve them for longer. Other sausages are dried without curing; they have a purer pork flavor.

FINOCCHIONA A Tuscan salami flavored with pepper and the region's wild fennel seeds, which make a powerful combination. Some versions are rolled in dried fennel leaves.

AHLE WURST The flavor of this German cured and dried "old sausage" comes from the slow maturation period, and the superb pork from especially heavy pigs. Sometimes it is smoked.

EICHSFELDER FELDKEICHER A cured and dried *rohwurst* ("raw sausage") from Germany, the traditional version was sewn into a pig's bladder, hence its drop-shape. It is smoked and dried for up to a year.

CHOURIÇO DE PORCO PRETO Made from the black Alentejo pig, this coarse-grained sausage is cured then oak-smoked and dried. It can be eaten raw but is also used in cooking.

KABANOS A very popular finger-thin hunter's sausage from Poland made from lean pork seasoned with pepper, juniper, caraway, garlic, and allspice. It is cured, smoked, and dried.

KIEŁBASA LISIECKA Made from coarsely chopped chunks of lean pork, this Polish cured sausage is flavored with pepper and garlic. It is then looped onto sticks and smoked and dried over hardwood.

LINGUIÇA A cured and dried sausage common throughout Portugal. Spices include garlic, paprika, oregano, and cumin. This is different from South American linguiça, which is only cured, not dried.

BERGSALAMI From Austria's mountainous regions, this fine-grained *rohwurst* is cured, then hot-smoked over beech and juniper, then dried for up to six weeks to produce its characteristic white mold.

MANGALICA Made from the meat of the curly-coated, fat Mangalica pig, this long Hungarian sausage is bright orange due to sweet paprika. It is cured, cold-smoked, and dried for three months.

SALAME TOSCANO This very salty Italian salami is made to be eaten with unsalted Tuscan bread. The dark red pork is studded with large pieces of fat.

ROSETTE DE LYON The pink meat gives this French sausage its name. The pork is liberally studded with fat. Jésus de Leon is similar and its bulbous shape comes from being dried in a pig's stomach.

SALCHICHÓN DE VIC A hard mountain sausage made from salted pork mixed with cracked black pepper, then lightly smoked and dried. Salchichón is popular throughout Spain and there are many versions.

PREPARING A SUCKLING PIG

One of the world's great celebration dishes, roast suckling pig combines a thin, crisp, crackling skin with succulent tender meat. A suckling pig can weigh from 11–34lb (5–15kg). Allow 1lb (450g) per person.

1 Make sure the supplier has cleaned the feet, ears, and snout. If not already done, remove all traces of hair. Rub salt all over the pig inside and out and leave overnight. The next day, pat it dry and stuff the cavity, but not too tightly as the stuffing will expand.

2 Fasten the stuffed cavity loosely with skewers, making sure that you keep them away from the edge of the cavity in case the skin tears. Then use string to pull the skin together as shown, criss-crossing it between the skewers and winding it around the outside as you go.

3 Truss the back legs. Thread a trussing needle with string and push it right through the center of the back legs and the body. Pressing down on the trotters helps to keep the legs in the right position as they are trussed.

4 Use one hand to hold the trotters together while you pierce through both of them as shown. Pull the ends of the string up fairly tightly and tie them together securely.

5 Now truss the forelegs. Push the trussing needle through the front legs, chest, and throat and tie. Again, use one hand to hold the legs next to the head while you push the trussing needle through.

6 Turn the pig the right way up and score the skin across the top of the body using a very sharp knife or scalpel. Make diagonal incisions about ¾in (2cm) apart on either side of the backbone. Do not pierce the meat.

7 Place the pig—still on its belly—in a large roasting pan. Rub it all over with oil and then salt. Heat the oven to 350°F (180°C). When cooking it, allow 20 minutes per lb (45 minutes per kg), and use a meat thermometer to check that the stuffing is cooked through.

8 Before cooking the pig, make some thick pockets of tin foil and cover the oiled ears and tail to prevent them from burning. Place the pig in the oven and baste it every half hour. When cooked, rest the pig in a warm place for 20–30 minutes.

SCOTCH EGGS

A classic British dish and popular picnic snack, these sausage-wrapped eggs are an indulgence like no other.

THE CUT Pork sausage

SERVES 6
PREP 20 mins   **COOK** 20 mins

8 large eggs

1lb 5oz (600g) pork sausage, casings removed

3 garlic cloves, minced

3½oz (100g) scallions, finely chopped

1¾oz (50g) chives, finely chopped

1 tbsp whole-grain mustard

1 tsp dried red pepper flakes

1½ tsp sea salt

1½ tsp freshly ground black pepper

1⅓ cups all-purpose flour

peanut oil, for frying

2 cups bread crumbs

1 Bring a saucepan of water to a boil, add 6 of the eggs, and boil for 3–5 minutes for a semi-soft yolk and 5–7 minutes for a firm yolk. Drain, run under cold water, and set aside to cool. Peel the eggs when cool enough to handle.

2 In a bowl, place the pork, garlic, onions, chives, mustard, one-third of the red pepper flakes, and half a teaspoon each of the salt and pepper. Mix to combine. In a separate bowl, place the flour, one-third of the red pepper flakes, and another half teaspoon each of the salt and pepper. Mix well.

3 Heat the oil in a deep-fat fryer or a large saucepan to 350°F (180°C). Divide the pork mixture into 6 equal portions. Flatten each portion and wrap it around a boiled egg, making sure the whole egg is covered.

4 Whisk the remaining 2 eggs in a small bowl. Place the bread crumbs in a shallow dish along with the remaining seasoning and red pepper flakes, and mix to combine. Dip each egg first in the flour mixture, then in the beaten eggs, and finally coat with the bread crumbs.

5 Deep-fry the eggs for 4–5 minutes each, turning occasionally, until well browned. Remove the eggs with a slotted spoon, drain on a plate lined with paper towels, and set aside to cool slightly. Serve hot.

SWEDISH MEATBALLS WITH GRAVY

Traditionally served with mashed potatoes and lingonberry jam, these mild meatballs with a rich gravy are the perfect comfort food.

THE CUT Ground pork

SERVES 4
PREP 10 mins, plus chilling   **COOK** 10–15 mins

FOR THE MEATBALLS

1lb (450g) ground pork

1 cup fresh white bread crumbs

½ onion, chilled and finely grated

1 tbsp whole milk

1 egg, beaten

1 tsp sugar

salt and freshly ground black pepper

2 tbsp butter

1 tbsp sunflower oil

mashed potatoes, to serve

FOR THE GRAVY

1 heaping tbsp all-purpose flour

1 cup beef stock

1 tsp red currant jelly

1 tbsp light cream

1 In a large bowl, mix the pork, bread crumbs, onion, milk, egg, sugar, and seasoning until well combined. Chill for at least 1 hour. Preheat the oven to 300°F (150°C).

2 Heat the butter and oil in a large frying pan. With damp hands, shape the pork mixture into walnut-sized balls. Cook the meatballs over low heat for 10 minutes, until browned all over and springy to the touch. Cook them in two batches to avoid overcrowding the pan.

3 When the meatballs are cooked, transfer them to the oven and cover loosely with foil to keep them warm. Remove the pan from the heat and sprinkle in the flour. Whisk it into the fat in the pan, then gradually whisk in the stock.

4 Return the pan to the heat and cook the gravy until it thickens. Reduce to a simmer, add the red currant jelly and cream, and cook for an additional 2–3 minutes. Check for seasoning and serve spooned over the meatballs and mashed potatoes.

STEAMED PORK DIM SUM

This popular light snack has its roots in the ancient Silk Road, where it was served at roadside teahouses.

 CUT Ground pork

MAKES 20–24 dumplings
PREP 30 mins, plus chilling **COOK** 15 mins

FOR THE DOUGH

1½ cups all-purpose flour, plus extra for dusting

1 tsp salt

1 egg, beaten with 1 tsp water

oil, for greasing

FOR THE FILLING

12oz (350g) ground pork

1 tbsp soy sauce

1 tbsp fish sauce

1 tsp sesame oil

1 scallion, finely chopped

1 tbsp rice wine

1 garlic clove, minced

1 tbsp minced fresh ginger

1 tsp sugar

1 egg

1 tsp cornstarch

1¾oz (50g) shiitake mushrooms

1 Sift the flour and salt into a large bowl. Make a well in the center, pour in the egg, and mix well to combine. Add ½ cup of water, a little at a time, until a dough forms. Continue to knead the dough until it is smooth, glossy, and elastic.

2 Place the dough on a lightly floured surface and knead for 5 minutes, until a smooth dough forms. Cover and chill in the fridge for 30 minutes.

3 For the filling, place all the ingredients in a large bowl and mix well to combine. Turn the dough onto a lightly floured surface, roll out very thin, and cut into 3–4in (7.5–10cm) squares.

4 To prepare the dumplings, place 1 tablespoon of the filling in the center of each square. Wet the edges of the dough and pleat it around the sides of the filling. Use your fingers to pinch a "waist" over the top of the dumpling, leaving the center open to help the filling cook. Gently press the dumpling to flatten the bottom.

5 Place the dumplings on a greased plate and steam over a pan of boiling water for 10–15 minutes, or until the filling has cooked through. Serve hot with soy sauce for dipping.

FRIKADELLER

Originally from Denmark, these moist patties are also popular in Germany. The creamy dill dip adds a lovely fresh note.

 CUT Ground pork

SERVES 4
PREP 30 mins, plus resting **COOK** 20–25 mins

FOR THE PATTIES

1lb (450g) ground lean pork

1¼ cups fresh brown bread crumbs

1 onion, finely chopped

¼ tsp ground allspice

1 egg

1 tbsp whole milk

2 tsp chopped dill

salt and freshly ground black pepper

1 tbsp sunflower oil, for frying

FOR THE DIP

4 tbsp sour cream

2 tsp chopped dill

1 Place all the ingredients, except the oil, in a bowl and mix well making sure the dill and onions are evenly incorporated. Divide the mixture into 12 equal portions, shape them into balls, and gently flatten into pattylike shapes. Place them on a plate and set aside to rest in a cool place for about 30 minutes.

2 Heat the oil in a large, nonstick frying pan over medium heat. Fry the patties for 5–10 minutes, until lightly brown on both sides. Then reduce the heat and cook for 5 more minutes to cook through. Remove from the pan, transfer to a plate, and keep warm. Cook the patties in two batches to avoid overcrowding the pan.

3 For the dip, mix the sour cream and dill in a small bowl. Serve the Frikadeller patties along with the dill cream dip and a mixed green salad.

PORK AND BEER STEW

A typical German stew blending savory beer with spices and thickened with rye bread, this is a rich and intense dish.

THE CUT Pork shoulder

SERVES 4
PREP 30 mins   **COOK** 1½ hrs

1lb 5oz (600g) pork shoulder, cut into cubes

2 tbsp peanut oil

1 large onion, thinly sliced

2 garlic cloves, minced

2 carrots, cut into thick batons

4½oz (125g) crimini mushrooms, sliced

¼ tsp ground allspice

1 bay leaf

1 cinnamon stick

¾ cup dark beer

¾ cup pork or chicken stock

1 cup rye bread crumbs

salt and freshly ground black pepper

chopped flat-leaf parsley, to garnish

1 Rinse the pork and pat dry with paper towels. Heat 1 tablespoon of the oil in a heavy-bottomed Dutch oven. Add the pork, in batches, and cook for about 10 minutes, until well-browned on all sides. Remove with a slotted spoon and set aside.

2 Add the remaining oil to the Dutch oven, reduce the heat, and add the onion. Cook for about 5 minutes, stirring, until the onion softens. Add the garlic and cook for 1 more minute. Then stir in the carrots and mushrooms, cook gently for 5 minutes, and add the allspice and bay leaf.

3 Return the meat to the Dutch oven and add the cinnamon stick, beer, stock, and bread crumbs. Bring to a boil and season to taste. Then reduce to a gentle simmer, cover partially, and cook for about 1 hour, until the pork is tender.

4 Remove the bay leaf and cinnamon stick and check for seasoning. Garnish with the parsley and serve with buttered green cabbage or kale.

BIGOS

To make this authentic Polish hunter's stew, it's worth using Polish sausages such as wiejska or kilometrova, but any smoked sausage will work well.

THE CUT Pork shoulder

SERVES 8
PREP 40 mins   **COOK** 2 hrs

½oz (15g) dried mushrooms, such as porcini

2 x 24oz (680g) jars of sauerkraut

9oz (250g) thick-cut bacon, chopped

2 large onions, roughly chopped

2¼lb (1 kg) pork shoulder, diced

10 dried prunes

8 juniper berries

½ tsp ground allspice

3 bay leaves

2 tbsp honey

1 tbsp tomato paste

4½ cups chicken stock

9oz (250g) smoked sausage, chopped into bite-size pieces

1 Soak the mushrooms in ¾ cup boiling water, cover, and set aside. Cook the sauerkraut in a large, heatproof Dutch oven over low heat for about 5–10 minutes. Meanwhile, cook half the bacon in a large nonstick frying pan. Once the fat is released, stir in the onions, reduce the heat, and cook for 5 minutes, stirring occasionally, until soft. Add the bacon mixture to the sauerkraut, stir well and set aside. Preheat the oven to 350°F (180°C).

2 Fry the remaining bacon in the pan for about 5 minutes. Remove with a slotted spoon, leaving the fat in the pan, and add to the sauerkraut. Then cook the diced pork in the pan over high heat for 5–10 minutes, until browned. Add it to the sauerkraut. Then stir in the mushrooms and the soaking water and add all the remaining ingredients, except the sausage. Place the casserole over high heat and bring to a boil. Then cover and cook in the oven for 1½ hours.

3 Remove from the oven, add the sausages, and stir to combine. Return to the oven and cook for 30 minutes, or until the pork is tender. Remove the bay leaves and juniper berries, and serve with small boiled potatoes.

BAVARIAN PORK ROAST

This German favorite features caraway seeds and a healthy dose of garlic, and is best when served with sauerkraut.

THE CUT Pork shoulder

SERVES 6
PREP 20 mins   **COOK** 4 hrs, plus resting

4lb (1.8kg) skin-on boneless pork shoulder

2 tbsp caraway seeds

1 tbsp paprika

1 tbsp each of salt and freshly ground black pepper

4 tbsp olive oil

1lb 2oz (500g) white onion, chopped

1lb 2oz (500g) carrots, sliced

1lb 2oz (500g) waxy potatoes, such as Yukon Golds or red potatoes

4 garlic cloves

1 cup vegetable stock (optional)

1 Preheat the oven to 325°F (160°C). Rinse the pork shoulder and pat dry with paper towels. Use a knife to lightly score the skin. Combine the caraway seeds, paprika, salt, pepper, and half the oil in a bowl. Coat the meat with two-thirds of the spice mixture.

2 Place the onion, carrots, potatoes, and garlic in a roasting pan and toss with the remaining oil and spice mix. Place the pork in the pan with its fat side up.

3 Roast the pork and vegetables in the oven for 3–4 hours, or until the internal temperature of the meat reaches 150°F (65°C). Add stock to the roasting pan to prevent the vegetables from drying out, if required.

4 Remove from the oven and let rest for at least 5 minutes before carving. Serve alongside the roasted vegetables, if preferred.

VARIATION

Bavarian-style roast beef Use the beef rump roast in place of the pork shoulder. For the marinade, use 2 tablespoons crushed allspice berries instead of the caraway seeds and 1 tablespoon chipotle paste instead of the paprika. Cook as above and serve with the roasted vegetables.

SLOW-COOKED PORK SHOULDER WITH CIDER GRAVY

Pork shoulder is an inexpensive and large cut, and roasts far better than a more traditional (but drier) pork leg. The boozy gravy adds a rich flavor to this simple dish.

THE CUT Pork shoulder

SERVES 6–8
PREP 10 mins, plus chilling
COOK 3 hrs, plus resting

4½lb (2kg) bone-in, skin-on pork shoulder

1 tbsp olive oil

salt and freshly ground black pepper

1¼ cups hard cider

¾ cup chicken stock

1 tbsp all-purpose flour

1 With a sharp knife, make criss-cross slits all over the skin of the pork, being careful not to cut through to the meat underneath. (You can ask your butcher to do this for you.) Rub the skin dry with paper towels and leave the meat to rest, uncovered, in the fridge for at least 4 hours, but preferably overnight. This will help the skin crisp while cooking.

2 Preheat the oven to 350°F (180°C). Place the meat skin-side up in a roasting pan and rub the oil and salt all over the top, being sure to get inside the slits in the skin.

3 Pour the cider and stock into the roasting pan, being careful not to splash the top of the meat. Cover the skin with a piece of parchment paper (this will help to keep the skin from sticking to the foil), then cover the whole roasting pan with foil, sealing it tightly so that no steam escapes.

4 Roast the pork for 2½ hours, then remove the foil and parchment paper, increase the oven temperature to 450°F (230°C), and roast for 30–40 minutes until the skin is crisp. Remove the pork from the oven and separate the crackling. Leave the crackling uncovered in the turned-off oven. Wrap the pork in foil to keep it warm while you make the gravy.

5 For the gravy, skim about ¼ cup of the pork fat from the top of the cooking juices into a saucepan and set it over low heat. Whisk in the flour and cook it for 2–3 minutes, whisking constantly, until it bubbles and starts to change color. Meanwhile, skim off and discard as much of the remaining fat as possible from the cooking liquid. Then pour the liquid into the pan a little at a time, whisking as you go, until

you have a thick, rich gravy. Check the seasoning. Bring it to a boil, reduce to a simmer, and cook for 5 minutes before serving with the pork and crackling.

NICE DEVICE

One of the best kitchen devices ever invented is the fat-separator, which has a spout at the bottom instead of the top. As the fat floats to the top of any liquid poured in, this measuring cup allows you to use as much of the natural juices as possible from a roast, while leaving the fat behind.

HUNGARIAN GOULASH

This traditional herdsman's supper is made unique by the use of paprika and caraway seeds.

 Pork shoulder

SERVES 6–8
PREP 30 mins   **COOK** 2 hrs

3 tbsp vegetable oil

1¾lb (800g) pork shoulder, cut into cubes

1 large onion, roughly chopped

1 garlic clove, crushed

½ tsp caraway seeds

1–2 tbsp paprika

2 ripe tomatoes, blanched, peeled, and diced

3 tbsp tomato paste

1 large red bell pepper, seeded and thinly sliced

2 large potatoes, peeled and cut into cubes

salt and freshly ground black pepper

chopped dill, to garnish

1 Heat the oil in a large, heatproof casserole over high heat. Add the meat, in batches, and cook until well-browned all over. Remove the meat with a slotted spoon, transfer to a plate lined with paper towels, and set aside.

2 Reduce the heat, add the onion, and cook for 1–2 minutes, until softened. Add the garlic, caraway seeds, paprika, and 2 tablespoons of water. Stir to mix the flavors and color.

3 Return the meat to the casserole and stir to combine all the ingredients. Add enough water to just cover the meat and bring to a boil. Then reduce the heat to a gentle simmer, cover, and cook for 1 hour, until the meat is tender.

4 Add the tomatoes and tomato paste, red bell pepper, and potatoes. Season well and bring to a boil. Then reduce to a simmer for 30 more minutes. Remove from the heat, garnish with chopped dill, and serve hot in deep bowls.

VARIATION

Chicken goulash Use chicken in place of the pork and green bell pepper in place of the red bell pepper. Replace the paprika with smoked paprika, and cook as above. Serve topped with sour cream and chopped fresh dill.

POSOLE

This traditional Mexican stew features hominy and is best served with lime wedges.

Pork shoulder

SERVES 8
PREP 20 mins   **COOK** 5 hrs, plus resting

2¼lb (1kg) boneless pork shoulder

2 tbsp ground cumin

½ tbsp garlic powder

½ tbsp smoked paprika

salt and freshly ground black pepper

7oz (200g) red onion, sliced

1 cup chicken stock

FOR THE POSOLE

¼ cup vegetable oil

4 garlic cloves, crushed

7oz (200g) red onion, chopped

20 cherry tomatoes, halved

2 x 14oz (400g) can diced tomatoes, with juices

4 cups chicken stock

3½oz (100g) hominy, drained

1¾oz (50g) dried pinto beans, rinsed and soaked in cold water overnight

1 tbsp dried oregano

1 tsp cumin seeds

1¾oz (50g) cilantro leaves, to garnish

3½oz (100g) grated cheddar cheese, to garnish

9oz (250g) white onion, chopped, to garnish

1 Preheat the oven to 275°F (140°C). For the pork, place the cumin, garlic powder, and smoked paprika in a small bowl and season well. Mix the spices and use to rub evenly on both sides of the pork. Place the pork and red onions in a small roasting pan, pour in the stock, and cover with foil. Transfer to the oven and roast for 5 hours.

2 Meanwhile, make the posole. Heat the oil in a large, heavy-based saucepan. Add the garlic and onions and sauté until tender. Add the remaining ingredients, season well, and stir to combine. Cover and simmer for 2 hours, stirring occasionally.

3 Remove the pork from the oven, leave it to rest for 30 minutes, then use a fork to shred the meat. Add the shredded meat, along with the onions to the posole. Season to taste. Serve the posole hot, garnished with cilantro, cheese, and white onion.

COCHINITA AL PIBIL

Inspired by the traditional Mexican dish of Mayan origin, which means "suckling pig cooked in a pit," this dish uses slow-cooked pork shoulder.

THE CUT Pork shoulder

SERVES 8
PREP 45 mins, plus overnight marinating
COOK 2½ hrs, plus resting

6lb (2.7kg) skin-on bone-in pork shoulder

3 tbsp garlic, finely chopped

grated zest of 1 orange, plus juice of 3 oranges

1 tbsp dried oregano

1 tbsp ground cumin

1 tbsp each of salt and freshly ground black pepper

8oz (225g) onions, thinly sliced

juice of 1 lime

juice of 1 lemon

½ cup dry sherry

1 Trim the excess fat from the shoulder and score the meat. Place the garlic, orange zest, oregano, cumin, salt, and pepper in a small bowl and combine to form a paste. Rub the mixture all over the pork, pushing it into the slits.

2 Place the onions in a large bowl and top with the pork. Mix the fruit juices and the sherry and pour over the pork. Cover the bowl and leave in a cool place to marinate overnight.

3 Preheat the oven to 325°F (160°C). Remove the pork from the bowl, reserving the marinade. Pat the pork dry with paper towels and set aside for about 2 hours to bring it to room temperature.

4 Transfer the pork and marinade to a roasting pan. Roast the pork in the oven for 2½ hours, basting with the marinade every 30 minutes, until the internal temperature reaches 165°F (75°C). Remove from the oven and allow to rest for 15 minutes before carving. To serve, carve the meat into slices and place on a platter, with the hot juices spooned over the slices.

POTTED PORK

Also known as *rilletes de porc*, this rich and savory spread is perfect with crusty bread and a spicy mustard.

THE CUT Pork shoulder

MAKES 2 pints (1.2 liters)
PREP 15 mins
COOK 4 hrs, plus resting and chilling

1 tbsp brown sugar

½ tsp dried thyme

½ tsp cinnamon

½ tsp cloves

½ tsp grated nutmeg

½ tsp ground ginger

½ tsp garlic powder

1 tbsp sea salt, plus extra to taste

2¼lb (1kg) pork shoulder

1½ cups butter

4 garlic cloves, crushed

3½oz (100g) shallots, finely chopped

1¾oz (50g) sage

freshly ground black pepper, to taste

1 Preheat the oven to 325°F (160°C). Place the sugar, thyme, cinnamon, cloves, nutmeg, ginger, garlic, and salt in a small bowl and mix well to combine. Rub both sides of the pork shoulder with the spice mixture and place in a roasting pan. Cover with foil and cook for 4 hours.

2 Melt the butter in a saucepan over low heat and skim off the foam. Remove the pork from the oven and set aside to rest for 30 minutes. Roughly shred the meat, place it in a food processor along with the garlic, shallots, sage, and half the melted butter. Pulse the mixture until it forms a smooth paste. Season to taste.

3 Spoon the mixture into pint glasses, with the remaining melted butter poured over. Seal and chill in the fridge for at least 1 hour. Serve chilled with sliced bread or crackers.

PORK WITH CLAMS

The marriage of pork, shellfish, and cured ham is particularly delicious in this Portuguese dish from the Alentejo region.

THE CUT Pork shoulder

SERVES 6
PREP 30 mins   **COOK** 2 hrs

2 tbsp olive oil

1lb 2oz (500g) boneless pork shoulder

1lb (450g) onions, finely chopped

6 garlic cloves, chopped

1 bay leaf

¼ tsp red pepper flakes

14oz (400g) can tomatoes

1 cup dry white wine

1¾oz (50g) presunto or prosciutto ham

6oz (175g) chouriço or chorizo sausages

70 small Venus clams or cockles, about 10oz (300g) in total

1 Heat the oil in a heavy-bottomed casserole over high heat. Cut the pork into 1in (2.5cm) pieces, add to the casserole, and cook for 10 minutes, until lightly browned on all sides. Reduce the heat and add the onions, garlic, bay leaf, and red pepper flakes. Then cook, stirring occasionally, for 5 more minutes.

2 Add the tomatoes, crushing them with the back of a wooden spoon. Stir in all but 2 tablespoons of the wine, bring to a boil, and then reduce to a gentle simmer. Cover and cook for 30 minutes.

3 Chop the presunto into small cubes and add to the casserole. Cover the stew and simmer for 30 minutes. Cut the chouriço into small chunks and add to the stew. Cover and cook for about 15 minutes, until the pork is tender.

4 Rinse the clams under cold running water and spread over the surface of the casserole. Drizzle over the remaining wine and stir it lightly into the sauce. Cover, increase the heat a little, and shake the pan firmly, for about 5 minutes to help open the clams. Discard any clams that do not open. Stir well to mix the ingredients, and remove the bay leaf. Serve with crusty bread and a green salad.

PORK CARNITAS

Slow cooking the pork tenderizes the meat and adds flavor to this spicy Mexican specialty.

THE CUT Pork shoulder

SERVES 6
PREP 20 mins   **COOK** 3½ hrs

2¼lb (1kg) boneless pork shoulder

1 tbsp chipotle paste or smoked paprika

1 tsp dried oregano

1 tsp ground cumin

1 tsp dried red pepper flakes

1 tsp garlic powder

salt and freshly ground black pepper

1lb 2oz (500g) white onion, thinly sliced

3 garlic cloves, crushed

3 tbsp olive oil

juice of 1 lime

1 Preheat the oven to 325°F (160°C). Rinse the pork and pat dry with paper towels. Place the spices and seasoning in a small bowl and mix well. Place the pork on a clean work surface and rub the spice mix over generously.

2 In a large roasting pan, heat the onions and garlic over medium heat. Place the pork on top and drizzle with 1 tablespoon of the oil and the lime juice. Cover the pan with foil and transfer to the oven. Roast the pork for 2½–3 hours or until the internal temperature reaches 150°F (65°C).

3 Remove the pan from the oven and set aside to rest for at least 5 minutes and to cool slightly. When cool enough to handle, use a fork and lightly shred the pork. Heat the remaining oil in a large frying pan and sauté the shredded pork over medium-high heat, until crisp. Serve with corn tortillas and salsa.

VARIATION

Slow-cooked chicken carnitas with guacamole Use boneless chicken breasts instead of the pork shoulder and cook as above. For the guacamole, mash 2 peeled avocados, 3½oz (100g) quartered cherry tomatoes, 1 chopped red onion, 2½oz (75g) chopped cilantro, salt, pepper, and the juice of 2 limes in a large bowl. Arrange the shredded chicken on a plate, top with the guacamole, and serve.

CANDIED PORK BUTT ROAST

Bottomed on an inexpensive cut of pork, this simple Chinese recipe imparts classic sweet and sour flavors.

THE CUT Pork butt roast

SERVES 6
PREP 20 mins   **COOK** 2½ hrs

1 bone-in pork butt roast, about 4½lb (2kg)

4in (10cm) piece of fresh ginger, peeled and thickly sliced

3 scallions, halved lengthwise

6 tbsp soy sauce

3 tbsp dry sherry

2 tbsp brown sugar

1 Place the pork in a large, heavy-bottomed saucepan. Cover with cold water, bring to a boil, and boil for 5 minutes. Drain and rinse the pork and return to the pan, skin-side down. Add the ginger, scallions, soy sauce, sherry, and sugar, and about 4 cups water. Bring to a boil, cover, and simmer for 1 hour moving the meat occasionally to prevent it from sticking to the bottom of the pan.

2 Turn the meat over and add enough water to cover one-third of the pork. Cover and bring to a boil. Then reduce to a simmer and cook for another 1 hour, moving the meat occasionally.

3 Remove the lid and increase the heat to allow the sauce to cook more. Baste the meat with the sauce as it thickens, making sure it does not stick to the bottom of the pan. When the sauce is of a coating texture, remove the meat from the pan.

4 To serve, carve the roast toward the bone and arrange the meat on a platter. Pour the sauce over and serve immediately.

SHAKE IT UP

To prevent the pork from sticking to the bottom of the pan, try placing it on a bamboo mat after the initial 5 minutes of cooking. An occasional prod of the meat or shaking of the pan will also work.

PORK AND COLLARD GREENS

This quick stir-fry makes the most of leafy seasonal produce and is best served with fluffy rice.

THE CUT Pork loin or tenderloin

SERVES 4
PREP 10 mins   **COOK** 10 mins

1 tbsp olive oil

12oz (350g) pork loin or tenderloin, cut into thin strips

4 garlic cloves, sliced

2 heads of collard greens, shredded

2 tsp onion seeds

salt and freshly ground black pepper

1 Heat the oil in a wok over medium-high heat. Add the pork and stir-fry for about 5 minutes, moving it around the wok as it heats up.

2 Add the garlic and greens and continue to stir-fry over medium-high heat for 1 minute, or until the greens have just wilted. Add the onion seeds, stir to combine, then season with salt and pepper. Serve immediately.

VARIATION

Squab breasts with collard greens and hoisin sauce Use 8 skinless squab breasts, cut into thin strips, instead of the pork and sunflower oil instead of olive oil. Stir-fry the meat for 2 minutes, then add 2 tablespoons of hoisin sauce, and stir-fry for 1 more minute. Then cook as above and add a dash of soy sauce, to taste, at the end.

WHOLE GLAZED HAM

A combination of marmalade and pineapple juice gives this succulent ham a wonderful sweet, sticky finish and makes it the perfect festive table centerpiece.

THE CUT Whole ham

SERVES 8–10
PREP 20 mins   **COOK** 2½ hrs

4½lb (2kg) piece of smoked boneless ham
3 heaping tbsp smooth marmalade
2 tbsp pineapple juice
1 tbsp honey
1 heaping tbsp light brown sugar
2 tbsp whole-grain mustard
salt and freshly ground black pepper

1 Preheat the oven to 325°F (160°C). Place the ham, skin-side up, on a rack in a large roasting pan. Pour water to a depth of 1in (3cm) into the pan. Cover tightly with foil and seal to ensure that no steam escapes. Cook in the oven for 2 hours.

2 Meanwhile, place the marmalade, pineapple juice, honey, brown sugar, and mustard in a large saucepan over medium heat. Season with salt and pepper and bring to a boil. Then reduce the heat to a simmer and cook for 5–7 minutes, until thickened.

3 Remove the ham from the oven and increase the oven temperature to 400°F (200°C). Remove the skin from the ham if necessary, leaving a thin layer of the fat. Cut a criss-cross pattern in the fat.

4 Brush some of the glaze over the ham. Return to the oven for 30 minutes, brushing with the glaze every 10 minutes, until brown and crispy. Remove from the oven and serve hot with mashed potatoes.

PORK LOIN COOKED IN MILK

Lactic acid helps to tenderize the meat and the lemon sauce enhances the flavor in this classic north Italian dish.

 Pork loin or tenderloin

SERVES 4
PREP 15 mins   **COOK** 2 hrs, plus resting

1lb 8oz (700g) boneless pork loin or tenderloin

sea salt and freshly ground black pepper

2 tbsp olive oil

4 tbsp unsalted butter

2 cups whole milk

5 garlic cloves, cut in half

1 tbsp chopped sage leaves

zest of 1 lemon, cut into strips

¾ cup heavy cream

1. Rub the pork with paper towels to remove excess moisture and season well. Heat the oil and butter in a large, lidded, heavy-bottomed saucepan. Add the pork and cook until well-browned all over. Meanwhile, heat the milk in a separate saucepan and set aside. Remove the pork from the pan and pour out half of the fat.

2 Reduce the heat and add the garlic and sage. Stir briefly, making sure the garlic doesn't burn. Return the pork to the pan and pour the heated milk over it. Add the lemon zest and bring to a boil. Reduce the heat to simmer, cover partially, and cook for 1½–2 hours. Remove from the heat.

3 Transfer the pork to a serving dish and set aside for 5 minutes. Add the cream to the pan and simmer for 5–10 minutes, until the sauce thickens. Remove from the heat. When cool enough to handle, cut the meat in thick slices and arrange on a serving dish. Scrape the brown bits from the bottom of the pan and add them to the sauce. These have a great flavor. Serve the pork with the milk and lemon sauce spooned over.

HERB APPEAL

If sage is not readily available, you can use fresh oregano or marjoram in its place.

MOLE SHREDDED PORK ENCHILADAS

Mole, a traditional Mexican sauce flavored with chile and dark chocolate, adds a deep, rich taste to this popular recipe.

 Pork loin or tenderloin

SERVES 4
PREP 20 mins   **COOK** 1½ hrs

2lb (900g) boneless pork loin or tenderloin

8oz (225g) grated Monterey Jack or cheddar cheese

4 large tortillas

FOR THE SAUCE

1 tsp olive oil

1 onion, finely chopped

3 garlic cloves, crushed

1oz (30g) semi-sweet chocolate, broken into pieces

2 x 14oz (400g) cans chopped tomatoes

1 tsp chipotle paste

pinch of cayenne pepper

pinch of ground cinnamon

pinch of sugar

salt and freshly ground black pepper

1 For the sauce, heat the oil in a large saucepan over medium heat. Add the onion and sauté for 4 minutes, until soft. Then add the garlic and sauté for an additional minute. Stir in the chocolate, tomatoes, chipotle, cayenne pepper, cinnamon, and sugar. Season well. Reduce the heat to simmer.

2 In a frying pan, seal the pork for about 30 seconds, on each side, over high heat. Add the pork to the sauce, turning once to coat, and simmer for 1 hour, stirring occasionally. Remove the pork from the sauce and shred the meat with a fork.

3 Preheat the oven to 350°F (180°C). Divide the meat and half the cheese between the tortillas. Roll up the tortillas tightly. Spoon half the mole sauce into a large heatproof casserole or baking dish. Lay the stuffed tortillas, seam-side down, in a row over the sauce. Top them with the remaining sauce and cheese and bake for 25 minutes. Serve hot with refried black beans and pico de gallo.

PROSCIUTTO-WRAPPED PORK TENDERLOIN WITH SAUSAGE AND GORGONZOLA STUFFING

A favorite at the holiday table, this dish features the most popular cuts of pork—the loin or tenderloin, salty prosciutto, and spiced sausage.

THE CUT Pork loin or tenderloin

SERVES 4
PREP 30 mins   **COOK** 2 hrs, plus resting

2 tbsp butter

3 garlic cloves, crushed

1¾oz (50g) shallots, sliced

5½oz (150g) sausage

1 tsp dried mixed herbs

1 tsp dried oregano

1 tsp dried rosemary

2½oz (75g) kale, roughly chopped

salt and freshly ground black pepper

½ tbsp crushed red pepper flakes

1oz (25g) crumbled Gorgonzola

10oz (300g) boneless pork loin or tenderloin

3½oz (100g) prosciutto

1 cup chicken stock

1. Melt the butter in a frying pan over medium heat. Add the garlic and shallots and sauté for 5 minutes, until browned. Stir in the sausage and half the herbs. Cook for 15–20 minutes, stirring occasionally, until the pork is browned. Stir in the kale and Gorgonzola, and reduce the heat to low. Preheat the oven to 350°F (180°C).

2 Place the tenderloin between two sheets of plastic wrap and pound with a meat tenderizer to a thickness of ¼in (5mm). Lay the tenderloin on a cutting board with 7 pieces of butcher's string placed horizontally under it at equal distance from each other. Spread the stuffing all over and gently roll the meat into a spiral. Wrap with the prosciutto to seal and tie with the string to secure.

3 Place the tenderloin in a roasting pan and cover with the stock. Sprinkle with the remaining spices and roast for 35–40 minutes or until browned. Rest for 15 minutes. Cut the tenderloin into thick slices, arrange on a serving platter, and serve warm.

ROAST PORK WITH SAGE AND ONION STUFFING

The marriage of sage and onion is a perfect foil for the sweetness of pork in this classic British dish.

THE CUT Pork loin

SERVES 10–12
PREP 30 mins   **COOK** 2 ½ hrs

3 tbsp butter

1 small onion, finely chopped

1¼ cups fresh white bread crumbs

1 tbsp chopped sage

salt and freshly ground black pepper

5lb (2.25kg) boneless pork loin

1 tsp sea salt

1 tsp all-purpose flour

2 tbsp white wine

2 cups pork or chicken stock

1 bay leaf

1 For the stuffing, heat the butter in a frying pan over medium heat and cook the onions for 5 minutes, or until soft but not browned. Stir in the bread crumbs and sage, and season lightly. Remove from the heat and set aside to cool.

2 Preheat the oven to 375°F (190°C). Lay the pork on a cutting board and use a kinfe to make ¾in (2cm) deep slashes at 1in (2.5cm) intervals from top to bottom in the skin. Rub in the sea salt. Turn the meat over, skin-side down, and cut a pocket about ¾in (2cm) deep along the length, season with salt and pepper, and spread the sage and onion stuffing into the pocket. Roll up tightly and tie with butcher's string.

3 Place the pork on a rack in a roasting pan and bake for 2 hours, basting with the fat every 45 minutes. Then transfer the pork to another roasting pan and reserve the fat. Increase the temperature to 450°F (230°C), return the pork to the oven, and cook for 10 more minutes to crisp up the crackling.

4 Meanwhile, to make the sauce, discard all but 1 tablespoon of the fat from the first roasting pan. Place over low heat, stir in the flour, scrape up the juices, and cook for 2–3 minutes. Then add the wine and stock, and stir to combine. Bring to a boil, add the bay leaf, and simmer until the sauce begins to thicken. Season and strain. To serve, remove the crackling and carve the meat in thick slices. Serve the gravy separately.

PORK CHOPS COOKED IN FOIL

Slow-cooking the pork chops tenderizes the meat and helps retain moisture.

THE CUT Pork chops

SERVES 4
PREP 15 mins   **COOK** 1 hr

4 tsp olive oil
4 pork chops
salt and freshly ground black pepper
1 large sweet apple
4 tsp honey
4 sprigs of marjoram or oregano
½ cup hard cider
mashed potatoes, to serve
green vegetables, to serve

1 Preheat the oven to 350°F (180°C). Cut 4 sheets of baking foil large enough to enclose the chops. Pour a teaspoon of oil on each one and spread over the middle. Dry the chops on paper towels, place in the center of each foil sheet, and season.

2 Cut the apple into quarters, take out the core, slice each piece into 4, and spread over the chops. Top each chop with a teaspoon of honey, a sprig of marjoram, and a splash of cider.

3 Fold the foil over to create a little enclosed parcel. Place on a baking sheet and cook in the oven for about 1 hour. Serve hot with mashed potatoes and green vegetables added to the foil parcels.

VARIATION

Slow-cooked pork belly Use pork belly instead of pork chops and prepare as above. Preheat the oven to 275°F (140°C) and slow cook the pork for up to 6 hours.

TONKATSU

This Japanese deep-fried breaded pork with a hot sauce is traditionally served with finely shredded white cabbage.

THE CUT Pork chops

SERVES 4
PREP 30 mins   **COOK** 15 mins

4 boneless pork chops
2 tbsp all-purpose flour
salt and freshly ground black pepper
2 eggs, beaten
½ cup panko bread crumbs
oil, for frying
1 small white cabbage, finely shredded

FOR THE SAUCE

¼ cup Worcestershire sauce
1 tbsp ketchup
1 tsp shoyu sauce

1 Use a knife to score the chops in vertical lines down to the fat. Place the flour in a small bowl and season with salt and pepper. Toss the pork chops in the flour and shake off the excess. Dip them in the beaten egg, and then coat evenly with bread crumbs.

2 Heat the oil in a deep-fat fryer to 350°F (180°C). Deep-fry the pork chops for 8 minutes, or until golden brown. Remove with a slotted spoon and drain on a plate lined with paper towels.

3 For the sauce, mix all the ingredients in a small bowl. Cut the pork in slices and serve on mounds of shredded cabbage, along with the sauce.

CHOUCROUTE GARNIE

Traditionally served with steamed potatoes, this classic dish from the Alsace region of France has a distinct German flavor, thanks to the pickled cabbage.

THE CUT Pork chops

SERVES 4
PREP 30 mins   **COOK** 2½ hrs

32oz (900g) jar of sauerkraut
2 tbsp lard
14oz (400g) mixed sausages, garlic or cured, cut into bite-size pieces
4 pork chops
1 large onion, thinly sliced
1 green sweet apple, peeled, cored, and sliced
2 garlic cloves, crushed
2 bay leaves
10 juniper berries
1 tbsp caraway seeds
2 cups dry white Alsace wine
finely chopped flat-leaf parsley, to garnish

1 Preheat the oven to 300°F (150°C). Rinse the sauerkraut in cold water and squeeze dry. Heat the lard in a large casserole over medium heat. Add the sausages and the chops and cook until well-browned all over. Do this in batches to retain the heat in the casserole. Remove the sausages and chops with a slotted spoon and set aside.

2 Reduce the heat. Add the onion and apple, and cook, stirring occasionally, until softened. Then add the sauerkraut and mix well. Add the garlic, bay leaves, juniper berries, and caraway seeds. Pour in the wine and 1 cup water and mix well.

3 Bring to a boil. Add the pork chops and reduce the heat. Allow to simmer for 10 minutes, then cover and place in the oven for 1 hour. Add the sausages and return to the oven for 1 more hour.

4 Remove from the oven and discard the bay leaf and juniper berries. To serve, place the sauerkraut in the center of a large platter. Arrange the pork chops around it and garnish with parsley.

VARIETY MIX

You can vary the sausage types from bratwurst to frankfurters or even Polish kielbasa. You can even add smoked ham for a different flavor.

BURMESE GOLDEN PORK

Chunky bits of pork mingle with spicy garlic, ginger, and chile flavors in this wholesome dish.

THE CUT Pork loin or leg

SERVES 4–6
PREP 30 mins   **COOK** 2 hrs

1 large onion, chopped

1 whole garlic bulb

3½oz (100g) fresh ginger, peeled

2¼lb (1kg) lean pork, cut into cubes

1 tsp salt

1 tbsp white wine vinegar

1 tsp chili powder

½ cup peanut oil

2 tsp toasted sesame oil

1 tsp ground turmeric

handful of cilantro leaves, to garnish

1 red chile, cut into strips, to garnish

1 Place the onion, garlic, and ginger in a food processor and pulse, or crush them using a mortar and pestle. Press the resulting mixture through a fine sieve, or squeeze them using a cheesecloth, to extract the liquid. Set the residue aside.

2 Place a saucepan over low heat, pour the extracted liquid and add the pork, salt, vinegar, chile, and half the peanut oil. Bring to a gentle simmer and cook over low heat for 1½ hours.

3 Place a small saucepan over low heat and add the remaining peanut oil and the sesame oil. Add the onion, garlic, and ginger residue and cook gently. Stir in the turmeric and cook over low heat for 5 minutes.

4 Pulse half the cooked pork in a food processor, then stir it into the cooked onion mixture and combine well. Add a little water if it seems dry. Add this mixture to the pork and stir well. Cook over low heat for an additional 20 minutes, until golden brown. Garnish with fresh cilantro or strips of red chile. Serve hot.

COOL COMFORT

Chill this dish in the fridge for a day or two to help the spices intensify and allow the flavors to develop fully.

PORK SATAY WITH PEANUT DIPPING SAUCE

Satay is the national dish of Indonesia and a favorite during festivals.

THE CUT Pork loin or tenderloin

SERVES 4
PREP 20 mins, plus marinating
COOK 30 mins

10oz (300g) white onion, chopped

1in (2.5cm) piece of fresh ginger, peeled and chopped

3 garlic cloves, finely chopped

juice of 1 lime

2 tbsp soy sauce

2 tbsp brown sugar

2 tsp red pepper flakes

1lb 8oz (700g) pork loin or tenderloin, cut into large chunks

1 tbsp vegetable oil

FOR THE SAUCE

4 tbsp peanut butter

2 tbsp soy sauce

4 garlic cloves

1 tbsp ground ginger

juice of 2 limes

4 tbsp vegetable oil

1 Place the onion, ginger, garlic, lime juice, soy sauce, sugar, and red pepper flakes in a food processor and pulse to form a smooth paste. Mix the pork with the paste in a bowl or plastic bag and chill in the fridge for 2 hours. Soak 4 bamboo skewers in water for at least 30 minutes.

2 Heat the oil in a large frying pan. Remove the pork from the marinade and thread onto the skewers. Cook over medium heat for 5–7 minutes, or until well-browned on all sides and cooked through.

3 For the sauce, put the peanut butter, soy sauce, garlic, ginger, and lime juice in a food processor and pulse until combined. Turn the processor on high and add the vegetable oil in a steady stream. Serve the pork hot with the peanut dipping sauce on the side.

CHINESE-SPICED PORK BELLY

A wonderful treatment turns an inexpensive cut of meat into an Asian feast, with the best crackling ever.

THE CUT Pork belly

SERVES 4
PREP 10 mins, plus marinating
COOK 1 hr 30 mins

1lb 10oz (750g) skin-on boneless pork belly

2 tbsp soy sauce

1 tbsp light brown sugar

1 tbsp five-spice powder

2 tsp salt

1 tsp sunflower oil

1 With a sharp knife, make criss-cross slits all over the skin of the pork, being careful not to cut through to the meat. Pat the skin dry with paper towels.

2 Mix the soy sauce, sugar, five-spice powder, and 1 teaspoon of salt into a thick paste and rub it over the meat side of the pork, keeping the skin dry. Chill in the fridge, skin-side up and uncovered, for at least 8 hours, or overnight.

3 Preheat the oven to 425°F (220°C). Line a roasting tray with foil and position a rack over it. Place the meat, skin-side up, on the rack and rub the skin with the oil and the remaining salt. Fill the roasting tray halfway wih boiling water.

4 Roast the pork at the top of the oven for 30 minutes, then reduce the temperature to 400°F (200°C) and roast for an additional 45 minutes–1 hour, until the skin turns crispy. Remove from the oven, carve into slices, and serve.

> ## DIP IT
>
> Mix soy sauce, grated ginger, Thai sweet chili sauce, and finely chopped scallions together with a little water and use as a dip for the sliced pork belly.

CHIPOTLE CINNAMON BACON

This sweet and savory bacon brings unexpected flair and flavors to the breakfast table.

THE CUT Pork belly

MAKES 1lb (450g) bacon
PREP 15 mins, plus 1 week marinating
COOK 1½ hrs, plus resting

1 cup brown sugar

1 tbsp molasses

2 tbsp sea salt

2 tsp Prague Powder No. 2 curing salt

1 tbsp cinnamon

1 tbsp chipotle powder or smoked paprika

4½lb (2kg) pork belly

YOU WILL ALSO NEED

17oz pack of hickory chips

charcoal, for the grill

1 Mix together the sugar, molasses, sea salt, curing salt, and spices. Rub the pork belly evenly with the mixture. Place in a plastic bag and refrigerate for at least one week.

2 Rinse the bacon thoroughly under cold running water. It should be firm to the touch. Soak the hickory chips in water for 1 hour, then wrap in foil.

3 Remove the rack from the barbecue and spread some charcoal in a ring around the edge. Place the foil-wrapped hickory chips in the center of the grill.

4 Light the charcoal and return the rack to the grill. Place the bacon, fat-side up, on the grill. Cover and cook for 1–1½ hours, until the internal temperature of the meat measures 150°F (65°C). If not, transfer it to an oven preheated to 300°F (150°C) and cook until the temperature reaches the required level.

5 Remove from the heat and allow to rest for 30 minutes. Slice and fry the bacon immediately, or store for up to 1 week in an airtight container in the fridge.

PORK BELLY PORCHETTA

This simple version of a classic Italian dish is made using pork belly infused with fresh herbs and fennel.

THE CUT Pork belly

SERVES 10–12
PREP 30 mins **COOK** 3½ hrs

10lb (5kg) rectangular piece of skin-on boneless pork belly

freshly ground black pepper

2 tbsp coarse salt

2 sprigs of thyme, shredded

2 tbsp roughly chopped rosemary

1 tbsp fennel seeds

10 garlic cloves, finely chopped

2 tbsp olive oil, plus extra for greasing

6 tbsp honey

juice of 2 limes

1 Preheat the oven to 480°F (250°C). Lay the pork belly skin-side down on a clean work surface. Sprinkle with pepper and half of the salt, rub well into the meat, and leave for 5 minutes.

2 Sprinkle the thyme, rosemary, and fennel seeds over the meat and then rub in with the garlic. Roll up the pork gently and tie crosswise with pieces of butcher's string at ½in (1cm) intervals through the length of the piece. Try to keep as much of the stuffing inside as possible.

3 Grease a roasting pan with a little oil and place the pork in it. Spread the remaining salt along with the oil all over the pork. Roast in the oven for 15 minutes skin-side down, then turn over and roast for another 15 minutes. Reduce the oven temperature to 300°F (150°C) and cook for 3 hours.

4 Remove the pork from the oven and coat with the honey and lime juice. Roll in the juices for a few minutes, then transfer the meat to a carving board. Stir up the remaining juices and pour into a warmed bowl. Cut the meat into thick slices, pour over the sauce, and serve with mashed potatoes and green peas.

PETIT SALE AUX LENTILLES

Simple to prepare, this classic French home-cured pork is traditionally boiled with lentils but can also be used in cassoulet and as a base for soups.

THE CUT Pork belly

SERVES 8
PREP 45 mins, plus curing **COOK** 1½–2 hrs

½ tsp black peppercorns

½ tsp juniper berries

2 sprigs of thyme

7 bay leaves

2 cups coarse sea salt

2 tsp Prague Powder No. 2 curing salt (optional)

4½lb (2kg) skin-on bone-in pork belly

12oz (350g) Puy lentils

10 small carrots (preferably Chantenay)

24 button onions, chopped

10 celery stalks, cut in 1in (2.5cm) lengths

4 tbsp butter

salt and freshly ground black pepper

2 tbsp chopped flat-leaf parsley, to garnish

1 Crush the peppercorns, juniper berries, 1 sprig of thyme, and 5 bay leaves together using a mortar and pestle. Then add salt and the curing salt (if using) and mix to combine.

2 Rinse the meat and pat dry with paper towels. Rub one-third of the salt mixture over the skin-side of the meat, then turn it over and rub the mixture into the other side.

3 Sprinkle half of the remaining salt mixture on a plastic tray and place the meat on it. Sprinkle the remaining half on and around the meat. Cover with plastic wrap, place a clean plastic tray on top, and weight it down with 2¼lb (1kg) weight. Leave for 8 hours in a cool place, turning every few hours.

4 Rinse the meat and place it in a large stock pot. Cover with cold water and bring to a boil. Drain and return the pork to the pan. Add 6 cups water and bring to a boil. Then reduce the heat and simmer for 30 minutes.

5 Rinse the lentils under cold water and add to the pork along with the carrots, onions, and celery. Add the remaining thyme and bay leaves, and simmer for 1 hour, until the lentils are tender.

6 Remove from the heat and take the pork out of the pot. Stir the butter into the pot and season to taste. Cut the pork into thick slices and place in a large dish. Sprinkle with parsley, and serve with the sauce.

HASLET

A traditional British meatloaf made with bread crumbs, this dish is best eaten the day after you have made it so the flavors can develop fully.

THE CUT Pork belly and bacon

SERVES 6–8
PREP 30 mins **COOK** 2 hrs, plus cooling

melted pork lard, for greasing

12oz (350g) ham, coarsely ground

12oz (350g) pork belly, coarsely ground

1 onion, chopped

2 cups fresh bread crumbs

1 egg, beaten

1 tsp mustard powder

2 tsp finely chopped sage

½ cup hard cider

salt and freshly ground black pepper

1 Preheat the oven to 350°F (180°C) and grease and line a 2lb (900g) loaf pan with parchment paper. Place a large bowl under the blade of a grinder. Using the fine blade, grind the meats together with the onion into the bowl. Add the remaining ingredients to the bowl and mix until well combined.

2 Place the mixture in the prepared loaf pan and press it down firmly with the back of a tablespoon, ensuring there are no gaps in the corners. Cover with foil, place the pan on a baking sheet, and bake in the oven for 2 hours, or until the internal temperature of the meat is 165°F (75°C)

3 Remove the haslet from the oven and set aside to cool. Once cooled, transfer it to a serving platter. Cut into slices and serve with crusty bread and traditional pickles such as piccalilli. It will keep in the fridge, wrapped in foil, for up to 3 days.

BACON JAM

This versatile savory jam can be used on anything, from breakfast sandwiches to roasted vegetables.

THE CUT Bacon

MAKES 1 pint (600ml) jar
PREP 10 mins   **COOK** 1 hr

1 tbsp butter

2 garlic cloves, crushed

1lb 2oz (500g) white onion, chopped

1lb 2oz (500g) thick-cut bacon, chopped

sea salt

1 tbsp chipotle paste

⅓ cup brown sugar

½ cup white wine

1 tbsp apple cider vinegar

1 tbsp pectin

1 Melt the butter in a heavy-bottomed frying pan over medium-low heat. Add the garlic, onion, and bacon to the pan. Season with sea salt and cook for about 20 minutes, stirring frequently, until the bacon caramelizes and becomes crisp.

2 Stir in the chipotle, brown sugar, wine, and vinegar, reduce the heat to simmer, and cook for 30 minutes. Then stir in the pectin and simmer for 10 more minutes.

3 Remove the pan from the heat. Transfer the hot jam to a 1 pint (600ml) jar or heatproof container. It will store for up to 2 weeks in the fridge.

JAM IT UP

For a delicious side dish, halve some Brussels sprouts and toss them into the hot jam. Roast for 45 minutes, or until they turn crisp.

ZWEIBELKUCHEN

Literally meaning "onion cake," this delicious onion and sour cream German tart is traditionally served during the grape harvest season.

THE CUT Bacon

SERVES 8
PREP 30 mins, plus rising
COOK 1 hr–1 hr 5 mins

4 tsp dried yeast

3 tbsp olive oil, plus extra for greasing

2¼ cups bread flour, plus extra for dusting

1 tsp salt

FOR THE FILLING

4 tbsp unsalted butter

2 tbsp olive oil

1lb 5oz (600g) onions, finely sliced

½ tsp caraway seeds

sea salt and freshly ground black pepper

⅔ cup sour cream

⅔ cup crème fraîche

3 large eggs

1 tbsp all-purpose flour

2½oz (75g) smoked bacon strips, chopped

1 For the crust, dissolve the yeast in 1 cup warm water. Add the oil and set aside. Sift the flour and salt into a large bowl and make a well in the center. Pour in the liquid mix, stirring constantly. Use your hands to bring the mixture together to form a soft dough.

2 On a floured surface, knead the dough for 10 minutes until soft, smooth, and elastic. Place in a greased bowl, cover with plastic wrap, and let it rise in a warm place for 1–2 hours, until it doubles.

3 For the filling, heat the butter and oil in a large, heavy-bottomed saucepan. Add the onions and caraway seeds, and season well. Cook gently for 20 minutes, covered, until the onions are soft, but not browned. Remove the lid and cook for 5 more minutes until any excess water evaporates.

4 In a separate bowl, whisk together the sour cream, crème fraîche, eggs, and flour, and season well. Add the onion mixture, mix well, and set aside to cool. When the dough has risen, turn it onto a floured work surface and gently punch it down. Lightly grease a rimmed baking sheet.

5 Roll the dough out to roughly the size of the baking sheet and use to line the bottom of it, making sure the pie has an upturned edge. Cover with lightly greased plastic wrap and let it rise in a warm place for 30 minutes until puffy in places.

6 Preheat the oven to 400°F (200°C). Gently push down the dough if it has risen too much around the edges. Spread the filling over the top, sprinkle with the chopped bacon, and bake on the top rack of the oven for 35–40 minutes, until golden brown. Remove from the oven and leave to cool for at least 5 minutes before serving. Serve warm or cold.

PASTA CARBONARA

Some say this rich and salty pasta dish was created to feed the hardworking charcoal miners of Italy, hence the name carbonara, derived from *carbanaro*, the Italian word for charcoal burner.

 THE CUT Bacon

SERVES 4
PREP 20 mins **COOK** 45 mins

2 tbsp olive oil

4 garlic cloves, crushed

1lb 2oz (500g) white onion, sliced

1lb 2oz (500g) thick-cut bacon, cut into cubes

7oz (200g) peas

1lb (450g) dried spaghetti

2 eggs

3½oz (100g) freshly grated Parmesan cheese

salt and freshly ground black pepper

1 Heat the oil in a frying pan. Add the garlic and onion, and sauté for 5–10 minutes over medium heat. Stir in the bacon and reduce the heat slightly. Allow the bacon to crisp, then add the peas and cook for an additional 5 minutes.

2 Meanwhile, cook the pasta according to package instructions until al dente. Strain and reserve some of the cooking liquid.

3 For the sauce, place the egg and grated Parmesan in a large bowl and whisk well to combine. Add a little pasta water to help loosen it if it looks too sticky.

4 Stir the pasta into the pan and cook for 5–10 minutes, making sure it is well coated in the bacon drippings. Remove the pan from the heat and stir in the egg and cheese sauce. Toss well to coat the pasta evenly. Season and serve immediately.

BRANDY BUZZ

Add a splash of brandy to the bacon once it has crisped up; continue cooking until the brandy has evaporated.

BARBECUED RIBS

Time spent on the grill guarantees a wonderfully succulent appetizer that will be the hit of any party.

SERVES 4
PREP 10 mins
COOK 1 hr 10 mins, plus resting

2 racks of babyback pork ribs, 1lb 10oz–2¼lb (750g–1kg) each

1¼ cups brown sugar

3 tbsp cayenne pepper

3 tbsp salt

1½ tbsp freshly ground white pepper

1½ tbsp mustard powder

VARIATION

Oven-roasted pork ribs Try cooking the ribs in the oven instead of on the grill. Preheat the oven to 350°F (180°C) at the beginning of step 1. Place the ribs on a baking sheet and cook in the oven for 1½ hours. Remove from the heat, take off the foil, and spoon over the cooking juices from the baking sheet. Then return the ribs to the oven for another 10 minutes to glaze. Serve hot.

1 Set the barbecue or charcoal grill to its highest setting. Combine the sugar, spices, and seasoning in a small bowl. Place the ribs, meat-side up, on a clean work surface and thoroughly rub over half the spice mix.

2 Place the ribs, meat-side down, on a large sheet of foil. Rub the remaining spice mix over the other side. Cover the ribs with foil and cook on the grill for 45 minutes to 1 hour.

3 Remove the ribs from the heat and take off the foil. Let rest for 1–2 minutes. Spoon over the cooking juices from the foil and return the ribs to the grill.

4 Cook the ribs on both sides for about 5–9 minutes to glaze and crisp up and until the internal temperature reaches 150°F (65°C). Remove from the heat and serve hot.

PORK SCHNITZEL WITH CREAMY MUSTARD SAUCE

This quick-to-make, tender pork cutlet with a light sauce is perfect for a midweek dinner.

 Boneless pork chops

SERVES 4
PREP 10 mins, plus chilling   **COOK** 10 mins

FOR THE SCHNITZEL

4 x 3½oz (100g) boneless pork chops
salt and freshly ground black pepper
1 tbsp all-purpose flour
1 egg, beaten
1 cup day-old white bread crumbs
1 tbsp olive oil
1 tbsp butter

FOR THE SAUCE

1 tbsp olive oil
½ onion, finely chopped
1 garlic clove, crushed
½ cup white wine
¾ cup heavy cream
1 tbsp Dijon mustard
pinch of sugar

1 If the pork is a little thick, pound it gently with a meat tenderizer, until it is about ¾in (2cm) thick all over. This also helps to tenderize the meat.

2 Season the flour and place it on a plate. Place the egg and bread crumbs in 2 separate shallow bowls. Dust the pork in the flour, shake off the excess, then dip it in the egg. Finally, coat it in the bread crumbs. Cover and chill for at least 30 minutes to help the coating stick to the meat.

3 Preheat the oven to 350°F (180°C). Heat the oil and butter in a large frying pan over medium-high heat. Add the pork and cook for 2–3 minutes on each side, until golden brown. Transfer to a baking sheet and place in the preheated in the oven to keep warm.

4 For the sauce, wipe the pan with paper towels, heat the oil, and cook the onion gently for 5 minutes. Add the garlic and cook for 1 minute. Then add the wine and allow it to reduce to almost nothing. Add the cream, mustard, and sugar, and simmer until the sauce thickens. Season to taste and serve poured over the pork.

MARINATED PORK LEG

A braised pork leg dish from Germany, the unique marinade gives it the tasty flavor of wild boar.

THE CUT Pork leg

SERVES 12
PREP 40 mins, plus 3 days marinating
COOK 4 hrs, plus resting

9lb (4kg) bone-in, skin-on pork leg
2 cups chicken or pork stock
¼ cup olive oil
¼ cup all-purpose flour

FOR THE MARINADE

4 cups red wine
¾ cup red wine vinegar
4 carrots, sliced
2 onions, thinly sliced
4 garlic cloves, minced
6 bay leaves
bunch of flat-leaf parsley
sprig of thyme
sprig of marjoram
1 tbsp black peppercorns
14 juniper berries, crushed
2 tsp coarse salt

FOR THE CABBAGE

1 tbsp olive oil
2 garlic cloves, minced
1 small white onion, diced
1 head of green cabbage, shredded
2 cups apple cider vinegar
2 tbsp salt
1 tbsp caraway seeds

1 For the marinade, place all the ingredients in a large saucepan and bring to a boil. Simmer for 5 minutes, remove from the heat, and let cool.

2 Score the skin of the pork and place in a large stock pot. Pour the marinade over the meat. Cover with a cloth and leave in a cool place for three days, turning occasionally, to make sure it is evenly covered with the marinade.

3 Preheat the oven to 325°F (160°C). Remove the pork from the marinade and pat dry with paper towels. Set the marinade aside. Heat the oil in a large casserole, add the pork, and cook until well-browned on all sides.

4 Meanwhile, heat the marinade, including the vegetables, in a separate pan. Remove the pork from the casserole with a slotted spoon, add the flour, and strain the hot marinade into the casserole. Stir to combine. Then pour in just enough stock to make a smooth, thick sauce.

5 Add the pork to the casserole and bring to a boil. Remove from the heat, cover, and transfer to the preheated oven. Cook the pork for 3–4 hours, until the meat is falling off the bone.

6 Meanwhile, for the cabbage, heat the oil in a deep, straight-sided frying pan or Dutch oven. Add the garlic and cook over medium heat until golden. Stir in the onion and cook for 10 minutes, or until translucent.

7 Add the cabbage to the pan along with ½ cup water, the vinegar, salt, and caraway seeds. Bring to a boil, reduce to a simmer, cover, and cook over low heat for 1½ hours. Remove from the heat.

8 Remove the meat from the casserole and keep warm on a serving dish. Skim the excess fat from the casserole and strain the sauce into a pan. Bring to a boil and adjust the seasoning. Add more stock if the sauce is too thick or boil for 1–2 minutes and reduce if too thin. Carve the meat into slices and serve with the sauce and spicy cabbage.

> ## MUSTARD TWIST
>
> Serve this dish with a mild, German-style, coarsely ground mustard to add a sweet, nutty flavor to the pork.

ASTURIAN BEAN STEW

A Spanish stew with a combination of beans and pork enriched with spices and smoked bacon.

THE CUT Ham

SERVES 6
PREP 30 mins, plus 12 hrs soaking of beans and meat
COOK 2 hrs

1lb 2oz (500g) ham

14oz (400g) dried fava beans or other large white beans

2 tbsp olive oil

5½oz (150g) smoked bacon, chopped

1 onion, finely chopped

1 garlic clove, crushed

1 bay leaf

pinch of saffron threads

½ tsp smoked paprika

freshly ground black pepper

2 Morcilla sausages or blood sausage

2 Spanish-style chorizo sausages

1 Place the ham in a large bowl and cover with water. Place in the fridge to soak for 12 hours, changing the water once. Rinse and soak the beans in cold water for 12 hours.

2 Heat the oil in a large, heatproof casserole. Add the bacon and cook, stirring occasionally, for 2 minutes. Then add the onion, reduce the heat, and cook for about 3 minutes, until soft. Stir in the garlic.

3 Drain the ham and beans, add them to the casserole, and pour in just enough water to cover the meat. Add the bay leaf, saffron threads, smoked paprika, and pepper. Bring to a boil, then reduce the heat. Simmer over low heat for 1½ hours, stirring occasionally. Add water if necessary. Add the Morcilla and chorizo sausages, stir to ensure they are evenly distributed, and cook for an additional 30 minutes.

4 Remove from the heat and take out the bay leaf. Transfer the ham and the sausages to a separate bowl and set aside to cool. Once cooled, cut the meat into chunks of about 1in (2½cm) and return to the casserole. Serve in shallow bowls with crusty bread. It is traditionally eaten with a wooden spoon.

PEA, HAM, AND POTATO SOUP

This simple, hearty, comforting soup can also be made with leftover ham, and it tastes even better the next day.

THE CUT Ham

SERVES 4–6
PREP 15 mins   **COOK** 2 hrs

2½lb (1.1kg) unsmoked ham

1 bay leaf

1 tbsp olive oil

1 onion, finely chopped

salt and freshly ground black pepper

1 tbsp Dijon mustard

3 garlic cloves, finely chopped

2 sprigs of rosemary

handful of thyme leaves only, plus extra to garnish

4 cups hot beef stock

1lb (450g) frozen peas

3 potatoes, peeled and chopped into bite-size pieces

1 Place the ham and bay leaf in a large saucepan, cover with 4 cups of water, and bring to a boil. Cover partially, reduce the heat to simmer, and cook for 1 hour or until the ham is cooked. Skim away any scum that forms at the surface. Discard the liquid, remove the ham, and set aside.

2 Heat the oil in a large heavy-bottomed pan over medium heat. Add the onion and cook for 3–4 minutes, until softened. Season, stir in the mustard, garlic, and herbs, and add a little stock. Bring to a boil, then add the peas and remaining stock. Bring to a boil, reduce the heat to a simmer, and cook for 45 minutes. Add hot water to the soup as needed.

3 Meanwhile, bring a separate pan of water to a boil. Add the potatoes, bring to a boil, then reduce the heat to a simmer. Cook for 12–15 minutes, until softened. Drain and set aside. Remove the rosemary from the soup and use an immersion blender to gently purée the peas.

4 Stir in the potatoes. Remove any fat from the ham, chop into bite-size pieces, and stir into the soup. Taste and adjust the seasoning, if needed. Garnish with the thyme leaves and serve with whole-wheat bread.

FEIJOADA

An authentic Brazilian worker's stew, this dish is made from a variety of fresh and cured pork cuts.

THE CUT Ham hock and pork ribs

SERVES 8
PREP 30 mins, plus 12 hrs soaking of beans and meat
COOK 3 hrs

1 smoked ham hock, about 1lb (450g)

6 salted pork ribs

1lb 2oz (500g) dried black beans

1 pig's foot, split

2 garlic cloves, finely chopped

4 bay leaves

14oz (400g) garlic pork sausages, cut into small chunks

4 small oranges, peeled and cut into wedges

1 Place the ham hock and salted ribs in a large bowl and cover with water. Soak them for 12 hours in the fridge, changing the water once. Rinse and soak the beans in cold water for 12 hours.

2 Drain the beans and place in a large, heatproof casserole. Add the ham hock, ribs, pig's foot, garlic, and bay leaves. Cover with water and bring to a boil. Reduce to simmer, skim off any scum, then cover and cook for 2½ hours.

3 Transfer a ladleful of the beans to a bowl and mash them with a fork. Return the mashed beans to the casserole and add the garlic sausages. Simmer for another 30 minutes or until the meat starts to fall off the bone. Remove from the heat.

4 Pick the meat from the hock and foot and discard the bones. Cut the meat into chunks and place on a warmed platter. Remove the bay leaves from the casserole. Ladle the beans and sausage stew over the meat and place the orange wedges around the sides. Serve with steamed long grain rice and collard greens.

PIGGING OUT

You can use any part of the pig for this recipe, such as ears, tails, or nose. Salted ribs are authentic, but if not available, fresh ones will suffice.

HAM HOCK WITH RED CABBAGE

Slow-cooked sweet cabbage is the perfect complement to ham and, with the addition of spices and dried fruit, transforms this humble piece of meat.

THE CUT Ham hock

SERVES 4–6
PREP 20 mins   **COOK** 3 hrs

2 ham hocks, about 3lb (1.35kg) each

1 small red cabbage, cored and finely shredded

2 onions, sliced

4 garlic cloves, finely chopped

a few sprigs of thyme

½ cup raisins

pinch of grated nutmeg

pinch of ground cinnamon

1¼ cups white wine vinegar

2 cups hot vegetable stock (optional)

salt and freshly ground black pepper

1 Preheat the oven to 325°F (160°C). Place the ham hocks in a large, heavy-bottomed saucepan and cover with water. Bring to a boil, then reduce to a simmer. Partially cover, and cook gently for 1 hour. Remove the hams and reserve the cooking liquid, if you wish to use it instead of the vegetable stock (it can be salty).

2 When the hams are cool enough to handle, remove the skin and discard, then place in a large, heatproof casserole. Add the remaining ingredients to the casserole, along with either the stock or the cooking liquid, and tuck the hams in neatly. Season with salt and pepper, cover, and place in the oven for 2 hours.

3 Check occasionally to ensure it does not dry out, adding a little hot water, if necessary. Remove the hams, shred the meat, and stir it into the casserole. Serve with baked or roasted potatoes.

VARIATION

Ham hock with white cabbage and celery Use 1 small, shredded white cabbage instead of the red, and add 2 chopped celery stalks along with the other ingredients in step 2. Omit the raisins, nutmeg, and cinnamon and add 1 tablespoon caraway seeds, and cook as above. Serve with plain boiled potatoes.

POT ROAST SMOKED HAM

Ham hock is amazing value and tasty, too. The Jerusalem artichokes add a nutty, creamy texture, but if they're not available you can use parsnips instead.

THE CUT Ham hock

SERVES 4–6
PREP 25 mins   **COOK** 3 hrs 15 mins

2 smoked ham hocks, about 3lb (1.35kg) each

1 bay leaf

1 tbsp olive oil

1 onion, finely chopped

salt and freshly ground black pepper

3 garlic cloves, finely chopped

a few sprigs of thyme

3 carrots, chopped

8oz (225g) Jerusalem artichokes, peeled and sliced

4½oz (125g) yellow split peas

½ cup hard cider

3 cups hot vegetable stock (optional)

1 Place the ham hocks and bay leaf in a large, heavy-bottomed saucepan. Cover with water and cook for about 2 hours, skimming away any scum that comes to the top of the pan. Remove the hams and, when cool enough to handle, peel away the skins and discard. Set the hams aside. Reserve the cooking liquid, if you wish to use it instead of the vegetable stock (it can be salty).

2 Preheat the oven to 350°F (180°C). Heat the oil in a large, heatproof casserole over medium heat. Add the onion and cook for 3–4 minutes, until soft. Season with salt and pepper, stir in the garlic, thyme, carrots, and artichokes, and cook for 1–2 minutes. Add the split peas and stir to coat. Increase the heat, pour in the cider, and let it bubble for 1 minute. Then add the stock or the cooking liquid and bring to a boil. Reduce to a simmer and add the hams to the casserole, tucking them down as much as possible.

3 Cover and place the casserole in the oven for about 1 hour, or until the peas are soft. Check occasionally to make sure it does not dry out too much, adding hot water if needed. Remove the casserole from the oven and, using a fork, slide the ham meat off the bones and stir it into the casserole. Discard the bones. Taste the casserole and season if necessary. Serve with fresh crusty bread.

COUNTRY HAM AND EGGS WITH RED-EYE GRAVY AND GRITS

A traditional breakfast in the South, the gravy combines the drippings from pan-fried ham and black coffee.

THE CUT Cured ham

SERVES 4
PREP 15 mins   **COOK** 30 mins

4 tbsp butter

8 slices of thick-cut salt-cured ham

4 large eggs

½ cup black coffee

FOR THE GRITS

2½ cups chicken stock

1 cup grits or coarse polenta

1 tbsp butter

1 tsp red pepper flakes

salt and freshly ground black pepper

1 cup heavy cream

1 For the grits, heat the chicken stock in a large saucepan. Stir in the grits, butter, red pepper flakes, and season. Cook for 10 minutes, or until it thickens. Stir in the cream and simmer for 5–10 minutes, stirring occasionally, until thickened.

2 In a frying pan, melt 1 tablespoon of the butter. Fry the ham slices for 2–3 minutes on each side, adding more butter if necessary. Remove the ham using a slotted spoon and place in a warm oven.

3 Meanwhile, melt a little butter in another pan. Fry the eggs, sunny-side up, for 3–6 minutes, or until the yolks have become firm.

4 To make the red-eye gravy, pour the coffee and any remaining butter into the pan in which the ham was fried. Increase the heat to medium-high and stir well to mix the ham drippings, butter, and coffee.

5 Place a generous helping of the grits, two slices of ham, and an egg on each plate and serve drizzled with the red-eye gravy.

CUBANO

A Latin variation of a grilled ham-and-cheese sandwich, the Cubano is one of the most popular street foods in Miami.

THE CUT Cooked ham and roast pork

SERVES 4
PREP 15 mins   **COOK** 20 mins

1 Cuban or French bread loaf

yellow mustard

4 slices of leftover roast pork

4 slices of ham

4 slices of Swiss cheese

4 dill pickles, sliced lengthwise

butter, softened

1 Cut the loaf into 4 x 6–8in (15–20cm) lengths, then slice each in half lengthwise. Lightly coat 4 slices of the bread with mustard and layer each with 1 slice of the roast pork, ham, and cheese. Add a pickle on top and cover with the remaining slices of bread. Brush the top of each sandwich with butter.

2 Place the sandwiches in a plancha grill, or sandwich press, and press down until the cheese has melted and the outside of the bread is crisp. Remove from the grill, cut each sandwich diagonally across, and serve hot.

CROQUE MONSIEUR

This classic Parisian café sandwich has been a favorite—for good reason—since the days of Proust.

THE CUT Cooked ham

SERVES 6
PREP 10 mins   **COOK** 25 mins

12 slices of French or Italian bread loaf
Dijon mustard
24 slices of ham
1 tbsp butter, for frying

FOR THE BÉCHAMEL

2 tbsp butter
3 tbsp flour
1¼ cups whole milk
½ tsp sea salt
1 tsp freshly ground black pepper
1 tsp nutmeg
7oz (200g) grated Gruyère cheese
2 tbsp freshly grated Parmesan cheese

1 Preheat the oven to 400°F (200°C). For the béchamel, melt the butter in a saucepan until it begins to bubble. Then whisk in the flour and cook, stirring constantly, for 2–3 minutes, or until smooth. Whisk in the milk, a little at a time, until it is the consistency of a sauce. Remove from the heat and season, then add the nutmeg, half the Gruyère, and the Parmesan.

2 Lightly coat each slice of the bread with the mustard. Top 6 slices of the bread with 4 slices of ham each. Sandwich together with the remaining 6 slices of bread.

3 Melt the butter in a frying pan, then add the sandwiches and fry for 2 minutes on each side. Transfer to an ovenproof pan and top with the béchamel sauce and remaining Gruyère.

4 Bake in the oven for 5 minutes. Heat the broiler on high and broil the sandwiches for 3 minutes, or until bubbling. Serve hot.

VARIATION

Croque madame Prepare the sandwich as above. Then heat 1 tablespoon of oil in a frying pan and fry 6 eggs, 1 at a time. To serve, place 1 fried egg on each sandwich, topped with 1 tablespoon of béchamel sauce.

TOAD IN THE HOLE WITH ONION GRAVY

These sausages encased in crispy batter are a classic British comfort food. You can also serve the gravy with grilled chops or mashed potatoes.

THE CUT Pork sausages

SERVES 4
PREP 25 mins   **COOK** 40–45 mins

FOR THE TOAD IN THE HOLE

1 cup all-purpose flour
salt and freshly ground black pepper
4 eggs
1¼ cups whole milk
½ tsp dried sage
½ tsp ground mustard
2 tbsp beef dripping
8 pork and herb sausages

FOR THE ONION GRAVY

2 tbsp olive oil
3 red onions, finely sliced
2 tbsp all-purpose flour
1¼ cups vegetable stock
splash of red wine (optional)

1 Preheat the oven to 400°F (200°C). Place the flour in a large mixing bowl and season well. Break the eggs, 1 at a time, into the flour, and stir with a fork to incorporate. Gradually add the milk, whisking vigorously after each addition. Stir in the sage and mustard. Set aside.

2 For the gravy, heat the oil in a small, nonstick pan over medium heat. Add the onions and cook for 5 minutes. Reduce the heat, cover, and cook gently for 30 minutes, stirring occasionally.

3 Meanwhile, place the pan drippings in a nonstick, heavy-bottomed roasting pan and heat for 5 minutes. Add the sausages and bake for 15 minutes. Space the sausages evenly in the pan, then pour over the batter. Return to the oven for 25–30 minutes, or until risen and golden brown.

4 Meanwhile, stir the flour into the onions and cook over medium heat for 2 minutes, stirring. Gradually pour in the stock, stirring constantly. Season to taste and add the wine (if using). Serve with slices of toad in the hole.

CHORIZO WITH PATATAS BRAVAS

A fiery tomato sauce meets a creamy aïoli, crisp chorizo, and hot fried potatoes in this Spanish tapas dish.

 Chorizo sausage

SERVES 4
PREP 15 mins   **COOK** 40 mins

6 tbsp olive oil

1lb 2oz (500g) onions, finely chopped

4 garlic cloves, crushed

3 tsp smoked paprika

1 tsp red pepper flakes

2 x 14oz (400g) can chopped tomatoes

juice of 1 lemon

salt and freshly ground black pepper

7oz (200g) Spanish-style chorizo sausage

1lb 2oz (500g) waxy potatoes, such as Yukon Gold, unpeeled and cut into cubes

1 tsp cayenne pepper

FOR THE AÏOLI

1 garlic clove, crushed

1 egg yolk

¾ cup olive oil

1 tbsp lemon juice

1 For the sauce, heat 2 tablespoons of oil in a lidded saucepan and add the onions and garlic. Cook over medium heat, until softened. Then stir in the smoked paprika, red pepper flakes, tomatoes, and lemon juice, and season well. Reduce the heat, cover, and simmer for 10 minutes. Remove from the heat and keep warm.

2 Place the chorizo in a large, nonstick frying pan. Cook for 7–10 minutes, until firm and well-browned, then remove with a slotted spoon and set aside. Add the potatoes, cayenne pepper, and the remaining oil to the pan. Stir to coat and cook over medium heat, stirring frequently, for 15 minutes. Slice the chorizo into chunks, add to the pan, and cook for 5 more minutes.

3 Meanwhile, make the aïoli. Place the garlic and egg yolk in a food processor along with a pinch of salt, and pulse to combine. With the processor on high, pour in the oil, a little at a time, until it forms a creamy sauce. Stir in the lemon juice.

4 Remove the potatoes and chorizo and place on a serving dish. Pour the sauce over and toss lightly to coat. Top with the garlic aïoli and serve hot.

CAJUN ANDOUILLE GUMBO

Rustic Cajun-style cooking is often a one-pot affair, and this hearty gumbo is a perfect example.

 Andouille sausage

SERVES 4
PREP 15 mins   **COOK** 1 hrs

2 tbsp olive oil

1 large onion, finely chopped

1 green bell pepper, seeded and cut into ¾in (2cm) cubes

2 garlic cloves, crushed

2 tbsp unsalted butter

3 tbsp all-purpose flour

2 x 14oz (400g) cans chopped tomatoes

2 cups hot fish or chicken stock

2 dried red chiles, finely chopped

1 tsp smoked paprika or ancho chili powder

7oz (200g) okra, trimmed and cut into ¾in (2cm) chunks

9oz (250g) andouille smoked sausage, peeled and cut into ¾in (2cm) chunks

salt and freshly ground black pepper

1 tbsp thyme leaves

1lb 2oz (500g) raw large shrimp, shelled and deveined

2 tbsp finely chopped flat-leaf parsley

1 Heat the oil in a large, heavy-bottomed saucepan. Add the onion and green pepper, and cook gently for 5 minutes, until soft, but not browned. Add the garlic and cook for an additional 2 minutes.

2 Add the butter and allow it to melt. Then stir in the flour and reduce the heat to low. Cook, stirring, for 5 minutes, until browned. Add the tomatoes, stock, chiles, smoked paprika, okra, and sausage, and bring to a boil. Taste and season with pepper and salt, if necessary.

3 Reduce the heat to a low simmer and add the thyme. Cook, uncovered, for 30 minutes, stirring occasionally, until the okra is soft and the gumbo is well thickened.

4 Increase the heat and add the shrimp. Cook the gumbo, uncovered, for an additional 5 minutes, until the shrimp are opaque and cooked through. Stir through the parsley. Serve with boiled rice.

BEEF AND VEAL

BEEF AND VEAL

SUCH LARGE CREATURES AS CATTLE ARE BOUND TO IMPRESS; THEY HAVE ALWAYS BEEN A SYMBOL OF RICHES AND POWER. FOR THOUSANDS OF YEARS, CATTLE HAS BEEN USED FOR DOWRIES AND GIFTS, AND ABOVE ALL FOR FEASTING.

CATTLE ARE GRAZING ANIMALS and cannot be raised as intensively as pigs or poultry (although feedlot systems, see below, are fairly intensive), which makes beef expensive. Ideally suited to moist, grass-producing areas, beef cattle fatten very well in cool climates, although British settlers in drier places such as America, Argentina, and Australia, fostered beef industries that are now significant producers.

A cool climate also makes it possible to age beef and further enhance its flavor. This tradition moved to America with European immigrants, and many famous American suppliers now specialize in dry-aging their beef for many weeks.

The dairy industry produces huge numbers of surplus male calves that are raised for beef and veal. However, because dairy cattle are selected to put their energy into producing milk, the beef they produce can be lean and of lower quality than the meat from beef breeds. Veal calves produce a particularly delicate and tender white meat.

Older breeding or milking cattle are all eventually used for meat, but this goes into the processing industry and usually only appears for sale as processed products.

PRODUCTION METHODS

• **Extensive or grass-fed beef** Some calves begin life indoors before going out to grass; others are born outside and stay on grass all their lives, although they may be housed during severe weather. They are rotated around grass paddocks that are usually fertilized to increase grass growth. Most grass-fed cattle are fed a grain supplement for a few weeks before slaughter to produce a better carcass. However, most beef labeled as "grass-fed" does not advertise this fact.
Diet: grass, with concentrates near the end of their lives.

• **Intensive or housed beef** Cattle are sometimes started off on grass but may then spend the rest of their lives indoors. They are kept in open-sided or ventilated sheds bedded with straw and fed ad lib on a mixed diet of cereals as well as hay, grass, or straw. They have adequate room to move about and lie down. Most will be cross-breeds.
Diet: concentrates, hay, straw, roots

• **Intensive feedlot beef** The US term for this production method—"concentrated animal feeding operations"—describes it well. Cattle begin life grazing, then for the last 3–4 months of their lives are moved to units, or feedlots, containing thousands of cattle where they are fed on high-energy diets. Antibiotics are used to control disease and to encourage rapid growth. Growth hormones are permitted in the US, but are banned in the EU.
Diet: concentrates

• **Organic beef** Cattle can be raised in any system, from extensive grass to intensive feedlots, but the feed must all be certified as organic and drug use is likely to be less than in the conventional equivalents. However, some organic marks allow drug use "when necessary," which is open to interpretation, although drug withdrawal periods must be adhered to.

BUYING BEEF

Good beef that has been well aged will be a dark ruby red with creamy white fat. Bright or pale red meat has usually not been hung. Grass-fed beef has slightly yellower fat than grain-fed beef. A lot of marbling (see p15) means that the beef will taste good and stay moist. Very lean beef has less flavor and is prone to drying out when not served pink.

BEEF BREEDS AND CATEGORIES

Beef is more often sold under the name of its breed than any other meat. The most famous is the Scottish Angus, now produced all over the world. But there are many other beef heroes: the Gelbvieh, Hereford, Limousin, Simmental, and Fleckvieh all produce outstanding beef, not to mention the Wagyu breeds used to make well-marbled Japanese beef. Other famous breeds are used for crossing: both the Piedmontese and Belgian Blue produce a double leg muscle and are very lean, while Friesian and Holstein cattle account for a large proportion of dairy beef.

Zebu, or Brahman, cattle have a hump on their neck; this helps them survive in hot countries. Originally from Asia, they are now also found in Africa and South America, notably Brazil where they were crossed with Charolais to produce the Chanchim.

• **Beef** Most beef comes from steers (castrated males) or heifers (young females). For faster growth, some steers are not castrated, a method that some people consider produces inferior beef. Beef from the dairy industry tends to be leaner but is not usually identified as such. Cross-bred beef is the norm, but if a particular breed is mentioned, it usually means the beef is of better quality.

• **Kobe beef** A Japanese speciality made from Wagyu cattle that are fed only on local grains and grasses to produce extraordinarily well-marbled meat that is very expensive. This style of beef is produced in other areas of Japan and in other countries, but should not be confused with the authentic version.
• **Veal** Bob, or bobby, veal comes from calves under one month old and usually just a few days old. To produce traditional white veal, calves are removed from their mother shortly after birth and fed on a milk formula. They are usually slaughtered at around 20 weeks. Some are confined in crates or stalls, while others are reared in groups in larger pens. Calf crates are banned in the EU and some states of the US.

Calves that stay with their mothers, or that are fed a more varied grain diet, or that eat grass as well as milk, have a variety of names depending on their production: rose veal, grain veal, and pasture or free-range veal. Red or ruby veal and calf meat is a little older with darker meat.

BUFFALO AND BISON

In the prairies of North America, vast herds of native bison roamed the country, but were nearly annihilated in the 19th century by hunting; about two million remain. Some early settlers called bison "buffalo," and the names are interchangeable in the US and the UK. However, bison are a completely different species from buffalo; their horns are distinctively different.
• **Buffalo** The most common species, the water buffalo, comes from Asia. They are primarily used for milk and for traction, although obviously produce meat, too. A few producers raise them exclusively for meat. Water buffalo milk is used to make Mozzarella in Italy. African buffalo are very distant relatives and are not domesticated.
• **Bison** A few enterprising entrepreneurs now raise bison for meat, although this is sometimes sold as "buffalo." It is usually extensively raised on grass and tends to be very lean.

BEEF CUTS

GOOD BEEF SHOULD BE DEEP DARK RED from being dry-aged (hung), and well marbled with fat, although excess fat should have been trimmed off already. If a beef breed is specified, this is a good indicator of quality. Bright red beef has not been aged and will have less flavor.

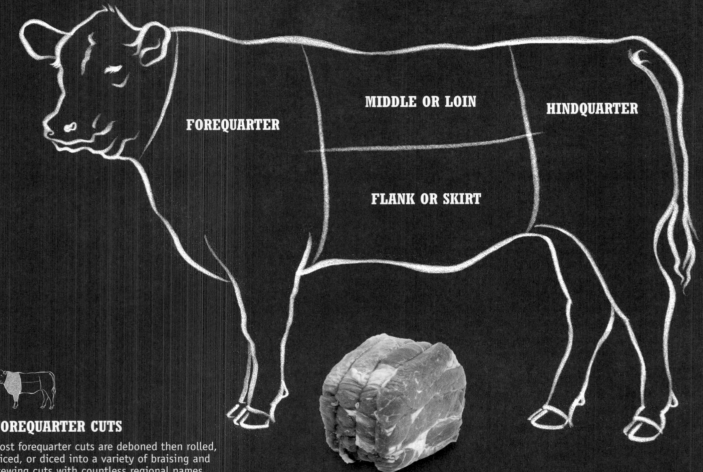

FOREQUARTER

MIDDLE OR LOIN

HINDQUARTER

FLANK OR SKIRT

FOREQUARTER CUTS

Most forequarter cuts are deboned then rolled, sliced, or diced into a variety of braising and stewing cuts with countless regional names. A few thin muscles can be grilled if served pink.

CHUCK AND BLADE Also known as shoulder as it comes from the upper part of the forequarter, this boneless, rolled cut makes a rich braising roast. Otherwise it is sliced or diced for stewing.

BONELESS SHOULDER STEAK
A well-marbled shoulder steak, cut from next to the bladebone, it has a seam of thick gristle running down the middle. With the gristle removed, it is called flatiron and can be grilled or stir-fried.

BRISKET This can be trimmed of excess fat then rolled (above) and braised, but is often brined and made into salt beef. A whole unrolled brisket is a popular cut for long, slow, hot-smoking.

Additional forequarter cuts

• **BONELESS ROLLED BACK RIB ROAST** From behind the neck, this slow-cooking cut has plenty of fat and connective tissue.

• **STEWING STEAK, DICED** Most parts of the shoulder can be diced or sliced for slow cooking.

• **GROUND** Ground forequarter has more fat while grinding the shank and hind leg yields a leaner product.

• **SHOULDER POT ROAST** A tough cut of meat that is usually braised or cooked in liquid to tenderize it.

• **CHUCK STEAK** Also known as a blade steak and is one of the more tender cuts from this section. You can braise it or roast it in the oven.

MIDDLE OR LOIN CUTS

It is difficult to find enough adjectives to describe the superb cuts that come from the beef loin. Whether bone-in or boneless, all are tender and flavorsome.

RIB EYE STEAK Cut from the forerib, this well-marbled steak is deservedly popular. Top cap or deckle, a thin muscle lying over the forerib, is sometimes sold separately for quick-frying.

FILET OR FILLET MIGNON Leaner than loin, this is the most tender cut. When fully trimmed, it makes a luxurious roast, although some prefer more marbled beef. It is also sliced into steaks.

STANDING RIB ROAST, ON THE BONE A superb bone-in roasting cut, this is similar to sirloin, but without the fillet and with more muscle and fat on the outside. It should be well marbled.

Additional middle or loin cuts

• **SIRLOIN ROAST, ON THE BONE** Similar to the standing rib roast but also includes the fillet muscle. T-bone steaks are slices of this cut.

• **BONELESS RIB EYE ROAST** A well-marbled, tender roast that is easy to carve.

• **SIRLOIN STEAK** A slice of a deboned sirloin, with marbling and outer fat; a premium steak.

• **STRIP STEAK** A lean steak from the eye muscle but with all the outer fat removed.

• **PORTERHOUSE STEAK** Cut from the rump end of the sirloin, this is a thick-cut bone-in steak.

FLANK OR SKIRT CUTS

Most cuts from this part of the carcass are used for processing as it is fatty with connective tissue. But there are several thin muscles that can be grilled or fried if served pink.

SHORT RIBS OR BOILING BEEF These chunky pieces of rib have a thick layer of meat and fat. They make good soup but increasingly are also cooked long and slow in a rich reduction sauce.

HANGER STEAK OR ONGLET A dark muscle from the diaphram, hanger does little work in the animal so is fairly tender. Other flank muscles are skirt and flank, both thin and fibrous. All can be cooked pink.

TRI-TIP A small triangular muscle from the end of the sirloin that makes good roasts and steaks or cubes for grilling. Another section of tri-tip forms part of the thick flank.

GROUND Fatty ground flank is used for sausages while grinding the shank and hind leg results in a leaner product.

HINDQUARTER CUTS

Beef from the hind leg is leaner than loin and forequarter cuts. It yields many fine but slightly cheaper steaks and roasts as well as braising cuts.

BONELESS RUMP Bridging the sirloin and leg, the rump is well marbled and makes excellent steaks and roasts. The thin muscle lying over the top is sold as minute steak or picanha.

TOP ROUND STEAK Not as tender or well-marbled as loin cuts, nevertheless top round makes good roasts and steaks. The thin muscle lying overtop is sometimes sold separately as top round cap or top cap.

SLICED SHANK This lean, boned out shin makes a hearty stew when diced, and has a lovely silky texture.

Additional hindquarter cuts

• **POINT STEAK** The pointed end of the rump muscle next to the sirloin—makes good steaks.

• **MINUTE STEAK** Cut from the rump cap, it is sliced thinly and cooked quickly to avoid toughness.

• **BONELESS RUMP ROAST** The most tender leg muscle, this cut makes economical steaks and rolled roasts.

• **BOTTOM ROUND ROAST** The larger of the two silverside muscles is generally braised but can be roasted.

• **SALMON CUT OR EYE OF ROUND** A slim muscle from the silverside, this is a neat log-shaped cut.

• **TOP RUMP OR THICK FLANK** Made up of several muscles including tri-tip, but is usually sliced for braising.

VEAL, BUFFALO, AND BISON CUTS

Veal, being young, is extremely tender and very pale. Bison and buffalo are slightly darker than beef, with proportionately more forequarter meat. Although in theory all the beef cuts (see pp144–5) could be produced, in reality far fewer cuts are offered. They are all very lean, so roasts need larding (see p232) if cooked beyond pink.

VEAL

Veal cuts are simply smaller versions of beef cuts, although more are used for roasts and steaks since the meat is so much more tender. The sinews in veal— especially white veal—are finer and less obtrusive than in beef. Rose veal and ruby veal comes from older animals, so the sinews in these meats will be slightly thicker.

FOREQUARTER CUTS

The forequarter of veal is almost exclusively used for braising and stewing, the most famous dish being *blanquette de veau* (see p182). The shank when sliced is used for osso buco.

DICED SHOULDER More tender than beef shoulder, this cut still benefits from gentle simmering. It suits delicately flavored dishes.

MIDDLE OR LOIN CUTS

These are the finest cuts of veal. As it is smaller than beef, some cuts are called by lamb or pork terms: the forerib is sometimes called rack, for example, and the bone-in steaks chops.

RIB CHOP The rib has more marbling than most veal cuts. Its creamy white fat adds flavor and succulence, and the meat, whether roast or chops, is superbly tender.

LOIN CHOP Loin chops are similar to T-bone steaks when they include the bone. When boneless, they are sometimes opened out into lean butterfly chops. Loin is leaner than rib.

HINDQUARTER CUTS

The hindquarter produces some of the largest muscles, so this is traditionally where cutlets are from. All hindquarter muscles tend to be leaner than loin.

FLANK STEAK – WHITE VEAL Milk-fed veal is the whitest and usually the youngest veal. A flank steak is a delicious cut and can cope with being sliced thickly. The rump can also be roasted.

FLANK STEAK – ROSE VEAL Rose veal has had access to grass, which makes the meat darker and the fat slightly more yellow. The calves may be older, but the meat is still very tender.

VEAL CUTLET A very thin, completely trimmed slice of a single muscle. Thicker slices can be flattened out to produce a thin cutlet, ready for coating in egg and bread crumbs.

BONELESS RUMP ROAST Sometimes called cushion, this forequarter roast is more tender than bottom round rump roast, so makes an excellent but quite lean cut. Can also be cut into steaks or diced for kebabs and fondues.

SHANK, SLICED ON THE BONE (OSSO BUCO) Although osso buco is cut from several different meats, veal shank is the original and authentic cut to use. Slowly braised, the bone marrow gives a rich finish to the dish.

Additional veal cuts

• **SHOULDER ROAST (FOREQUARTER)** Far leaner than beef shoulder, this needs larding before being gently braised.

• **GROUND (FOREQUARTER)** Leaner and milder than beef, ground veal is good for pasta sauces.

• **BRAISING STEAK (FOREQUARTER OR HINDQUARTER)** Comes from the leg or from the shoulder; the leg is more lean and tender.

• **CUTLET (MIDDLE OR LOIN)** A restaurant favorite, these trimmed chops are from the forerib or best end.

• **FILLET (MIDDLE OR LOIN)** A very tender and lean cut, especially once exterior fat is removed.

• **SIRLOIN ROAST (MIDDLE OR LOIN)** Also called filet or chump end, this is a prime boneless roasting cut.

• **FRENCH RACK (MIDDLE OR LOIN)** A luxury cut from the forerib—a six-rib rack weighs about 3lb 3oz (1.5kg).

• **VEAL BREAST (FLANK)** From the flank, breast is a good cut for stuffing. It has layers of fat.

• **SILVERSIDE (HINDQUARTER)** From lower down the leg than a cutlet, this cut can be roasted or braised.

BUFFALO AND BISON

In the United States, bison meat is often (but not always) called buffalo so it is worth checking which species is being sold, alhough the meats are similar. Italy and the US are the major exporters of both bison and buffalo. The best buffalo comes from animals grown for meat rather than ex-milking cows. In Asia, buffalo could come from older working animals and the meat could therefore be tougher.

FOREQUARTER CUTS

The forequarter of both buffalo and bison is proportionately larger than the forequarter of beef. However, like beef, most is used for making rich stews and braises, or to grind.

SHOULDER ROAST The best part comes from behind the neck. Not the most tender cut, it is well endowed with fat and connective tissue to keep it succulent as a slow-roast.

MIDDLE OR LOIN CUTS

The middle or loin section of bison and buffalo contains the same tender cuts as beef, although you are less likely to encounter excess exterior fat.

RIB EYE ROAST, BONELESS From the fore end of the loin, this roast is likely to have a little more fat than most cuts. Even so, it is more successfully cooked rare or pink.

HINDQUARTER CUTS

The hindquarter cuts of bison and buffalo tend to be even leaner than beef, so it is advisable to cook it like venison and serve steaks pink.

FLANK STEAK Despite a covering of fat on the outside of the steak, the meat itself is very lean so should be cooked like venison and served pink to keep it from toughening.

Additional buffalo and bison cuts

• **DICED SHOULDER (FOREQUARTER)** With their large shoulders, there is a wide choice of diced meat for stewing.

• **BRISKET (FOREQUARTER)** There is some fat on a whole brisket, which keeps it moist if left on.

• **FILLET (MIDDLE OR LOIN)** The most tender cut for roasts and steaks. Often sold as tenderloin.

• **LOIN EYE (MIDDLE OR LOIN)** Sometimes called striploin, this is the loin or eye muscle, fully trimmed of fat.

• **TOPSIDE (HINDQUARTER)** A lean cut that is best served either pink or larded and slow-cooked.

PRESERVED BEEF

MANY OF THESE PRESERVED BEEF PRODUCTS are unsmoked to emphasize the flavor of the beef. They are often more expensive than their pork counterparts. Beef sausages often contain pork fat to add juiciness and reduce cost, but some are made without pork to satisfy the kosher and halal markets.

SALT BEEF This was originally made to preserve beef for long sea voyages. The meat is soaked in a strong, spiced brine for some weeks and its bright red color comes from adding sodium nitrite to the brine.

PASTRAMI An American sandwich meat made from salt-cured beef brisket that is covered in a spice mix and then smoked and cooked. It can be eaten hot or cold.

CARNE DE SOL Also called *jabá,* this speciality of northeastern Brazil is made from beef that is salted and then left to dry in the sun. The name means "meat of the sun."

BRESAOLA From the Italian Alps, bresaola is made from beef from the hind leg that is salted and flavored with juniper berries for a few days before being dried.

BÜNDNERFLEISCH Also called *viande de Grisons*, this dried beef comes from Switzerland. Boneless beef is marinated in a spiced wine brine and then air-dried. It is not usually smoked.

CECINA This is made in Spain and Mexico. In Mexico, sheets of beef are salted, marinated, and sun-dried. Spanish *Cecina de Leon* is beef leg meat that is cured, smoked, and dried.

JERKY is a variation of South American *charqui*—salted and wind-dried strips of meat. Jerky is marinated in a hot, spicy mixture and is sometimes smoked as well.

GRUZINSKAYA A cold-smoked cured and dried beef sausage from the Russian Caucasus flavored with sugar, brandy, and typical spices such as fenugreek, coriander, turmeric, dill, and basil.

HOFER REINDFLEISHWURST This German *rohwurst* is traditionally made from lean beef, although pork is also used now. It is well spiced with garlic, cloves, and black pepper, then it is cured and briefly dried.

CHISTORRA A very long, thin Spanish sausage made with beef and also pork. Its red color comes from the addition of paprika and it can be a fresh or a dried sausage. It is served as a tapa.

SOUDJOUK Also spelled *sujuk* or *sukuk*, this mahogany-red dried beef sausage comes from Lebanon, Turkey, and Syria. It is flavored with garlic, fenugreek, allspice, cumin, sumac, and paprika.

VEAL SALAME Not a traditional Italian salami, this is often made for the Halal and Kosher markets, so the veal is mixed with beef fat before being cured, packed into skins, and dried.

GENDARME A rectangular-sectioned dried sausage from Alsace made of beef, pork skin, and pork fat. It is highly seasoned with hot spices and wine, then heavily smoked, pressed, and dried.

SALAMETTI SWISS A small, plump sausage from Switzerland, this *rohwurst* is made of beef mixed with pork and well flavored with pepper and sometimes wine. It is cured and dried.

MAKING SALT BEEF

Salt beef is easy to make. See page 21 for useful tips on salting and brining. Prague powder (curing salt) can be bought online—it is not essential but gives salted meat its characteristic red color.

1 For 5lb (2.25kg) rolled brisket, dissolve 2⅔ cups salt and 2 tbsp Prague Powder No.1 in 17½ cups of hot water. Add 2 tbsp ground black peppercorns and allspice, 1 tbsp ground ginger, 2 bay leaves, and 1 sprig of thyme and let it cool.

2 Immerse the brisket completely in the cold brine. Use a weight to keep it submerged. Store in the fridge for a week, turning it each day to distribute the salt, then drain and rinse in clean water.

3 Place the beef in a pan of fresh water, bring slowly to a boil, and simmer gently for between two and four hours depending on size. When tender, transfer the beef to a warm dish. Cover and keep warm.

4 Serve hot or let cool before slicing. Traditional accompaniments include carrots and mashed potatoes (if served hot), or gherkins, pickles, and sauerkraut (if cold).

MAKING PASTRAMI

Brisket needs long, slow smoking. If your smoker cannot cook slowly enough, then transfer the meat to a conventional oven to complete the cooking after 1–2 hours' smoking.

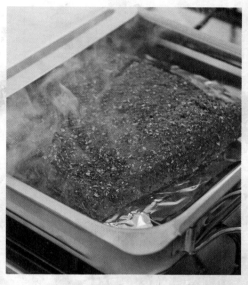

1 Unroll the brisket. Follow steps 1 and 2 for Salt Beef (opposite), but add 2 tbsp ground coriander seeds and 1¼ cups brown sugar as well. Remove the brisket after 4 days and rinse in clean water.

2 Mix together 1 tbsp each of ground black peppercorns and ground coriander seeds. Rub this mixture into the surface of the meat and especially into the fat. Leave overnight in the fridge.

3 Smoke the spiced brisket as slowly as possible for 1–2 hours until the internal temperature reads 160°F (70°C). See pp22–23 for information on hot smoking meat. There are various smokers you can use, such as this oven-top version.

4 Transfer the brisket to a rack and place this over a roasting pan. Add ½in (1cm) water to the roasting pan. This will make steam while it is in the oven.

5 Preheat the oven to 230°F (120°C). Envelop the whole pan in foil to make a sealed tent that allows plenty of air around the meat. Place the brisket in the oven.

6 Steam gently for 2–3 hours, or until the internal temperature of the thickest part is 160°F (70°C) and the meat is meltingly tender. Eat hot or cold.

SPICY BEEF AND PEA PATTIES

These patties can be eaten both hot or cold and make a great picnic snack.

THE CUT Ground beef

SERVES 4
PREP 15 mins   **COOK** 15–20 mins

3 tbsp olive oil

1 tbsp grated fresh ginger

1 onion, chopped

2 garlic cloves, minced

1 tsp ground cumin

2 tsp ground coriander

7oz (200g) frozen peas, defrosted

1lb 2oz (500g) ground beef

1 large egg, beaten

⅓ cup fine bread crumbs

sea salt and freshly ground black pepper

1 red chile, seeded and finely chopped

small handful of cilantro leaves

2 tbsp chopped mint leaves

1 Heat 1 tablespoon of oil in a large frying pan. Add the ginger, onion, garlic, cumin, and coriander. Cook for about 3 minutes, stirring frequently, until the onions are soft but not brown. Put the mixture into a large bowl and leave to cool.

2 Once the mixture has cooled, add the peas, beef, egg, and bread crumbs to the bowl. Season with salt and pepper and mix well. Then add the chile, cilantro, and mint and mix to combine.

3 Shape the meat mixture into small patties. Heat the remaining oil in a frying pan and fry the patties for 3 minutes on each side, until browned and cooked through. Do this in batches to avoid overcrowding the pan. Remove with a slotted spoon and drain on a plate lined with paper towels. Serve hot with mustard or pickles.

CHILI CON CARNE

A Mexican classic, this spicy recipe transforms kidney beans and beef into a firm favorite.

THE CUT Ground beef

SERVES 4
PREP 25 mins   **COOK** 1 hr 45 mins

2 tbsp olive oil

1 onion, finely chopped

1 celery stalk, finely chopped

1 green bell pepper, finely chopped

2 garlic cloves, minced

1lb 2oz (500g) ground beef

1 tsp dried oregano

2 tsp smoked paprika

½ tsp cayenne pepper

1 tsp ground cumin

1 tsp brown sugar

salt and freshly ground black pepper

14oz (400g) can chopped tomatoes

1 cup beef stock

1 tbsp tomato paste

14oz (400g) can kidney beans, drained and rinsed

1 Heat the oil in a large heatproof casserole or Dutch oven over medium heat. Add the onions, celery, and green bell pepper and cook for 10 minutes, until they start to color at the edges. Then add the garlic and cook for 1 more minute.

2 Increase the heat to high and add the beef. Cook for 5–8 minutes, or until well-browned, breaking up any clumps with a wooden spoon. Then add the oregano, spices, sugar, and season. Cook until the spices are fragrant.

3 Add the tomatoes, stock, and tomato paste. Bring to a boil, then reduce the heat to low. Cover and cook for 1 hour. Then add the kidney beans and cook, uncovered, for an additional 30 minutes, until the sauce has thickened slightly. Remove from the heat and serve hot with rice, sour cream, and grated Cheddar cheese, if desired.

CLASSIC BURGERS

Using very lean meat can make a burger dry. Mixing in a little fat with the meat keeps it juicy, basting it from within while it cooks.

THE CUT Ground beef

SERVES 4
PREP 20 mins, plus chilling   **COOK** 10 mins

14oz (400g) ground beef

¼ cup fresh white bread crumbs

1 large egg yolk

½ red onion, finely chopped

½ tsp dried mustard powder

½ tsp celery salt

1 tsp Worcestershire sauce

sea salt and freshly ground black pepper

4 hamburger buns, halved

1 head lettuce, shredded, to serve

2 tomatoes, thickly sliced, to serve

1 small red onion, finely sliced, to serve

1 pickle, finely sliced, to serve

4 tbsp spicy tomato relish, to serve

1 Place the ground beef, bread crumbs, egg yolk, onion, mustard powder, celery salt, and Worcestershire sauce in a large bowl. Season with pepper and mix until well combined.

2 Use damp hands to divide the mixture into 4 evenly sized balls. Roll each between your palms until smooth, then flatten them to a thickness of 1¼in (3cm) to form large, fat disks.

3 Pat in the edges of the burgers to neaten them up and place on a plate. Cover with plastic wrap and chill in the fridge for 30 minutes. Prepare the charcoal grill.

4 Generously season both sides of the burgers with sea salt. Cook the burgers over a hot grill for 6–8 minutes, flipping them as needed, until the meat is springy to the touch and the edges charred. The internal temperature of the burgers should be 165°F (75°C).

5 Grill the buns for 1–2 minutes, on the insides only, until lightly toasted. Serve the burgers and buns with the lettuce, tomatoes, sliced onions, pickles, and relish.

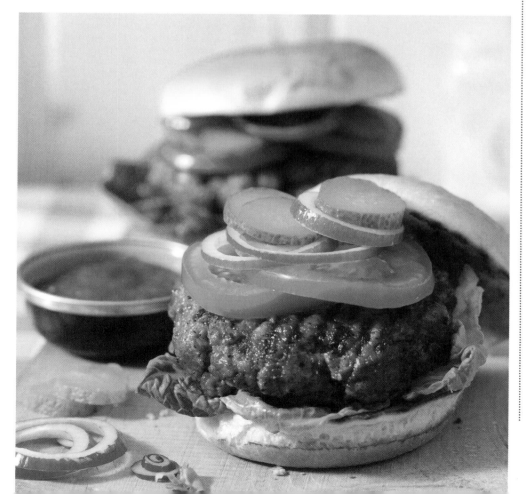

FLAT IRON STEAK WITH BLACK OLIVE BUTTER

This lesser-known steak cut is small, sweet to taste, and best when cooked rare.

THE CUT Flat iron steak

SERVES 4
PREP 10 mins, plus marinating and chilling
COOK 10 mins, plus resting

2 tbsp canola oil

3 tbsp red wine

2 tbsp chopped rosemary

1 garlic clove, minced

4 flat iron steaks, thinly sliced

sea salt and freshly ground black pepper

FOR THE BUTTER

11 tbsp unsalted butter, softened

2 tbsp chopped flat-leaf parsley

1¾oz (50g) pitted black olives, drained and roughly chopped

1 garlic clove, crushed

freshly cracked black peppercorns, to taste

1 Place the oil, red wine, rosemary, and garlic in a shallow dish and whisk together. Add the steaks and mix to coat. Cover and chill in the fridge for 2–3 hours.

2 Meanwhile, for the butter, place all the ingredients, except the cracked peppercorns, in a large bowl. Mash the ingredients well using a fork and season lightly with cracked peppercorns. Mix to combine.

3 Form the mixture into a sausage shape, and place on a piece of parchment paper. Roll the paper up into a tube and twist each end to seal. Chill the butter in the fridge for 30 minutes.

4 Preheat a grill pan to its highest setting. Remove the steaks from the marinade and place on a lined plate till they reach room temperature. Place the steaks on the grill pan and cook for 2–3 minutes, on each side, for a rare steak.

5 Remove from the heat and let rest on a plate for 3–5 minutes. Remove the butter from the fridge and cut into 8 thick slices. Serve the steaks topped with 2 slices of the black olive butter.

CARBONADE OF BEEF WITH ALE

This hearty dish of Flemish origin uses the deep flavor of dark ale to give a wonderfully sweet and sour sauce.

THE CUT Beef braising steak

SERVES 4–6
PREP 40 mins
COOK 2 hrs 10 mins–2 hrs 40 mins

3 tbsp all-purpose flour, seasoned

2¼lb (1kg) beef braising steak, trimmed and cut into 1½in (4cm) pieces

2–3 tbsp olive oil

2 onions, finely sliced

2 carrots, peeled and sliced

1 tbsp tomato paste

2 garlic cloves, crushed

1¼ cups brown ale

1½ cups beef stock

2 tsp soft brown sugar

1 tbsp red wine vinegar

2 bay leaves

sprig of thyme

handful of flat-leaf parsley, roughly chopped

sea salt and freshly ground black pepper

FOR THE CROUTONS

6 slices of French bread

1 garlic clove, halved

1 tbsp olive oil

2–3 tsp Dijon mustard

1 Preheat the oven to 350°F (180°C). For the croutons, place the bread slices on a clean work surface and rub both sides with the garlic thoroughly. Drizzle the oil over a large baking sheet and place the bread slices on it.

2 Turn the slices over to coat evenly with the oil. Bake the bread in the oven for 15–20 minutes, until crisp and crunchy. Remove from the oven and set aside. Reduce the oven temperature to 300°F (150°C).

3 Place the flour in a large shallow dish. Add the beef pieces, toss to coat evenly, and shake off any excess. Heat 2 tablespoons of oil in a large heatproof casserole over medium heat.

4 Add the beef to the casserole and cook, stirring frequently, for about 8 minutes or until golden brown all over. Do this in batches to avoid overcrowding the pan. Add more oil between batches, if needed. Remove the beef with a slotted spoon and place on a plate. Set aside and keep warm.

5 Reduce the heat to low. Add the onions and carrots, and cook for 6–8 minutes, stirring occasionally, until lightly colored. Then add the tomato paste and garlic and cook, stirring constantly, for about 1 minute.

6 Then add the beef, ale, stock, brown sugar, vinegar, bay leaves, thyme, and half the parsley. Season and bring to a boil. Cover and transfer to the oven. Cook the beef in the oven for 2–2½ hours, stirring occasionally, until tender and cooked through.

7 Remove from the heat. Taste and adjust the seasoning, if necessary. Spread the Dijon mustard over each crouton and arrange them on top of the meat. Return the casserole to the oven for an additional 10 minutes to crisp up the croutons. Serve garnished with the remaining parsley.

FILIPINO BEEF STEW

This traditional dish uses a wonderful combination of Asian flavors to enhance the flavor of beef.

THE CUT Beef braising steak

SERVES 4
PREP 20 mins   **COOK** 2½ hrs

4 tbsp sunflower oil

1 tbsp annatto seeds

2¼lb (1kg) beef braising steak, cut into 1in (2.5cm) pieces

2 large onions, sliced

6 garlic cloves, crushed

2 tbsp white wine vinegar

2 cups beef stock

2 bay leaves

1 tbsp palm sugar, grated

2 x 14oz (400g) can coconut milk

2 tsp sea salt

½ tbsp freshly ground black pepper

2 tbsp Thai fish sauce

2 tbsp soy sauce

2 tbsp ground rice, dry roasted until golden brown

4 tbsp crushed roasted peanuts

9oz (250g) eggplant, cut into chunks

9oz (250g) celery root, peeled and cut into chunks

5½oz (150g) green beans, ends trimmed

6 scallions, trimmed and shredded, to garnish

1 Heat the oil in a large saucepan. Add the annatto seeds and fry, covered, until the oil is red. Drain the oil through a sieve and discard the seeds. Return the oil to the pan. Add the meat to the pan and cook for 6–8 minutes until well-browned. Do this in batches to avoid overcrowding the pan. Remove the meat with a slotted spoon and drain on a plate lined with paper towels.

2 Add the onions and garlic, reduce the heat to low, and cook for 5 minutes, until the onions are soft and lightly colored. Return the meat to the casserole and stir to mix. Add the vinegar, stock, bay leaves, sugar, coconut milk, and season. Bring to a boil, and add the fish sauce and soy sauce. Reduce the heat to simmer, cover, and cook for 1¾–2 hours, until the meat is tender.

3 Add the rice and peanuts to the stew and stir to mix. Then add all the vegetables and cook, stirring constantly, until tender. Remove the bay leaves. Garnish with scallions, and serve hot.

DAUBE OF BEEF WITH PRUNES

Slow cooking produces a wonderfully sweet sauce and melt-in-your-mouth beef in this classic French dish.

THE CUT Beef braising steak

SERVES 4
PREP 25 mins
COOK 2 hrs 15 mins–2 hrs 45 mins

2 tbsp all-purpose flour, seasoned with salt and pepper

1 tsp dried mixed herbs

2lb (900g) beef braising steak, trimmed and diced

2–4 tbsp olive oil

2 onions, thinly sliced

2 garlic cloves, minced

2 carrots, sliced into matchsticks

2 bay leaves

zest of 1 orange, cut into pieces

sprig of rosemary

3½oz (100g) dried pitted prunes

sea salt and freshly ground black pepper

2 cups beef stock

⅔ cup red wine

1 tbsp tomato paste

1 tsp white wine vinegar

handful of cilantro leaves, roughly chopped, to garnish

1 Preheat the oven to 275°F (140°C). Place the flour and dried herbs in a shallow dish. Add the beef pieces, toss to coat, and shake off any excess. Heat 2 tablespoons of oil in a large, nonstick frying pan. Add the onions and cook for 6–8 minutes, until soft and golden brown. Remove with a slotted spoon and place in a large heatproof casserole.

2 Add the beef to the pan and cook, stirring, for 5 minutes, or until golden brown. Do this in batches to avoid overcrowding the pan and add more oil, if necessary. Remove with a slotted spoon and add to the casserole. Then add the garlic, carrots, bay leaves, orange zest, rosemary, and prunes to the casserole. Season and mix well.

3 Stir the stock, wine, tomato paste, and vinegar into the casserole. Place the casserole over high heat and bring to a boil. Then cover and transfer to the oven. Cook in the oven for 2–2½ hours or until tender. Remove from the oven and season to taste. Garnish with the cilantro and serve hot with creamy mashed potatoes.

POTTED BEEF

The beef in this traditional dish has the texture of a coarse pâté and a delicious buttery taste.

THE CUT Beef braising steak

MAKES 2 cups
PREP 10 mins   **COOK** 5 hrs

1lb (450g) beef braising steak, trimmed of excess fat, sinew removed, and cut into chunks

sea salt and freshly ground black pepper

1 tsp grated nutmeg

1 bay leaf

pinch cayenne pepper

1 blade of mace

½ tbsp anchovy paste

9 tbsp butter, plus 4 tbsp extra for the topping

1 Preheat the oven to 250°F (130°C). Place the meat in an ovenproof dish. Sprinkle with the black pepper, nutmeg, bay leaf, cayenne pepper, and mace. Drizzle with the anchovy paste and lay the butter on top. Cover tightly with foil and cook for 2–3 hours, then remove from the oven and stir to mix. Return to the oven for another 2 hours or until the meat is tender, and beginning to flake.

2 Remove from the oven and let rest for 30 minutes. Transfer the meat to a food processor, pulse until smooth, and season to taste. Remove the bay leaf and mace from the cooking juices and stir it into the beef. Divide the mixture between a few ramekins and lightly press it down with the back of a spoon to firmly pack it in. Cover with plastic wrap and place in the fridge to solidify.

3 Heat the extra butter in a small saucepan over low heat until melted. Add a layer of the melted butter to each ramekin and chill in the fridge for 12 hours. Serve with bread, pickled walnuts, and chutney. It will keep in the fridge in airtight containers for 5–7 days.

BEEF GOULASH

This traditional Hungarian stew makes the most of green bell peppers and tomatoes to enrich the flavor of the dish.

THE CUT Beef braising steak

SERVES 4
PREP 25–30 mins   **COOK** 2 hrs 45 mins

1 tbsp vegetable oil

2oz (60g) smoked bacon, diced

6 onions, about 1lb 10oz (750g) in total, chopped

2 tbsp paprika

1lb 10oz (750g) beef braising steak, cut into 1½in (4cm) cubes

2 garlic cloves, finely chopped

½ tsp caraway seeds

2 tomatoes, seeded and chopped

2 green bell peppers, sliced

salt and freshly ground black pepper

⅓ cup all-purpose flour

1 egg, beaten

½ cup sour cream (optional)

1 Heat the oil in a large heatproof casserole. Add the bacon and cook for 3–5 minutes, stirring, until it is lightly browned and the fat has rendered. Stir in the onions. Cover the mixture with a piece of foil and then with the lid. Cook over low heat, stirring occasionally, for 20–25 minutes until the onions are soft and translucent.

2 Preheat the oven to 350°F (180°C). Add the paprika to the casserole and cook for 2 minutes, stirring to make sure it does not burn. Add the meat pieces, garlic, caraway seeds, and 2 cups water and stir to mix. Bring to a boil, stirring, then cover and transfer to the oven. Cook in the oven for 1–1½ hours until the beef is almost tender.

3 Remove from the oven, stir in the tomatoes and peppers, and season. Cover and return to the oven for another 30–45 minutes until the meat is very soft and the stew rich and thick. Remove from the heat. Taste and adjust the seasoning.

4 Place the flour and a little salt in a bowl. Stir in the egg and mix to combine. Place the casserole over high heat and bring to a boil. Drop teaspoons of the flour mix into the goulash, reduce the heat to a simmer, and cook for 5–7 minutes until the dumplings are cooked through. Ladle the goulash and dumplings into warmed soup bowls and top with a spoonful of sour cream, if using. Serve hot.

KERALA BEEF

This fabulous curry from the southern Indian state of Kerala uses popular local ingredients such as coconut, turmeric, and curry leaves to produce a distinctively hot, spicy, and aromatic dish.

THE CUT Beef braising steak

SERVES 4–6
PREP 20 mins, plus marinating
COOK 1 hr 45 mins – 2 hrs 15 mins

2in (5cm) cinnamon stick

12 black peppercorns

6 cloves

1 tbsp fennel seeds

1½ tbsp coriander seeds

6 cardamom pods, seeds removed

1 tsp ground turmeric

1 tsp fine salt

2¼lb (1kg) beef braising steak, trimmed and cut into 1in (2.5cm) chunks

1in (2.5cm) piece of fresh ginger, peeled and finely grated

4 garlic cloves, finely sliced

2 green chiles, seeded and finely chopped

2 onions, thinly sliced

20 fresh curry leaves, or 16 dried curry leaves

½ cup shredded coconut

¼ cup sunflower, canola, or coconut oil

½ tbsp mustard seeds

handful of cilantro, to garnish

handful of thinly sliced dried coconut, to garnish

1 Heat a small frying pan over medium heat. Add the cinnamon, peppercorns, cloves, fennel, coriander, and cardamom seeds to the pan. Roast the spices, stirring frequently, until lightly colored and fragrant. Remove from the heat and let cool for 2–3 minutes.

2 Use a mortar and pestle to grind the roasted spices to a fine powder and transfer to a large bowl. Add the turmeric and salt and mix well. Add the meat, ginger, garlic, chiles, and half the onion and curry leaves. Mix to coat the meat. Cover and leave to chill in the fridge for 1 hour. Preheat the oven to 325°F (160°C).

3 Transfer the meat and marinade to a large heatproof casserole. Add 1½ cups cold water and bring to a boil, then cover and transfer to the oven. Cook in the oven for 1½–2 hours, until the beef is tender. Remove the casserole from the oven and place it, uncovered, over high heat. Bring to a boil and cook until all the liquid has evaporated, stirring constantly to prevent the curry from sticking to the bottom. Remove and set aside.

4 Heat a large non-stick frying pan. Add the coconut and toast for 2–3 minutes, stirring constantly, making sure it does not burn. Add the oil, mustard seeds, and remaining onion to the pan. Cook for 3–4 minutes or until the onion is golden brown. Add the beef mixture and remaining curry leaves. Stir-fry until the beef is well-browned and looks dry, but glossy. Serve garnished with cilantro and dried coconut.

BOILED BEEF BRISKET WITH HERB DUMPLINGS

This traditional British dish is an excellent way of using a cheaper cut of beef. The vegetables and well-spiced dumplings serve as a delicious accompaniment to the brisket.

THE CUT Beef brisket

SERVES 4–6
PREP 20 mins **COOK** 2 hrs 50 mins

4½lb (2kg) rolled beef brisket

5½–7 cups beef stock

sea salt and freshly ground black pepper

1 large onion, studded with 4 cloves

3 carrots, peeled and chopped into
1½in (4cm) chunks

1 bouquet garni

10 black peppercorns

1 celery stalk, chopped into 1½in (4cm) lengths

½ cinnamon stick

2 star anise (optional)

3 leeks, rinsed, trimmed, and chopped into
1½in (4cm) lengths

FOR THE DUMPLINGS

1 cup self-rising flour

4 tbsp shredded beef suet

1 tsp mixed dried herbs

handful of flat-leaf parsley, chopped

1 tsp horseradish

1 Place the beef in a large, lidded saucepan. Pour in just enough stock to cover the meat and season with 1 teaspoon salt. Place over medium heat and bring slowly to a boil, skimming off any foam that rises to the surface.

2 Reduce the heat to a simmer, then add the onions, carrots, bouquet garni, peppercorns, celery, cinnamon, and star anise, if using. Cover and cook for 1¾ hours, skimming the surface occasionally. Add the leeks and stir lightly to mix. Cover and cook for another 45 minutes.

3 Meanwhile, for the dumplings, place all the ingredients in a large bowl. Season with salt and pepper and add 5–6 tablespoons water. Mix all the ingredients to form an elastic dough. Divide the dough into 8 small evenly sized pieces and roll them into balls.

4 Remove the meat from the pan and let rest in a warm place. Remove and discard the bouquet garni, peppercorns, cinnamon stick, and star anise. Taste and adjust the seasoning, if needed.

5 Add the dumplings, cover, and cook for 15–20 minutes or until the dumplings expand and rise to the top of the pan. Remove them with a slotted spoon and place on a plate. Strain the stock and reserve the vegetables. Slice the beef, arrange it on warm plates, and serve warm with the vegetables, dumplings, and some of the stock poured over.

SPICED BEEF SKIRT WITH BEETS, CRÈME FRAÎCHE, AND HORSERADISH

The addition of beets in this recipe adds an earthy flavor and helps to tenderize the beef. The horseradish adds a lovely piquancy to the dish.

THE CUT Beef skirt

SERVES 4–6
PREP 20 mins **COOK** 3 hrs, plus resting

2 tbsp all-purpose flour, seasoned with
salt and pepper

2¼lb (1kg) beef skirt, cut into
1½in (4cm) pieces

2 tbsp canola oil

pat of butter

1 large onion, diced

2 garlic cloves, crushed

½ red chile, seeded and
finely diced (optional)

3 tbsp red wine vinegar

¾ cup red wine

2¼ cups beef stock

1 tbsp balsamic vinegar

8 juniper berries, crushed

6 allspice berries, crushed

1 bay leaf

1 tsp chopped thyme leaves

3 tsp brown sugar

8 small beets, peeled and halved

sea salt and freshly ground black pepper

1 tbsp cornstarch, mixed with a little warm
water (optional)

2 tbsp crème fraîche

2 tbsp dry mustard

3 tbsp creamed horseradish

1 Preheat the oven to 325°F (150°C). Place the flour in a large shallow dish. Add the beef pieces, toss to coat evenly, and shake off any excess.

2 Heat the oil and butter in a large heatproof casserole over high heat. Add the beef and cook for 5–8 minutes or until well-browned. Remove with a slotted spoon, place on a plate, and set aside.

3 Reduce the heat to medium. Add the onions, garlic, and chile (if using) to the casserole. Cook

for 5–10 minutes, stirring occasionally, until the onions are softened. Increase the heat and pour in the wine, stock, and vinegar. Stir to mix and bring to a boil.

4 Stir in the juniper berries, allspice berries, bay leaf, thyme, and sugar. Return the meat to the casserole along with the beets, season with salt and pepper, and stir lightly to mix. Cover and transfer to the oven. Cook the beef in the oven for 2–2½ hours.

5 Remove from the oven and let rest for 10 minutes. Remove the bay leaf and skim the surface of any extra fat. If the sauce seems thin, thicken with the cornstarch. Combine the crème fraîche, mustard, and horseradish in a bowl and stir into the casserole. Serve with mashed potatoes and celeriac.

DRY-RUBBED STEAK WITH CHIMICHURRI SAUCE

Crusty on the outside and juicy on the inside, this sweet and spicy steak is wonderfully paired with a fresh and tart green sauce of Argentinean origin.

THE CUT Beef skirt or flat iron

SERVES 4
PREP 15 mins, plus chilling
COOK 8–20 mins, plus resting

1 tbsp light brown sugar

1 tbsp chopped thyme leaves

½ tsp mustard powder

¼ tsp garlic salt

¼ tsp smoked paprika or ancho chile powder

salt and freshly ground black pepper

1 beef skirt, about 1½lb (675g)

FOR THE CHIMICHURRI SAUCE

6 tbsp olive oil, plus extra for brushing

1½ tbsp red wine vinegar

1 tbsp lemon juice

¼ cup flat-leaf parsley leaves, roughly chopped

2 tbsp cilantro, roughly chopped

1 tbsp oregano leaves, roughly chopped

2 garlic cloves, chopped

1 tsp dried red chile flakes

1 Place the sugar, thyme, mustard, garlic salt, and smoked paprika in a food processor. Season with pepper and grind to form a fine powder. Place the steak on a large piece of plastic wrap and rub the mixture all over. Wrap tightly in the plastic wrap and chill for at least 1 hour.

2 For the sauce, place all the ingredients in a large serving bowl and mix well to combine. Cover with plastic wrap and chill for at least 1 hour to allow the flavors to develop.

3 Remove the steak and the sauce from the fridge and bring to room temperature. Set the barbecue to its highest setting. Brush the steak with a little oil and grill on both sides until cooked to your liking—4–6 minutes on each side for rare, 6–8 minutes on each side for medium, and 8–10 minutes on each side for well-done.

4 Remove the steak from the heat, cover loosely with foil, and let rest for at least 10 minutes. Cut the steak into thick slices and serve with the chimichurri sauce.

MAPLE AND MUSTARD CRUSTED RIB OF BEEF

Cooking the meat on the bone adds flavor and keeps the roast moist in this impressive dish and the mustard crust complements it well.

THE CUT Beef fore rib

SERVES 4–6
PREP 30 mins   **COOK** 2 hrs, plus resting

2-rib fore rib of beef, about 4½lb (2kg)

3 tbsp canola oil, plus extra for greasing

sea salt and freshly ground black pepper

½ cup fine bread crumbs

1 tbsp finely chopped rosemary

2 tbsp finely chopped flat-leaf parsley

small bunch of thyme leaves, finely chopped

3 large carrots, roughly chopped into small rounds

1lb 2oz (500g) shallots

2 celery stalks, roughly chopped

4 garlic cloves

1¾ cups red wine

2 tbsp maple syrup

3 tbsp Dijon mustard, plus 1 tsp extra

½ cup port wine

2 cups beef stock

4 tsp cornstarch, mixed with a little warm water

2 tsp red currant jelly

1 Preheat the oven to 400°F (200°C). Rub the beef with 2 tablespoons of oil and season well. Fry the beef in a large frying pan until just brown all over. Remove from the heat. Place the bread crumbs, rosemary, parsley, and half the thyme in a large bowl. Season, mix well, and press the mixture over the fat on the beef until evenly coated.

2 Place the carrots, shallots, celery, garlic, and remaining thyme and oil in a large roasting pan and mix well. Place the beef on top of the vegetables and cover with an oiled sheet of foil. Roast in the oven for 30 minutes. Then remove the pan from the oven and add half the red wine and a splash of water. Reduce the oven

temperature to 350°F (180°C) and roast for an additional 40 minutes, adding more water if necessary.

3 Meanwhile, mix the maple syrup and mustard in a small bowl. Remove the pan from the oven and take off the foil. Coat the crust with the maple and mustard mixture, and press down lightly. Return the pan to the oven for an additional 30 minutes, until the internal temperature of the meat reaches 140°F (60°C). Remove from the oven. Place the beef on a serving dish and let rest for at least 30 minutes.

4 Remove and discard any excess fat from the pan. Add the port wine, stock, and remaining red wine. Place the pan over high heat and bring to a boil. Then strain and discard the vegetables. Reduce the heat, add the cornstarch mixture, and cook the sauce until thickened. Then add the jelly and remaining mustard, season, and serve with the beef.

ROTISSERIE OF RIB EYE BEEF

If you don't have a rotisserie, you can cook this dish in the oven rotisserie or on a barbecue grill.

 Beef rib eye

SERVES 8
PREP 20 mins, plus marinating
COOK 45 mins–1 hour

3¼lb (1.5kg) beef rib eye

FOR THE MARINADE

1 tbsp coarse freshly ground black pepper

1 tbsp chopped rosemary leaves

3 garlic cloves, ground into a smooth paste

2 tsp celery seeds

3 tbsp canola oil

2 tsp brown sugar

zest and juice of 1 lemon

sea salt

FOR THE SAUCE

3 tbsp sour cream or crème fraîche

5 tbsp horseradish sauce

1 tbsp heavy cream

1 tsp sugar

squeeze of 1 lemon

sea salt and freshly ground black pepper

1 Roll the beef into a neat round shape and tie at intervals with a butcher's string. For the marinade, mix all the ingredients in a bowl. Rub into the meat, covering the whole roast, and leave to marinate for 1–2 hours. Set the rotisserie at its medium setting.

2 Thread the beef onto the rotisserie skewer and place on the rotisserie. Season and cook for about 1 hour for a rare piece of beef. Reduce the heat if the meat browns too quickly. Leave to rest in a warm place for 20 minutes.

3 For the sauce, mix all the ingredients in a bowl and season well. Cut the beef into thin slices and serve along with the sauce.

VARIATION

Roasted rib eye beef Preheat the oven to 375°F (190°C). Cook the beef in the oven to your liking—1 hour for rare, 1 hour 40 minutes for medium, and 2 hours for well-done. Remove, cover with foil, and rest for 20 minutes. Serve as above.

CORNISH PASTIES

These tasty meat and potato pies were originally made as a portable meal for field workers to carry with them.

 Beef skirt

MAKES 4
PREP 20 mins, plus chilling   **COOK** 40–45 mins

FOR THE SHORTCRUST PASTRY

7 tbsp lard, chilled and diced

4 tbsp unsalted butter, chilled and diced

1½ cups all-purpose flour, plus extra for dusting

½ tsp salt

1 large egg, beaten, to glaze

FOR THE FILLING

9oz (250g) beef skirt steak, trimmed and cut into ½in (1cm) cubes

2¾oz (80g) rutabaga, peeled and cut into ¼in (5mm) cubes

3½oz (100g) waxy potatoes, such as Yukon Gold, peeled and cut into ¼in (5mm) cubes

1 large onion, finely chopped

splash of Worcestershire sauce

1 tsp all-purpose flour

sea salt and freshly ground black pepper

1 For the pastry, rub the lard and butter into the flour until the mixture resembles fine bread crumbs. Add the salt and enough cold water to bring the mixture together into a soft dough. On a lightly floured surface, knead the dough briefly, then wrap in plastic wrap and chill in the fridge for 30 minutes.

2 Preheat the oven to 375°F (190°C). Mix the filling ingredients together and season well. Roll out the pastry on a well-floured surface to ¼in (5mm) thick. Then fold it in half and flatten it to ¼in (5mm) thick again. Use a side plate, or saucer, and cut 4 circles from the dough. Pile one-quarter of the filling into each circle, leaving a ¾in (2cm) border all around.

3 Brush the border of the pastry with a little beaten egg. Pull both edges up over the filling and press together to seal. Crimp the sealed edge with your fingers to form a decorative ridge along the top. Brush a little beaten egg all over the finished pasties.

4 Bake in the middle of the oven for 40–45 minutes, until golden brown. Cool for at least 15 minutes before serving warm or cold.

CARIBBEAN JERK BEEF

Native to Jamaica, jerk refers to the way a piece of meat is seasoned with spices and then cooked over pimento wood slowly for a long time.

 Beef rib eye or sirloin

SERVES 4
PREP 20 mins, plus marinating and resting
COOK 10–15 mins, plus resting

4 x 8oz (225g) rib eye steak or sirloin steak

sea salt

FOR THE MARINADE

4 tbsp canola oil

1 tbsp white wine vinegar

3 garlic cloves, chopped

1–2 Scotch bonnet chiles, seeded and roughly chopped

2 tbsp ground allspice

1 tbsp smoked paprika

1 tbsp chopped fresh ginger

1 tsp ground cinnamon

2 tsp brown sugar

1 tsp dried thyme

FOR THE RELISH

9oz (250g) pineapple, peeled and finely chopped

1 red chile, seeded and finely chopped

small handful of cilantro leaves, chopped

juice of 1 lime

1 small red onion, finely chopped

1 For the marinade, place all the ingredients in a food processor and pulse until they form a thick paste. Add more oil if it looks too dry. Rub both sides of each steak with the marinade. Leave to marinate in the fridge for 2 hours, or overnight.

2 Set the barbecue grill to its highest setting. Remove the steaks from the fridge and rest them for at least 25 minutes at room temperature. Season with salt on each side. Cook the steaks on the grill for 3 minutes on each side, allowing a crust to form. Then move them to a cool part of the grill and cook for an additional 2 minutes.

3 Remove from the heat and leave to rest for about 5 minutes. For the relish, mix all the ingredients in a large bowl and let rest for about 20 minutes or for up to 3 hours. Serve the steaks hot with the relish.

BEEF CARPACCIO

In this recipe, lean beef fillet is semi-frozen so it is easy to cut into paper-thin slices, so thin, it's said, that light will shine through them.

 Beef fillet

SERVES 4
PREP 20–25 mins, plus freezing

1lb 2oz (500g) beef fillet

8 canned anchovy fillets

1½oz (45g) drained capers

4½oz (125g) arugula

4½oz (125g) Parmesan cheese

1 small onion, very finely diced

juice of 2 lemons

½ cup extra virgin olive oil, or to taste

freshly ground black pepper

1 Wrap the fillet tightly in foil, twisting the ends to seal and forming a cracker shape. Freeze for 2½–3 hours, until firm but not solid.

2 Meanwhile, drain the anchovies and spread out on paper towels. If the capers are large, chop them coarsely. Wash and dry the arugula, then strip out and discard any tough stalks. Set aside.

3 Remove the beef from the freezer and discard the foil. If the meat is too hard to cut, let it thaw slightly at room temperature. Using a very sharp knife, cut paper-thin slices of meat from the fillet, slicing as much of the meat as you can. There will be a little left at the end.

4 Arrange the beef slices, overlapping, on 4 plates. Shave over the Parmesan using a vegetable peeler. Divide the anchovies, onion, and capers between the plates. Drizzle the lemon juice over, sprinkle with the olive oil, and top with the arugula. Serve at room temperature with a sprinkling of pepper.

FILLET STEAK WITH BLUE CHEESE SAUCE

This traditional recipe uses Roquefort cheese to make a classic French sauce. However, you can use any other blue-veined cheese instead.

 Beef fillet

SERVES 4
PREP 10 mins, plus resting   **COOK** 15 mins

4 x 7oz (200g) beef fillet steak

1 tbsp canola oil

sea salt and freshly ground black pepper

FOR THE SAUCE

4 tbsp unsalted butter

2 shallots, finely diced

4 tbsp dry white wine

1 tbsp brandy

2 tbsp rich beef stock

¾ cup heavy cream

3½oz (100g) Roquefort cheese, crumbled

1 Rub the steaks with oil and season well. Heat a heavy-bottomed frying pan and fry the steaks on each side, 2–3 minutes for rare, 4–5 minutes for medium, and 5–6 minutes for well-done. Remove from the heat and let rest in a warm place for 3–5 minutes.

2 For the sauce, heat half the butter in a small frying pan over low heat. Add the shallots, and cook for about 5 minutes, until softened. Then add the wine and brandy, and bring to a boil.

3 Add the stock to the pan and cook the sauce until reduced by half. Then add the cream, mix well, and reduce the heat to simmer. Cook for about 5 minutes, then whisk in the remaining butter and the cheese. Remove from the heat and strain through a sieve. Season to taste and serve along with the fillet steak.

GRILLED BALSAMIC STEAK WITH BEETS

This recipe uses balsamic vinegar to highlight the flavor of the beef. The addition of a fresh salad of beets, cherry tomatoes, and scallions adds color and crunch to the dish.

THE CUT Beef fillet

SERVES 4
PREP 20 mins, plus marinating
COOK 5–10 mins, plus resting

2 tbsp olive oil

1 tbsp red wine

2 garlic cloves, cut into slivers

2 tbsp balsamic vinegar

2 red onions, cut into rings

1 sprig of thyme

1 tsp cracked black peppercorns

4 x 8oz (225g) fillet steaks

canola oil, for brushing

sea salt

FOR THE CRÈME FRAÎCHE

2 tbsp crème fraîche

2 tbsp creamed horseradish

1 small beet, cooked and finely diced

freshly ground black pepper

FOR THE SALAD

4 cooked beets, sliced into fine strips

handful of cilantro leaves, chopped

12 cherry tomatoes, cut in half

1 bunch of scallions, trimmed and cut into diagonal slices

1 tsp finely sliced red chile (optional)

2 large handfuls of baby ruby chard leaves

3 tbsp olive oil

juice of 1 lemon

2 tsp of honey

1 Place the olive oil, wine, garlic, balsamic vinegar, red onions, thyme, and peppercorns in a large bowl and mix well. Add the steaks, toss to coat, and let marinate for 2 hours.

2 Remove the steaks from the marinade and pat dry with paper towels. Reserve the marinade. Heat a grill pan to its highest setting. Brush the steaks with a little canola oil and season with salt. Cook the steaks for 2¹/₂ minutes, on each

side, for rare. Reduce the heat if they are cooking too quickly. Cook the steaks for longer if you prefer them medium or well-done. Then remove from the heat and leave to rest for 5 minutes.

3 Pour the marinade into the grill pan and cook for 1–2 minutes over low heat, until the onions have softened. Then remove from the heat and set aside.

4 For the crème fraîche, mix all the ingredients in a bowl until well combined and season with salt and pepper. Set aside.

5 For the salad, mix the beets, cilantro, cherry tomatoes, scallions, chile (if using), and chard leaves in a bowl. Place the olive oil, lemon juice, honey, and the seasoning in a separate bowl and whisk to make the dressing.

6 Toss the dressing through the salad. Place the salad on 4 plates, top with the steaks and the red onions and drizzle any remaining beef juices over the steaks. Serve with the horseradish sauce.

PAN-FRIED FILLET OF BEEF

Using the light and low-fat fillet cut of beef, this dish perfectly pairs a tender steak with sweet caramelized garlic and crisp potato and parsnip rösti.

THE CUT Beef fillet

SERVES 4
PREP 30 mins   **COOK** 20–30 mins, plus resting

2 tbsp unsalted butter

¼ cup light brown sugar

2 sprigs of thyme

1 tbsp white wine

1 tbsp white wine vinegar

2 garlic bulbs, blanched and dried

4 x 8oz (225g) beef fillet steaks

1 tbsp olive oil, for brushing

sea salt and freshly ground black pepper

FOR THE RÖSTI

2 large potatoes, peeled and grated

2 large parsnips, peeled, cored, and grated

5 tbsp unsalted butter, melted, plus 2 tbsp extra for frying

pinch of cayenne pepper

1–2 tbsp olive oil

1 Melt the butter in a small, heavy-based saucepan over medium heat. Add the sugar, thyme, wine, and vinegar. Cook the mixture until it starts to thicken and caramelize, swirling the pan so it colors evenly.

2 Add 1 tablespoon of water to the pan. Then add the garlic and stir to coat in the mixture, and cook for 3–5 minutes, until softened but still retaining its shape. Remove from the heat and set aside to cool, adding a little more water if it looks too sticky.

3 For the rösti, squeeze out any excess liquid from the potatoes and parsnips and place them in a clean bowl. Add the butter and cayenne pepper, season well, and mix. Heat the remaining butter and the oil in a nonstick frying pan. Divide the

potato mixture into 4 portions. Add 1 portion to the pan, press down well, and fry for 2–3 minutes on each side, until golden brown. Remove and keep warm. Repeat with the remaining portions.

4 Lightly brush the steaks with oil and season well. Heat a heavy-bottomed pan over high heat. Cook the steaks on each side until cooked to your liking—2–3 minutes on each side for rare, 3–4 minutes on each side for medium, and 5–6 minutes on each side for well-done. Remove from heat and let rest in a warm place for 3–5 minutes.

5 Place a rösti on each plate and top with a steak and some caramelized garlic. Drizzle over the cooking juices from the steak and garlic. Serve hot with horseradish or mustard.

FIERY BEEF FILLET WITH ROASTED VEGETABLES

This colorful dish is a fusion of seasonal vegetables with the tender beef fillet.

THE CUT Beef fillet

SERVES 4–6
PREP 20 mins   **COOK** 40 mins, plus resting

2¼lb (1kg) beef fillet, trimmed

3 tbsp canola oil

sea salt and freshly ground black pepper

2 tbsp Madras curry paste

2 tbsp thick Greek-style yogurt

handful of cilantro leaves, chopped

1 tbsp black peppercorns

2 tbsp cumin seeds

1 tbsp coriander seeds

FOR THE VEGETABLES

1 eggplant, sliced lengthwise

2 zucchini, sliced

2 red bell peppers, seeded and cut into pieces

1 small butternut squash, seeded and sliced lengthwise

2 tbsp Madras curry paste

4 tbsp canola oil

FOR THE YOGURT

1½ cups Greek-style yogurt

½ cucumber, peeled, seeded, and finely chopped

1 garlic clove, minced

2 tbsp shredded mint leaves

1 Preheat the oven to 400°F (200°C). Heat a large frying pan over high heat. Brush the beef with 1 tablespoon of oil. Add the beef to the pan and brown on all sides. Season, remove from the heat, and let cool.

2 Mix the curry paste, yogurt, and cilantro in a bowl. Rub the mixture over the meat. Use a mortar and pestle to crush the peppercorns, cumin, and coriander seeds. Sprinkle the spices over the meat evenly, place it in a roasting pan, and drizzle with the remaining oil. Cook in the oven for 35–40 minutes.

3 Meanwhile, place all the vegetables in a separate roasting pan. Mix the curry paste with the oil. Add the spice mix to the vegetables, toss to coat, and place the roasting pan below the beef in the oven. Roast in the oven for 20–25 minutes.

4 Remove the beef and vegetables from the oven. Leave the beef to rest in a warm place for 15 minutes and keep the vegetables warm. For the yogurt, place all the ingredients in a bowl and mix well. Slice the beef into thick steaks, pour over any cooking juices, and serve with the vegetables and yogurt.

BOEUF EN CROÛTE

Also known as Beef Wellington, this rich and luxurious dish is easy to make
and perfect for entertaining. Steps 1–4 can be carried out a day in advance.

THE CUT **Beef fillet**

SERVES 6
PREP 45 mins
COOK 42–60 mins, plus resting

2¼lb (1kg) beef filet, cut from the thick end, trimmed

salt and freshly ground black pepper

2 tbsp sunflower oil

3 tbsp butter

2 shallots, finely chopped

1 garlic clove, crushed

9oz (250g) mixed wild mushrooms, finely chopped

1 tbsp brandy or Madeira

all-purpose flour, for dusting

1lb 2oz (500g) puff pastry

1 egg beaten, to glaze

1 Preheat the oven to 425°F (220°C). Season the meat with salt and pepper. Heat the oil in a large frying pan. Add the beef and cook until browned all over.

2 Transfer the beef to a roasting pan and roast in the oven for 10 minutes. Remove from the oven and set aside to cool. Weighting the meat as it cools will help to make a better shape. Leave the oven on.

3 On a lightly floured surface, roll out one-third of the pastry to a rectangle about 2in (5cm) larger than the base of the beef. Place it on large baking sheet and prick with a fork. Transfer to the oven and bake for 12–15 minutes until crisp. Let cool.

4 Melt the butter in a saucepan. Add the shallots and garlic and cook for 2–3 minutes, stirring until softened. Add the mushrooms and keep stirring for 4–5 minutes until the juices evaporate. Add the brandy. Bring to a boil and boil for 30 seconds. Remove from the heat and set aside to cool.

5 Spread one-third of the mushroom mixture over the cooked pastry. Place the beef on top and spread the remaining mushroom mixture over the meat. Lightly brush the edges of the pastry with a little of the beaten egg. Roll out the remaining pastry and use it to cover the beef, tucking the uncooked pastry underneath the edges of the cooked pastry, pressing it to seal.

6 Heat the oven to 425°F (220°C). Brush the uncooked pastry with the remaining beaten egg. Slit the top for the steam to escape. Bake until cooked to your liking—30 minutes for rare and 45 minutes for well-done. Cover the pastry loosely with foil if it starts to brown too quickly. Remove from the oven and let stand for 10 minutes. Use a sharp knife to slice it.

SPICED CHILI BEEF FILET WITH RED WINE AND MUSHROOM SAUCE

Serve this hearty roast with buttered spinach, sour cream, and a tangy tomato salsa.

 Beef filet

SERVES 4
PREP 5 mins, plus marinating   **COOK** 1 hr

1 tbsp Mexican chile powder or hot chile powder

1 tbsp cumin seeds, toasted

2 tbsp extra virgin olive oil

handful of cilantro, chopped

sea salt and freshly ground black pepper

2¼lb (1kg) beef filet

3 tbsp olive oil

1 large red chile, seeded and chopped

1 onion, finely chopped

2 garlic cloves, crushed

2 cups red wine

1lb 2oz (500g) mushrooms, cleaned and sliced

1 tbsp tomato paste

1 tbsp honey

1 cup beef or chicken stock

1 tbsp cilantro, chopped

vegetable oil, for greasing

handful of flat-leaf parsley, to garnish

1 Combine the chile powder, cumin, extra virgin olive oil, cilantro, and a little black pepper in a bowl, rub the mixture over the filet, and let marinate for at least 2 hours, or overnight.

2 Preheat the oven to 400°F (200°C). Heat the 2 tablespoons of the olive oil in a saucepan over low heat. Add the chile, onions, and garlic, and cook for 5 minutes, until soft. Add the wine, increase the heat, and cook until reduced by half.

3 Heat the remaining oil in a separate pan and cook the mushrooms until soft. Add the tomato paste and honey and cook for 1 minute, then add the stock and stir in the cilantro. Add to the wine mixture and simmer for 10–15 minutes, until the sauce is thick and glossy.

4 Heat a large frying pan. Brush the filet with the vegetable oil, seal on all sides, and season. Remove from the heat and place in a roasting pan. Cook in the oven for 30–40 minutes. Remove and let rest. Garnish with the parsley and serve hot with the sauce and mashed potatoes.

VIETNAMESE BEEF SOUP

Slow-cooked beef stock flavored with gentle spices makes this dish special. You can add extra scallions, chiles, or julienned carrots and bean sprouts.

 Beef filet steak

SERVES 4–6
PREP 15 mins   **COOK** 1 hr 15 mins

1½lb (675g) meaty beef bones

1 tbsp dark soy sauce

1 tbsp olive oil

1 star anise

1 tsp black peppercorns

1 cinnamon stick

½ tbsp Thai fish sauce

1 onion, finely chopped

3 garlic cloves, finely chopped

1 chile, seeded and finely chopped

1 lemongrass stalk, trimmed, tough outer leaves removed and finely chopped

1in (2.5cm) piece of fresh ginger, peeled and finely sliced

salt and freshly ground black pepper

12oz (350g) filet steak, finely sliced across the grain

2oz (60g) vermicelli noodles, soaked in hot water for 5 minutes (or as per the package's instructions) and drained

bunch of green scallions, trimmed and finely sliced

1 Place the beef bones in a large bowl, pour in the soy sauce, and toss lightly to coat. Heat a little oil in a large heavy-bottomed saucepan over medium-high heat. Add the bones and cook for about 15 minutes, stirring occasionally, until the meat is no longer pink.

2 Transfer the bones to a large, lidded stock pan, pour in 5 cups water, and add the star anise, peppercorns, cinnamon, and fish sauce. Bring to a boil, then reduce the heat to a simmer. Cover partially and cook for 1 hour. Strain the stock through a sieve into a pan, adding water to make 3 cups, if necessary, and set aside.

3 Heat the remaining oil in a large heavy-bottomed pan. Add the onions to the pan and cook for 3–4 minutes, until softened but do not brown. Stir in the garlic, chile, and lemongrass and cook for another 1 minute.

4 Pour in the beef stock, add the ginger, and adjust the seasoning, if needed. Gently simmer for 2–3 minutes, then add the sliced steak and cook for 2–3 minutes. Add the noodles and scallions, stir to mix, and remove from the heat. Ladle the soup into warmed bowls and serve hot.

BEEF STROGANOFF

A popular dish of sautéed pieces of beef served with a sour cream sauce, it dates back to mid 19th-century Russia.

THE CUT Beef filet

SERVES 4–6
PREP 10 mins   **COOK** 15–20 mins

4 tbsp butter

2 tbsp olive oil

1 large onion, finely diced

sea salt and freshly ground black pepper

8oz (225g) crimini mushrooms, sliced

pinch of grated nutmeg

1lb 10oz (750g) beef filet, cut into thin strips

1 tbsp brandy

2 tsp Dijon mustard

pinch of hot paprika

¾ cup sour cream

½ cup heavy cream

dash of beef stock

1 Melt half the butter and 1 tablespoon of the oil in a large frying pan over medium heat. Add the onions and season with salt and pepper. Cook for 5 minutes or until the onions are softened but not colored.

2 Pour the remaining oil into the pan. Add the mushrooms and nutmeg, season well, and cook for about 5 minutes. Remove the onions and mushrooms with a slotted spoon, place on a plate lined with paper towels, and set aside.

3 Melt the remaining butter in the pan over high heat. Add the strips of beef. When the butter starts to foam up, cook for 2–3 minutes, until brown on the outside but still pink inside. Then add the brandy and set it alight to burn off the alcohol.

4 Return the onions and mushrooms to the pan and cook for 2–3 minutes. Add the mustard, paprika, sour cream, heavy cream, and stock. Stir to mix and cook until it bubbles slightly. Taste and adjust the seasoning if needed, and serve immediately with buttered rice.

BEEF TARTARE

Made from chopped beef and served with a raw egg on top, this dish was popular in early 20th-century France. You can also use beef sirloin and venison loin.

THE CUT Beef filet

SERVES 2
PREP 15 mins

14oz (400g) aged beef filet, chilled

6 cornichons, finely chopped

1 tbsp capers, rinsed and finely chopped

1 tbsp finely chopped flat-leaf parsley

2 shallots, finely chopped

1 tsp Dijon mustard

2 anchovy fillets, rinsed and finely chopped (optional)

tabasco sauce, to taste

sea salt and freshly ground black pepper

2 eggs

1 Finely trim off the exterior of the beef filet, then cut it into thin slices across the grain using a very sharp knife (see p18). Dice the beef into very small pieces and place in a large bowl.

2 Add the cornichons, capers, parsley, shallots, mustard, anchovies, and tabasco sauce to the bowl. Season and mix gently with a fork. Taste and adjust the seasoning, if needed.

3 Divide the beef mixture into two equal portions and place each on a square of parchment paper or saucers. Crack the eggs and separate the whites from the yolks. Place one yolk on top of each portion of the beef tartare. Serve with sourdough toast or duck fat fries and a lamb's lettuce salad.

WASABI BEEF AND BOK CHOY

Japanese wasabi paste, a type of hot mustard, is extremely strong, so you only need a little of it to lift the flavor of the grilled beef steaks.

THE CUT Beef sirloin steak

SERVES 4
PREP 10 mins **COOK** 10 mins, plus resting

3 tbsp olive oil

2 tsp wasabi paste

4 x 7oz (200g) beef sirloin steaks

7oz (200g) bok choy, cut lengthwise into 8 pieces

5 garlic cloves, grated or finely chopped

1 tbsp dark soy sauce

salt and freshly ground black pepper

1 Place 1 tablespoon of oil and the wasabi paste in a shallow bowl and mix to combine. Add the steaks and mix to coat evenly. Heat 1 tablespoon of oil in a large frying pan over medium-high heat and cook the steaks to your liking—2–3 minutes on each side for medium-rare or 5 minutes on each side for well-done. Remove and leave to rest in a warm place for 5 minutes.

2 Add the remaining oil to the pan, reduce the heat to low, and add the bok choy. Cook for 1–2 minutes, turning once or twice, then add the garlic and soy sauce. Fry for 1 more minute or until the bok choy has just wilted. Cut the steak into ½in (1cm) slices, season, and place on a plate. Serve hot with the bok choy.

COUNTRY FRIED STEAK WITH PEPPER GRAVY

Also known as "chicken fried steak" for its similarity to fried chicken, this dish is home cooking at its best.

THE CUT Beef sirloin steak

SERVES 4
PREP 15 mins, plus overnight marinating
COOK 35 mins

1 cup whole milk

salt and freshly ground black pepper

1 tsp cayenne pepper

4 x 5½oz (150g) tenderized rump or sirloin steaks

1 large egg

1⅔ cups all-purpose flour, seasoned with salt and pepper

⅔ cup peanut or sunflower oil, for frying

FOR THE GRAVY

¼ cup all-purpose flour

2 cups whole milk

FOR THE FRIES

2¼lb (1kg) waxy potatoes, such as Yukon Gold, cut into wedges

4 smoked bacon strips

1 onion, chopped

2 garlic cloves, minced

pinch of red pepper flakes

1 Place the milk in a large bowl. Season with salt and pepper, add a pinch of cayenne pepper, and mix well. Add the steaks, toss lightly to coat, and let marinate in the fridge overnight.

2 Remove the steaks from the marinade. Beat the egg with a little of the milk marinade in a small bowl. Combine the flour and the remaining cayenne pepper in a bowl. Heat the oil in a frying pan over high heat. Toss the steaks in the flour, then dip into the milk mixture, and again in the flour. Fry for 3–5 minutes, on each side or until golden brown and cooked through. Remove and set aside. Drain two-thirds of the oil from the pan. Add the flour and whisk to form a thick paste. Then slowly add the milk, 1 cup at a time, stirring constantly, until it forms a thick gravy. Remove and season generously with pepper.

3 For the fries, cook the potatoes in a pan of boiling water for 20 minutes. Then drain and set aside to cool. When cool enough to handle, cut them into ¾in (2cm) strips, leaving the skins on. Fry the bacon in a large, nonstick frying pan, until crisp. Remove from the pan and crumble the bacon. Add the potatoes, onions, garlic, red pepper flakes, and bacon to the pan. Season and cook over medium heat, until the potatoes are crisp. Serve the steaks with a generous portion of the gravy and fries on the side.

THAI BEEF SALAD

This colorful salad is healthy, easy to cook, and has a wonderful tangy flavor.

THE CUT Beef sirloin steak

SERVES 4
PREP 15 mins **COOK** 10 mins, plus resting

2 x 8oz (225g) beef sirloin steaks, thick cut

vegetable oil, for brushing

sea salt and freshly ground black pepper

lime wedges, to serve

FOR THE DRESSING

2 tbsp Thai fish sauce

3 tbsp lime juice

1 large garlic clove, thinly sliced

1 tbsp soy sauce

2 tsp brown sugar or palm sugar

2 tsp peanuts, toasted and chopped

1 tbsp peanut oil

2 bird's eye chiles, seeded and finely chopped

FOR THE SALAD

1 heart of romaine lettuce, rinsed, dried, and finely sliced

10 cherry tomatoes, cut in half

3 shallots, finely sliced

4 scallions, trimmed and sliced diagonally

handful of cilantro leaves, chopped

small handful of Thai basil leaves or mint leaves

½ cucumber, halved, seeded and sliced diagonally

1 For the dressing, mix the fish sauce, lime juice, garlic, soy sauce, sugar, peanuts, oil, and chiles, in a bowl and stir until the sugar has dissolved. For the salad, place all the ingredients in a bowl and toss to mix. Set aside.

2 Heat a grill pan to its highest setting. Brush the steaks with oil and season with salt and pepper. Cook the steaks on the grill pan for 3–4 minutes on each side, depending on how you like your steak.

3 Remove from the heat and let rest for about 5 minutes. Cut the steaks into thin slices and add to the salad. Then add the dressing, toss to coat, and transfer to a large serving platter. Serve the salad with lime wedges.

GINGER, HONEY, AND SOY-GLAZED BEEF SIRLOIN

A spicy marinade with a fresh, juicy mango and chile salsa that perfectly complements the succulent steak.

 Beef sirloin

SERVES 4
PREP 30 mins, plus marinating
COOK 10–15 mins, plus resting

3 tbsp soy sauce

5 tbsp honey

½ tsp five-spice powder

¾in (2cm) piece of fresh ginger, peeled and finely grated

1 garlic clove, cut in half

sea salt and freshly ground black pepper

4 x 8oz (225g) beef sirloin steaks

2 tbsp canola oil

FOR THE SALSA

1 large ripe mango, peeled and diced

1 red chile, seeded and finely sliced

1 red onion, finely diced

juice of 1 lime

small bunch of cilantro, roughly chopped

1 Place the soy sauce, honey, five-spice powder, ginger, and garlic in a bowl and mix well. Season with pepper and add the steaks. Rub the mixture into both sides of the steak and let marinate in the fridge for 20–30 minutes. Preheat the oven to 400°F (200°C).

2 Heat the oil in a grill pan over medium heat. Season the steaks with salt and cook on the pan for 1 minute on each side. Transfer to the oven and cook to your liking—1 minute for rare, 3–4 minutes for medium, and 5 minutes for well done.

3 Remove from the pan and rest for 3–5 minutes in a warm place. For the salsa, mix all the ingredients in a bowl, season, and leave for 1–2 minutes. Serve the steaks hot with the salsa on the side. This salsa can be made up to 3 hours in advance.

STEAK AND WILD MUSHROOM PIE

This delicious and hearty steak pie is both comforting and extravagant. Slow cooking the beef and mushrooms together gives the dish a wonderful earthy flavor.

 Beef braising steak

SERVES 4–6
PREP 50–55 mins, plus chilling
COOK 2½–3 hrs

1lb 2oz (500g) mixed wild mushrooms, fresh, or 2½oz (75g) dried wild mushrooms

¼ cup all-purpose flour, seasoned with salt and pepper

salt and freshly ground black pepper

2¼lb (1kg) beef braising steak, cut into 1in (2.5cm) cubes

4 shallots, finely chopped

3 cups beef stock or water

6 parsley sprigs, leaves finely chopped

FOR THE DOUGH

2 cups all-purpose flour, plus extra for dusting

½ tsp fine salt

12 tbsp unsalted butter, diced

1 egg, beaten, to glaze

1 Preheat the oven to 350°F (180°C). Soak the mushrooms in water for about 30 minutes, then drain and slice them in half. Place the flour in a shallow dish, add the meat, and toss to coat. Place the meat, mushrooms, and shallots in a large heatproof casserole. Add the stock and bring to a boil, stirring constantly. Cover and cook in the oven for 2–2¼ hours, until tender.

2 Meanwhile, for the dough, sift the flour and salt into a bowl. Rub in one-third of the butter until the mixture resembles bread crumbs. Add ½ cup water and bring it together to form a dough. Chill for 15 minutes.

3 On a lightly floured surface, roll out the dough to a 6 x 15in (15 x 38cm) rectangle. Dot the rest of the butter over two-thirds of the dough. Fold the unbuttered side over half the buttered side, then fold the remaining buttered side over to enclose the butter between layers of dough. Turn the dough over and use a rolling pin to seal the edges. Wrap in plastic wrap and chill for 15 minutes, then roll it out to 6 x 18in (15 x 45cm) and fold it again as above. Seal and chill for 15 minutes. Repeat this process three more times, chilling for 15 minutes between each turn.

4 Add the parsley to the meat, season, and pour into a 2-quart pie dish. Increase the oven temperature to 425°F (220°C). Roll out the dough on a floured surface to a size larger than the pie dish. Cut a strip from the edge, dampen the rim of the dish, and press the strip onto it. Place the rolled out dough over the pie, seal, and brush with the beaten egg. Make a hole in the center of the pie and add a pie funnel to allow steam to escape. Chill for 15 minutes then bake for 25–35 minutes, until golden brown. Cover the top with foil if it starts to brown too quickly. Remove from the heat and serve hot.

BEEF FAJITAS WITH GUACAMOLE AND TOMATO SALSA

A popular Tex-Mex recipe, this dish pairs the flavorful flank steak with cajun spices and fresh, tangy sauces.

THE CUT Beef flank steak

SERVES 4
PREP 25 mins   **COOK** 10–15 mins, plus resting

4 x 6oz (175g) beef flank steak, ¾in (2cm) thick

1 tbsp olive oil

4 tsp Cajun spice

sea salt and freshly ground black pepper

8 flour tortillas

4 tbsp sour cream, to serve

FOR THE SALSA

1lb (450g) tomatoes, peeled

handful of cilantro, chopped

½ red onion, finely chopped

1 green chile, seeded and finely chopped

3 tbsp lime juice

FOR THE GUACAMOLE

2 ripe avocados, halved and pits removed

2 tbsp lime juice

1 tbsp olive oil

1 red onion, finely chopped

1 garlic clove, crushed with sea salt

1 small green chile, seeded and finely chopped

1 For the salsa, roughly chop the tomatoes, removing the core from around the stem but not the seeds. Place the tomatoes in a bowl and add the cilantro, onions, chile, and lime juice. Season and mix well.

2 For the guacamole, scoop the avocado flesh into a bowl and mash gently with a fork. Add the lime juice, oil, onions, garlic, and chile and mix well. Taste and season, if needed. Cover with plastic wrap and place in the fridge to avoid it turning brown.

3 Place a grill pan over high heat. Place the oil and Cajun spice in a small bowl and mix well. Rub the steaks with the oil mix evenly. Cook the steaks until cooked to your liking—2–2½ minutes on each side for rare, 3–3½ minutes on each side for medium-rare, about 4 minutes on each side for medium, and about 5 minutes on each side for well-done. Remove from the heat and let rest for 3–5 minutes in a warm place.

4 Warm the tortillas in a dry frying pan. Cut the steaks into strips and divide the meat between the tortillas. Top with the guacamole and salsa, and roll up the tortillas. Serve hot with sour cream.

STEAK AU POIVRE

A classic French Bistro dish, this pepper steak recipe dates back to the 19th century.

THE CUT Beef filet or sirloin

SERVES 4
PREP 10 mins   **COOK** 15 mins, plus resting

3 tbsp black peppercorns

4 x 7oz (200g) beef filet or sirloin steaks, 1½–2in (4–5cm) thick

sea salt

1 tbsp olive oil

3 shallots, finely chopped

½ cup brandy or Cognac

⅔ cup rich beef stock

⅔ cup heavy cream

6 tbsp unsalted butter, chilled and cut into cubes, plus a pat extra

1 Crush the peppercorns using a pestle and mortar and place in a shallow dish. Add the steaks, toss to coat, then season with salt. Heat the oil in a large heavy-bottomed frying pan over medium heat.

2 Cook the steaks in the frying pan until cooked to your liking—2½–3 minutes on each side for rare, 3–4 minutes on each side for medium-rare, and 5–6 minutes on each side for medium to well-done. Make sure you don't burn the pepper when cooking the steak for more than 4 minutes. Remove from the heat and let rest for about 5 minutes in a warm place.

3 Reduce the heat to low and add a pat of butter to the pan. Add the shallots and cook for about 5 minutes, then add the brandy and increase the heat to help ignite it and allow the alcohol to burn off.

4 Add the stock and cream. Bring to a boil rapidly and cook until the liquid is reduced by half and has thickened enough to coat the back of a spoon. Whisk in the butter and season to taste. Pour the sauce over the steaks and serve with duck fat fries and a green salad.

THE ULTIMATE STEAK

Good-quality steak needs very little embellishment. Frying is a simple method of cooking it that produces great results. The thickness of the steak will affect the cooking time.

THE CUT Beef rib-eye steaks

SERVES 1
PREP 30 mins **COOK** 8–14 mins, plus resting

1½in (2 x 3cm) thick beef rib-eye steaks
1–2 tbsp butter, softened
salt and freshly ground black pepper

COOKING STEAK TO PERFECTION

BLUE Cook for 2–3 minutes in total, until just seared and the steak feels very soft when pressed. The interior of the steak should be reddish purple. The meat inside is cool and no blood runs out.

RARE Cook for 6–8 minutes in total, until drops of blood appear on the surface and the steak feels spongy. The interior of the steak should be red and it will be warm. If rested, the blood will disperse evenly.

MEDIUM Cook for 10–12 minutes in total, including resting, which makes it evenly pink. Stop frying when drops of juice become visible on the surface. The steak offers resistance and the interior is pink.

WELL DONE Cook for 12–14 minutes in total. If resting time is included in the 14 minutes, the steak will stay moist. When done, it is well browned, feels firm, and the juices are clearly visible on the surface.

1 Heat a heavy-bottomed frying pan over high heat. Heat 1–2 tbsp of butter in the pan until it simmers. Use tongs to carefully lay the steaks in the pan, taking care in case the fat splashes. Press down the steaks with a slotted spatula to ensure that they are in contact with the pan. Then reduce the heat slightly, to avoid the fat burning, and sear untouched for 1–2 minutes.

2 Use the tongs to lift the steaks and check the underside. If well browned, turn them over and brown the other side, seasoning the browned side with salt and pepper. If the steak is not yet well browned, turn the heat up slightly and make sure they are browned before turning them over to brown the other side. Blue steaks need no further cooking.

TESTING FOR DONENESS

With experience, the cook can simply prod a steak or roast with a fork to know how well cooked it is. Here is a guide to how it should feel. If you are still unsure, you can always slice into a steak and take a look.

RARE Hold your hand with the fingers extended gently forward. Prod the muscle between the thumb and forefinger to feel how soft it is. This is how a rare steak should feel. If the fingers are held limp, this is how a blue steak will feel.

MEDIUM Stretch out your fingers as far as they will go. Now prod between the thumb and first finger where shown. This is how a medium steak feels. It will become firmer while resting, so can be taken out of the pan when softer than this.

WELL DONE Clench your fist tightly and prod between the thumb and forefinger. The muscle feels much firmer; this is well-done meat. Resting is important for well-done meat as it removes any pinkness but retains some moisture.

3 Continue to fry the steaks, turning them every 1–2 minutes, until cooked to your liking (see left for cooking times). Reduce the heat if the butter starts to burn. Remember that thinner steaks cook more quickly. Lightly press the steaks with your finger to check for doneness (see right) and remove from the pan. Leave to rest on a warmed plate for 3–5 minutes before serving.

ROAST BEEF

Roast beef, Yorkshire puddings, and gravy make this a quintessential British Sunday lunch.

THE CUT Rump roast

SERVES 4–6
PREP 10 mins
COOK 1 hr 45 mins, plus resting

3lb 3oz (1.5kg) bottom round rump roast

salt and freshly ground black pepper

1 tbsp olive oil

2 tbsp beef dripping (optional)

2 tbsp all-purpose flour

1¼ cups beef or vegetable stock

Yorkshire puddings, to serve

1 Preheat the oven to 400°F (200°C). Season the beef with salt and pepper. Heat the oil in a medium, heavy-bottomed roasting pan. Add the beef and cook until seared on all sides.

2 Place the beef in a roasting pan, transfer to the oven, and roast for 20 minutes. Reduce the oven temperature to 325°F (160°C) and cook the beef for 1 hour 10 minutes for rare, or 1 hour 25 minutes for medium-rare.

3 Remove the roast from the pan, place on a warmed plate, and cover with foil. Set aside for at least 20 minutes to allow the meat to rest, making it moist and easy to carve.

4 Meanwhile, place the roasting pan on the stove top and warm the cooking juices through (if you don't have any juices, add the dripping). Stir in the flour and cook for 2–3 minutes, stirring to form a smooth paste. Gradually add the stock, stirring, to make a rich gravy. Pour in any juices from the rested beef and stir well. Carve the meat and serve with Yorkshire puddings and the gravy.

CLEVER LEFTOVERS

Leftover roast beef and roast potatoes can make the basis of a delicious hash. Try serving it with a beet, orange, and watercress salad and some Horseradish crème fraîche.

CHINESE SPICED BEEF AND NOODLE SOUP

This well-spiced, aromatic, and cleansing soup makes for a great snack or a light main course.

THE CUT Beef shank

SERVES 4
PREP 30 mins
COOK 2 hrs 50 mins–3 hrs 50 mins

3½oz (100g) dried egg Chinese noodles

3 tsp brown sugar

2 tbsp light soy sauce

½ tbsp dark soy sauce

2 tbsp shaoxing rice wine

3 tsp chili bean sauce

a handful of bean sprouts

4 Napa cabbage leaves, shredded

2 scallions, finely sliced

a small handful of cilantro

FOR THE BEEF STOCK

2 beef shank bones, about 8in (20cm) long

2 banana shallots, halved lengthwise

3 whole carrots, halved

8 black peppercorns

FOR THE SOUP

2 tbsp peanut oil

1 onion, chopped

¾in (2cm) piece of fresh ginger, grated

2 garlic cloves, crushed

1–2 red bird's eye chile

1lb 2oz (500g) beef shank, cut into ⅛in (3cm) cubes

1 star anise

1 tsp Chinese five-spice powder

½ cinnamon stick

sea salt and freshly ground black pepper

1 Preheat the oven to 400°F (200°C). For the beef stock, place the shank bones in a roasting pan. Add the shallots and carrots, transfer to the oven, and roast the bones and vegetables for 35–40 minutes, until the bones are browned but not burnt.

2 Remove from the oven and transfer the bones and vegetables to a large saucepan. Pour in 3 cups of water, add the peppercorns, and bring to a boil. Reduce the heat to a simmer and cook for 1 hour. Skim away any froth that rises to the surface. Strain the stock, discard the bones, and reserve the carrots and stock.

3 Meanwhile, for the soup, heat the oil in a large saucepan over medium heat. Add the onion and cook until soft, then add the ginger, garlic, and chiles and cook for another 1 minute.

4 Add the beef to the pan and cook until well-browned, then add all the remaining soup ingredients along with the stock and season with salt and pepper. Bring to a gentle simmer. Cook for 1–2 hours, until the meat is tender, adding more stock if needed. Then strain the liquid into a clean pan. Transfer the meat to a platter and set aside. Discard the star anise and cinnamon stick.

5 Bring a large pot of water to a boil and cook the noodles according to package instructions. Drain and rinse under cold water. Set aside.

6 Add the carrots to the stock, reserved earlier, and cook for about 5 minutes. Mix the brown sugar, light and dark soy sauce, rice wine, and chili bean sauce in a small bowl and stir it into the soup.

7 Return the meat to the pan and bring to a gentle simmer for 1 minute. Remove from the heat. Just before serving, divide the noodles and bean sprouts between 4 deep bowls. Stir the Napa cabbage into the soup and ladle the hot soup over each bowl. Garnish with chopped scallions and cilantro and serve immediately.

BRAISED BEEF SHANK IN RED WINE

In this rich and luxurious stew, beef shank is slow cooked to a melt-in-your-mouth, flavorful tenderness. Simple and delicious, it makes for real comfort food.

THE CUT Beef shank

SERVES 6–8
PREP 45 mins **COOK** 2½ hrs

4 tbsp canola oil, plus extra if needed

7oz (200g) bacon strips, chopped

18 small shallots

7oz (200g) crimini mushrooms, quartered

1 onion, finely chopped

3 garlic cloves, chopped

3½oz (200g) white mushrooms, chopped

3lb 3oz (1.5kg) beef shank, trimmed and cut into 2in (5cm) chunks

3 tbsp all-purpose flour, seasoned with salt and pepper

2½ cups red wine

1 x 14oz (400g) can of chopped tomatoes

1¾ cups beef stock

sprig of thyme

1 large bay leaf

2 tbsp chopped flat-leaf parsley

sea salt and freshly ground black pepper

1 Preheat the oven to 300°F (150°C). Heat 2 tablespoons of the oil in a heavy-bottomed frying pan. Add the bacon and cook gently until browned, then transfer to a large casserole or Dutch oven. Add the shallots to the pan and cook until golden. Transfer to the casserole, then cook the crimini mushrooms until golden and add to the casserole. Cook the onions and garlic in the pan until golden, then add the white mushrooms and cook until softened. Add more oil if needed. Transfer to the casserole.

2 Heat the remaining oil in a saucepan. Toss the beef in the flour, cook in the pan until browned, and transfer to the casserole. Discard the fat from the pan, add one-quarter of the wine, and bring to a boil, scraping any residue from the bottom. Add the tomatoes, return to a boil, then transfer to the casserole along with the thyme, bay leaf, 1 tablespoon of parsley, and remaining wine and stock. Mix well and season.

3 Cover and cook in the oven for about 2–2½ hours, stirring occasionally and adding more stock if necessary. Remove from the oven, taste and adjust the seasoning, and take out the thyme and bay leaf. Thicken the sauce, if preferred, and serve garnished with the remaining parsley.

BOEUF BOURGUIGNON

A simplified version of a French classic, the beef here is meltingly rich and tender.

THE CUT Beef shank

SERVES 4–6
PREP 30 mins **COOK** 2 hrs 45 mins

4 tbsp olive oil

3½oz (100g) slices bacon, chopped

2 onions, finely chopped

4 thin carrots, cut into ¾in (2cm) slices

1 celery stalk, finely chopped

5½oz (150g) button mushrooms, halved if large

2¼lb (1kg) stewing beef, such as shank, cut into 1in (3cm) cubes

2 tbsp all-purpose flour, seasoned with salt and pepper

salt and freshly ground black pepper

1½ cups red wine

1 cup beef stock

1 bouquet garni

buttered noodles, to serve

1 Preheat the oven to 300°F (150°C). Heat 2 tablespoons of the oil in a large casserole. Cook the bacon for 1–2 minutes until lightly browned. Add the onions, carrots, celery, and mushrooms and cook for 5 minutes. Set aside.

2 Pat the beef with paper towels to remove excess blood. Mix with the flour until well coated and shake off any excess. Heat the remaining oil in the pan and cook the beef until well-browned. Do this in batches to avoid overcrowding the pan. Set aside.

3 Pour the wine and stock into the pan, stirring to dislodge any meaty residue. Season well, add the bouquet garni, and return the meat and vegetables to the pan. Cover and cook in the oven for 2½ hours, until very tender. Remove the bouquet garni and serve with buttered noodles.

WINE ICE CUBES

Freeze leftover wine in ice-cube trays for use in cooking. Once frozen, transfer to a freezer bag. Add a cube or two to a casserole or stew for added flavor.

BRAISED BRISKET OF BUFFALO

Onions and beer provide the texture and flavor for the sauce in this slow-cooked dish.

THE CUT Buffalo brisket

SERVES 6–8
PREP 15 mins   **COOK** 3–4 hrs

3lb 3oz (1.5kg) buffalo brisket

1 tsp salt

½ tsp freshly ground black pepper

2 tbsp olive oil

4 onions, sliced

1 bay leaf

1½ cups light beer

1 tbsp balsamic vinegar

1 Preheat the oven to 325°F (160°C). Pat the meat dry with paper towels to remove any excess blood. Season with the salt and pepper. Heat the oil in a large, deep casserole, add the meat, and cook for about 10 minutes until browned all over. Remove with a slotted spoon, place on a plate lined with paper towels, and set aside.

2 Add the onions to the casserole and cook until browned. Then return the meat to the casserole and add the bay leaf, beer, and vinegar. Pour in just enough water to cover the meat and bring to a boil, then cover and transfer to the oven for 3½ hours.

3 Remove from the oven and let rest, uncovered, for 15 minutes. Transfer the meat to a carving board and cut into thick slices. Arrange the meat on a large platter and pour over the cooking juices. Serve with roast vegetables and mashed potatoes.

MOIST MEAT

Buffalo meat is leaner than beef, so cook it whole in a liquid. This helps keep the moisture in.

ROAST RACK OF VEAL WITH PESTO

Make this dish visually appealing by criss-crossing two ribs of veal to make a Guard of Honor before roasting. It is lovely served with sautéed potatoes.

THE CUT Rib of veal

SERVES 4
PREP 10 mins
COOK 1 hr 15 mins, plus resting

4 tbsp butter, plus a pat extra

3 tbsp olive oil

6-rib roast of veal, trimmed

sea salt and freshly ground black pepper

2 onions, halved

4 garlic cloves, crushed

a few sprigs of rosemary

1 bay leaf

1 cup white wine

1 Preheat the oven to 350°F (180°C). Heat the butter and oil in a roasting pan over high heat. Add the veal to the pan and cook until browned all over. Season with salt and pepper.

2 Add the onions, garlic, rosemary, and bay leaf. Pour in the wine and roast in the oven for 45 minutes to 1 hour, basting regularly with the juices. Remove from the oven, place the rib on a serving dish, and let rest for 10 minutes.

3 Meanwhile, place the roasting pan over low heat to reduce the cooking juices. Add the butter and whisk well to combine. Taste and adjust the seasoning, if needed. Carve the veal and serve along with the cooking juices.

RED BISON CURRY

A fresh-tasting Thai curry, this dish uses the prime cut of meat. Cooked quickly, the meat retains its flavor and texture.

THE CUT Bison sirloin

SERVES 4
PREP 20 mins   **COOK** 25 mins

1 tbsp vegetable oil

1lb (450g) bison sirloin steak, cut into strips

1 x 14oz (400ml) can coconut milk

½ cup beef stock

1 tbsp Thai fish sauce such as Nam Pla

1 tbsp brown sugar

3 tbsp red curry paste

1 bell pepper, seeded and sliced

1 carrot, sliced

4oz (115g) crimini mushrooms, sliced

1 tbsp chopped basil leaves

1 Heat the oil in a large frying pan over medium heat. Add the meat and cook for about 5 minutes, until well-browned. Remove with a slotted spoon, place on a plate, and set aside.

2 Add the coconut milk, stock, fish sauce, sugar, and curry paste to the pan. Whisk to combine all the ingredients, reduce the heat to a simmer, and cook for about 5 minutes.

3 Add all the vegetables and cook, stirring occasionally, for another 10 minutes, until the vegetables are soft and the sauce has thickened slightly. Return the meat to the pan and add the basil. Serve hot with jasmine rice.

VARIATION

Red beef curry Use beef sirloin steak in place of the bison and 3½oz (100g) sliced snow peas or okra in place of the carrots. Cook as above and serve hot.

VEAL SCALLOPINI WITH SALSA VERDE

A typical Italian dish, it is traditionally served with salsa verde or a tomato or wine sauce.

THE CUT Veal sirloin

SERVES 4
PREP 15–20 mins   **COOK** 5 mins, plus resting

4 x 6¼oz (180g) veal sirloin medallions

8 slices prosciutto

12 sage leaves

freshly ground black pepper

2 tbsp unsalted butter

a dash of olive oil (optional)

FOR THE SALSA

3 tbsp finely chopped flat-leaf parsley

grated zest and juice of 1 small lemon

2 tbsp capers, drained and rinsed, if in salt, and finely chopped

2 garlic cloves, crushed

⅔ cup olive oil

½ tsp Dijon mustard

sea salt

1 Place the veal between two sheets of plastic wrap and flatten slightly using a rolling pin or mallet. Remove from the plastic wrap and set aside. Spread out two slices of prosciutto on a plate and top with 3 sage leaves. Place the veal on top of the sage leaves and season with pepper. Wrap the prosciutto around the veal and repeat with each medallion.

2 Meanwhile, for the salsa, place the parsley, lemon zest, capers, and garlic in a bowl. Add the lemon juice, oil, and mustard. Toss well to coat, and taste and adjust the seasoning, if needed.

3 Heat the butter in a large frying pan. Add the veal, and when the butter starts to foam, cook until golden on both sides. Add the oil, if required. Let the veal rest for 2 minutes and serve with the salsa verde.

VEAL CUTLETS WITH PEPPERS

This dish is a northern Italian classic. Give the cutlets enough room in the pan or they will steam instead of developing a crisp crust.

THE CUT Veal cutlet

SERVES 6
PREP 20–25 mins, plus chilling
COOK 9–12 mins

6 veal cutlets, about 13oz (375g) in total

¼ cup all-purpose flour, seasoned with salt and pepper

2 large eggs, lightly beaten

¼ cup dried bread crumbs

2oz (60g) freshly grated Parmesan cheese

4 tbsp olive oil, plus extra if needed

1 garlic clove, finely chopped

2 small green bell peppers, seeded and cut into strips

2 small red bell peppers, seeded and cut into strips

salt and freshly ground black pepper

7–10 sprigs of oregano, leaves picked and finely chopped, plus extra to serve

2 tbsp butter

1 lemon, sliced, to serve

1 Place the veal pieces between two sheets of plastic wrap and flatten using a rolling pin or mallet until they are ⅛in (3mm) thick. Remove from the plastic wrap and set aside.

2 Sift the flour onto a large plate. Place the beaten eggs in a shallow dish. Mix the bread crumbs and Parmesan in a small bowl and spread on another sheet of parchment paper. Coat the meat in the flour and shake off any excess. Then dip them in the egg and finally coat with the bread crumbs and cheese mixture. Chill in the fridge for 30 minutes.

3 Heat 2 tablespoons of the oil in a frying pan. Add the garlic and peppers, season, and sauté until soft, stirring occasionally. Remove from the heat, add the oregano, and keep warm.

4 Heat the butter and remaining oil in a large frying pan over medium-high heat. Fry the cutlets for 1–2 minutes on both sides until golden brown and no longer pink in the center. Reduce the heat if the crumbs start to burn. Do this in batches to avoid overcrowding the pan, adding more oil between batches, if necessary. Transfer to a plate lined with paper towels and keep warm. Serve with the peppers, lemon slices, and a sprig of oregano.

VEAL SCHNITZEL WITH FRIED EGG, CAPERS, AND PARSLEY

The national dish of Austria, it is usually served with a green salad, lemon, and parsley.

THE CUT Veal sirloin

SERVES 4
PREP 20 mins, plus chilling   **COOK** 15 mins

4 veal sirloin steaks, 7oz (200g) each

2 tbsp all-purpose flour, seasoned with salt and pepper

2 large eggs, lightly beaten

1¾ cups bread crumbs

2 tbsp butter

2 tbsp clarified butter

2 tbsp olive oil

4 eggs, to serve

1 tbsp capers, rinsed

1 tbsp chopped flat-leaf parsley

1 Place the steaks between two sheets of plastic wrap and flatten using a rolling pin or mallet until it is ⅛in (3mm) in thickness. Remove from the plastic wrap and set aside.

2 Place the flour in a large bowl. Place the beaten eggs in a separate bowl and put the bread crumbs on a plate. Coat each piece of veal in the flour and shake off any excess. Then dip them in the egg and finally coat with the bread crumbs. Chill in the fridge for 30 minutes.

3 Remove the veal pieces from the fridge. Heat the butter and half the oil in a deep-sided frying pan. Add the veal pieces and fry for 2–3 minutes on each side, until crisp and golden brown. Remove with a slotted spoon and place on a plate. Set aside and keep warm.

4 Heat the remaining oil in a separate frying pan and fry the eggs. To serve, place each piece of veal on a warm plate, top with the capers, parsley, and a fried egg. Serve with a green salad, a little clarified warm butter, and a lemon wedge.

ROAST VEAL WITH LEMON, OLIVES, AND CHERRY TOMATOES

Perfect for the summer months, this delicious roast has a unique balance of sweet, salty, and sharp flavors.

 Veal filet

SERVES 6
PREP 20 mins   **COOK** 1½ hrs, plus resting

zest of 1 lemon

2¼lb (1kg) veal filet

2 tbsp olive oil

sea salt and freshly ground black pepper

2 onions, chopped

¾ cup white wine

4 garlic cloves, thinly sliced

1 preserved lemon, rinsed and cut into 4 wedges

9oz (250g) cherry tomatoes on the vine

1¾oz (50g) black olives

1¾oz (50g) green olives

2 sprigs of lemon thyme

2 sprigs of rosemary

a pat of butter

handful of flat-leaf parsley, roughly chopped, to garnish

1 Preheat the oven to 300°F (150°C). Rub lemon zest all over the meat. Heat the oil in a roasting pan over high heat. Add the meat and cook on both sides, until well-browned. Season with salt and pepper.

2 Add the onions and 2–3 tablespoons of the wine to the pan. Baste the meat with the cooking juices. Pour in the rest of the wine and transfer the roasting pan to the oven. Roast the veal for 50–60 minutes, basting every 15–20 minutes with the cooking juices.

3 Remove from the oven and transfer the meat to a serving dish and let rest in a warm place. Add the garlic, lemon wedges, tomatoes, black and green olives, thyme, and rosemary to the pan. Return to the oven for another 15 minutes.

4 Remove the roasting pan from the oven, add the butter, and stir gently into the mixture. Taste to adjust the seasoning. Carve the veal into slices and place them on a plate with the olives, lemon, and tomatoes. Pour in the buttery juices, garnish with some parsley, and serve hot.

BLANQUETTE DE VEAU

This classic French dish has a rich, creamy sauce that is thickened with the careful addition of egg yolks.

 Veal shoulder

SERVES 4
PREP 15 mins   **COOK** 1 hr 40 mins

1lb 5oz (600g) veal, cut into 1½in (4cm) pieces

1 bouquet garni

1 celery stalk, roughly chopped

1 carrot, roughly chopped

salt and freshly ground black pepper

½ cup white wine

12 button onions

10oz (300g) button mushrooms

2 egg yolks

¼ cup heavy cream

handful of flat-leaf parsley leaves, chopped, to garnish

1 Place the meat, bouquet garni, celery, and carrot in a 2-quart heavy-bottomed heatproof casserole. Season well and add the wine, then pour in 2 cups water, bring to a boil, and skim off any foam that rises to the surface.

2 Reduce the heat, cover, and simmer for 1 hour, stirring occasionally. Add the onions and mushrooms and bring to a boil. Cover and simmer for 30 minutes. Remove the bouquet garni.

3 Whisk together the egg yolks and cream in a bowl and whisk in a little of the cooking juices. Slowly pour the egg and cream mixture into the casserole, stirring constantly. Cook gently until the sauce thickens. Remove from the heat, scatter the parsley over the meat, and serve with steamed green vegetables and mixed basmati and wild rice.

GOAN VEAL KEBABS

Inspired by Portuguese cuisine, Goan dishes usually contain coconut, rice, intense spices and, of course, chile.

 Veal cutlet

SERVES 4–6
PREP 15 mins, plus marinating and soaking
COOK 15 mins, plus resting

2¼lb (1kg) veal cutlet, cut into 1½in (4cm) strips

sea salt and freshly ground black pepper

FOR THE MARINADE

2in (5cm) cinnamon stick

10 cloves

2 large dried red chiles, torn into small pieces

2in (5cm) piece of fresh ginger, roughly grated

1 large onion, chopped

1 tsp turmeric powder

2 tbsp tamarind paste

2 tsp brown sugar

½ cup cider vinegar

2 tbsp canola oil

4 garlic cloves, crushed

1 tsp salt

½ tsp freshly ground black pepper

1 For the marinade, crush the cinnamon and cloves in a mortar and pestle. Toast the mixture in a dry frying pan over low heat until fragrant, then add the red chile. Remove from the heat and set aside to cool. Place the rest of the ingredients in a food processor, along with the spice mix, and pulse to form a smooth paste.

2 Transfer the mixture to a large bowl, add the meat, and mix well. Cover and chill in the fridge for 2 hours. Meanwhile, soak 6 wooden skewers in cold water for 30 minutes. Turn the grill to its highest setting or heat a ridged grill pan over high heat.

3 Remove the meat from the fridge and thread it onto the skewers. Cook the kebabs on the grill or ridged grill pan, turning regularly, for 6–8 minutes or until cooked through. Season the meat from time to time.

4 Remove from the heat and rest the kebabs for 2–3 minutes. Serve hot with toasted fresh coconut naan breads and mint yogurt.

SPINACH-STUFFED VEAL

These stuffed rolls can be cooked up to two days ahead, covered and refrigerated. Their flavor will mellow over time.

 Veal cutlet

SERVES 4
PREP 45–50 mins **COOK** 30–40 mins

1lb 2oz (500g) spinach leaves, trimmed

4 tbsp olive oil, plus extra if needed

½ cup walnuts, chopped

1oz (30g) freshly grated Parmesan cheese

grated nutmeg

8 garlic cloves, finely chopped

salt and freshly ground black pepper

8 veal cutlets, about 1lb 6oz (625g) in total

1 onion, thinly sliced

1 carrot, thinly sliced

2 celery stalks, thinly sliced

1 cup dry white wine

1 cup chicken stock

1 Bring a saucepan of water to a boil, add the spinach, simmer for 1–2 minutes, then drain. Squeeze to remove excess water, then chop. Heat 2 tablespoons of the oil in a frying pan and add the spinach. Stir until all the moisture has evaporated. Remove from the heat and add the walnuts, Parmesan, nutmeg, and half the garlic. Stir well. Taste and adjust the seasoning.

2 Place the veal pieces between two sheets of plastic wrap and flatten using a rolling pin or mallet till ⅛in (3mm) in thickness. Remove from the plastic wrap and set aside. Place the cutlets on a clean work surface and season with salt and pepper. Divide the spinach stuffing evenly between the veal cutlets. Roll up the meat, tucking in the ends, and tie the rolls with pieces of butcher's string.

3 Heat the remaining oil in a frying pan over high heat. Add the veal rolls and cook for 2–3 minutes, turning occasionally, until well browned all over. Remove with a slotted spoon, transfer to a plate, and set aside.

4 Stir the onion and remaining garlic into the pan and cook until softened. Add the carrot and celery, reduce the heat, and cook for 8–10 minutes, until tender. Pour in the wine, bring to a boil, and simmer to reduce by half.

5 Return the meat to the pan and add the stock. Cover and simmer for 30–40 minutes, until tender. Strain the liquid into a saucepan, reserving the vegetables, and boil until reduced to ⅔ cup. Slice the veal rolls and serve with the sauce.

LAMB AND GOAT

LAMB AND GOAT

WE HAVE VISIONS OF SHEEP GRAZING SALT-WASHED MARSHES NEAR THE SEA OR SURVIVING ON THE ROCKY SHORELINES OF NORTHERN ISLANDS. WE ALSO THINK OF GOATS CLIMBING UP TREES TO FORAGE FOR SCARCE LEAVES IN DRY, INHOSPITABLE SCRUBLAND.

BOTH SHEEP AND GOATS are remarkably efficient at living off some of the poorest pastures in the world. Since they are small animals, they are easy to keep and were domesticated before cattle or pigs, providing us with wool, milk, and delicious meat.

Until recently, however, most sheep were primarily kept for milk and wool. Meat was a by-product that generally came from animals that were older than the ones we eat today. Lamb was a luxury item, used— and still used—for feasting: at Muslim weddings, births, and on religious holidays,

for Jewish Passover, and at the Easter meal for Christians. In many countries, though, lamb is not a common meat.

Goats have been a major source of meat, as well as milk, throughout the arid regions of Africa and, especially, Asia. These regions contain about 60 percent of the world's population. Elsewhere, some goats are reared specifically for meat, but most are kept in dairy units where excess young males are sold for meat. Mature goat meat is widely available where there is a thriving milk industry.

PRODUCTION AND FEED

Sheep and goats are both ruminants. Goats are browsers rather than grazers and prefer leaves and shrubs, whereas sheep prefer short vegetation. When raised for milk production, they will have a higher energy diet and are more likely to be reared indoors, with food such as hay and alfalfa, along with concentrates, as feed. But in many hot countries they are still herded and grazed on whatever vegetation is available.

Sheep and goats raised specifically for meat are largely grazed outside. Some sheep are raised in the hills, sometimes on salt marshes or on seashores. The vegetation in these special environments gives a distinctive and much prized flavor to the meat. Large flocks of sheep are reared on ranches in South America, Australia, and New Zealand, which has the highest density of sheep in the world. Sheep and meat goats are also raised fairly intensively in fertilized, grass paddocks as part of arable rotations. Root crops, such as rutabagas or turnips and fodder beet, are fed in the winter, and concentrates may also be given, either during lambing or kidding, or to finish the fattening process before slaughter. However, the chances of lamb and young goat being intensively reared are far fewer than with other species.

DIPS AND DOSES

Where sheep and goats are free-ranging there are few serious health issues, but during periods or systems of more intensive management, sheep and goats are usually

UNTIL RECENTLY, MOST SHEEP WERE KEPT FOR MILK AND WOOL. MEAT WAS A BY-PRODUCT, SO IT GENERALLY CAME FROM ANIMALS OLDER THAN THOSE WE NOW EAT.

dosed to prevent or treat parasites, flies, and foot rot. Controversial sheep dips, such as those using organophosphates, can be harmful to the environment and, most people think, to farmers as well. They need careful handling and many would like to see them banned.

ORGANIC LAMB

Like other livestock, organic lamb can be raised in a number of ways, although feed must be organic. Some very extensively raised lamb may not carry an organic mark, but may well be just as "organic" as some certified lamb. Organophosphates have been permitted on organic farms in some countries where other suitable treatments are absent.

LAMB AND GOAT BREEDS

• **Sheep** Of the hundreds of sheep breeds, many—like the famous Spanish Merino—are wool breeds. Others are bred for milk production. In most lamb-producing countries, meat breeds are crosses between hardy breeds and productive ones.

Britain has more breeds of sheep than any other country and many breeds, such as Romney, Suffolk, and Cheviot, are seen in flocks across the world. The Dorset Horn crossed with the Blackhead Persian sheep created the popular Dorper breed. Similarly, the Texel, a large breed from the Netherlands, has been adopted in many countries as a fast-growing meat-producing sheep. Each country has its special heritage breeds, such as the Herdwick, the Welsh Mountain sheep, and the Scottish Blackface.

Fat-tailed sheep: This is a special group of breeds from Asia, the Middle East, and Africa where they thrive in arid conditions. They are reared for meat, but their main speciality is their very long tails that have been selected to produce especially delicious fat which is highly prized.

• **Goat meat breeds** Outside Asia and Africa, specialized meat production is comparatively new and most goats are dairy breeds. The South African Boer is

one of the most common meat breeds (it is a cross between native and imported breeds), followed by the Spanish and Anglo Nubian, a multipurpose breed developed by crossing Indian and Middle Eastern goats.

LAMB AND GOAT CATEGORIES

• **Milk-fed lamb or baby lamb:** This is 4–10 weeks old and has a very delicate flavor.
• **Spring lamb:** This is 3–6 months old, although since so much lamb is sold very young anyway, the term is not often used.
• **Lamb:** Lamb meat can be up to one year old and has a mild, but distinctive, flavor.
• **Hogget or yearling mutton:** At 1–2 years old, the meat from a hogget is still tender, but it has a more pronounced flavor than lamb, with a little more fat.
• **Mutton:** This comes from sheep of two years of age and upward, so is more variable. The fat and meat has a much stronger "sheep" taste. Mutton can be tough if very old.
• **Kid (young goat)** Up to 14 months old, goat meat has a delicate flavor similar to

young lamb. It has several names. Milk-fed goat, or baby goat, is usually well under three months old and often eaten before it starts grazing. Capretto and cabrito are used to describe the meat from young goats in the 2–12 month age range, and chevon is about 6–14 months old.
• **Goat:** An adult goat is more than 14 months old. When older than about three years, its meat can have a powerful flavor, especially if it comes from a male. Old goat meat is sometimes called mutton.

BUYING LAMB AND GOAT

Young lamb does not have a great deal of fat, but well-finished lamb can contain a lot, particularly in the forequarter cuts. The back legs are always the leanest part. Hogget is likely to be fatter than lamb. Mutton fat is harder than lamb fat and has a stronger taste. Most goat meat is fairly lean.

LAMB AND GOAT CUTS

The meat from these extensively reared animals tastes sweet and their versatile meat is perhaps not as common as it should be. Although goat and old mutton can be cut exactly like lamb, they are generally cut more simply. Hogget and younger mutton is cut as lamb.

FOREQUARTER

MIDDLE OR SADDLE

LEG

BREAST AND FLANK

GOAT AND KID

Goat is much leaner than lamb and mutton. Young goat meat is sometimes called chevon or cabrita to distinguish it from older, stronger, goat meat. Kid is 4–14 months old.

- **WHOLE LEG** A prime cut, the leg can be roasted or braised whole or deboned and rolled. Whole legs weigh around 4½lb (2kg).

- **WHOLE SADDLE, BONE-IN WITHOUT RIBS** The most tender cut, the saddle can be roasted whole, divided into a rack or chops for grilling and barbecuing, or boned out and trimmed for a neat premium roast.

- **WHOLE SHOULDER** A whole shoulder is at its best slowly cooked in foil until the meat falls off the bone. The shank can be removed, but cooked slowly it becomes tender too.

- **DICED GOAT** Perfect for curries and stews, diced goat meat is usually boneless. Some recipes ask for diced goat meat with the bone in but this may need to be ordered.

- **KID** Milk-fed kid has a delicate, pale meat and is particularly tender, but older kid meat is also tender and mild-flavored. Sold whole and in primals (leg, shoulder, and saddle).

FOREQUARTER CUTS

Many traditional dishes use slow-cooked forequarter cuts as their flavor is superb. Sliced neck, shoulder, and shank all have different textures. Most cuts can be grilled or broiled as well.

DICED FOREQUARTER
There are many uses for diced lamb, from kebabs to stews. The fat content means the meat is kept moist, whether quickly or slowly cooked. Diced leg is far leaner.

ARM CHOP These are also sold without the bone. Good for the grill, but also delicious when slow-cooked as the meat stays succulent. Bandsaw-cut chops may have bone splinters.

WHOLE SHOULDER, BONE-IN WITH SHANK This cut is quite thin so cooks quickly but the high fat content means it is better cooked to well-done. Try slashing the meat and rubbing in flavorings.

Additional forequarter cuts

- **SHOULDER, DEBONED AND ROLLED** This cut is good roasted or braised, although it has more fat than the leg.

- **NECK FILET** A neat little cut that can be quickly roasted. Perfect for two.

- **SLICED NECK** The perfect cut for Irish stew; the bones keep the meat sweet.

MIDDLE OR SADDLE CUTS

These tender cuts are the best part of the lamb. Boneless loin steaks may be called noisettes or medallions, and small log-shaped loin roasts may be called a pavé.

BEST END OR RACK This cut can be cooked as a whole piece and sliced into chops at the table if it has been chined. French trimming the ends (see p193) gives a neat appearance.

DOUBLE LOIN CHOPS Cut from the rump end of the loin and with the backbone chined, these chops have both loin and filet meat and are the most succulent of all the chops.

LOIN OF LAMB, LARDER TRIMMED Also called cannon, this perfectly trimmed tender muscle is lamb at its most elegant. Best cooked to rosy pink and especially good with an herb crust.

Additional middle or saddle cuts

• **LOIN ROAST** A premium cut from the best part of the back (from the sirloin to the start of the ribs), cut just like venison.

• **BARNSLEY CHOPS** This slice of saddle makes a generous portion; it has both loin and filet meat.

• **BUTTERFLY STEAKS** These steaks must be completely trimmed or they curl up when cooking.

BREAST AND FLANK CUTS

Breast and flank fat is harder than pork fat, so flavors and cooking methods need to take this into account.

GROUND Ground lamb is poplular for inexpensive dishes such as shepherd's pie, meatballs, and koftes. Ground flank is very fatty, ground shoulder is less so, but ground leg is the leanest.

BREAST AND FLANK This fatty cut has thick connective tissue so needs slow cooking. It can also be cooked on the grill. The breast can be stuffed and rolled for an inexpensive dish.

LEG CUTS

Leg meat is leaner than loin and shoulder meat but has just enough fat to keep it moist whether cooked pink or well-done. Diced leg makes excellent kebabs and tagine.

WHOLE LEG, ON THE BONE A whole leg is the perfect size for a family. The sirloin half is easier to carve without the pelvic bone. The other half may have the shank removed.

SIRLOIN CHOPS Despite their name, sirloin chops are usually boneless. From the top of the leg, they are very tender with a good flavor. They can be pan-fried, grilled, or braised.

SHANK, BONE-IN A popular pub cut, this little cut needs slow cooking. With caramelized root vegetables and some red wine, it produces a wonderfully rich dish. One shank makes a generous serving.

Additional leg cuts

• **ROLLED LEG OF LAMB** A whole rolled leg sometimes includes the shank but smaller roasts are always boneless.

• **BUTTERFLIED LEG** Legs are slashed deeply and opened out so they can be rubbed with flavorings (see p192).

• **BONELESS LEG STEAK** Perfect for grilling or pan-frying, this is a fairly lean cut of lamb.

PRESERVED LAMB AND GOAT

PRESERVED LAMB PRODUCTS are found where lamb is most common: in northern European countries and around the Mediterranean fringe. Goat products tend to come from southern Europe, Asia, and Africa, where goats are herded in large numbers. Many of these tasty preparations are dark in color and have an intense flavor.

REESTIT MUTTON From the Shetland Islands, reestit mutton is brined and then hung to dry in the rafters where the peaty smoke imparts a special flavor.

PASTIRMA From the Middle East, Balkans and Turkey, pastirma is prepared from salted lamb and goat, washed, dried and pressed, covered in a paste of hot spices and further dried.

MERGUEZ OR MIRQAZ A spicy cured or dried sausage common throughout North Africa. Lamb and goat are flavored with lemon, harissa, and hot chiles, which make it bright red.

FÅREPØLS This Norwegian dried sausage is made of mutton and pork and sometimes includes the blood. Flavorings include ginger or juniper and, typically, syrup.

RYYNIMAKKARA Made with cooked oats or barley groats and flavored with ginger, cloves, and pepper, this Finnish sausage originally contained no meat. Nowadays, however, it contains lamb among other meats.

SPEKEPØLSE A common cured, smoked, and dried Danish sausage; many forms exist. As well as lamb, pork and even vegetables such as cabbage or potatoes are also added.

MARANHO OR BURLHÕES This Portuguese sausage is cooked in the goat's stomach. It is flavored with rice, ham, paprika, and mint.

LOUKANIKO A Greek lamb sausage often containing pork as well. Flavorings include pepper, cumin, sometimes orange peel, and either leeks or oregano.

BILTONG This is made in South Africa from many meats, including goat and mutton. The meat is sprinkled with vinegar, lightly spiced, and then dried in the sun.

BUTTERFLYING A LEG

A leg is deboned to spread the meat out more evenly and thinly so is ideal for broiling and barbecuing. The pelvic bone is at the widest, meatiest end, the shank at the narrowest.

1 Place the lamb fleshiest side down. Grip the end of the pelvic bone in one hand and work around it with the tip of a boning knife to expose the bones. Now make an incision at the pelvic bone and cut through the skin and meat along the entire length of the thigh bone.

2 Cut the meat away from the thighbone, using short strokes and keeping the knife tilted toward the bone. Use the tip of the blade to avoid slashing the meat. As the meat falls away, pull the bone upward.

3 Once the whole thighbone is exposed, pull it right up from the shank bone and cut away all the meat from the bone and cartilage around the knuckle joint. If any cartilage comes off with the meat, cut it off and discard it.

4 Cut the meat away from the shank bone (it is easy to see the edge of the bone) and cut through any remaining meat and tendons. All 3 leg bones can now be lifted out in one piece.

5 Open out the meat and lay it flat. Using a stroking movement, cut into the thickest part of the largest muscles to make everything as uniform a thickness as possible.

6 Open out the slashed "wings" to make a roughly square shape. If it is to be rolled, then slivers can be cut from over-thick areas and tucked into the thinnest parts to make an even shape.

FRENCH TRIMMING A RACK

A rack, or "carré," is an elegant cut that makes the most of the single lean eye muscle and is easy to carve into portions. It can be cooked unadorned or have a crust applied to the outside.

1 On one side of the meat there may be a soft, cartilaginous piece of shoulderblade under the skin. If so, lift the flap and cut it out with a flexible boning knife, holding the knife blade flat to avoid cutting into the muscle.

2 Slip the boning knife beneath the membrane of skin and outer fat, and rip it off with your other hand. Shave off excess fat, or remove all the fat and sinew until only the eye muscle remains.

3 With a small, very sharp knife, cut between the ribs with the blade right next to the bones to cut out the strips of meat, fat, and papery sinew that holds them together.

4 Holding the knife blade about 1½in (4cm) away from the main eye muscle, slice off the fatty flap. If you prefer really lean meat, cut closer to the muscle. Reserve the flap and trimmings to make stock.

5 Lay the rib bones on the cutting board. Take a cleaver and, with one stroke, chop off the ends of the bones so that they all come off in a straight line. With a utility or chef's knife, carefully strip off the fine skin that surrounds the bones for an attractive presentation.

6 Hold the cut upright. With a saw or cleaver, cut off the backbone (or "chine") from the rack. Try to do this with just 1 or 2 clean and accurate strokes. If you leave any traces of backbone, it will prevent you from slicing the cutlets apart after cooking.

GRILLED LAMB KOFTAS

These easy-to-make authentic Greek lamb koftas are fresh, spicy, and bursting with flavor.

THE CUT Ground lamb

SERVES 8
PREP 30 mins, plus resting
COOK 8–12 mins

1 large onion, grated

1 tbsp coarse salt

2lb (900g) finely ground lamb

2 large eggs, lightly beaten

2 tbsp chopped cilantro leaves

2 tsp ground cumin

1 tsp dried thyme

½ tsp ground allspice

freshly ground black pepper

olive oil, for greasing

1 Place the onions and salt in a bowl, mix well, and leave for 15 minutes. Then use a fine sieve to squeeze the juice from the salted onions, and discard juice.

2 Add the lamb, eggs, cilantro, cumin, thyme, allspice, and pepper to the bowl. Mix to combine all the ingredients, kneading the mixture lightly for 2–3 minutes. Cover and let rest for 30 minutes at room temperature.

3 Heat a grill pan over medium heat. Oil 8 metal skewers. Divide the lamb mixture into 8 equal portions and shape each into a sausage shape. Slide the sausages onto the skewers, smoothing the ends down so they do not slip off while cooking. Brush a little oil on each kofta.

4 Cook the koftas on the grill pan for about 8 minutes, turning occasionally, until browned and evenly cooked on the outside, but still a little pink on the inside. These koftas will be cooked to medium-rare. If you prefer them well-done, cook for 2–3 minutes more. Slide the koftas off the skewers and leave to cool slightly for 2–3 minutes. Serve hot with pita bread and some sliced tomatoes.

VARIATION

Grilled goat koftas Use ground goat meat instead of lamb and prepare as above. Broil the koftas instead of cooking over a grill pan and serve with spiced flatbreads and Greek-style yogurt.

MOUSSAKA

This delicious Greek recipe may take a while to prepare, but the layers of sauces, grilled vegetables, and lamb really make it well worth the time spent.

THE CUT Ground lamb

SERVES 4
PREP 1 hr   **COOK** 2 hrs 25 mins, plus resting

12oz (350g) waxy potatoes, such as Yukon Golds, peeled

1 large eggplant, cut lengthwise into ½in (1cm) thick slices

FOR THE SAUCE

2 tbsp olive oil, plus extra for brushing

1 onion, finely chopped

2 garlic cloves, finely chopped

1lb (450g) ground lamb

14oz (400g) can chopped tomatoes

¾ cup beef, lamb, or chicken stock

⅓ cup of red wine (optional)

2 tbsp finely chopped flat-leaf parsley

½ tsp dried thyme

½ tsp dried oregano

½ tsp ground cinnamon

salt and freshly ground black pepper

FOR THE BÉCHAMEL

4 tbsp butter

¼ cup all-purpose flour

1½ cups whole milk

pinch of grated nutmeg

1oz (25g) freshly grated Parmesan cheese

1 large egg, beaten

1 For the sauce, heat the oil in a large, heavy-bottomed saucepan over medium heat. Add the onion and cook for about 5 minutes, until softened. Then add the garlic and cook for 1 more minute. Increase the heat, add the lamb and cook until well-browned. Then add the tomatoes, stock, wine (if using), herbs, and cinnamon. Season and bring to a boil. Then reduce the heat to simmer, and cook for 1–1 hour 15 minutes, until the liquid evaporates.

2 Meanwhile, boil the potatoes in a large pan of salted water, until cooked through. Drain, slice lengthwise, and set aside. Set the broiler to its highest setting. Spread the eggplant slices on a baking sheet, brush with the oil, and broil until browned. Turn, brush the other side with oil, and broil until browned. Set aside.

3 Preheat the oven to 350°F (180°C). For the béchamel, melt the butter in a small pan over medium heat. Whisk in the flour and cook for 2 minutes. Then remove from the heat and gradually whisk in the milk. Return to the heat and cook, stirring, until thickened. Add the nutmeg and Parmesan, season well, and cook over low heat for 10 minutes. Remove from the heat and whisk in the beaten egg.

4 Spread half the meat in an 8in (20cm) square ovenproof dish. Cover with half the eggplant, then half the béchamel. Arrange the potatoes in an overlapping layer, then add the rest of the meat, eggplant, and béchamel. Bake for 1 hour until golden brown. Leave to rest and serve hot.

FORFAR BRIDIES

A traditional Scottish pie, ideal for eating when out and about in the hills, at a soccer game, or on a picnic.

CUT Ground lamb

SERVES 4
PREP 20 mins, plus chilling and resting
COOK 40 mins

FOR THE PASTRY

1⅓ cups bread flour

½ cup all-purpose flour, plus extra for dusting

½ tsp salt

12 tbsp butter, chilled and diced

FOR THE FILLING

1lb 2oz (500g) ground lamb

5 tbsp cold beef suet or lard, grated

1 onion, finely chopped

1 tbsp chopped flat-leaf parsley

salt and freshly ground black pepper

1 For the pastry, place all the ingredients in a food processor and pulse until the mixture resembles fine bread crumbs. Transfer the mixture to a large bowl, add 3–4 tablespoons of ice water, and mix to form a soft dough. Bring together to form a rough dough, wrap in plastic wrap, and chill for 2 hours.

2 Preheat the oven to 400°F (200°C). For the filling, place all the ingredients in a large bowl and mix well to combine. Remove the pastry from the fridge and divide it into 4 equal portions. On a lightly floured surface, roll each portion out into an oval shape. Place one-quarter of the meat mixture onto one side of each pastry oval, leaving a border around the edges.

3 Moisten the edges of the pastry ovals with water. Fold the pastry over to enclose the filling and crimp the edges with a fork to neaten and seal. Make a small hole on the top of each pie to allow steam to escape and leave to rest for 1 hour. Place on a baking sheet and bake for 40 minutes. These pies can be served warm or cold.

VARIATION

Beef bridies Use ground beef in place of lamb and marjoram in place of parsley. Add 1 teaspoon mustard to the filling and cook the pies as above.

LAMB BURGERS WITH ROASTED TOMATO RELISH

The addition of cream and fresh herbs to the lamb makes for burgers that are very succulent and full of flavor.

CUT Ground lamb

SERVES 4
PREP 20 mins, plus chilling
COOK 8–10 mins, plus resting

1lb 2oz (500g) lean ground lamb

handful of cilantro leaves, finely chopped

2 shallots, finely chopped

1 tsp ground cumin

1 red chile, seeded and finely chopped

2 garlic cloves, crushed and finely chopped

1 tsp ground cinnamon

1 tbsp chopped flat-leaf parsley

1 tbsp chopped mint

pinch of ground allspice

1 tbsp heavy cream

2 tbsp fine bread crumbs

grated zest of 1 lemon

sea salt and freshly ground black pepper

canola oil, for brushing

FOR THE RELISH

1lb (450g) cherry tomatoes

1 red onion, finely diced

1 garlic clove, finely chopped

3 tbsp olive oil

1 tsp of sugar

handful of cilantro leaves, chopped

1 Place all the burger ingredients in a large bowl and mix lightly to combine. Make four round, 1in (3cm) thick patties without compressing the meat too much. Chill the patties for 30 minutes.

2 Heat a heavy-bottomed nonstick frying pan over medium heat. Brush the patties lightly with oil and fry them until cooked to your liking— 4 minutes on each side for medium and 5 minutes on each side for well-done. Let rest for about 2 minutes.

3 For the relish, place all the ingredients, except the cilantro, in a frying pan and cook for 8–10 minutes, until soft. Cool the mixture slightly, then squeeze the tomato flesh out of the skins and transfer to a bowl. Add the onions and garlic to the bowl and stir in the cilantro. Serve the patties in hamburger buns along with the relish.

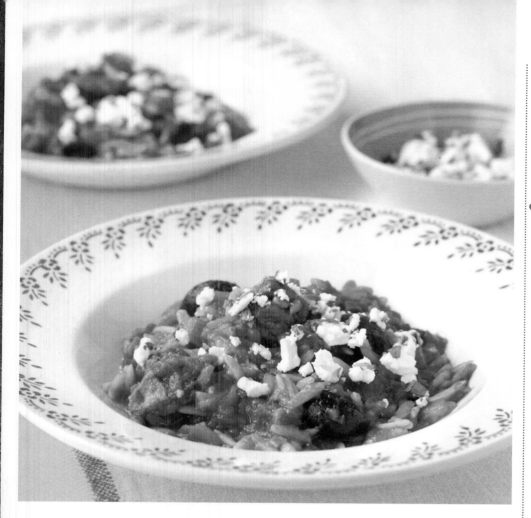

LAMB KEBABS WITH YOGURT AND POMEGRANATE

These Greek-inspired kebabs are easy to make and are traditionally served with a refreshing yogurt dressing.

THECUT Lamb shoulder

SERVES 4
PREP 30 mins, plus marinating
COOK 10 mins

12oz (350g) lean lamb shoulder, cut into cubes

½ tsp ground cumin

½ tsp ground coriander

½ tsp garam masala

¼ tsp ground cinnamon

olive oil, for brushing

seeds from 1 pomegranate, to serve

FOR THE DRESSING

1 shallot, finely chopped

1 garlic clove, chopped

1 tbsp chopped mint

½ cucumber, peeled, seeded, and chopped

1¼ cup Greek-style yogurt

pinch of salt

1 Place the lamb in a large bowl. Add the cumin, coriander, garam masala, and cinnamon to the bowl and mix to coat the meat in the spices. Leave to marinate for 30 minutes.

2 For the dressing, place the shallots, garlic, mint, cucumber, and yogurt in a large serving bowl. Add the salt, mix well to combine, and set aside.

3 Heat a large heavy-bottomed frying pan or a grill pan. Divide the lamb cubes into 4 equal portions and thread them onto 4 skewers. Brush the pan with a little oil and grill the meat for 8 minutes, turning regularly, until well-browned.

4 Remove from the heat. Sprinkle over the pomegranate seeds, remove the kebas fom the skewers, and transfer to a serving plater. Serve with a dollop of the yogurt dressing, couscous, and pita bread.

GREEK LAMB STEW

A complete meal in itself, this rich and hearty stew only needs some crusty bread to soak up the delicious juices.

THECUT Lamb shoulder

SERVES 4
PREP 30 mins   **COOK** 20–25 mins

2 tbsp olive oil

1lb 9oz (700g) boneless shoulder or neck fillet of lamb, trimmed and cut into bite-sized pieces

1 red onion, finely chopped

2 garlic cloves, finely chopped

¾ cup dry white wine

2 x 14oz (400g) can chopped tomatoes

3½oz (100g) pitted Kalamata olives

3 sprigs of thyme

3½oz (100g) kritharáki or orzo pasta

3½oz (100g) feta cheese, crumbled

small bunch of mint leaves, finely chopped

salt and freshly ground black pepper

1 Preheat the oven to 300°F (150°C). Heat 1 tablespoon of oil in a large, heavy-bottomed heatproof casserole or Dutch oven over medium heat. Cook the meat until browned. Do this in batches to avoid overcrowding the pan. Remove with a slotted spoon and set aside on a plate lined with paper towels.

2 Add the remaining oil to the casserole. Then add the onion and cook for 5 minutes, stirring occasionally, until softened. Add the garlic and cook for 2 more minutes.

3 Add the wine and tomatoes to the casserole and stir to mix. Return the lamb to the pan, add the olives and thyme, and bring to a boil. Season well, cover, and cook in the oven for 1½ hours.

4 Remove from the oven, discard the thyme, then add in the pasta, and stir. Adjust the seasoning and return to the oven for 15 minutes. Mix the feta and mint in a small dish. Serve the stew hot with the cheese mixture sprinkled over.

LAMB AND BARLEY STEW

A richly satisfying dish, its flavor intensifies greatly after keeping for a day or two.

THE CUT Leg of lamb

SERVES 4
PREP 30 mins   **COOK** 2 hrs

3 tbsp oil or lamb fat

salt and freshly ground black pepper

1lb (450g) leg of lamb, diced

1 onion, finely sliced

2 carrots, sliced

2 celery stalks, finely sliced

2 garlic cloves, crushed

1 tbsp all-purpose flour

1¼ cups white wine

1 tbsp tomato paste

2 strips lemon peel

1 bay leaf

sprig of thyme

1oz (30g) pearl barley

1 tbsp chopped flat-leaf parsley

1 Preheat the oven to 325°F (160°C). Heat 2 tablespoons of oil in a large heatproof casserole. Season the lamb, and cook for 4–5 minutes, until well-browned. Do this in batches to avoid overcrowding the pan. Remove with a slotted spoon and set aside on a plate lined with paper towels.

2 Reduce the heat and add the remaining oil to the casserole. Add the onions, carrots, and celery and cook, stirring constantly, until softened. Stir in the garlic and cook for 1 more minute.

3 Return the meat to the casserole, stir in the flour, and mix through. Then add the wine, tomato paste, lemon peel, bay leaf, and thyme. Pour in just enough water to cover and bring to a boil. Then add the barley, stirring to combine. Cover and cook in the oven for 1½ hours until the lamb is tender.

4 Remove from the oven and take out the bay leaf, thyme, and lemon peel. Taste and adjust the seasoning, if needed. Stir in the parsley and serve with mashed potatoes and greens.

VARIATION

Goat and barley stew Use goat in place of the lamb, oatmeal in place of the flour, and cider in place of the wine. Cook as above and serve hot.

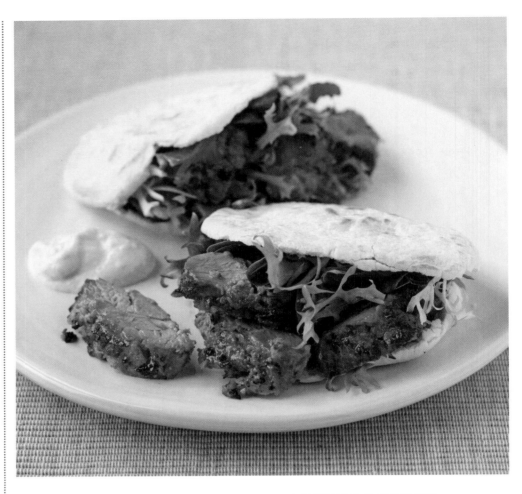

LAMB FILLET BASTED WITH ANCHOVY PASTE

Anchovies give the lamb a punchy flavor in this dish. You can use store-bought anchovy paste or make your own as shown here.

THE CUT Lamb neck

SERVES 4
PREP 15 mins, plus marinating
COOK 20 mins, plus resting

1 whole lamb neck fillet, about 1½lb (675g)

2 scallions, trimmed and roughly chopped

1 x 5oz (140g) jar salted anchovies in oil, drained

2 tbsp capers in vinegar, drained

3 tbsp olive oil

1 Set the broiler to its medium setting. Score the lamb fillet in a criss-cross pattern about ½in (1cm) deep. Place onions, anchovies, capers, and olive oil in a food processor and pulse to a fine paste.

2 Place the lamb in a large shallow dish and coat with the anchovy paste, making sure it gets into the scores. Let marinate in the fridge for about 30 minutes.

3 Cook the lamb fillet in the lower part of the broiler for 15–20 minutes, turning occasionally, until browned and cooked to your liking.

4 Remove from the heat, transfer to a plate, and let rest in a warm place for at least 10 minutes. Cut the meat into ½in (1cm) slices and serve with warm pita bread, hummus, and seasonal salad leaves.

LANCASHIRE HOTPOT

A traditional dish from the northwest of England, it uses the rich-tasting neck of lamb and kidneys.

THE CUT Neck of lamb

SERVES 4
PREP 15 mins   **COOK** 2½ hrs

4 lamb kidneys

2¼lb (1kg) neck end of lamb or lamb shanks

salt and freshly ground black pepper

1 tbsp vegetable oil

3 tsp butter, plus 1 tsp extra for greasing

2¼lb (1kg) floury potatoes, such as Russets, thinly sliced

3 onions, finely sliced

2 sprigs of thyme

2 bay leaves

1 tsp superfine sugar

1¾ cups lamb stock

1 Preheat the oven to 325°F (160°C). Slice the kidneys in half horizontally. Then remove the skins and cut out the cores. Season the kidneys and lamb with salt and pepper.

2 Heat the oil in a frying pan over high heat, add all the meat, and cook for about 10 minutes, until browned. Remove with a slotted spoon and set aside on a plate lined with paper towels.

3 Grease the bottom of a large casserole dish. Use half the potato to arrange an overlapping layer at the bottom and season lightly. Then layer with the meats, onions, thyme, and bay leaves. Sprinkle over the sugar.

4 Top with the remaining potatoes, overlapping, to fully cover the meat. Pour in just enough stock to cover the meat, leaving the top layer of the potatoes dry. Season lightly.

5 Melt the butter in a saucepan and brush over the top of the potatoes. Cover and cook in the oven for 2 hours. Then remove the lid, increase the temperature to 400°F (200°C), and cook for an additional 30 minutes to brown the edges of the potatoes. Remove from the heat and take out the thyme and bay leaves. Serve hot with cabbage or greens.

IRISH STEW

An economical dish that uses inexpensive cuts, it has a long cooking time, which ensures a rich and intense flavor.

THE CUT Neck or shoulder of lamb

SERVES 4
PREP 25 mins   **COOK** 3 hrs

2lb (900g) stewing lamb from the neck or shoulder, trimmed and cut into 1in (3cm) pieces

½ cup pearl barley

1 large onion, roughly chopped

3 carrots, roughly sliced

7oz (200g) rutabaga, roughly chopped

4 potatoes, roughly chopped

4 sprigs of thyme

salt and freshly ground black pepper

3½ cups hot lamb stock

1 Place half the meat in a large, heavy-bottomed casserole. Top with half the barley, half the vegetables, 2 sprigs of thyme, and season well. Repeat the layers using up the remaining meat, barley, vegetables, and thyme. Season well.

2 Pour over the stock, place the casserole over high heat, and bring to a boil. Skim off any scum that rises to the surface.

3 Reduce the heat to a simmer, cover, and cook for 3 hours, stirring occasionally. Taste and adjust the seasoning, if needed. Remove from the heat and serve hot in bowls with crusty bread.

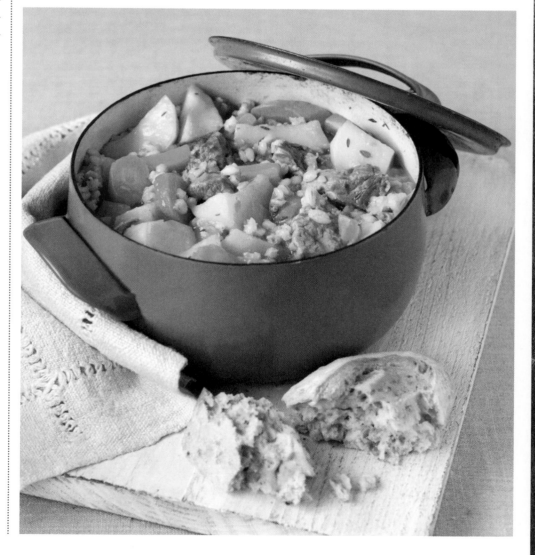

TAGINE BIL MISHMISH

This tagine "with apricots" is a take on a traditional Moroccan dish. The dried apricots and orange juice help produce its distinct flavor.

THE CUT Lamb shoulder

SERVES 4
PREP 10 mins, plus marinating
COOK 1½ hrs

1 onion, thinly sliced

1 tsp ground coriander

1 tsp ground cumin

1 tsp ground ginger

1 tsp dried thyme

2 tbsp sunflower oil or peanut oil

2lb (900g) boneless lamb shoulder, cut into 1in (2.5cm) cubes

2 tbsp all-purpose flour

1¼ cups orange juice

2 cups hot chicken stock

1 cup dried apricots

salt and freshly ground black pepper

handful of mint leaves, roughly chopped, to garnish (optional)

1 Place the onions, coriander, cumin, ginger, thyme, and 1 tablespoon of the oil in a large non-metallic bowl. Mix to combine. Then add the lamb and mix to coat in the marinade. Cover and let marinate in the fridge for at least 3 hours or overnight.

2 Preheat the oven to 325°F (160°C). Place the flour in a small bowl and stir in the orange juice until smooth. Set aside. Heat the remaining oil in a large frying pan over high heat. Add the lamb mixture and cook, stirring frequently, for about 5 minutes or until well-browned.

3 Transfer the lamb to a large heatproof tagine. Add the flour mixture and stir. Pour in the stock, return to the heat, and bring to a boil, stirring constantly. Remove from the heat, cover, and cook in the oven for 1 hour.

4 Remove from the oven and stir in the apricots. Cover and cook in the oven for another 20 minutes or until the lamb is tender. Remove and adjust the seasoning, if needed. Sprinkle with the mint leaves, if using, and serve hot.

ROASTED LAMB LOIN WITH GOAT CHEESE

The lavender in this dish provides a light aromatic touch to the robust flavor of the lamb, resulting in a beautifully balanced dish.

 Lamb loin

SERVES 4–6
PREP 25 mins, plus marinating
COOK 25 mins, plus resting

4 boneless lamb loins, about 5½oz (150g) each, trimmed

3 tsp whole-grain mustard

2 sprigs lavender leaves, roughly chopped

2 tbsp chives, roughly chopped

3½oz (100g) soft rindless goat cheese

1 tbsp heavy cream, plus extra if needed

1 tsp black peppercorns, cracked

2 tbsp canola oil, for frying

¾oz (20g) arugula leaves

12 asparagus spears, trimmed, blanched, and halved

1 tbsp flat-leaf parsley, chopped

1 tbsp oregano leaves, chopped

FOR THE CROUTONS

2 slices of ½in (1cm) thick whole-wheat bread, crusts removed

1 tbsp butter, softened

½ garlic clove, crushed

FOR THE VINAIGRETTE

3 tbsp whole-grain mustard

3 tbsp canola oil

3 tbsp apple cider vinegar

juice of 1 lemon

2 tsp honey

sea salt and freshly ground black pepper

1 Cook the lamb loins in a dry hot frying pan until well-browned. Remove from the heat and let cool. When cool enough to handle, coat the lamb in the mustard, and sprinkle with the lavender and 1 tablespoon chives. Wrap tightly in plastic wrap and chill in the fridge for 30 minutes. Preheat the oven to 375°F (190°C).

2 For the croutons, cut the bread into ½in (1cm) cubes. Melt the butter in a small pan with the garlic, add the bread, and stir until thoroughly coated. Transfer to a small baking sheet and bake for about 8 minutes.

3 For the vinaigrette, place all the ingredients in a small bowl, whisk to combine, and set aside. Place the goat cheese and cream in another bowl and use a fork to lightly beat the mixture until soft peaks form. Add more cream, if needed, to help loosen the mixture. Add the peppercorns and remaining chives, mix well, and set aside.

4 Heat the oil in a frying pan and cook the lamb for 1–2 minutes on each side, until an even crust forms. Bake on a baking sheet for 8–10 minutes. Remove and let rest for 10–15 minutes.

5 Mix the arugula, asparagus, parsley, oregano, and croutons in a bowl. Place the salad in the center of a plate and add three spoonfuls of the creamed goat cheese around it. Cut each lamb loin in half diagonally and place over the salad. Drizzle with the vinaigrette and serve hot.

LAMB FILLET WITH TOMATO AND BASIL SALAD

Garlic, chile, rosemary, and parsley combine to add piquancy to this flash-grilled marinated lamb. The colorful salad adds a refreshing punch to the dish.

 Lamb fillet

SERVES 4
PREP 15 mins, plus marinating
COOK 20 mins, plus resting

3 tbsp olive oil

1 large garlic clove, crushed

1½ tbsp finely chopped flat-leaf parsley, plus extra to garnish

sprig of rosemary, leaves picked

small pinch of dried red pepper flakes

5¾oz (165g) lamb fillet, trimmed

salt and freshly ground black pepper

drizzle of extra virgin olive oil, to serve

FOR THE SALAD

2 ripe plum tomatoes, cut into quarters lengthwise

9oz (250g) cherry tomatoes on the vine, separated but still with their stems

4½oz (125g) yellow bell or cherry tomatoes, halved

small handful of basil leaves

1 small garlic clove, crushed

½ small red onion, thinly sliced into rings

1½ tbsp extra virgin olive oil

1 Place the olive oil, garlic, parsley, rosemary, and red pepper flakes in a bowl. Season and mix well. Add the lamb and mix to coat the meat in the marinade. Chill in the fridge for at least 1 hour.

2 Heat the gas or charcoal grill. Grill the lamb over medium heat for 8–10 minutes on each side for medium-rare, or until cooked to your liking. Transfer to a plate, cover with foil, and let rest in a warm place for 20 minutes.

3 For the salad, place all the ingredients in a bowl, season, and toss gently. Slice the lamb diagonally and arrange on a platter. Scatter with the parsley and a drizzle of extra virgin olive oil. Serve hot with the salad.

LAMB CHOPS IN PAPER WITH FENNEL

These chops are enclosed in paper parcels while cooking. This lets them steam in their own juices, using minimum fat for maximum flavor.

THE CUT Lamb loin chops

SERVES 4
PREP 25–30 mins   **COOK** 35–40 mins

2¼lb (1kg) fennel bulbs, stalks and roots trimmed and any tough outer layers removed

4 tbsp olive oil

2 garlic cloves, finely chopped

1 x 14oz (400g) can chopped tomatoes

3 tbsp pastis

salt and freshly ground black pepper

4 lamb loin chops, each 1in (2.5cm) thick, tails cut and reserved, about 1lb 6oz (625g) in total

melted butter, for brushing

1 egg, beaten with ½ tsp salt, to glaze

1 Thinly slice each fennel bulb, reserving some green fronds for the garnish. Heat 2 tablespoons of oil in a frying pan over medium heat. Add the fennel and garlic and cook for 6–8 minutes, until the fennel begins to soften.

2 Add three-quarters of the tomatoes and the pastis to the pan. Season well and cook, stirring occasionally, for 20–25 minutes until the mixture is thick and most of the moisture has evaporated.

3 Meanwhile, season the lamb chops and tails with salt and pepper. Heat the remaining oil in

a separate frying pan over high heat. Cook the meat for 1–2 minutes on each side, until well-browned. Remove with a slotted spoon, place on a plate lined with paper towels, and set aside.

4 Fold a large sheet of parchment paper measuring about 12 x 15in (30 x 37.5cm) in half, and draw a curve to make a heart shape when unfolded, large enough to leave a 3in (7.5cm) border around a chop. Cut out the heart shape with scissors. Repeat to make 4 paper hearts.

5 Preheat the oven to 375°F (190°C). Open out and brush each paper heart with the butter, leaving a border of about 1in (2.5cm) unbuttered. Brush the unbuttered border of each paper heart with the beaten egg.

6 Divide the fennel mixture between the 4 paper hearts, placing it over 1 half. Top with a lamb chop and tail, spoon a little of the reserved tomato over, and top with a fennel frond. Fold the other half of the paper over the filling and stick the 2 sides of the hearts together. Make small pleats to seal the edges of the paper parcels and twist the ends to finish.

7 Place the parcels on a baking sheet and bake for 10–14 minutes until puffed up and brown. Serve the parcels hot with steamed asparagus on the side, allowing each diner to open their own parcel.

LAMB LOIN WITH RED BELL PEPPERS

A colorful dish, this tender prime cut of meat provides a sweet counterpoint to the flavor of the pepper.

THE CUT Lamb loin

SERVES 4–6
PREP 30 mins   **COOK** 15 mins

4 red bell peppers

4 lamb loins, about 7oz (200g) each, trimmed and sinew removed

salt and freshly ground black pepper

3 tbsp olive oil

½ cup white wine

1 cup lamb or chicken stock

8 tbsp butter, chilled and diced

handful of basil leaves, to garnish

1 Set a grill pan over medium heat. Wash the bell peppers and pat dry with paper towels. Roast the bell peppers, turning occasionally, for about 15 minutes or until the skin is blackened and loose in places. Let cool, then rub the skin off. Cut the peppers in quarters and discard the seeds. Chop the flesh into 1in (2.5cm) pieces and set aside.

2 Pat the lamb dry with paper towels to remove any excess blood and season well. Heat the oil in a large heavy-bottomed frying pan over high heat. Add the lamb and cook for 5 minutes until well-browned. Then reduce the heat and cook for an additional 3–4 minutes, turning over once. Remove with a slotted spoon and drain on a plate lined with paper towels. Cover and set aside in a warm place.

3 Increase the heat and pour the wine into the pan. Bring to a boil and cook until reduced by half. Add the stock and boil again until reduced by half again. Then add the peppers, heat through, and remove the pan from the heat. Stir in the butter to form a light sauce. Taste and adjust the seasoning, if needed.

4 Slice the lamb loins at an angle into 3 or 4 pieces each. Arrange on hot plates and top with the bell peppers and sauce. Garnish with a few torn basil leaves and serve hot.

RACK OF LAMB WITH PARSLEY CRUMB

Medium is considered the best way to cook a rack of lamb, with the meat at its most succulent. The bread crumbs mixed with parsley give a crisp finish to this dish.

THE CUT Rack of lamb

SERVES 6
PREP 35–40 mins   **COOK** 25–30 mins

2 racks of lamb, chine bones removed, about 1lb 10oz–2¼lb (750g–1kg) each

2 garlic cloves, cut into slivers

2 tbsp olive oil

salt and freshly ground black pepper

4 slices of white bread, crusts removed

3 tbsp butter

small bunch of flat-leaf parsley, leaves only, finely chopped

FOR THE GRAVY

½ cup white wine

1 cup lamb, beef, or chicken stock

1–2 tbsp cornstarch, mixed with a little warm water (optional)

1 Preheat the oven to 450°F (230°C). French trim both the racks of lamb (see p193). Then make several incisions in the meat using the sharp point of a knife and push the garlic slivers into the slits. Transfer the racks to a large roasting pan and place them with the ribs facing down. Wrap the bones in foil to prevent them from burning. Spoon the oil over the meat and sprinkle with salt and pepper.

2 Roast the rack in the oven for 25–30 minutes, basting with the cooking juices at least twice, until the meat shrinks away from the bones and the internal temperature of the meat reaches 140°F (60°C).

3 For the parsley crumb, place the bread in a food processor and pulse to form crumbs. Melt the butter in a frying pan, add the bread crumbs, and cook for 2–3 minutes, stirring, until just golden. Stir in the parsley and season.

4 Transfer the racks to a cutting board. Discard the foil covering the bones, then cover the racks with more foil and set aside to rest. Set the broiler at its highest setting.

5 For the gravy, discard the fat from the roasting pan. Add the wine and boil until reduced by half, stirring to dissolve the roasting juices from the bottom of the pan. Add the stock and boil for 5–7 minutes, until the gravy is well flavored. Season to taste, strain, and keep warm. For a thicker gravy, add the constarch to the sauce and mix well.

6 Press the bread crumb mixture on to the top of the racks and baste with the roasting juices. Broil the racks, bread crumb-side up, for 1–2 minutes until lightly browned, making sure the bread crumb coating does not burn. Carve and serve on warmed plates with the gravy on the side.

RACK OF LAMB WITH CELERY ROOT GALETTES

This dish makes for easy entertaining and involves no carving. Celery root is a worthy accompaniment for lamb.

THE CUT Rack of lamb

SERVES 4
PREP 30 mins   **COOK** 45–55 mins

4 tbsp butter, plus a pat of butter extra

4 x 3-rib mini racks of lamb, trimmed

1 small onion, chopped

1 carrot, finely chopped

2 bacon strips, chopped

1 garlic clove, crushed

1¼ cups red wine

1 tbsp tomato paste

1 tbsp chopped flat-leaf parsley

1¼ cups lamb stock

1 tbsp red currant or quince jelly

sea salt and freshly ground black pepper

FOR THE GALETTES

10oz (300g) waxy potatoes, such as Yukon Gold, thinly sliced

1 celery root, peeled and thinly sliced

4 tbsp butter, melted

½ tsp celery salt

freshly ground white pepper

1 tbsp chopped rosemary leaves

1 Preheat the oven to 350°F (180°C) and line a baking sheet with parchment paper. For the galettes, place the potato and celery root in a large bowl. Pour the melted butter over the top, season with the celery salt and white pepper, and sprinkle over the rosemary.

2 Place the celery root on the baking sheet in 4 overlapping disklike shapes, roughly 5in (12cm) in diameter. Place the potato in neat overlapping circles over each disk. Make sure the galettes are spaced out evenly to avoid sticking to each other during cooking. Bake for 40–45 minutes until tender.

3 For the lamb, heat half the butter in a heavy-bottomed saucepan. Sauté the onions, carrots, bacon, and garlic for 2 minutes, until soft. Add the wine, tomato paste, and parsley and cook for 5–10 minutes to reduce by half. Add the stock and jelly, and cook for 5 minutes to reduce by a third. Strain, return to the pan, beat in the remaining butter, and season.

4 Increase the temperature to 400°F (200°C). Heat the oil and a pat of butter in a frying pan. Add the racks and cook for about 5 minutes, until well-browned. Season and cook in the oven for about 10–15 minutes. To serve, place the lamb on the galettes and drizzle over the cooking juices.

BROILED LAMB CUTLETS AND EGGPLANT WITH RED CABBAGE SLAW

Red cabbage coleslaw gives this broiled lamb and eggplant dish a refreshingly different twist.

 Lamb cutlet

SERVES 4
PREP 25 mins   **COOK** 10 mins, plus resting

12 lamb cutlets, trimmed

2 tbsp olive oil

salt and freshly ground black pepper

1 eggplant, about 10oz (300g), thinly sliced lengthwise

½ small red cabbage

3½oz (100g) thin green beans, trimmed, blanched, and thinly sliced diagonally

1 small cucumber, thinly sliced or shaved lengthwise

1 small red onion, thinly sliced in rounds

2 celery stalks, peeled and thinly sliced diagonally

⅓ cup hazelnuts, chopped

small handful of chives, snipped

2 tbsp extra virgin olive oil

1 tsp balsamic vinegar

1 Set the broiler at its medium setting. Brush the lamb cutlets with oil and season with salt and pepper. Broil the cutlets for 3–5 minutes on each side or until cooked to your liking. Remove from the heat, transfer to a plate, and set aside to rest in a warm place.

2 Increase the broiler to high. Brush the eggplant slices with a little oil and season with pepper. Broil the eggplant for about 3 minutes on each side until golden. Remove from the heat and transfer to the plate along with the lamb.

3 Finely slice or shred the red cabbage and place in a large bowl. Add all the remaining ingredients, season with salt and pepper, and toss gently. Serve the lamb cutlets and the eggplant slices with the cabbage coleslaw on the side.

SLOW-COOKED LAMB RIBS WITH FATTOUSH SALAD

The spices in the marinade cut through the meaty richness of the ribs from the lamb breasts.

 Lamb breast ribs

SERVES 4–6
PREP 30 mins, plus marinating
COOK 3½–4 hrs

FOR THE RIBS

4½lb (2kg) lamb ribs from the breast

1 cup white wine

2 garlic cloves, crushed

3 cinnamon sticks

1 tsp salt

2 star anise

6 black peppercorns

FOR THE MARINADE

1 tsp cumin seeds

2 tsp coriander seeds

3 cardamom pods, seeds removed

1 tsp ground cinnamon

½ tsp ground allspice

1 red chile, seeded and chopped

2 garlic cloves, crushed

grated zest and juice of 1 lemon

½ cup olive oil

2 tbsp honey

handful of cilantro leaves, chopped

FOR THE SALAD

1 cucumber, peeled, halved lengthwise, seeded, and diced

bunch of radishes, trimmed and thinly sliced

1 red onion, finely chopped

7oz (200g) cherry tomatoes, quartered

seeds from 1 small pomegranate

bunch of flat-leaf parsley, leaves only, roughly chopped

1 tbsp sumac powder, plus extra if needed

juice of 1 lemon, plus extra if needed

sea salt and freshly ground black pepper

2 pita breads

1 tbsp olive oil

1 Preheat the oven to 400°F (200°C). For the lamb, place all the ingredients in a large roasting pan, add just enough water to cover, and bring to a boil. Cover tightly and bake in the oven for 2 hours or until tender. Drain and cool. Discard the cooking liquid.

2 Heat a frying pan over medium heat. Add the cumin, coriander, and cardamom seeds and roast, stirring constantly, until fragrant. Remove from the heat, cool slightly, and crush in a mortar and pestle.

3 Transfer the crushed spices to a large nonmetallic bowl. Add all the remaining marinade ingredients and mix well. Cut the lamb into single ribs and add to the bowl. Mix to coat the ribs in the marinade. Chill in the fridge for at least two hours or overnight.

4 Preheat the oven to 275°F (140°C). Place the lamb ribs in a large roasting pan, cover with foil, and roast in the oven for 1 hour. Then remove from the oven, take off the foil, and turn the ribs over. Return the pan to the oven for an additional 30 minutes. Then remove from the heat.

5 For the salad, place all the ingredients, except the pita bread and oil, in a large bowl. Heat a frying pan over medium heat and warm the pita bread on both sides. Remove from the pan, cut it into small cubes, and add to the salad. Then add the oil and toss to coat. Taste and add more lemon juice or sumac powder, if desired. Place the ribs on a plate and serve hot with the salad and flatbread.

THAI-SPICED LAMB SALAD WITH LIME DRESSING

The bright, vibrant colors of this spicy lamb salad really sing out, making it perfect for a summer lunch.

THE CUT Lamb chump or leg

SERVES 4
PREP 10 mins **COOK** 7–10 mins, plus resting

grated zest and juice of 5 limes

3 tsp palm sugar or brown sugar

1 red chile, seeded and finely chopped

½ tsp Thai fish sauce

1 tsp tamarind

3 tbsp peanut oil

1lb 2oz (500g) boneless lamb chump or leg

3½oz (100g) Thai glass noodles, cooked

3 shallots, finely sliced

handful of cilantro leaves

12 Thai basil leaves

small handful of mint leaves

⅓ cup roasted peanuts, coarsely ground

1 For the dressing, place the lime zest and juice, sugar, chile, fish sauce, tamarind, and 1 tablespoon of oil in a small bowl. Mix to combine all the ingredients and dissolve the sugar. Set aside.

2 Cut the lamb into 6 equal strips. Heat a grill pan and add the remaining oil. Sear the lamb for about 2 minutes on each side. Do not overcook the lamb, it should be rare. Leave to rest for 3 minutes.

3 Slice the lamb thinly and place in a large bowl. Add the glass noodles, dressing, shallots, herbs, and peanuts, and toss to combine. Divide the salad between 4 plates and serve immediately.

HAY-ROASTED LEG OF LAMB WITH ANCHOVIES AND CAPER SAUCE

Cooking with hay imparts a wonderful grassy and smoky flavor to the meat. It also keeps the meat succulent.

THE CUT Leg of lamb

SERVES 8–10
PREP 30 mins, plus chilling and resting
COOK 2 hrs, plus resting

2 handfuls of clean hay

16 cups white bread flour

6½lb (3–3.5kg) leg of lamb, bone left whole

10 good quality anchovies in salt, rinsed

8 garlic cloves, cut into slivers

2 tbsp butter, melted, plus extra for greasing

grated zest of 1 lemon and juice of half a lemon

sea salt and freshly ground black pepper

bunch of thyme

bunch of rosemary

1 egg, beaten

FOR THE SAUCE

2 cups chicken stock

2–3 tbsp small capers in vinegar, drained and chopped

splash of red wine or sherry vinegar

2 large handfuls of mint leaves, finely chopped

large pat of butter, chilled and diced

2 tsp red currant jelly

1–2 tsp arrowroot, mixed with a little water (optional)

1 Preheat the oven to 350°F (180°C) and grease a large baking sheet. Soak the hay in cold water for 15 minutes. Place the flour in a mixer, add 3½ cups water, and pulse for about 5 minutes to form a dough. Chill the dough in the fridge for 30 minutes.

2 Make small slits all over the leg of lamb. Slice the anchovies in half and use to wrap the garlic slivers. Insert them into the slits on the lamb.

3 Divide the dough into 2 portions and roll each out to a size large enough to cover the lamb and about ½in (1cm) in thickness. Lay one pastry piece over the baking sheet. Squeeze out the water from the hay, and spread it over the pastry, leaving a border of at least 2in (5cm) around the edges.

4 Place the lamb on the hay and brush with the melted butter. Sprinkle the lemon zest and juice over the lamb. Season and place the herbs on top. Lift the hay up and wrap evenly around the lamb. Brush the edges of the dough with cold water. Place the second piece of pastry on top of the lamb, making sure the bone protrudes out to allow heat to penetrate into the center of the meat. Pinch, roll, and crimp the edge of the dough together. Brush with the beaten egg and leave to rest for about 20 minutes.

5 Place the lamb in the oven and bake for about 2 hours. Then remove from the oven and check for doneness. The internal temperature of the meat should be 140°F (60°C) for medium and 150°F (65°C) for well-done. Cook for an additional 10–15 minutes, if needed, then remove from the heat. Leave to rest for 30 minutes, then crack open the crust, remove the hay, and pour out any juice or fat into a small saucepan.

6 For the sauce, heat the fat and juice in a saucepan over medium heat. Add the stock, and stir to deglaze. Cook the sauce until reduced by half. Then remove from the heat and strain into a bowl. Return the sauce to the pan and cook over medium heat for 3–4 minutes.

7 Add the capers, vinegar, mint, butter, and red currant jelly. Stir well and season to taste with salt and pepper. If the sauce tastes a little bitter, add a bit more of the red currant jelly. If the sauce seems too thin, thicken it with a little arrowroot. Place the lamb on a large platter, pour over the caper sauce and serve hot.

ON THE SIDE

This dish can be served with mashed cannellini and rosemary beans, boulangerie potatoes, or dauphinoise gratin. Buttered kale or spinach are also great accompaniments.

LAMB CUTLETS WITH BUTTERNUT SQUASH, BEANS, AND MINT

The sweet, dense orange flesh of butternut squash marries well with the tender lamb in this autumnal dish.

THE CUT Lamb cutlets

SERVES 4
PREP 15 mins   **COOK** 30 mins

2 tbsp olive oil

pinch of five-spice powder

pinch of cayenne pepper

salt and freshly ground black pepper

8 lamb cutlets

1 butternut squash, halved, seeded, peeled, and roughly chopped

10 cherry tomatoes

4½oz (125g) thin green beans, trimmed

handful of mint leaves, roughly chopped

1 Preheat the oven to 400°F (200°C). Pour half the oil in a small bowl and add the five-spice powder and cayenne pepper. Season with salt and pepper and mix well.

2 Brush the cutlets with half the spice mix and place in a roasting pan. Add the squash to the remaining spice mix and toss lightly to coat. Add the squash to the pan. Cook in the oven for 20–30 minutes, or until the lamb is cooked to your liking and the squash is golden.

3 Meanwhile, place the tomatoes and beans in a bowl and toss with the remaining oil. Add to the roasting pan for the last 10 minutes of cooking so they are just lightly charred in places. Remove from the heat, sprinkle with mint, and serve hot.

VARIATION

Pork chops with sweet potatoes, beans, and thyme
Use 4 lean pork chops instead of the lamb cutlets and 1 teaspoon of Cajun spice instead of the five-spice powder and cayenne pepper. Substitute 1 large sweet potato, peeled and cut into chunks, instead of the butternut squash. Cook for 30–40 minutes until tender, adding the cherry tomatoes and beans for the last 10 minutes of cooking, as before. Sprinkle with a handful of thyme leaves instead of mint and serve hot.

GRILLED LAMB WITH MINT HOLLANDAISE

In this recipe, a herby hollandaise sauce adds a lovely, buttery contrast to the crispy meat.

THE CUT Lamb leg steak

SERVES 4
PREP 30 mins · **COOK** 45 mins, plus resting

9oz (250g) asparagus, cleaned and trimmed

7oz (200g) zucchini, cut diagonally

1 large red bell pepper, seeded and cut into eight pieces

1 red onion, cut into eight wedges

4 tbsp olive oil

4 lamb leg steaks, about 7oz (200g) each

2 large garlic cloves, cut in half

sea salt and freshly ground black pepper

FOR THE HOLLANDAISE

6 black peppercorns, coarsely crushed

1 shallot, finely chopped

$\frac{2}{3}$ cup white wine

$\frac{1}{2}$ cup white wine vinegar

4 egg yolks

18 tbsp unsalted butter, chilled and diced

2 tbsp chopped mint leaves

1 Preheat the broiler to its highest setting. Place the vegetables in a bowl, add 3 tablespoons of oil, and toss to coat. Season and broil them until charred and just soft. Adjust the seasoning if needed, set aside, and keep warm.

2 Rub the lamb steaks with the garlic and the remaining oil. Cook the steaks for about 4–5 minutes on each side, until pink. Let rest for 3–5 minutes in a warm place.

3 For the hollandaise, place the peppercorns, shallots, wine, and vinegar in a large saucepan over medium heat. Bring to a boil and boil rapidly, until reduced to 1 tablespoon of liquid.

4 Meanwhile, place a stainless steel or glass bowl over a saucepan of simmering water. Strain the reduced vinegar mixture into the bowl, discarding the peppercorns and shallots. Whisk in the egg yolks, until thick and just warm. Do not overheat the yolks or they will scramble.

5 Add the butter slowly, whisking to make a thick, smooth sauce. Season, add the mint, and spoon the sauce into bowls. Slice the steaks and serve with the vegetables and mint hollandaise.

LAMB WITH LEMON AND OLIVES

Using whole lemons adds a sharpness of flavor to this dish and the olives give it a nice Mediterranean touch.

THE CUT Leg of lamb

SERVES 4
PREP 10 mins   **COOK** 35 mins, plus resting

3 tbsp olive oil

bunch of scallions, trimmed and finely chopped

1lb 2oz (500g) boneless lean leg of lamb, cut into bite-sized pieces

6 garlic cloves, finely sliced

1 lemon, cut into eighths

1 tsp chopped rosemary leaves

handful of flat-leaf parsley, chopped

1 tsp paprika

3 tbsp green olives, pitted

salt and freshly ground black pepper

1 Preheat the oven to 400°F (200°C). Heat the oil in a frying pan over medium heat. Add the scallions and cook for 5 minutes, or until softened. Then add the lamb and cook, stirring occasionally, for 5 minutes, or until no longer pink.

2 Add the garlic and lemon and cook for 1 minute, then add the remaining ingredients and cook for about 2 minutes, stirring well. Transfer the mixture to a small baking dish, packing it in tightly. Add 2 tablespoons of water, mix well, and then bake for 20 minutes.

3 Remove from the oven and let rest for about 10 minutes. Serve with fresh crusty bread and a crisp green salad.

BARBECUED MOROCCAN LEG OF LAMB

A favorite barbecue food, leg of lamb makes a perfect grilled roast. Butterfly it for extra flavor.

THE CUT Leg of lamb

SERVES 4
PREP 20 mins, plus marinating and chilling
COOK 40 mins, plus sealing

2 tsp ground cinnamon

3 tsp ground coriander

3 tsp ground cumin

¼ cup harissa paste

1 tbsp ground turmeric

4 garlic cloves, crushed

½ cup olive oil, plus 2 tbsp extra for frying

¼ cup finely chopped flat-leaf parsley

2 large handfuls of cilantro, finely chopped

¼ cup lemon juice and zest of 1 lemon

3lb 3oz–4½lb (1½–2kg) boneless leg of lamb

2 cups full-fat yogurt

FOR THE COUSCOUS

1 cup orange juice

¼ cup lemon juice

2 tsp ground cinnamon

2 cups instant couscous

5 tbsp butter

3 tbsp olive oil

7oz (200g) frozen peas, blanched for 2 minutes

1 x 14oz (400g) can chickpeas, rinsed and drained

1 cup pistachios, chopped

⅓ cup currants

6 scallions, trimmed and finely sliced

3 tbsp chopped flat-leaf parsley

3 tbsp chopped cilantro

3 tbsp chopped mint leaves

sea salt and freshly ground black pepper

1 In a small bowl, mix all the spices, half the turmeric, and half the garlic. Pour the oil into a large bowl and add half the spice mix. Then add the parsley, cilantro, lemon juice, and zest. Mix well, then add the lamb, coating it in the spice mix. Chill for 1 hour.

2 Preheat the oven to 375°F (190°C). Place the yogurt in a large bowl, add the remaining spice mix, and stir to combine. Cover and chill in the fridge for about 1 hour. Remove the lamb from the marinade. Heat the oil in a frying pan. Add the lamb and cook for 3–4 minutes on both sides, until well-browned.

3 Transfer the lamb to a large ovenproof dish and cook in the oven for about 40 minutes. Preheat the grill to 375°F (190°C). Remove the lamb from the oven and cook on the grill for another 15–20 minutes, depending on your taste. Then remove from the heat, cover with foil, and let rest for 15 minutes.

4 For the couscous, pour the orange and lemon juice into a large measuring cup and add enough water to increase the total quantity to 2 cups. Pour into a saucepan, add the cinnamon, and bring to a boil. Remove from the heat. Add the couscous and stir to mix. Cover and leave for 5 minutes, then add the butter and olive oil and use a fork to fluff up the couscous.

5 Add the peas, chickpeas, pistachios, currants, scallions, parsley, cilantro, and mint to the couscous. Mix well and season with salt and pepper. Slice the meat across the grain and arrange on a serving dish. Serve hot with the couscous and spicy yogurt along with some arugula.

VARIATION

Barbecued Moroccan goat Use a leg of goat in place of the lamb and pine nuts in place of the pistachios. Cook as above and serve warm with the spicy yogurt and couscous.

LEG OF LAMB COOKED IN RED WINE

The mushrooms and tomatoes make a great base for the luscious sauce in this perfect family dish.

THE CUT Leg of lamb

SERVES 6–8
PREP 20 mins   **COOK** 2 hrs, plus resting

5lb (2.25kg) boneless leg of lamb

2 garlic cloves, cut into thin slivers

salt and freshly ground black pepper

1 large onion, thinly sliced

2 tbsp olive oil

1 x 14oz (400g) can chopped tomatoes

½ tsp dried oregano

½ tsp dried thyme

2 bay leaves

3¼ cups red burgundy wine

2 tsp butter

8oz (225g) button mushrooms, sliced

1 Preheat the oven to 450°F (230°C). Score the lamb and slide in the slivers of garlic and the salt and pepper. Scatter the onion over the bottom of a roasting pan, place the lamb on top, and pour over the oil. Roast in the oven for 20 minutes.

2 Remove the pan from the oven and reduce the heat to 350°F (180°C). Arrange the tomatoes around the lamb, add the herbs, and pour in half the wine. Return the pan to the oven and cook for another 1 hour.

3 Heat the butter in a frying pan, add the mushrooms, and sauté for 2–3 minutes until lightly browned. Add to the pan and pour in the remaining wine. Return the pan to the oven and cook for 30 minutes.

4 Remove the lamb from the roasting pan, cover with foil, and let rest for 15 minutes. Place the roasting pan over medium heat and cook the sauce for 10 minutes, stirring, to reduce. Remove from the heat and strain into a saucepan, pushing the vegetables through with the back of a ladle.

5 Discard any leftover vegetables and return the pan to the heat. Reduce the heat to a simmer and cook, stirring occasionally, until the sauce has thickened. Season with salt and pepper and remove from the heat. Carve the lamb and arrange on a serving dish. Serve hot with the sauce, roasted carrots, and boiled potatoes.

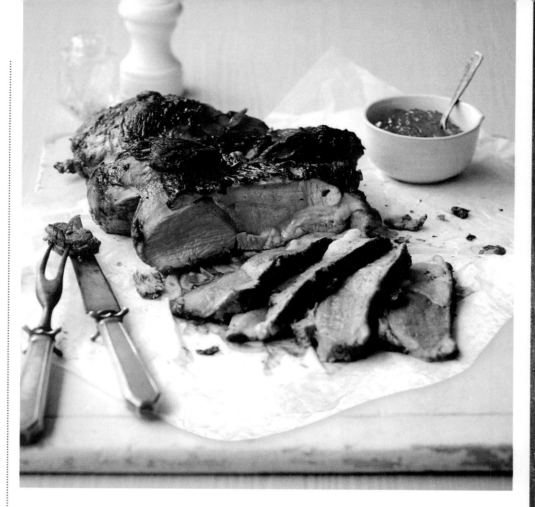

BUTTERFLIED LEG OF LAMB

A fruity herb-based marinade and boneless meat makes for very quick cooking and easy serving.

THE CUT Leg of lamb

SERVES 6–8
PREP 30 mins, plus marinating
COOK 40 mins, plus resting

¾ cup red wine

3 tbsp marmalade

2 tbsp red wine vinegar

1 small onion, finely chopped

2 tsp dried marjoram

2 tsp dried rosemary

1 large bay leaf

1 tsp sea salt

¼ tsp ground ginger

2 garlic cloves, crushed

6½lb (3kg) boneless leg of lamb, butterflied (see p192)

1 For the marinade, place all the ingredients except the meat in a saucepan and simmer for 15 minutes over low heat. Remove from the heat and let cool slightly. Place the lamb skin-side down in a large, lidded plastic container and pour the marinade over it. Cover and let marinate in a cool place for 8 hours, turning occasionally.

2 Set a large grill pan or barbecue to medium heat. Pat the meat dry with paper towels and place it, fat-side down, on the pan. Cook the lamb for 10 minutes, then turn over and brush with a little marinade. Cook for another 10 minutes, then turn and brush with the marinade once more. Cook for another 20 minutes, turning and basting with the marinade.

3 Remove from the heat and let rest for at least 15 minutes. Carve the meat into slices and serve with hot pepper jelly and a crisp salad.

VARIATION

Butterflied leg of roe deer Use a butterflied leg of roe deer in place of the lamb, redcurrant jelly in place of marmalade, and 4 crushed juniper berries in place of the marjoram. Cook as above and serve hot.

ROAST LEG OF LAMB

In this aromatic roast dish, the juices from the lamb provide the basis for the simple yet flavorful gravy that accompanies it. See p192 for how to debone a leg.

SERVES 6–8
PREP 40 mins
COOK 1½ hrs

5lb (2.25kg) leg of lamb, bones removed and reserved

1 onion, roughly chopped

1 large carrot, roughly chopped

2 garlic cloves, unpeeled and crushed

3 sprigs of thyme

3 tbsp olive oil

salt and freshly ground black pepper

2 tsp chopped rosemary

1 tsp chopped marjoram

1 tsp tomato paste

1 Preheat the oven to 400°F (200°C). Place the bones, onions, carrots, garlic, and thyme in a large roasting pan. Drizzle with 2 tablespoons of oil and toss to coat the bones and vegetables. Transfer the roasting pan to the oven and roast for 10 minutes, or until browned.

2 Meanwhile, season the lamb and rub with the remaining oil. Remove the roasting pan from the oven and place the lamb on the roasted bone and vegetable mixture. Return the pan to the oven to roast for 40 minutes, occasionally basting the meat with the cooking juices.

3 Remove from the oven and pour out one-third of the fat. Add 2 cups water and sprinkle with the herbs. Reduce the temperature to 350°F (180°C), return the pan to the oven, and cook for 40 minutes, occasionally basting with the cooking juices. Remove and transfer the lamb to a serving dish. Cover with foil and set aside to rest in a warm place.

4 Place the roasting pan over medium heat, add the tomato paste, and scrape up the pan juices. Reduce the heat and simmer for 5 minutes, until reduced to a light gravy. Strain, discarding the bones and pushing the vegetables through the sieve to add texture to the sauce. Taste and adjust the seasoning if needed. Carve the meat and serve along with the gravy.

TURKISH LAMB AND POMEGRANATE PILAF

Fragrant and full of color, this pilaf has layers of flavor. Add in different fruits and nuts for variety—dates and almonds are often used in Turkish cuisine.

THE CUT Leg of lamb

SERVES 4–6
PREP 15 mins   **COOK** 1 hr

2 tbsp olive oil, plus extra for drizzling

1½lb (675g) leg of lamb, cut into bite-size pieces

1 onion, finely chopped

salt and freshly ground black pepper

3 garlic cloves, finely chopped

1 green chile, seeded and finely sliced

1 tsp dried mint

1 tsp ground cinnamon

⅓ cup raisins or golden raisins

12oz (350g) instant basmati rice

3 cups hot lamb stock

½ cup hazelnuts, toasted and roughly chopped

small handful of dill, finely chopped

seeds from 1 pomegranate

2½oz (75g) feta cheese, crumbled (optional)

1 Heat the oil in a large heatproof casserole over medium-high heat, add the lamb, in batches, and cook for 6–8 minutes until browned on all sides. Remove with a slotted spoon and set aside.

2 Add the onions to the casserole and cook over medium heat for 3–4 minutes until soft. Season with salt and pepper, stir in the garlic, chile, mint, and cinnamon, and cook for another 2 minutes. Stir in the raisins.

3 Add the rice and stir through, so all the grains are coated and the juices soaked up. Return the lamb to the casserole, pour in the stock, and reduce to a simmer. Partially cover and cook for 30–40 minutes, adding a little more hot stock if it begins to dry out. Taste and adjust the seasoning, then stir in the hazelnuts and dill, and scatter with the pomegranate seeds. Top with crumbled feta (if using) and serve hot.

LAMB SHANKS WITH BUTTER BEANS AND CELERY

Pot-roasting keeps the meat moist and the creamy beans add a deep contrast of flavor.

THE CUT Lamb shanks

SERVES 4
PREP 20 mins, plus overnight soaking
COOK 1½ hrs

2 tbsp olive oil

4 bone-in lamb shanks, about 7oz (200g) each

salt and freshly ground black pepper

1 onion, cut in 4 circles

1 cup lamb or chicken stock

8oz (225g) dried butter beans, soaked overnight

1 garlic clove

2 cups whole milk

grated nutmeg

2 tbsp heavy cream

9 celery stalks, diced

1 tbsp chopped flat-leaf parsley

1 Heat the oil in a large, heatproof casserole. Season the lamb shanks, add to the casserole, and cook for 6–8 minutes, until well-browned. Remove with a slotted spoon. Pour out and reserve 1 tablespoon of fat from the pan.

2 Preheat the oven to 350°F (180°C). Spread the onion circles over the bottom of the casserole and place a lamb shank on each onion. Pour in the stock and bring to a boil. Cover and place in the oven for 1 hour 15 minutes, turning the shanks frequently, until the meat is tender.

3 Pinch the beans out of their skins. Discard the skins, rinse the beans, and drain. Place in a large, lidded saucepan. Add the garlic and milk and bring to simmering point, but do not boil. Reduce the heat to a simmer, add the nutmeg, and season with salt and pepper. Cover partially and cook for about 1 hour, stirring occasionally, until the beans are tender and the milk has reduced. Pour in the cream.

4 In a large frying pan, heat the remaining oil and the reserved lamb fat. Add the celery and cook for 4–5 minutes, until lightly browned. Stir into the bean mixture with the parsley. Spread the bean mixture at the bottom of 4 hot bowls. Place a shank over the beans and pour over some of the cooking juices from the casserole. Serve hot.

MOROCCAN MUTTON WITH PRUNES AND APRICOTS

The unusual combination of meat with honey and dried fruits, and the addition of the nutty flavored Argan oil lends exotic flavors to this traditional Berber dish.

THE CUT Mutton shoulder

SERVES 4
PREP 15 mins, plus soaking   **COOK** 3½ hrs

½ cup dried prunes, pitted

½ cup dried apricots, pitted and halved

⅔ cup black tea

2 tbsp argan oil or vegetable oil

2¼lb (1kg) boneless mutton shoulder, cut into cubes

2 onions, finely chopped

½ tsp ground turmeric

½ tsp ground ginger

1½ tsp ground cinnamon

½ tsp ground cumin

½ tsp Ras el hanout powder

2 tbsp honey

¾ cup lamb or chicken stock

4 tbsp Greek-style yogurt

1 tbsp chopped mint

½ cup sliced almonds, toasted

1 Preheat the oven to 325°F (160°C). In a small bowl, place the prunes and apricots and pour the black tea over them. Cover and leave to soak for 30 minutes.

2 Heat 1 tablespoon of oil in a large, heatproof casserole over medium heat. Add the meat and cook for 7–8 minutes, until well-browned. Remove with a slotted spoon and set aside.

3 Pour the remaining oil into the pan. Add the onions and cook, stirring occasionally, for 4–5 minutes, until lightly colored and softened. Stir in the spices and cook for 2 minutes more.

4 Return the meat to the casserole. Add the honey, stock, and the dried fruits with their soaking liquid. Stir until well-combined and bring to a simmer, but do not boil. Cover and cook in the oven for 3 hours or until the meat is tender.

5 Remove from the oven. Place the yogurt and mint in a small bowl and mix well to combine. To serve, sprinkle the almonds over the meat and serve with a dollop of the yogurt and couscous.

MUTTON HAM

An unusual alternative to ham from a pig, this leaner, tender ham is a great winter filler.

THE CUT Leg of mutton

SERVES 10
PREP 30 mins, plus 7 days curing
COOK 3–4 hrs, plus overnight resting and cooling

1 cup sea salt

½ cup dark brown sugar

2 tsp Prague powder No.2 curing salt

1 tbsp coriander seeds

1 tbsp allspice berries

5 juniper berries

12–13 black peppercorns

1 bone-in leg of mutton, about 5½lb (2.5kg)

1 leek, chopped

1 large onion, unpeeled and cut in 2 pieces lengthwise

4 carrots, chopped

6 cloves, stuck into the onion pieces

2 celery stalks, chopped

bunch of parsley

sprig of thyme

¾ cup molasses

1 In a bowl, mix the salt, sugar, and curing salt. Use a mortar and pestle to grind the coriander seeds, allspice berries, juniper berries, and 10 peppercorns to a coarse paste. Add to the salt and sugar mixture.

2 Place the mutton leg in a large ceramic dish and thoroughly rub the spice mix all over. Cover with a dish towel and place in a cool place. Leave to cure for 7 days, turning the leg daily and rubbing in any liquid it yields. Use vinyl gloves to handle the meat to prevent it from spoiling.

3 Rinse the mutton in cold water to remove excess salt. Place the vegetables, herbs, and remaining peppercorns in a large stock pot. Add the ham and molasses and pour in just enough water to cover the meat. Bring to a boil, then reduce the heat, and simmer for 3–4 hours.

4 Remove from the heat and leave to cool in the liquid for 1 hour or until completely cold. Remove the ham from the pot and discard the rest. Wrap the ham tightly with a dish towel and place on a plastic tray. Cover with another plastic tray and weigh it down with 2¼lb (1kg) weights. Leave overnight. Slice and serve with a salad, pickle, and baked potatoes.

MUTTON CURRY WITH COCONUT AND GINGER

The combination of coconut and cashew nuts in this vibrantly flavored dish gives it contrasting textures.

THE CUT Mutton shoulder

SERVES 6
PREP 15–20 mins   **COOK** 1½–2 hrs

1 cup unsweetened dried coconut

2 tsp chopped fresh ginger

1 onion, chopped

1 garlic clove

4 red chiles, seeded and chopped

1 tbsp chopped cilantro leaves

1 tsp ground turmeric

2 tbsp plain yogurt

1 tbsp coriander seeds

1 tbsp sesame seeds

2 tbsp vegetable oil

2lb (900g) mutton shoulder, cut into cubes

¼ tsp grated ginger

4oz (115g) cashews, finely chopped

1 Use a mortar and pestle to grind the coconut, chopped ginger, onions, garlic, chiles, coriander, and turmeric to form a paste. Place in a bowl, add the yogurt, and mix to combine. Set aside.

2 Heat a lidded, heavy-bottomed saucepan over medium-low heat. Place the coriander and sesame seeds on a cutting board and crush them with the back of a spoon. Add to the pan and roast for 2–3 minutes, stirring lightly, until browned. Remove from the heat and set aside.

3 Clean the pan with paper towels. Add the oil and place over medium heat. Add the meat to the pan, sprinkle over the grated ginger, and mix. Cook for 3–4 minutes until well-browned. Then add the yogurt and spice paste, stir to coat, and cook for 2–3 minutes.

4 Add the roasted spices and just enough water to cover the meat. Reduce the heat, cover, and simmer for 1½ hours or until the mutton is tender. Serve over rice, sprinkled with cashews.

KASHMIRI MUTTON WITH TURNIPS

Slow cooking the meat results in a succulent and flavorful dish. Keep the meat and turnips the same size for added appeal.

THE CUT Leg of mutton

SERVES 6
PREP 15 mins **COOK** 2 hrs

2lb (900g) lean leg of mutton, cut into cubes

2 tbsp vegetable oil

1 tsp grated ginger

¾ cup full-fat yogurt

4 small turnips, quartered

¼ tsp salt

1 tsp garam masala

1 tsp ground turmeric

½ tsp chili powder

2 tsp ground coriander

1 tsp sugar

2 tbsp chopped cilantro leaves

1 Pat the meat dry with paper towels to remove any excess blood. Heat the oil in a large casserole over high heat. Add the mutton, sprinkle over the ginger, and cook for about 5 minutes, until well-browned. Do this in batches to avoid overcrowding the pan.

2 Add the yogurt and stir to coat the meat. Allow to scorch a little for added flavor in the curry. Add a little water, then stir in the turnips, salt, and spices. Then add just enough water to cover and bring to a boil.

3 Reduce the heat to a simmer, cover, and cook for about 1½ hours, until tender. Stir in the sugar and half the cilantro. Garnish with the remaining cilantro and serve with chapattis to soak up the sauce.

GIGOT OF MUTTON COOKED IN MILK WITH CAPERS

The luscious sauce enriched with savory cooking juices and herbs is a real winter warmer. This dish is great served with mashed potatoes and peas.

THE CUT Leg of mutton

SERVES 8
PREP 30 mins **COOK** 2–3 hrs, plus resting

5½lb (2.5kg) boneless leg of mutton, trimmed

3½ cups whole milk

2 large onions, studded with 2 cloves each

2 carrots, chopped

sprig of rosemary

1 bay leaf

6 black peppercorns

sprig of thyme

FOR THE SAUCE

2 tbsp butter

2 tbsp all-purpose flour

3 tbsp capers in vinegar, plus a little of the vinegar juice

2 tbsp chopped flat-leaf parsley

salt and freshly ground black pepper

1 Place the leg of mutton in a large stock pot and pour the milk over. Add the vegetables and herbs to the pan, cover, and bring to a boil. Reduce the heat to a simmer and cook for 2–3 hours, until the meat is cooked through and the juices run clear when the meat is pierced at its thickest point. Remove the meat from the pot and set aside to rest in a warm place.

2 For the sauce, strain the cooking stock. Pour half the milky stock back into the pot, place it over low heat, and simmer for 10 minutes. Melt the butter in a separate saucepan and stir in the flour. Cook gently for 1–2 minutes. Add the hot milky stock, a little at a time, and stir slowly until it forms a smooth sauce. Then add the capers and parsley, and adjust the seasoning. To serve, cut thick slices from the mutton leg and arrange on a platter with the sauce poured over.

NO WASTE!

Freeze the remaining cooking stock from the sauce. Use ¾ of the milky stock along with 1 cup water to prepare caper sauce as above. Pour this sauce over left over roast lamb and serve hot.

SCANDINAVIAN LEG OF MUTTON WITH HONEY MUSTARD AND ROOTS

A grand dish, this is simple to prepare as all the vegetables are cooked with the meat.

THE CUT Leg of mutton

SERVES 6–8
PREP 30 mins
COOK 1 hr 50 mins, plus resting

6lb (2.7 kg) leg of mutton

1lb (450g) parsnips, cut into even-sized chunks

1lb (450g) kohlrabi, cut into even-sized chunks

1lb 2oz (500g) red-skinned potatoes, quartered

1lb (450g) carrots, cut into even-sized chunks

4 onions, quartered

1 whole garlic bulb, unpeeled and crushed with the back of a knife

1 cup dark beer

1 cup lamb or beef stock

1 tbsp olive oil

sea salt

2 tsp chopped rosemary

3 tbsp Swedish honey mustard

1 Preheat the oven to 400°F (200°C). Remove the leg of mutton from the fridge at least 2 hours before cooking, to bring it up to room temperature.

2 Place all the vegetables and garlic in a large, deep-roasting pan. Pour in the beer, stock, and oil. Sprinkle over the salt and rosemary.

3 Pat the leg dry with paper towels and rub with some salt and the honey mustard. Place it on a rack above the vegetables so that the fat and juices run into the roasting pan.

4 Transfer the pan to the oven and roast for 20 minutes, then reduce the heat to 350°F (180°C) and cook for an additional 1½ hours or until the internal temperature of the meat reaches 140°F (60°C).

5 Remove from the oven and leave the meat to rest for at least 20 minutes in a warm place. Arrange the vegetables in a large serving tray. Carve the meat into slices and serve on top of the vegetables. Squeeze the garlic out from the skins and spread over the meat.

GOAT STEW WITH CABBAGE

The meat and cabbage, flavored with caraway, are cooked separately and combined just before serving.

THE CUT Leg of goat

SERVES 4
PREP 30 mins   **COOK** 2 hrs

3 tbsp vegetable oil

3 tsp butter

2¼lb (1kg) leg of goat, cut into cubes

1 large onion, roughly chopped

2 garlic cloves, chopped

2 tsp tomato paste

¼ tsp ground cloves

¼ tsp grated ginger

pinch of cayenne pepper

4 carrots, thickly sliced

juice of 1 lemon

2 cups lamb or beef stock

2 sprigs of thyme

1 bay leaf

1 cabbage

salt

2 tsp caraway seeds

1 Heat the oil and 1 teaspoon of the butter in a large heatproof casserole. Add the meat, and cook until well-browned. Then add the onions and garlic, and cook until the onions have softened.

2 Stir in the tomato paste, cloves, ginger, and cayenne pepper, and cook for 1 more minute. Then add the carrots, lemon juice, stock, thyme, and bay leaf, and bring to a boil. Reduce the heat, cover, and simmer for 1½–2 hours.

3 Meanwhile, cut the cabbage into quarters, remove the core, and shred very finely. Place in a large bowl of salted water for half an hour. Then drain all but a few tablespoons of the cabbage soaking water.

4 Melt 2 teaspoons of butter in a large saucepan over medium heat. Add the cabbage and stir to coat in the butter. Cover and steam for 4 minutes. Then stir in the caraway seeds and cook, uncovered, until all the water has evaporated.

5 Remove from the heat and discard the thyme and bay leaf. Mix the goat stew and cabbage together and serve hot in bowls.

HONEYED GOAT SHOULDER WITH FLAGEOLET BEANS

The creamy texture of the beans perfectly complements the sweetness of the meat, which has a subtle herby flavor.

THE CUT Goat shoulder

SERVES 4
PREP 5 mins   **COOK** 2 hrs, plus resting

juice and zest of 1 lemon

2 tbsp honey

1 tsp olive oil

½ garlic bulb

2¼lb (1kg) goat shoulder

sea salt and freshly ground black pepper

⅔ cup chicken or vegetable stock, plus extra if needed

4 sprigs each of thyme, rosemary, and oregano

FOR THE FLAGEOLET BEANS

2 tbsp butter

1 onion, finely chopped

1 garlic clove, finely chopped

2 x 14oz (400g) can flageolet beans, drained

1 tsp rosemary leaves, finely chopped

½ cup chicken or vegetable stock

3 tbsp heavy cream

1 Preheat the oven to 350°F (180°C). Line a roasting pan with parchment paper. Mix the lemon juice and zest, honey, and oil in a bowl and set aside. Place the garlic bulb in the center of the pan, then place the meat on top and rub over the lemon and honey mix. Season, pour in the stock, and place the herbs over the top.

2 Cook in the oven for 1½ hours. Check the meat after 1 hour. If it is browning too much, turn down the oven temperature. If the stock has evaporated, add in more. Remove from the oven and allow to rest for 20 minutes.

3 For the flageolet beans, melt the butter in a frying pan, add the onions and garlic, and sweat for 5–10 minutes, until soft but not colored. Add the flageolet beans and rosemary, and stir well to coat in the onion mixture.

4 Add the stock, bring to a boil, and simmer for 3 minutes, until thick. Add the cream, boil for 1 more minute, and season. Carve the meat and arrange on a serving dish. Serve with the flageolet beans and the cooking juices.

WEST INDIAN CURRIED GOAT

Lime juice helps to tenderize the meat before cooking, and Jamaican rum and butter enrich the spicy sauce.

 Leg of goat

SERVES 4
PREP 10 mins, plus marinating
COOK 1½–2 hrs

2¼lb (1kg) leg of goat, cut into cubes
juice of 2 limes
3 large onions, finely chopped
2 tsp chopped chives
2 tsp chopped flat-leaf parsley
1 whole red chile
½ tsp ground ginger
1 tsp ground allspice
2 tbsp vegetable oil
1 tsp cumin seeds
5 garlic cloves, chopped
2 tbsp curry powder
2 tbsp tomato paste
2 x 14oz (400g) can coconut milk
2 sprigs of thyme
1 bay leaf
1 tbsp dark rum
2 tsp butter, chilled and diced

1 Place the meat in a large bowl, pour over the lime juice, and leave to marinate for 15 minutes. Place the onions, chives, parsley, chile, and ground spices in a bowl and mix to combine.

2 Heat the oil in a large heavy-bottomed saucepan, add the cumin and toast to release the flavors. Reduce the heat, stir in the garlic and curry powder, and cook for 1–2 minutes. Add the tomato paste and the coconut milk and bring to a boil.

3 Add the meat and lime juice to the pan. Then stir in the onion and herb mix. Add the thyme and bay leaf, stir thoroughly, and bring to a boil.

4 Reduce the heat to a simmer and cook, uncovered for 40 minutes or until the meat is cooked through. Check and top up with water if the liquid evaporates too quickly. Remove from the heat and stir in the rum and butter. Serve with red beans and rice.

GOAT, ALE, AND MUSHROOM POT PIE

Slow-cooking the goat meat with ale, rosemary, and bay leaf intensifies its flavor in this delicious pie dish.

CUT Goat shoulder

SERVES 4–6
PREP 30 mins   **COOK** 1 hr 40–45 mins

2 tbsp all-purpose flour, seasoned with salt and pepper
2¼lb (1 kg) goat shoulder, cut into bite-size pieces
2 tbsp canola oil, plus extra if needed
12 pearl onions
2 carrots, peeled and diced
9oz (250g) crimini mushrooms, quartered
2 garlic cloves, finely chopped
2 tbsp tomato paste
¼ tsp ground allspice
⅔ cup ale
2 cups meat stock
1 sprig of rosemary
1 bay leaf
sea salt and freshly ground black pepper
2 tsp brown sugar
1 large sheet store-bought puff pastry
1 egg, lightly beaten

1 Preheat the oven to 300°F (150°C). Place the flour in a large bowl, add the meat, and toss to coat lightly. Heat the oil in a large pan and cook the meat until golden brown on all sides. Transfer the meat to a large heatproof casserole and set aside.

2 Add more oil to the pan, if needed, and cook the onions, carrots, and mushrooms, stirring occasionally until lightly browned. Add the garlic, tomato paste, and allspice. Mix well and add to the casserole. Add the ale, stock, rosemary, and bay leaf. Bring to a boil, season, and add the sugar. Cook for an additional 5–10 minutes to reduce the gravy, then transfer to the oven.

3 Cook in the oven for 1 hour 20 minutes, or until the meat is just cooked. Season with salt and pepper. Increase the temperature to 425°F (220°C). Place the meat and the vegetables in a 2-quart pie dish with a pie funnel in the center and let cool.

4 Cut a 1in (2cm) wide strip of pastry. Brush the rim of the pie dish with the beaten egg, press the strip on the rim, and brush again with egg. Cover the dish with the pastry, making a hole for the funnel. Press the edges together, trim the pastry, and flute all around. Brush the top with egg, place on a baking sheet, and bake in the center of the oven for 20–25 minutes, until golden brown and crisp.

GAME

GAME

IN THIS BOOK, "GAME" INCLUDES ANIMALS AND BIRDS THAT ARE HUNTED FOR FOOD. HOWEVER, SOME GAME SPECIES ARE NOW ALSO REARED, BOTH ON A DOMESTIC SCALE AND QUITE INTENSIVELY. ALSO INCLUDED ARE SOME SPECIES THAT ARE NOT WILD BUT WHOSE FLESH IS VERY LEAN AND COOKS LIKE WILD GAME.

GAME IS BROADLY DIVIDED into furred game (animals) and feathered game (birds), and the latter are further divided into land birds and waterfowl.

Wild game is likely to vary in age and condition; it could be young and tender or old and tough, too thin or over fat, or anywhere in between. Therefore assessment and preparation are crucial. Farmed game is more consistent and comes from younger animals. Often (but not always) milder in flavor, it can be made more intense by careful hanging.

A HEALTHY MEAT

Game meats are what human beings evolved to eat; they are the best possible meat for our health. Since they have not been selectively bred, and because their diet consists largely of wild food, the profile of their meat is perfect. It is very low in fat, and what fat there is has a favorable saturated-to-unsaturated ratio. Also, any fat tends to be on the outside of the meat, so can be trimmed easily. Darker game meats contain more iron than any domestic meat and valuable vitamins, such as B6 and B12, as well as potassium, phosphorus, riboflavin, niacin, and zinc. However,

although their diet is mostly wild, as with any wild animal that lives close to intensive farmland, there is always a possibility that they could have eaten recently sprayed crops.

FURRED GAME

- **Venison** There are 40 species of deer, some smaller than a lamb, others larger than cattle. With careful butchery and good cooking, even old venison can be turned into a gourmet meal.
- **Wild boar** Found in many countries, wild boar is also farmed for meat and crossed with domestic pigs. The meat from feral pigs may be sold as wild boar.
- **Kangaroo** Great numbers of kangaroo were culled in Australia as pests. Nowadays, culling is carried out more carefully under license and the meat is exported worldwide.
- **Rabbit** Wild rabbits exist in many parts of the world and are also widely reared commercially and privately. Domestic rabbits are much larger than wild ones. There is no close season (see opposite for more about game seasons).
- **Hare** Some hares live in open grassland, others in the mountains, and in some countries they are farmed. They are not usually sold when rearing young.
- **Guinea pig** Most commonly reared in Peru, guinea pigs are regarded there as a delicacy. They are also eaten in parts of Asia and served in ethnic restaurants.
- **Horse** Most comes from ex-riding or working animals that are usually quite old, although some meat from wild horses comes from younger beasts.

- **Squirrel** Squirrels live in temperate woodland. Reds are a protected species in most countries. Grays are larger and more commonly eaten; they are trapped or shot. There is no closed season.

FEATHERED GAME

- **Pheasant** A popular game bird, wild pheasant exist in most continents, eating seeds and insects. They are also reared and released for sport; while captive their food consists of commercial rations.
- **Grouse** Grouse species include willow, hazel, red-legged grouse, the larger black grouse, and capercaillie. They inhabit forests and mountains of the Northern hemisphere.
- **Partridge** Partridges exist in most parts of the Northern hemisphere on agricultural margins where they eat seeds and insects. They are also widely reared for release into the wild for shooting.
- **Pigeon** Found the world over, there are around 300 species of pigeon. They eat seeds, plants, and fruit. They are also commercially reared; these young birds are called squabs.
- **Guinea Fowl** Originally from Africa, guinea fowl were domesticated for centuries

in Europe and are now sold around the world. Although considered game, most guinea fowl are now intensively reared.

• **Quail** The common quail is native to the Middle East and Mediterranean but most countries have native species that migrate in huge numbers. They are also farmed intensively in large numbers.

• **Ostrich** Native to Africa, the ostrich's diet is mainly vegetarian with a few insects. They are now farmed in many countries where they eat commercial rations as well as grass.

• **Wild goose** Wild geese probably fly further in their migrations than any other bird, so unless you have one hatched that year, the meat could be tough. There are many different species.

• **Mallard** (large wild duck) Of all the waterfowl, mallard is the best known and widespread, migrating to all continents of the world. Their diet consists mainly of vegetation, seeds, and grain crops with some crustaceans.

• **Snipe** One of the smallest of the game birds, snipe live on marshy uplands and fields; they are very difficult to shoot. They are often eaten with their entrails intact.

• **Teal** One of the smallest duck species, teal are renowned for their flavor. Any duck shot by the seashore may have a fishy flavor; those shot inland taste the best.

• **Woodcock** Living in deciduous or mixed coniferous woodland, large numbers migrate out of Northern Scandinavia and Russia to Europe and North America. They are notoriously difficult to shoot.

GAME SEASONS

In most countries, game animals and birds have a "closed season": a period during which the animal may not be killed or its

meat sold. There are also some species that can never be bought and sold. In some countries, such as the United States, it is illegal to sell any indigenous wild game; nevertheless it is eaten in large quantities.

Closed seasons are designed to protect animals while they breed and rear their young. However, some species that have become pests due to overpopulation have no closed seasons. Farmed game is often exempt from close seasons; when in doubt, check online or with the local authority. Each country has its own laws, although the spring and summer are typically the periods during which closed seasons apply.

Wild game is usually regarded as a winter treat, and traditional recipes tend to reflect this. But species that have no season, or are exempt, may be bought and cooked all year round. So remember that because game meat is so lean, it makes superb and refreshing summer eating when people prefer to eat less fatty food. New recipes reflect this lighter approach to these meats.

BUYING GAME

Where protected wild game can be sold, it can only be bought in season. Often, game has to be bought from a licensed game dealer, who may be the hunter, a game farmer, or a butcher. Some supermarkets sell a limited selection, as do farmers' markets, and it can usually be obtained online. Wild game that has no season is usually at its best in the late summer and fall.

Small game animals (such as hare and rabbit, etc.) are usually sold whole and skinned, although occasionally they are cut into pieces. Large game animals,

such as deer and boar, are butchered like domestic meats, although usually there is a smaller variety of cuts.

Game birds were traditionally sold with their feathers on and undrawn (not gutted); today most are sold oven-ready. Male birds are bigger than females and so, regardless of sex, it is better to cook two or more of the same age and size so that they cook evenly. In the case of larger game birds, increasingly it is the deboned breasts that are sold. Occasionally, the skinned crown of a bird is sold to be roasted on its own; these need to be barded with bacon or fat. Small game birds are sometimes sold butterflied, i.e. split down the middle and opened out so that they will cook evenly when broiled or barbecued.

Unfortunately, some dealers handle game badly, so avoid any that is badly bruised, has too much torn skin, or broken legs.

CHECKING FOR SHOT

When game has been shot with guns there is always the possibility of finding pellets, fragments of bullets, or bone shards in the meat, although this rarely applies to farmed game. Pellets and fragments of bullet or bone can damage the teeth if they are bitten into, so always examine the meat carefully: shot damage is indicated by areas of bruising and holes in the skin. Make sure any feathers drawn into the holes are removed along with the pellets. Removing the breasts from game birds makes it easier to see any pellets.

FURRED GAME CUTS

GAME MEAT IS VERY LEAN AND CAN TOUGHEN if incorrectly cooked. Farmed game is more tender. Cook roasts and steaks pink or rare and cook stews gently (see the venison cooking chart on p45). Recipes for game can usually be interchanged successfully, especially where the meat is of the same color.

MIDDLE OR SADDLE CUTS

Venison saddle (the whole back) provides the finest textured and most tender meat of all, either as a bone-in cut, or as boneless, de-sinewed loin and fillet.

VENISON

Venison from wild deer varies in size and age so can be big or small, tender or tough. Farmed deer are usually tender. Allow 5½–7oz (150–200g) boneless meat per person.

FOREQUARTER

MIDDLE OR SADDLE

HINDQUARTER

WHOLE SADDLE CUT The finest roasting cut. When from older deer, the outer skin and silvery sinews are often removed before cooking.

LOIN, LARDER TRIMMED Easy to cook and reliably tender, though best if not overcooked. Medallion steaks are cut from this joint.

FOREQUARTER CUTS

Most of the forequarter is used for stewing and ground meat, although the shoulder of young deer makes good roasts and frying steaks. Venison shoulder is extemely lean.

FILLET OR TENDERLOIN Even more tender than loin, this small muscle is only cut from larger deer. The chain steak should be removed.

GROUND Ground venison is tasty but lean, so add fat or vegetables for succulence. Good for meatballs, burgers, and a variety of dishes.

DICED VENISON Diced shoulder venison is used for stews and pies. Diced haunch can be stewed, or stir-fried if from young deer.

HINDQUARTER CUTS

The back leg (haunch) is very lean. Young deer can be roasted on the bone but older deer have thick sinews and benefit from being separated into individual de-sinewed muscles.

WHOLE LEG, BONE-IN. Roasting the whole leg is a good way to cook a small deer.

RUMP ROAST Large deer legs are often boned and trimmed to make a lean, flavorsome roast. Best cooked medium or rare.

STRIP STEAK From young deer this makes a tender grilling steak, cooked pink, otherwise it is best fried or braised.

Additional venison cuts

• **SHOULDER ROAST, BONED AND ROLLED** Braise slowly for a rich dish. Being lean it needs larding and basting.

• **FRENCH RACK** The eye muscle ensures this cut will be tender. Cook quickly to pink.

• **CUTLETS** Grill or fry if young, braise if old.

• **LOIN STEAKS** Cut from the saddle and trimmed; the most tender steak of all.

• **HAUNCH CHOPS AND STEAKS** Small deer hanches can be sliced with or without bone. Grill or fry.

• **WHOLE SALMON CUT PAVÉ** A useful small muscle from the silverside. Roast, or slice into medallions.

• **THICK FLANK, ROAST AND STEAKS** Remove the outer cap then roast, or slice into frying or braising steak.

• **SHANK, ON-BONE AND TRIMMED** Takes longer to cook than lamb shank but is delicious and succulent.

• **OSSO BUCO** Takes longer to cook than veal but makes a very rich dish.

RABBIT

Wild rabbit can be tough unless young. Farmed rabbits are much bigger and more tender. Allow 8–12oz (250–350g) per person; the back legs and saddle have the most meat.

On wild rabbit, the forequarter .... has very little meat on it; farmed rabbit shoulders are more meaty and tender.

HARE

The back legs and saddle are the most meaty cuts. A whole adult feeds 6–8 people, a leveret (young hare) 4–5. Ask for the blood if making a civet. Lowland hares have the best flavor.

.... It is advisable to remove the thin outer skin, especially from the saddle.

WILD BOAR

The meat of wild boar and feral pigs is dark and lean. Young wild boar, called marcassin, make the best eating; older boar can be very tough.

KANGAROO

Kangaroo is not unlike venison in both taste and texture, and, like venison, can vary in age. Steaks and stew are the most common cuts. Allow 5½–7oz (150–200g) boneless meat per person.

HORSE

A slightly sweet, rich meat, horse is a very good source of iron. Steaks, stewing meat, and ground meat are the most common cuts.

SQUIRREL

Gray is the most commonly eaten species. They are difficult animals to skin. The flavor is best when they are fat from eating nuts and berries. Allow one squirrel per person.

GUINEA PIG

Most commonly seen in Peru and some Asian countries. The flavor is not unlike rabbit or dark chicken meat, although it is fattier. One feeds 1–2 people.

FEATHERED GAME CUTS

Game birds that migrate long distances can be tough unless they are hatched during the year. They should be either cooked quite pink or else braised or simmered gently. The meat also makes very tasty ground dishes. Young birds are more versatile and can also be roasted, or grilled if butterflied (see p61).

PARTRIDGE

Red partridge are the most common, although gray and chukar partridge have better flavor. Young birds have paler flesh and are more tender than old ones. Allow one per person.

PHEASANT

Pheasant meat is paler than most game birds. When not hung, it tastes similar to free-range chicken. Yellow fat means they have been feeding on corn. A hen pheasant feeds 2–3, a cock 3–4.

QUAIL

Most quail available for sale are intensively farmed and so are young and tender. Best butterflied (see p61), or stuffed and roasted. Allow one per person.

PHEASANT BREAST
Remove the silver sinew to prevent the meat from curling in the pan.

GROUSE

Grouse are never farmed and their diet gives the dark flesh a unique flavor that is particularly renowned. It is often served with the feet still attached. Allow one per person.

PIGEON

Wild pigeon has lean, dark red meat that needs careful cooking. Domestic squabs are much younger, fatter, and more tender. Allow one pigeon or 2–3 breasts per person.

PIGEON BREAST This is delicious cooked pink and sliced thinly.

MALLARD

Mallard (large wild ducks) have dark flesh and are far smaller and leaner than domestic ducks, so need careful cooking or the meat can become dry. A mallard feeds 1–2 people.

WHOLE MALLARD Once plucked, it is not easy to know how old a wild bird may be and therefore whether it should be roasted or braised. If the skin tears easily, it is young; if not, it is old.

MALLARD BREAST Wild duck breasts are thin and cook extremely quickly, especially when there is no fat on them.

TEAL (SMALL DUCK)

These tiny birds are renowned for their flavor. Like all wild duck, they are lean and need careful cooking so they don't dry out. Allow one per person.

WOODCOCK

Woodcock are considered one of the most delicious game birds, especially when cooked with the entrails (or "trail") intact and the head on. May need to be ordered in advance. Allow one per person.

GUINEA FOWL

Guinea fowl has a flavor halfway between chicken and pheasant. Although tender, the meat is quite lean and inclined to be dry if not cooked carefully. One feeds four people.

OSTRICH

Ostrich meat is dark and lean. Young farmed ostrich tastes like mild venison and is tender. However, they are long-lived birds so wild ones can be tough.

SNIPE

Often cooked with their entrails (or "trail") intact, so mention this when ordering otherwise they will be plucked and drawn. May need to be ordered in advance. Allow 1–2 per person.

WILD GOOSE

Wild goose can be quite tough. However, its meat is dark and flavorsome, and full of iron; it makes good ground meat and stew. One goose breast will feed 2–3 people.

PRESERVED GAME

THE RANGE OF PRESERVED GAME MEATS must be among the oldest in the world, dating from before domesticated animals. Today, countries with populations of large game animals are the ones with the greatest variety of preserved game products, with venison and wild boar being the most common.

ALHEIRA DE CACA A delicate pale smoked sausage from Portugal made from game meats bound with bread crumbs sometimes flavored with paprika and garlic.

SMOKED VENISON Venison is dry cured and smoked for eating raw in Scandinavia, Austria, Switzerland, and Scotland.

SLINZEGA Made in Valtellina in the Italian Alps, Slinzega is similar to bresaola (see p148) but uses smaller strips of meat. Traditionally it was made with horse meat but is also made with venison or pork.

PEMMICAN A traditional native American preparation, pemmican is made by pounding dried game meats with melted fat and wild berries. It was widely eaten by early explorers and is still marketed.

CHARQUI This South American jerky is made from thin slices of salted and wind-dried meat, usually llama or horse and sometimes beef. North American jerky is usually marinated in spicy dressings before being dried and sometimes smoked.

KUIVALIHA Also known as *kapaliha*, this is made from strips of meat, often reindeer venison, that are dried over a few weeks in Finland when the spring weather is appropriate.

MORREPØLSE There are many different recipes for this dried sausage. Popular ingredients are venison and deer heart. Sometimes it is mixed with pork and can include the blood. Flavorings include ginger or juniper and, typically, syrup.

SALAME DI CINGHIALE Salame can be made from any game meat. The lean, dark meat produces a rich flavor. Wild boar damage crops and vineyards, so throughout the winter they are pursued by hunters and preserved as salame.

VILDSVINSLAMI This wild boar salami is made from one of the two most popular wild meats in Sweden; venison being the other one. Both are dark, lean meats with an intense flavor and they are often flavored with juniper and garlic.

DROEWORS Thses are slim, quickly dried sausages that should contain very little fat, so ostrich or game meat such as gazelle is popular. The meat is uncured, but homemade versions sometimes use vinegar to prevent spoilage, which adds to the flavor. They are usually spicy but not hot.

ALGKORV AND REINSDYRPØLSE These venison sausages are typical of Norway and Sweden. They are made from both elk (*algkorv*) and reindeer (*renkorv*), which in Norway are called *reinsdyrpølse*. Flavorings include juniper or cloves, cinnamon, and ginger and they can be fresh or dried.

SAUCISSON SEC DE CHEVAL The meat of this saucisson is dark and lean, with a strong beefy flavor. France is one of the few European countries where horse meat is still available in supermarkets and at markets. *Saucisson sec de lievre* (hare) is also made.

KEEPING GAME MEAT MOIST

Game meat is usually very lean and therefore it is less forgiving of being cooked incorrectly. Below are some ways of making sure that the meat stays moist.

KEEP THE MEAT PINK

When grilling, frying, or roasting lean meat, the easiest way to keep it moist is to make sure there are still pink juices in the meat. Lean meat has no marbling of fat, so it can turn from moist to dry very quickly, but pink meat cannot be dry. The secret is to part-cook the meat then rest it until rare or medium rare: roast, grill, or fry the meat at high heat to brown it. Then finish the cooking by resting the meat at a low temperature that evenly distributes the juices. Use a meat thermometer to check how the meat has cooked (see p29).

BUTTERFLIED BIRDS

Poultry or feathered game can be butterflied—split in half and opened out—to allow the different thicknesses of meat to cook more quickly and evenly (see p61).

COOK IN A LIQUID

Cooking lean meat gently in a liquid will ensure it stays moist. Stew small pieces of meat in a liquid to keep the meat moist and add extra flavor. Poach whole birds or a cut in liquid, and make sure that the hot meat stays in the liquid while it cools so that it absorbs moisture. Then drain off the liquid, slice the meat or remove it from the bone, and gently warm it up in the liquid or a sauce to serve.

ADD SUCCULENT TEXTURES

Serve the meat with vegetables with a slippery texture—such as cooked onions, mushrooms, peppers, prunes, eggplant, and apricots—either as side dishes or cooked with the meat. These not only add flavors, but can make eating game even more sumptuous.

USE CREAMY SAUCES

Creamy sauces are ideal for any meat that is inclined to be dry as they can make the meat feel more succulent. See pp30–31 for suggestions. Small pieces of meat have proportionately more surface covered with sauce than large pieces, so they feel moister in the mouth.

LARDING MEAT

It is not necessary to lard meat that is to be served pink. Larding meat—inserting fat into it—makes it succulent; it is most effective when meat is cooked to well done, for example when braising and pot-roasting.

USE A LARDING NEEDLE TO "SEW" LONG STRIPS OF PORK back fat into the meat. Push it right into the center, so all the meat gets lubricated. Alternatively, make deep holes in the meat with a small sharp knife and slide frozen strips of fat into them.

BARDING MEAT

Barding protects the outer surface of meat from drying out while being roasted. It is quite unnecessary to bard any meat when cooking it pink or rare—unless it is spit-roasted, or a really large cut that needs protection.

USE BUTCHER'S STRING TO TIE SHEETS OF PORK FAT, bacon, or vegetable leaves over the meat before cooking. Remove them toward the end of cooking to brown the surface of the meat. Avoid using strong flavors on delicate game.

DEBONING A RABBIT

Rabbit is best skinned (see pp306–7) as soon as it is shot. If sold in fur, wash the carcass after skinning. Young wild rabbit and farmed rabbit has tender flesh that can be roasted. Stew or simmer old rabbit.

1 Place the rabbit on its back on the work surface. Using kitchen scissors, cut away the liver from the cavity and set aside.

2 Next, remove the leg by cutting through the ball and socket joint in the direction of the backbone, with a very sharp boning knife.

3 Repeat this with the other leg and set it aside. Turn the rabbit over and cut off each foreleg as close to the rib cage as possible.

4 Once all the legs have been removed, use a sharp chef's knife to cut away the backbone that is now visible. Press hard on the knife in order to make a clean cut through the bone.

5 Flip the rabbit over onto its back again, and cut right up through the breastbone using sharp kitchen scissors. The breast meat should separate into two even sections.

6 Turn the rabbit over once more, tucking the breast sections neatly underneath. Make a clean cut with a chef's knife so that there are just 4 ribs attached to the loin.

CIVET OF VENISON

The delicious flavors of bacon in the sauce balance wonderfully with the venison in this dish. Preparing all the garnish is well worth the trouble.

THE CUT Venison shoulder

SERVES 8
PREP 1 hr, plus overnight marinating
COOK 2 hrs 15 mins

1½ cups red wine

1 onion, thinly sliced

3 tbsp brandy

3 tbsp olive oil

salt and freshly ground black pepper

3lb 3oz (1.5 kg) stewing venison, diced

FOR THE SAUCE

4 tbsp butter

8oz (225g) bacon, chopped

2 large onions, chopped

1 large carrot, peeled and diced

2 garlic cloves, crushed

2 tbsp all-purpose flour

1 bay leaf

sprig of thyme

7oz (200g) crimini mushrooms, sliced

2 cups game or chicken stock

FOR THE GARNISH

16 tbsp butter

2 tsp sugar

24 small onions or shallots

⅔ cup game or chicken stock

24 small crimini mushrooms

8 slices white bread, cut into triangles and crusts removed

chopped flat-leaf parsley, to garnish

1 Place the red wine, onion, brandy, and oil in a large bowl. Season with salt and pepper and mix to combine all the ingredients. Add the venison, mix well, and leave in a cool place overnight.

2 Preheat the oven to 350°F (180°C). For the sauce, heat the butter in a large heatproof casserole over medium heat. Add the bacon and cook for 5 minutes until well-browned. Then add the onions and carrots and stir for about 5 minutes until lightly browned. Drain the meat and reserve the marinade. Pat dry with paper towels and add to the casserole. Increase the temperature and stir to mix.

3 Add the garlic and flour to the casserole and stir well for 1–2 minutes to coat. Strain the marinade, and add to the casserole along with the herbs and mushrooms. Add just enough stock to cover and bring to a boil. Place in the oven for 1½ hours.

4 Meanwhile, for the garnish, melt 4 tablespoons of the butter and the sugar in a heavy-based saucepan and add the onions. Lightly shake the pan to coat the onions. Add just enough stock to cover and boil rapidly to cook, until the liquid evaporates, leaving the onions coated in caramel. Remove from the heat and set aside.

5 Heat another 4 tbsp butter in a separate pan. Add the mushrooms and cook until lightly browned. Season with salt and pepper.

6 Cook the bread in the remaining butter until brown and crisp. Place the meat in a large shallow serving dish, top with the mushrooms and caramelized onions, and arrange the fried bread triangles around the edge. Garnish with parsley and serve alongside mashed potatoes and green vegetables.

VENISON, SHALLOT, AND CHESTNUT HOTPOT

Lean venison, sweet chestnuts, dried mushrooms, and shallots come together in this dish to make a rich, robust casserole full of flavor.

THE CUT Venison shoulder or haunch

SERVES 4
PREP 30 mins   **COOK** 2 hrs 15 mins

2 tbsp all-purpose flour

2 tbsp thyme leaves

salt and freshly ground black pepper

1¼lb (550g) boneless shoulder or haunch of venison, cut into bite-size pieces

pat of butter

2 tbsp olive oil

4½oz (125g) bacon strips, sliced

4½oz (125g) shallots

¾ cup of red wine

1¾oz (50g) dried mushrooms, such as shiitake, oyster, or porcini, soaked in 1¼ cups warm water for 20 minutes

4½oz (125g) cooked chestnuts

2 cups hot vegetable stock

3 sprigs of rosemary

1 Preheat the oven to 300°F (150°C). Place the flour, thyme, and seasoning in a bowl, add the venison pieces, and toss well to coat. Heat the butter with 1 tablespoon of the oil in a cast-iron pan. Add the venison, and cook over medium heat, stirring frequently for 6–8 minutes, or until lightly colored. Remove with a slotted spoon and set aside.

2 Add the bacon to the pan and stir for 5 minutes, or until well-browned and crisp. Remove with a slotted spoon and set aside. Then add the remaining oil to the pan. Add the shallots and cook over medium-low heat for 8 minutes, or until soft and turning golden. Return the meat to the pan, season with pepper, then add the wine and boil for 2 minutes. Stir to scrape up the crispy bits from the bottom of the pan.

3 Drain the mushrooms, reserving the liquid, and add to the pan. Then strain the reserved liquid and add to the pan. Stir in the chestnuts, pour in the stock, and add the rosemary. Cover and place in the oven for 2 hours or until the meat is tender, adding a little hot water if necessary. Serve hot.

BRAISED SHOULDER OF VENISON

Thyme is an excellent companion for the meat, and the onions cut across the grain provide a silky sauce.

THE CUT Venison shoulder

SERVES 4–6
PREP 15 mins **COOK** 2 hrs

3lb (1.35kg) bone-in venison shoulder

2 tbsp vegetable oil

2 tbsp butter

10oz (300g) onions, sliced across the grain

1 tsp sugar

4 sprigs of thyme

1 bay leaf

salt and freshly ground black pepper

1 Preheat the oven to 350°F (180°C). Season the shoulder with the salt and pepper. Heat the oil in a large, lidded saucepan. Add the meat and cook for about 10 minutes, until well-browned all over. Remove the meat with a slotted spoon and set aside.

2 Melt the butter in the pan, and add onions, sugar, and a little salt and pepper. Stir to mix and cook for about 8 minutes, until colored. Make sure the mixture does not burn.

3 Return the meat to the pan and add about 2 cups water. Then add the herbs and season well. Bring to a boil, then transfer to the oven, and cook for 2½ hours. Remove from the oven and keep warm.

4 Strain the sauce, pushing the juices and onions through a sieve with the back of a ladle. Remove the bay leaf, and taste and adjust the seasoning if required. Carve the meat into slices and serve hot with the sauce poured on top.

VARIATION

Braised shoulder of lamb Use a bone-in shoulder of lamb in place of the venison and replace the thyme with rosemary. Add 2 teaspoon red currant jelly with the water in step 3 and cook as above.

VENISON AND RED WINE STEW

Venison is a good source of low-fat protein, and its treatment in this recipe gives it a rich, satisfying flavor.

THE CUT Venison shoulder

SERVES 4
PREP 15 mins
COOK 2 hrs 30 mins – 2 hrs 45 mins

3 tbsp olive oil

4 shallots, halved

2 celery stalks, finely chopped

1 carrot, finely chopped

2 garlic cloves, finely chopped

2 tbsp all-purpose flour

½ tsp grated nutmeg

½ tsp ground allspice

salt and freshly ground black pepper

1½lb (675g) boneless shoulder or other stewing venison, cut into bite-size chunks

4 tbsp red currant jelly

finely grated zest and juice of 1 orange

1¼ cups red wine

⅔ cup beef stock

1 bay leaf

1 Preheat the oven to 300°F (150°C). Heat 1 tablespoon of the oil in a heatproof casserole and cook the shallots, celery, and carrots for 3 minutes. Add the garlic and cook for 2–3 minutes more. Remove with a slotted spoon and set aside.

2 Place the flour, nutmeg, and allspice in a large plastic bag, season well, and add the meat. Shake the bag lightly to coat the meat. Put it into a sieve, and shake to remove excess flour.

3 Add the remaining 2 tablespoons of oil to the casserole. Add the meat and cook for 8–10 minutes over medium heat, until well-browned all over. Do this in batches to avoid overcrowding the pan. Remove with a slotted spoon and set aside. Add the red currant jelly, orange zest, and juice, wine, stock, and bay leaf to the casserole. Season and stir until the jelly has melted.

4 Return the vegetables and meat to the casserole, stir, and reduce the heat to simmer. Cover and cook in the oven for 2–2½ hours or until the meat is tender. Remove the bay leaf and serve hot with potato and mashed celery root.

BARBECUED HAUNCH OF VENISON

A lovely dish for a summer evening, the freshness of the marinade lightens the richness of the meat.

THE CUT Venison haunch

SERVES 10–12
PREP 15 mins   **COOK** 30 mins, plus resting

4 garlic cloves

2 chiles, seeded

3 sprigs of rosemary, chopped

2 tbsp honey

2 tbsp canola oil

1 small piece of fresh ginger, crushed

juice of 2 limes

8–10lb (4–5kg) whole haunch of venison, butterflied

sea salt and freshly ground black pepper

1 Using a mortar and pestle, pound the garlic, chiles, and rosemary until coarsely ground. Transfer to a small bowl and add the honey, oil, and ginger. Place the marinade in a plastic bag large enough to hold the haunch. Pour in the lime juice, then put the haunch in and seal, rubbing the mixture into the skin through the bag. Leave for 1 hour at room temperature.

2 Preheat the grill to its medium setting. Remove the haunch from the bag and season with salt and pepper. Cook the haunch on each side for 15 minutes, until well-browned. Remove and let rest on a carving platter for at least 10 minutes. Carve into thin slices and serve hot.

CINGHIALE IN DOLCE FORTE

A classic Italian dish for wild boar—the orange and chile add a real touch of spice.

THE CUT Wild boar haunch

SERVES 6
PREP 45 mins, plus 2 days marinating
COOK 2¹⁄₂–3 hrs

3lb 3oz (1.5 kg) wild boar, cut into 1in (3cm) cubes

3 tbsp olive oil

1 onion, finely chopped

2 tsp ground chile

2¹⁄₂oz (75g) prunes, pitted

1 tbsp raisins

¹⁄₂ cup chicken stock

zest of 1 orange

1 tbsp brown sugar

1¾oz (50g) dark chocolate

salt and freshly ground black pepper

FOR THE MARINADE

2 cups red wine

¹⁄₂ cup red wine vinegar

1 bay leaf

sprig of thyme

1 carrot, chopped

1 onion, chopped

1 celery stalk, chopped

2 tsp ground cinnamon

2 tsp grated nutmeg

2 tsp ground allspice

1 For the marinade, place all the ingredients, except the spices, in a large, heavy-bottomed saucepan. Then add half the spices, bring to a boil, and let cool. Place the meat in an airtight plastic container, pour the marinade over, and chill for 2 days.

2 Strain the marinade, remove the meat, and pat dry with paper towels. Reserve the liquid and discard the vegetables. Heat the oil in a lidded, heavy-bottomed pan over medium heat. Add the meat, in batches, and cook for 4–5 minutes until well-browned.

3 Add the onion and cook for 3–4 minutes until softened. Stir in the remaining spices, the chile, prunes, raisins, reserved liquid, and stock. Bring to a boil then reduce the heat to a simmer. Skim off the fat, cover, and cook for 2 hours, or until the meat is cooked through.

4 Stir in the orange zest, sugar, and chocolate. Taste and adjust the seasoning, if needed. Serve hot with polenta.

VENISON CUTLETS WITH CHANTERELLES

This truly rich but earthy flavored dish is given depth with shallots and cream.

THE CUT Venison cutlet or steak

SERVES 4
PREP 30 mins   **COOK** 25 mins

8 venison cutlets or steaks

salt and freshly ground black pepper

1 tbsp sunflower oil

8 tbsp butter

1 shallot, finely chopped

1lb (450g) chanterelles, trimmed and sliced

¹⁄₂ cup game stock

¹⁄₂ cup heavy cream

1 Pat the cutlets dry with paper towels to remove any excess blood. Season well with salt and pepper. Heat the oil and half the butter in a large, heavy-bottomed saucepan. Add the cutlets as the butter foams up and cook for 5–10 minutes, until well-browned on both sides. Do this in batches to avoid overcrowding the pan.

2 Reduce the heat and cook the cutlets for an additional 5 minutes. Then remove with a slotted spoon, set aside on a plate, and keep warm. Add the remaining butter to the pan. Stir in the shallots and the chanterelles and cook for 5 minutes, stirring occasionally.

3 Add the stock and cook until reduced by half. Stir in the cream and season. As the sauce thickens, remove from the heat. Stir in any juices that have collected from the resting cutlets. Serve with two cutlets on each plate, with the sauce swirled around.

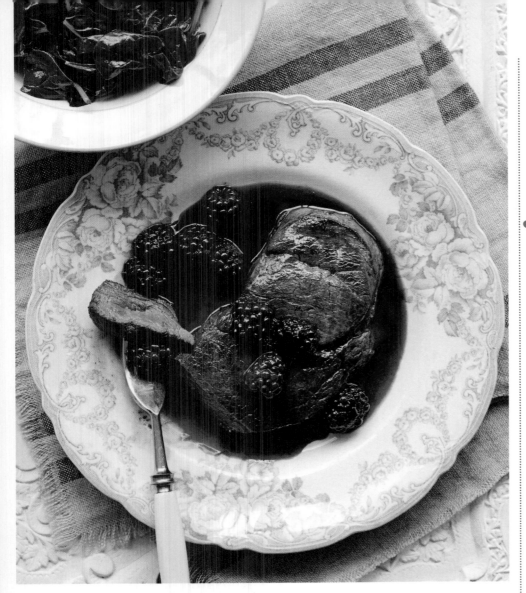

VENISON SAUSAGES, CELERY ROOT GRATIN, AND BRAISED RED CABBAGE

This hearty dish is full of flavors and textures and makes for some wonderful comfort food.

THE CUT Venison sausage

SERVES 4
PREP 25 mins   **COOK** 2 hrs

4 tbsp unsalted butter

2 tbsp sugar

1 tsp salt

6 tbsp rice wine vinegar, white wine vinegar, or apple cider vinegar

1 red cabbage, finely shredded (about 2¼lb [1kg])

2 sweet apples, peeled, cored, and grated

2 heaping tbsp red currant jelly

FOR THE GRATIN

2 tbsp unsalted butter, softened

1½lb (650g) celery root (trimmed weight), peeled and thinly sliced

2 garlic cloves, crushed

salt and freshly ground black pepper

1¾ cups half and half

8–12 venison sausages

1 Preheat the oven to 325°F (160°C). Place the butter, sugar, salt, vinegar, and 6 tablespoons water in a large, heatproof casserole. Bring to a boil, and simmer for 1 minute.

2 Add the cabbage, and return to a boil. Cover tightly with 2 layers of foil and the lid, place on the lowest rack of the oven, and cook for 1½ hours. Then stir in the apples and jelly, adding water if it looks dry. Replace the foil and lid, and return to the oven for 30 more minutes.

3 Meanwhile, for the gratin, lightly grease a large, shallow, ovenproof dish with butter, and layer in half the celery root. Sprinkle in the garlic, season well, and layer in the remaining celery root. Pour in the half and half and dot with the remaining butter.

4 Cook the gratin on the top rack of the oven for 1 hour 15 minutes, until soft when pierced with a knife. Broil the sausages for 5–10 minutes, turning, until browned all over. Serve with the gratin and cabbage.

VENISON STEAK WITH BLACKBERRIES

A simple method of cooking this lean meat quickly, the blackberries in the dish provide a tangy accompaniment.

THE CUT Venison haunch steak

SSERVES 4
PREP 5 mins   **COOK** 15 mins

4 venison haunch steaks, about 7oz (200g) each

salt and freshly ground black pepper

1 tbsp sunflower oil

4 tbsp butter, chilled and diced

¼ cup blackberry wine or red wine

2 tbsp red currant jelly

5½oz (150g) blackberries

1 Pat the steaks dry with paper towels to remove any excess blood. Season well. Heat the oil and 1 teaspoon of butter in a heavy-bottomed pan over medium heat. Place the steaks in the hot pan and cook for 4–5 minutes on each side.

2 Reduce the heat and cook for another 5 minutes, turning once, until well-browned. Remove the meat from the pan, cover with foil, and set aside. Then add the wine, red currant jelly, and blackberries to the pan. Bring to a boil, stirring gently to melt the jelly.

3 Once the sauce has thickened, remove from the heat and whisk in the remaining butter. Do not boil the sauce again, or else the butter will separate. Serve the steaks with the sauce poured over them.

WILD BOAR CURRY

This dry, spicy curry is a Sri Lankan delicacy. The addition of fennel seeds and ginger gives a lovely aroma.

THE CUT Wild boar haunch

SERVES 6
PREP 20 mins   **COOK** 2–3 hrs

3lb (1.35 kg) wild boar, cut into cubes

salt and freshly ground black pepper

2 tbsp sunflower oil

6 small onions, thinly sliced

2 red chiles, seeded and chopped

1 tsp fennel seeds

6 garlic cloves, sliced

1in (2.5cm) piece of fresh ginger, peeled and finely chopped

½ tsp ground turmeric

1 tbsp wine vinegar

1 tsp salt

juice of 1 lime

1 Place all the ingredients, except the lime juice, in a large heavy-bottomed saucepan. Add 1¼ cups water to just about cover the meat, and bring to a boil.

2 Reduce the heat to simmer and cook gently for 2–3 hours or until tender and well-cooked, stirring occasionally. Make sure the liquid does not dry out before the meat is cooked through.

3 Remove from the heat and stir in the lime juice. Serve hot with boiled or steamed rice.

KANGAROO TAIL AND CHICKPEA SOUP

A typical Australian outback recipe that is simple but full of flavor and textures. Perfect for chilly winter evenings.

THE CUT Kangaroo tail

SERVES 4
PREP 20 mins   **COOK** 2 hrs

1 tbsp olive oil

1 kangaroo tail, cut into pieces

1 onion, diced

5 garlic cloves, crushed

1 x 14oz (400g) can chopped tomatoes

1 x 1 tbsp tomato paste

2 star anise

14oz (400g) can chickpeas, drained

1 carrot, diced

2 cups beef or chicken stock

3 bay leaves

salt and freshly ground black pepper

1 tbsp chopped mint, to garnish

1 Heat the oil in a heatproof casserole. Add the meat pieces and cook over medium heat for 4–5 minutes, stirring occasionally, until well-browned. Remove and set aside.

2 Reduce the heat, add the onions, and cook for 3–4 minutes, stirring, until lightly colored and softened. Add the garlic and stir for 1 minute. Add the tomatoes, tomato paste, star anise, chickpeas, and carrot.

3 Return the meat to the casserole and add enough stock to cover the meat. Add the bay leaves and stir to mix. Reduce the heat to a simmer, cover, and cook for 1½ hours, or until the meat is tender. Season. Ladle into bowls, sprinkle over the mint, and serve.

VARIATION

Oxtail soup Use oxtail in place of the kangaroo tail, cooked navy beans in place of the chickpeas, and cook as above.

RABBIT PIE WITH LEMON AND SAGE

A lovely old recipe from southwest England, in which a crust is created from bread crumbs flavored with lemon and sage.

THE CUT Whole rabbit

SERVES 6
PREP 15 mins   **COOK** 2 hrs

2 rabbits, about 6½ lb (3kg) in total, cut into 6 pieces each (see p233)

all-purpose flour, seasoned with salt and pepper, for dusting

4 cups fresh bread crumbs

6 large onions, finely chopped

zest of 1 lemon

2 tbsp finely chopped sage

salt and freshly ground black pepper

2 eggs, beaten

2 tbsp milk

5 bacon strips

1 Preheat the oven to 400°F (200°C). Dust the rabbit pieces with the flour, and place in a straight-sided casserole.

2 Place the bread crumbs, onions, lemon zest, and sage in a large bowl. Season with salt and pepper, add the beaten eggs and milk, and mix well to combine and bind.

3 Cover the rabbit with the bacon and spread the stuffing over the top. Cook in the oven for 2 hours. Cover with foil if it starts to brown too early. Serve hot alongside green beans.

VARIATION

Chicken pie with lemon and tarragon Use chicken drumsticks in place of the rabbit and tarragon in place of the sage. Mix 1 teaspoon of English mustard with the milk and add to the casserole along with the other ingredients in step 2. Assemble the pie as above, but cook it in the oven for 1 hour instead of 2 hours.

RABBIT WITH MUSTARD

A French classic with a piquant contrast in flavors—good with both farmed and wild rabbits.

THE CUT Whole rabbit

SERVES 3–4
PREP 15 mins   **COOK** 1–1½ hrs

1 tbsp olive oil

2 tbsp Dijon mustard

salt and freshly ground black pepper

1 rabbit, about 3lb 3oz (1.5kg), cut into 6 pieces (see p233)

¼ cup dry white wine

¼ cup heavy cream

1 Preheat the oven to 450°F (230°C). In a large bowl, mix the oil, mustard, ½ teaspoon salt, and a sprinkle of pepper. Dip the rabbit pieces in the mixture and mix until well coated. Place the pieces in a gratin dish and cook in the oven for 5 minutes.

2 Remove from the oven. Add ½ cup water, cover with foil, and return to the oven, reducing the heat to 325°F (160°C). Cook for 1 hour, or until the meat is tender. Remove the meat pieces from the dish, cover with foil, and set aside.

3 Pour the wine in the gratin dish and cook over high heat for 3–5 minutes, stirring to dislodge any bits that may have stuck to the bottom. When the wine has reduced by one-third, stir in the cream, reduce the heat, and season to taste. Cook for 3–5 minutes, or until the sauce is thick enough to coat the back of a spoon. Strain the sauce. Place the rabbit pieces in a serving dish, pour the sauce over the top, and serve hot.

VARIATION

Braised chicken legs with mustard Use 3lb 3oz (1.5kg) chicken legs instead of the rabbit. Marinate as before, then cook in a large, heavy-bottomed pan for 7–8 minutes, until well-browned on all sides. Make the sauce as before. Arrange the chicken legs on a plate, pour the sauce over, and serve with small boiled potatoes and seasonal vegetables.

RABBIT SALAD

Luscious rabbit meat is a perfect foil for the crunchy, brightly colored salad of fresh seasonal produce.

CUT Rabbit saddle

SERVES 4
PREP 30 mins   **COOK** 10 mins

2 bone-in rabbit saddles, about 8oz (225g) each

salt and freshly ground black pepper

1 tbsp peanut oil

2 carrots, cut crosswise into 2in (5cm) pieces

1 celery stalk, peeled

2 white turnips

handful of sorrel leaves

2 tsp sunflower seeds

1 tsp butter

FOR THE DRESSING

2 tbsp extra virgin olive oil

juice of ½ lemon

½ tsp Dijon mustard

1 Remove the skin flaps from the sides of the saddles. Use a sharp knife to remove the fine membrane that covers the flesh of the saddle. Pat the meat dry with paper towels to remove any excess blood. Season with salt and pepper.

2 Heat the oil in a lidded saucepan. Place the saddles, skin-side down, and cook for 4 minutes, until well-browned. Flip, reduce the heat, cover, and cook for 15–20 minutes. Remove from the pan, cover with foil, and set aside.

3 Slice the carrot pieces lengthwise into 3–4 pieces, depending on the thickness. Then slice them into thin matchsticks. Slice the celery and turnips in the same way.

4 For the dressing, mix all the ingredients in a large bowl. Add the vegetables and sorrel leaves, toss to coat, and set aside. Remove each loin of rabbit, cutting parallel to the bone, and cut the 2 fillets from under the bone. Cut the meat into bite-size chunks.

5 Melt the butter in a pan, add the sunflower seeds, and stir until the butter starts foaming. To serve, place a small mound of the salad on a plate and top with the rabbit slices. Add a spoonful of sunflower seeds and a drizzle of the foaming butter.

HARE STEW WITH MUSHROOMS

A young hare is marinated in olive oil and garlic and then cooked simply with earthy mushrooms.

CUT Whole hare

SERVES 4
PREP 30 mins, plus marinating
COOK 1 hr 5 mins

1 leveret (young hare), cut into 8 pieces (see p233)

2 tbsp butter

3½oz (100g) bacon strips, chopped

1 tbsp brandy

1 cup game stock

4 tomatoes, peeled, seeded, and chopped

4oz (115g) crimini mushrooms, trimmed and sliced

FOR THE MARINADE

½ cup olive oil

salt and freshly ground black pepper

3 garlic cloves, unpeeled and crushed

juice of 1 lemon

1 Place all the marinade ingredients in a large bowl and mix to combine. Add the leveret, mix to coat, and let marinate for 4 hours in the fridge.

2 Melt the butter in a large, lidded saucepan over low heat. Add the bacon and cook for 5–10 minutes, until lightly colored.

3 Remove the meat from the marinade and reserve the liquid. Increase the heat to medium, add the meat, and stir to coat. Cook for 15 minutes, turning occasionally, until well-browned all over.

4 Pour the brandy into the pan. Remove and discard the garlic from the marinade. Add the marinade to the pan, then add the stock, tomatoes, and mushrooms. Season well and reduce the heat to simmer. Cover and cook for 40 minutes, until the meat is tender. Remove from the heat and serve hot with spätzle or pappardelle.

HARE TENDERLOIN WITH BEETS

This simple and colorful dish brings together a creamy beet sauce and the rich, earthy flavor of hare.

THE CUT Hare tenderloin

SERVES 4
PREP 45 mins, plus overnight marinating
COOK 30 mins, plus resting

2 hare tenderloins

2 tsp olive oil

12oz (350g) cooked beets, thinly sliced

2 tbsp chopped shallots

2 tbsp red wine vinegar

1 cup heavy cream

1 tsp Dijon mustard

snipped chives, to garnish

FOR THE MARINADE

2 cups red wine

1 carrot, diced

1 large onion, finely chopped

sprig of rosemary

1 bay leaf

½ tsp salt

8 black peppercorns

8 juniper berries

2 cloves

1 Use a knife to remove the membrane covering the tenderloins. Combine the marinade ingredients in a large bowl, add the meat, and mix to coat. Cover, refrigerate, and leave overnight.

2 Preheat the oven to 475°F (250°C). Remove the meat from the marinade and pat dry with paper towels. Strain the marinade, retain the liquid, and discard the rest.

3 Heat the oil in a large heavy-bottomed pan over high heat. Add the meat and cook for 3–4 minutes, until well-browned. Remove from the pan and transfer to a large roasting pan.

4 Place the roasting pan in the oven and cook for 10–15 minutes. The meat should still be pink. Cover with foil and let rest in a warm place. Remove about three-quarters of the fat from the pan.

5 Place the roasting pan over medium heat. Add the beets and cook for 1–2 minutes. Then add the shallots and cook for 2 minutes, stirring occasionally, until softened. Pour in the vinegar and ¼ cup of the marinade, and cook for about 1 minute.

6 Add the cream and mustard to the sauce. Stir to mix and season well. Cook the sauce, stirring, until reduced to a light coating consistency, but do not cook it for long.

7 Remove from the heat and keep warm. Remove the loins from the top of the tenderloin and the fillets from the bottom. Carve the meat lengthwise and serve with the beet sauce.

HARE IN CHOCOLATE SAUCE

This classic Italian dish uses a small amount of chocolate to enhance the flavor of the hare.

 THE CUT Whole hare

SERVES 6
PREP 45 mins **COOK** 2½ hrs, plus resting

1 hare, cut into 12 pieces (see p233)

¼ cup all-purpose flour, seasoned with salt and pepper

1 tbsp canola oil

6 tbsp butter

4oz (115g) bacon, chopped

1 large onion, thinly sliced

salt and freshly ground black pepper

sprig of marjoram

4 cups chicken stock

½ cup sugar

½ cup white wine vinegar

2oz (60g) chocolate, at least 75 percent cocoa solids

⅓ cup pine nuts

⅓ cup raisins

1 Preheat the oven to 325°F (160°C). Pat the hare pieces dry with paper towels to remove any excess blood. Place the flour in a shallow bowl. Add the meat, toss to coat, and shake off any excess.

2 Heat the oil and half the butter in a large, heatproof casserole. Add the meat when the butter begins to foam, and cook for about 10 minutes, until well-browned all over. Remove with a slotted spoon and set aside.

3 Reduce the heat and add the remaining butter to the casserole. Add the bacon and onion, and cook, stirring, until softened. Then add the marjoram and stock and bring to a boil.

4 Cover and place in the oven for 1½ hours. Remove from the oven, mix the sugar and vinegar in a small bowl, and stir into the casserole. Return the casserole to the oven for 30 minutes.

5 Remove from the oven and grate the chocolate into the casserole. Stir in the pine nuts and raisins, and let rest for 15 minutes. Serve warm with polenta and a green salad.

PHEASANT BREAST WITH SMOKED PAPRIKA

In this simple Spanish dish the pheasant is given an alluring smoky taste by the addition of paprika in the sauce.

THE CUT Pheasant breast

SERVES 4
PREP 10 mins **COOK** 30 mins

4 skinless pheasant breasts

2 tbsp butter

2 shallots, finely chopped

2 garlic cloves, chopped

1 tsp smoked paprika

½ cup dry vermouth

⅔ cup heavy cream

pinch of salt

juice of ½ a lemon

1 Pat the pheasant breasts dry with paper towels to remove any excess blood. Heat the butter in a lidded heavy-bottomed saucepan over medium heat. Add the pheasant breasts when the butter begins to foam, making sure the side that had the skin is facing down. Cook for about 10 minutes, until lightly colored. Then reduce the heat to low and turn them over. Cover and cook for an additional 5 minutes. Remove from the pan and keep warm.

2 Add the shallots and garlic to the pan, cook for 5 minutes until softened, and add the smoked paprika. Scrape up the juices from the bottom of the pan and stir well. Pour in the wine and bring to a boil.

3 Then pour in the heavy cream, reduce the heat to simmer, and cook gently until the sauce coats the back of a spoon. Taste and adjust the seasoning and add the lemon juice. Remove from the heat and strain the sauce, reserving the liquid. Place the breasts in a serving dish, pour the sauce over them, and serve with pilaf rice.

FAISAN NORMANDE

A traditional recipe from northern France, the gamey taste of the bird is balanced by crisp apples and a creamy brandy sauce.

THE CUT Whole pheasant

SERVES 2
PREP 20 mins   **COOK** 1 hr

1 young pheasant
4 tbsp butter, softened
1 tbsp sunflower oil
5 tbsp Calvados
1 cup heavy cream
salt and freshly ground black pepper
2 sweet apples, such as Gala or Golden Delicious, peeled, cored, and cut into wedges

1 Preheat the oven to 350°F (180°C). Season the meat and spread 1 tablespoon of the butter over the legs and breast. Heat the oil in an oval casserole over low heat. Add the pheasant, breast-side down, and cook each breast for 5 minutes, until browned. Then turn the bird onto its back, cover, and cook in the oven for 40–45 minutes.

2 Remove from the oven, transfer the pheasant to a serving dish, and keep warm. Strain off most of the fat from the casserole. Then pour over the calvados, bring to a boil, and cook for 2 minutes, until the alcohol has evaporated. Add the cream and continue to reduce the sauce by boiling, until the sauce coats the back of a spoon. Taste and adjust the seasoning.

3 Heat the remaining butter in a frying pan. Add the apples and cook until lightly browned but still retaining their shape. Place the pheasant in a serving dish with the apples arranged around it and serve with the sauce.

POT ROAST PHEASANT WITH BACON

Pot roasting helps to retain the moisture and the bacon adds flavor to this very lean bird.

THE CUT Whole pheasant

SERVES 2
PREP 20 mins
COOK 1 hr 20 mins, plus resting

1 young pheasant
2 bacon strips
2 tbsp sunflower oil
4 tbsp butter
sprig of thyme
1 bay leaf
1¼ cups white wine
salt and freshly ground black pepper

1 Place the bacon over the breasts of the pheasant and tie with a string to hold it in place. Preheat the oven to 350°F (180°C).

2 Heat the oil and butter in a heavy-bottomed heatproof casserole or Dutch oven over medium heat. Add the pheasant, breast-side down, and cook each breast for 5 minutes, until browned.

3 Then turn the bird onto its back. Add the thyme, bay leaf, and wine, lifting the pheasant slightly to get some liquid under it. Cover partially, transfer the casserole to the oven, and cook for 45 minutes.

4 Remove from the heat and let rest, covered, for 15 minutes. Then remove the pheasant and set aside. Place the casserole over high heat and boil the sauce for 5 minutes, or until thickened. Stir well and strain into a warmed bowl.

5 Cut the string from the pheasant and remove the legs. Place the legs on 2 separate plates. Carve the meat from the breast into thick slices and place on the legs. Top with the bacon, pour the sauce over, and serve with braised red cabbage.

PÂTÉ DE GIBIER EN CROÛTE

Made with a hot water crust, this delicious raised game pie provides a magnificent centerpiece for any party or occasion. The stock can be made a day in advance and then gently warmed.

THECUT **Mixed game**

SERVES 8–10
PREP 2½ hrs, plus overnight marinating, resting, and cooling
COOK 1½ hrs, plus chilling

FOR THE FILLING

1lb (450g) game livers, such as pheasant, hare, and rabbit, or lamb livers

3 tbsp vermouth

8oz (225g) boneless lean game meat, such as venison, pheasant, or rabbit

4oz (115g) pork fat

1 venison heart, trimmed

3 slices thick-cut bacon

1 shallot, finely chopped

1 garlic clove, crushed

1 egg, beaten

¼ tsp ground cloves

¼ tsp ground allspice

salt and freshly ground black pepper

FOR THE DOUGH

3 cups all-purpose flour

¼ tsp salt

¾ cup lard, diced

⅔ cup milk

1 egg yolk, beaten, plus 1 egg beaten to glaze

FOR THE JELLY STOCK

2 large onions

2 pig trotters

2lb (900g) pork bones

1 large carrot

1 celery stalk

2 bay leaves

2 tbsp dry sherry

1 For the filling, trim the livers of discoloration and connective threads. Roughly chop them, place in a bowl, and pour in the vermouth. Cover and let marinate in a cool place overnight. Place the game pieces, pork fat, venison heart, and bacon in a food processor and pulse until ground.

2 Transfer the ground mixture to a bowl and add the shallots and garlic, then pour in the egg and add the spices to the bowl. Season the mixture with salt and pepper and mix well. Cover and let marinate in a cool place overnight.

3 For the dough, sift the flour and salt into a bowl, mix, and make a well in the center. Boil the lard and milk in a pan. Pour the hot liquid into the well and use a wooden spoon to mix to form a smooth dough. Add the beaten yolk as it cools and combine well. When cool enough to handle, roll the dough out to about ½in (1cm) thick. Fold it in three and roll out again. Cover with plastic wrap and let rest in a cool place for 30 minutes.

4 For the jelly stock, place all the ingredients in a pan, cover with water, and bring to a boil. Reduce the heat to a simmer and cook for 2 hours. Strain, season with 1 teaspoon salt and a good grinding of pepper, and cook until reduced to about 2½ cups. Remove from the heat, skim off the fat, and let cool. Preheat the oven to 350°F (180°C). Meanwhile, line a pie or loaf pan with two-thirds of the dough.

5 Mix the livers with the game mixture and press into the pan. Roll out the remaining dough and use to cover the mixture. Brush the edges with a little water and squeeze them together. Brush the top with a little beaten egg, decorate it with dough trimmings, and brush with the remaining egg. Slit a small hole in the middle of the dough large enough to hold a funnel. Bake for 1½ hours.

6 Remove the pie from the oven and let cool in the pan. When both the pâté and the stock are cool, but not cold, use a funnel to slowly pour the stock into the pâté through the hole. Allow the stock to settle into the mold. Chill in the fridge for at least 12 hours. To remove the pie from the pan, wrap the pan in a hot wet kitchen towel, then run a knife around the edge of the pan before turning it out. It will keep in the fridge for several days.

GEORGIAN PHEASANT

An unusual dish from the Caucasus region, this recipe uses oranges and sweet wine to create an aromatic sauce.

THE CUT Whole pheasant

SERVES 2–3
PREP 30 mins   **COOK** 1 hr 15 mins

2lb (900g) muscat grapes

juice of 4 oranges

½ cup Georgian wine or Hungarian Tokay

1 green tea bag

2 cups walnut halves

1 pheasant

6 tbsp butter

salt and freshly ground black pepper

¼ cup all-purpose flour

handful of chopped flat-leaf parsley, to garnish

1 Preheat the oven to 375°F (190°C). Place the grapes in a food processor and pulse until it reaches the consistency of a purée. Strain and place in a large bowl. Add the orange juice and wine and mix to combine.

2 Place the tea bag in a small bowl and pour in ½ cup boiling water. Brew the tea for 5 minutes, then strain and discard the tea bag. Spread the walnuts at the bottom of a large casserole. Place the pheasant on top and pour the grape mixture over the top.

3 Place the casserole over medium heat, add half the butter, and pour over the tea. Add just enough water, if needed, to ensure the liquid covers the bird. Season with salt and pepper and bring to a boil. Cover and cook in the oven for 1 hour.

4 Remove from the oven, transfer the pheasant to a serving dish, and set aside. Strain the liquid into a wide saucepan and bring to a boil over high heat. Cook the liquid until reduced by half.

5 Meanwhile, mix the flour and remaining butter in a small bowl to form a paste. Add the flour paste to the pan, a little at a time, whisking constantly to form a sauce. Slice the pheasant breasts and cut the legs in two. To serve, pour the sauce over the meat and garnish with parsley.

ROAST GROUSE

Considered to be the king of game birds, in this dish the rich, coarse meat of the grouse is flavored with heather and served with liver pâté and toast.

THE CUT Whole grouse

SERVES 4
PREP 30 mins   **COOK** 30 mins

4 tsp blueberries

8 tbsp butter

4 sprigs of heather (optional)

4 young grouse, drawn with the livers reserved

salt and freshly ground black pepper

flour, for dusting

2 bacon strips

4 small slices of toast

⅔ cup game or chicken stock

1 Preheat the oven to 425°F (220°C). Place the blueberries, half the butter, and heather (if using) in the body cavities of each bird. Sprinkle evenly with salt and pepper and dust with the flour, shaking off any excess.

2 Place the remaining butter with the bacon in a roasting pan and place in the oven, until the fat has melted. Add the grouse to the pan and baste with the drippings. Roast the grouse in the oven for 10 minutes, then remove and baste again. Return to the oven, reduce the heat to 350°F (180°C) and cook for an additional 10 minutes.

3 Remove from the oven. Transfer the grouse and bacon to a serving dish and keep warm. Place the roasting pan over medium heat, add the grouse livers, and cook for 5 minutes. Remove from the pan and crush them with the back of a fork to form a paste. Spread the liver pâté on the toasts.

4 Pour off the excess fat from the pan, add the stock, and simmer to reduce by half. Taste and adjust the seasoning, if needed, and strain into a warmed bowl. Place each grouse on a separate plate, along with 1 toast and half a strip of bacon. Serve warm with the gravy on the side.

VARIATION

Roast squab You can use a young, fairly plump squab in place of the grouse and prepare as above.

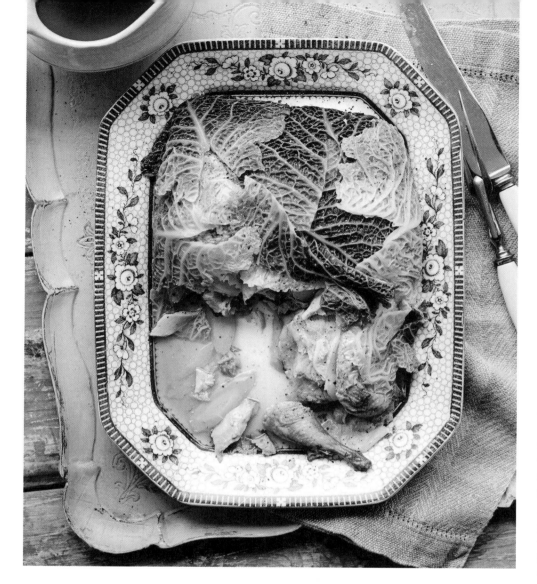

CHARTREUSE OF PARTRIDGE

The combination of bird, bacon, and cabbage is simply stunning in this vintage French dish.

THE CUT Whole partridge

SERVES 6
PREP 1 hr   **COOK** 2 hrs, plus resting

6 French partridges

salt and freshly ground black pepper

1 tbsp vegetable oil

8 tbsp butter

2 Savoy cabbages

1lb (450g) bacon

1 bay leaf

sprig of thyme

4 large carrots

1½ cups game or chicken stock

⅓ cup dry white wine

1 Preheat the oven to 450°F (230°C). Season the partridges with salt and pepper. Heat the oil and 2 tbsp of the butter in a roasting pan over medium heat. Add the partridges and cook until well-browned. Then transfer to the oven and roast them, breast-side up, for 15–20 minutes. Remove from the oven, transfer to a serving dish, and leave to rest for 15 minutes. When the partridges are cool enough to handle, remove the legs and breasts, and discard the rest.

2 Boil a large pan of water and add a teaspoon of salt. Remove the outer leaves of the cabbage, discard the discolored ones, and reserve the hearts. Rinse the leaves in cold water and plunge in the boiling water for about 3 minutes.

Then drain in a colander and run under cold water to arrest the cooking. Drain the cold leaves and dry on a clean dish towel.

3 Heat another 2 tbsp of butter in the roasting pan over medium heat. Add the bacon and cook until well colored. Cut the cabbage hearts into quarters, making sure you keep the central core intact. Move the bacon to the sides of the pan, add the cabbage hearts, and cook until lightly colored.

4 Add the bay leaf, thyme, carrots, and just enough water to cover the vegetables and bring to a boil. Cover with foil and place in the oven. Reduce the temperature to 400°F (200°C) and braise for 1 hour. Remove the vegetables and bacon with a slotted spoon and set aside. When cool enough to handle, slice the bacon and carrots and remove the stalks from the braised cabbage.

5 Increase the temperature to 425°F (220°C). Grease a 10 x 5in (25 x 12cm) ovenproof dish with the remaining butter. Trim the stalks of the blanched cabbage leaves. Place the largest and most intact leaf at the bottom of the dish and keep another one for the top. Line the dish with the leaves overhanging at the top to allow for a fold in, making sure they overlap and there are no gaps.

6 Spread two quarters of the braised cabbage over the base of the dish and season lightly with salt and pepper. Layer evenly with the breast meat. Cover with another two quarters of braised cabbage, season lightly with pepper, and top with the bacon slices. Add a third layer of cabbage, season lightly, and top with the carrots and legs. Season and cover with the last of the braised cabbage, pushing it down gently to make sure everything is in place. Top with the last cabbage leaf, bring in the overhanging leaves to seal, and bake for 30 minutes.

7 For the sauce, bring the stock and wine to a boil in a saucepan and cook until reduced by half. Season and pour into a warm bowl. Turn the Chartreuse out onto a large plate and serve with the sauce and plain boiled potatoes.

ROAST PARTRIDGE, WITH LEGS BRAISED IN PUY LENTILS

In this modern method of cooking the bird, the legs are cooked longer, with the crowns served pink. The lentils in the dish help make it hearty and satisfying.

THE CUT Whole partridge

SERVES 4
PREP 30 mins   **COOK** 1½ hrs, plus resting

4 partridges, legs and crowns separated

1 tbsp vegetable oil

1 tsp butter

1 celery stalk, coarsely chopped

1 large carrot, diced

1 onion, chopped

10oz (300g) Puy lentils, rinsed

2 tbsp red wine

1 bay leaf

sprig of thyme

4 bacon strips

1 Heat the oil in a small, heatproof casserole or Dutch oven, add the partridge legs and cook for 5–10 minutes over high heat, until well-browned. Remove from the heat and set aside. Reduce the heat, add the butter, and stir in the celery, carrots, and onions. Cook for 5 minutes, stirring to color lightly. Preheat the oven to 400°F (200°C).

2 Add the lentils and continue to cook for 5 minutes, stirring to combine. Pour in the red wine and add the herbs, bring to a boil, and return the legs to the casserole. Add just enough water to cover the meat and bring to a boil. Reduce the heat to a simmer, cover, and cook for 1 hour, until the meat falls off the bone.

3 Meanwhile, wrap each crown with 1 strip of bacon, season well, and roast in the oven for 15–20 minutes. Remove and leave to rest in a warm place for 30 minutes.

4 Remove the legs from the casserole and boil the liquid until reduced by half, leaving the lentils coated in a thin layer of sauce. Taste and adjust the seasoning, and remove from the heat. Use a fork to lightly shred the meat from the legs and return to the casserole. Stir to combine. To serve, ladle a large helping of the lentils and leg meat on 4 plates, slice the breast meat from the bone and place on top.

SQUAB PASTILLA

This traditional and popular street food found in the markets of Marrakech, is a blend of sweet, sour, and exotic flavors, all in one dish.

THE CUT Whole squab

SERVES 4
PREP 30 mins   **COOK** 2 hrs

10 tbsp butter, softened

3 squab

3 red onions, thinly sliced

small bunch of cilantro

small bunch of flat-leaf parsley

pinch of saffron threads

1 tbsp honey, plus extra to taste

1 cinnamon stick

salt and freshly ground black pepper

⅓ cup almonds, toasted and coarsely chopped

6 eggs, lightly beaten

1 tsp orange flower water

12 sheets ready-made phyllo pastry

2 tbsp confectioners' sugar, for dusting

1 tbsp ground cinnamon, for dusting

1 Melt 6 tbsp of the butter in a wide, lidded saucepan. Tie the squabs with a piece of butcher's string. Add the squabs, onions, herbs, saffron, honey, and cinnamon stick to the pan. Season, cover with 2½ cups water, and bring to a boil. Reduce the heat to low, cover, and cook for 1 hour.

2 Remove the squabs. Increase the heat and cook for 10 minutes, uncovered, to reduce the liquid. Meanwhile, use a fork to roughly shred the meat off the bones. Discard the bones. Return the shredded meat to the pan and remove and discard the herbs. Reduce the liquid until it just covers the bottom of the pan.

3 Add the almonds and 4 of the beaten eggs to the pan and stir to mix. Cook lightly, stirring, until curds of cooked egg form. Taste and season with salt or add honey if it needs sweetening. Then add the orange flower water, remove from the heat, and set aside to cool. Preheat the oven to 300°F (150°C).

4 Melt the remaining butter in a small pan. Lay four sheets of the pastry on a clean work surface. Lightly brush each of the sheets with the melted butter, place another sheet on top of the first, and brush with more butter. Repeat the pastry layers until all the sheets are used up.

5 Use a slotted spoon to place a quarter of the meat mixture in the center of each pastry pile. Fold the corners of the pastry over the mixture to make a five-sided circular sealed parcel. Brush each parcel with the remaining melted butter. Then brush with the beaten egg and place them on a baking sheet. Transfer to the oven and bake for 45 minutes. Remove from the oven and serve hot, dusted with confectioners' sugar and cinnamon.

THAI SWEET AND SOUR SQUAB

The tangy vegetable sauce adds color and flavor to this simple Thai dish. Chopping the vegetables into similar-sized pieces adds to the visual appeal of this dish.

THE CUT Squab breast

SERVES 4
PREP 30 mins   **COOK** 40 mins

2 tbsp white wine vinegar

1 tbsp soy sauce

½ tbsp all-purpose flour

1 tbsp vegetable oil

8 squab breasts

4 garlic cloves, crushed

½ tsp salt

1 onion, thinly chopped

2 red bell peppers, seeded and chopped

1 x 14oz (400g) can chopped tomatoes

1 small cucumber, peeled, seeded, and chopped

2 tbsp chopped cilantro leaves

1 Place the vinegar, soy sauce, and flour in a bowl. Mix to form a thin lumpy paste and set aside. Heat the oil in a lidded, heavy-bottomed saucepan over medium heat. Add the squab breasts and cook for 1–2 minutes on both sides.

2 Add the garlic and the salt, and stir to mix for 1 minute. Then add the onions and bell peppers and cook for 5 minutes, stirring frequently to coat in the juices.

3 Add the tomatoes and cucumber and stir to combine. Pour in the vinegar paste, mix thoroughly, and bring to a boil. Then reduce the heat to a simmer, cover and cook for 30 minutes, stirring occasionally, until the sauce takes on a glossy sheen. Remove from the heat, garnish with chopped cilantro, and serve hot with rice.

SALAD OF SQUAB BREAST

A selection of herbs and colored leaves makes this salad a refreshing first course.

THE CUT Squab breast

SERVES 4
PREP 15 mins   **COOK** 10 mins, plus resting

4 squab breasts

salt and freshly ground black pepper

1 tsp canola oil

1 tsp butter

4½oz (125g) mixed salad leaves, such as mesclun, arugula, baby chard, sorrel, and spinach, washed, dried, and stalks removed

4½oz (125g) mixed herbs, such as chervil, tarragon, and flat-leaf parsley, washed, dried, and stalks removed

FOR THE DRESSING

½ cup olive oil

2 tbsp white wine vinegar

1 tsp whole-grain mustard

1 Pat the squab breasts dry with paper towels to remove any excess blood. Season with salt and pepper.

2 Heat the oil and butter in a heavy-bottomed saucepan. When the butter starts to foam, add the squab breasts, skin-side down, and cook for about 2 minutes, until well-browned.

3 Reduce the heat and turn over the squab breasts. Cover partially and cook for another 2 minutes. Remove from the heat and let rest for 5 minutes.

4 For the dressing, mix all the ingredients in a large bowl. Chop the mixed salad leaves and herbs into bite-size pieces, add them to the dressing, and toss to coat. Divide the greens equally on four plates. Slice the squab breasts vertically and place on top of the greens. Serve immediately.

VARIATION

Salad of chicken breast Use 2 skin-on chicken breasts in place of the squab breasts. Pan-fry the meat for 10–15 minutes, then remove and rest for 5 minutes. Slice them vertically and serve as above with the dressing and greens.

GAME CASSEROLE

This highly flavored stew with mushrooms, celery, and carrots is best served with creamy mashed potatoes.

THE CUT Mixed game

SERVES 4
PREP 30 mins   **COOK** 1 hr 15 mins

1½lb (675g) (boned weight) mixed game, such as pheasant, venison, and duck, cut into bite-size pieces

all-purpose flour, for dusting

salt and freshly ground black pepper

1 tbsp olive oil

1 tbsp brandy

1 onion, finely chopped

2 garlic cloves, grated or finely chopped

2 celery stalks, finely diced

2 carrots, finely diced

1 bouquet garni

9½oz (275g) crimini mushrooms, quartered

½ cup dry white wine

2 tsp red currant jelly

2½ cups hot chicken stock

1 Preheat the oven to 350°F (180°C). Dust the meat lightly with a little flour, then season well with salt and pepper. Heat half the oil in a cast-iron pan, add the meat, and cook over medium heat, stirring occasionally, for 6–8 minutes, or until browned on all sides. Remove with a slotted spoon and place in a casserole.

2 Add the brandy to the pan and stir to deglaze. Then add the rest of the oil, if needed, and the onions. Cook over low heat for 6 minutes, or until soft. Stir in the garlic, celery, carrots, and bouquet garni and cook over low heat, stirring occasionally, for 8 minutes, or until tender.

3 Stir in the mushrooms, then increase the heat, add the wine, and boil for 2 minutes while the alcohol evaporates. Pour the mixture into the casserole with the meat, then stir in the red currant jelly. Pour in the stock, cover with a lid, and cook in the oven for 1 hour, or until the meat is tender. Add hot water during the cooking, if needed.

BRAISED QUAIL LUCULLUS

Named after a Roman epicure gourmet, this dish uses a light grape and wine sauce to enhance the delicate flavor of quail.

THE CUT Whole quail

SERVES 4
PREP 30 mins   **COOK** 1 hr

8 quails

16 bacon strips

2 tbsp vegetable oil

2 tbsp butter

1 onion, chopped

¾ cup white wine

1¼ cups chicken stock

2 tbsp brandy

20 seedless green grapes, peeled

salt and freshly ground black pepper

juice of 1 lemon

1 tbsp chopped flat-leaf parsley, to garnish

1 Wrap each quail in 2 strips of bacon and tie securely with butcher's string. Heat the oil and 1 tablespoon of butter in a large, lidded heavy-bottomed saucepan. Add the birds and cook for 8–10 minutes, until well-browned. Do this in batches to avoid overcrowding the pan. Remove with a slotted spoon and set aside.

2 Add the onion to the pan and stir for about 5 minutes, until softened and evenly browned. Reduce the heat, add the wine, and return the quails to the pan. Cook gently for 10 minutes, occasionally basting with the wine as it reduces. Then pour in the stock, cover, and simmer for about 20 minutes, until just cooked.

3 Remove the quails with a slotted spoon and set aside. Add the brandy and grapes and simmer for 5–10 minutes to reduce the sauce by half. Taste and adjust the seasoning, if needed, and remove from the heat. Stir in the lemon juice and remaining butter to form a light sauce.

4 Cut the strings from the quail but leave the bacon intact. Divide the quails on 4 plates with the grapes. Pour in the sauce, garnish with the parsley, and serve hot with plain boiled potatoes and green vegetables.

GUINEA FOWL WITH SMOKED BACON

This stunning dish brings together powerfully flavored ingredients that lift the gamey flavor of the bird.

THE CUT Whole guinea fowl

SERVES 4
PREP 1 hr, plus overnight marinating
COOK 40 mins

1 guinea fowl, about 2½lb (1.1kg), cut into 10 pieces

freshly ground black pepper

10 thin smoked bacon strips

3 tbsp peanut oil

2 tbsp butter

1 tbsp all-purpose flour

3½ cups chicken stock

5½oz (160g) baby onions

5 tbsp heavy cream

2 tbsp Crème de cassis

FOR THE MARINADE

3½ cups full-bodied red wine such as Rioja, Bordeaux, or Merlot wine

sprig of rosemary

1 bay leaf

sprig of thyme

1 garlic clove, unpeeled and crushed

1 Season the meat with pepper. Wrap each piece in a strip of bacon and fix it in place with a toothpick. Mix the marinade ingredients in a large bowl. Add the meat, mix to coat, and chill in the fridge overnight.

2 Remove the meat from the marinade and pat dry with paper towels. Strain the garlic and herbs from the marinade, set aside, and reserve the liquid. Heat the oil in a frying pan, add the meat, and cook for 4 minutes on each side, until well-browned, making sure the pieces are still wrapped in the bacon. Remove from the pan.

3 Heat the butter in a heatproof casserole and add the browned meat. Add the strained garlic and herbs and shake the pan gently to mix. Sprinkle in the flour and stir for 1–2 minutes to coat. Then pour in the marinade and stock, and add the onions. Bring to a boil, reduce the heat to simmer, and cook for about 20 minutes.

4 Remove the meat and onions. Remove the toothpicks, making sure the bacon is still wrapped, if possible. Cook the sauce for 10 minutes to reduce a little. Then add the cream and Crème de cassis, bring to a boil, and cook for 10 more minutes, until reduced by half. Strain through a fine sieve. Arrange the meat alongside the onions, pour the sauce over the top, and serve with mashed potatoes garnished with chopped herbs.

OSTRICH STEAKS

The flavor of the breast steaks, a lean meat, is greatly enhanced with an easy to prepare marinade.

THE CUT Ostrich breast steak

SERVES 4
PREP 15 mins, plus marinating
COOK 10 mins, plus resting

4 ostrich breast steaks, about 5oz (140g) each

1 tbsp canola oil, plus extra for brushing

2 tbsp Worcestershire sauce

1 garlic clove, minced

sprig of rosemary, coarsely chopped

salt and freshly ground black pepper

¼ tsp sumac

1 Place all the ingredients, except the steaks, in a large bowl and mix well to combine. Pour the marinade into a plastic bag, add the steaks, and seal the bag. Shake the bag gently to coat the meat. Leave to marinate for 30 minutes at room temperature.

2 Preheat a grill pan or broiler to its highest setting. Remove the steaks from the marinade, pat dry with paper towels, and brush lightly with the oil.

3 Grill the steaks for about 4 minutes on each side, until lightly colored. Then reduce the heat to low and cook for an additional 4 minutes on each side, until well done. Then leave the steaks, skin-side up, on the grill for an additional 5 minutes. Leave to rest for 5 minutes, then serve hot with some grilled mushrooms and fries.

MATCH UP

A mild mustard sauce, grilled mushrooms, or a crunchy green salad with a light dressing would be the perfect accompaniments to the delicate flavor of the ostrich.

BREAST OF WILD GOOSE

This lean bird is kept moist by being wrapped in foil and cooked with vermouth; the resulting juices make for a fine sauce.

THE CUT Wild goose breast

SERVES 2
PREP 15 mins   **COOK** 2 hrs

2 tsp canola oil

1 onion, finely sliced

2 sprigs of rosemary

2 skinless wild goose breasts, about 6oz (175g) each

salt and freshly ground black pepper

¼ cup dry vermouth

¼ cup heavy cream

1 tsp lemon juice (optional)

1 Preheat the oven to 325°F (160°C). Cut two squares of foil, about 12in (30cm) each, and brush the center with the oil. Place half a sliced onion, a sprig of rosemary, and then the goose breast on each sheet. Season well and drizzle the vermouth over them. Roll up the edges of the foil to enclose, place on a baking sheet, and cook in the oven for 2 hours.

2 Open the packages a little at one end. Pour the juices into a small saucepan, bring to a boil, and cook until reduced by half. Reduce the heat to simmer, add the cream, and cook until the sauce coats the back of a spoon. Taste and adjust the seasoning, and add a little lemon juice if needed. Slice the meat thinly and serve with the sauce poured on top.

VARIATION

Breast of wild duck You can use 2 skinless wild duck breasts in place of the goose breasts and thyme in place of the rosemary and cook as above.

SLOW ROASTED WILD GOOSE

Soft fruit and butter provide the moisture required to cook a wild goose and add a contrasting flavor as well.

 Whole wild goose

SERVES 4
PREP 30 mins   **COOK** 2 hrs, plus resting

8 tbsp butter, softened

4oz (115g) blackberries

1 cup raisins

1 orange, cut in half and zest grated

1 garlic clove, crushed

salt and freshly ground black pepper

1 skinless wild goose, about 5½lb (2.5kg)

1 large onion, sliced in rings

1 bay leaf

6 bacon strips

1 Preheat the oven to 350ºF (180ºC). Place the butter, fruits, orange zest, and garlic, in a large bowl. Season with salt and pepper, mix to combine, and form into a ball. Place the stuffing in the body cavity of the goose. Use one orange half to firmly seal the cavity of the bird.

2 Place 2 large sheets of foil on a clean work surface. Layer the center of the sheet with the onions and place the bay leaf on top. Then place the goose, breast-side up, on top. Spread 4 strips of bacon over the breast and 2 over the legs.

3 Wrap the goose in the foil to ensure that it is fully enclosed. Leave just a little space to allow air and heat to escape. Place in a roasting pan and roast in the oven for 1 hour. Then unwrap the foil, turn the bird over, and reseal the parcel. Return to the oven for 1 more hour.

4 Remove from the oven, open the foil parcel a little, and pour off about 1¼ cups of the liquid into a small saucepan. Turn the bird over so it is breast-side up and leave to rest for 15 minutes. Boil the cooking juices, taste and adjust the seasoning, and squeeze over the juice from the remaining orange half, if necessary. Carve the goose into slices and serve with the gravy on the side.

BREASTS OF WILD DUCK WITH SAUCE BIGARADE

Bigarade is the Provençal word for the Seville or bitter orange, a perfect match for this wild fowl.

THE CUT **Wild duck breast**

SERVES 4
PREP 15 mins   **COOK** 30–35 mins

4 wild duck breasts

salt and freshly ground black pepper

2 tsp all-purpose flour

1 cup game stock

zest and juice of 2 Seville oranges

1 tbsp Grand Marnier

1 tbsp sherry vinegar

1 tsp sugar

1 Heat the oil in a heavy-bottom saucepan over high heat. Pat the duck breasts dry with paper towels to remove any excess blood. Season all over, place skin-side down in the pan, and sear for 2–3 minutes. Turn the meat over and reduce the heat. Cover and cook for 5 minutes. Remove with a slotted spoon, cover with foil, and leave to rest in a warm place.

2 Stir the flour into the pan and cook for 1–2 minutes to color lightly. Pour in the stock, orange juice, Grand Marnier, and sherry vinegar. Reduce the heat to simmer and cook until the sauce just coats the back of a spoon. Taste and adjust the seasoning, add the sugar, and strain into a small pan. Then add the zest, simmer for 1–2 minutes, and remove from the heat. Carve the meat into thin slices and serve with the sauce and wild rice.

GAME TERRINE

Lined with bacon and with lean fillets of game through the middle, this terrine makes an impressive dish. It is best served a day later to allow the flavors to fully develop.

THE CUT Mixed game

SERVES 8–10
PREP 35–40 mins, plus marinating   **COOK** 1 hr

2 boneless pheasant breasts

3 tbsp Benedictine or drambuie

1lb (450g) ground lean game, such as venison or pheasant

2¼lb (1kg) ground pork belly

2 tsp salt

½ tsp freshly ground black pepper

4 garlic cloves, crushed

2 tsp Worcestershire sauce

30 pistachios, shelled

15–20 bacon strips

2 bay leaves

1 Slice the pheasant breasts lengthwise into strips. Rub the pieces with the Benedictine and let marinate in a cool place for 1 hour. Preheat the oven to 375°F (190°C).

2 Place the ground game and pork in a large bowl and mix well. Add the salt, pepper, garlic, and Worcestershire sauce. Pour in the Benedictine from the marinade, add the pistachios, and mix well to combine. Line an earthenware terrine with the bacon, leaving enough of an overhang to allow it to fold over the top when the terrine is filled.

3 Place one-third of the ground mixture over the bacon, pushing it firmly into the corners so that there are no air pockets. Top with half the pheasant strips, and another third of the ground mixture, and press down firmly. Place the remaining pheasant strips over the top and add the remaining ground mixture. Fold the bacon over to cover the mixture completely. Cut extra pieces of bacon to fill in if there are any gaps. Place the bay leaves on top and cover with foil.

4 Place the terrine on a baking sheet and cook in the oven for 1 hour, or until the juices run clear when pierced with a skewer. Let cool and refrigerate. To serve, cut into slices and serve with toast.

SALMIS OF WILD DUCK

A traditional method of serving game birds, this dish uses the livers to make a rich sauce.

THE CUT Whole wild duck

SERVES 4
PREP 45 mins   **COOK** 1 hr, plus resting

4 bacon strips

2 wild ducks, legs removed and livers retained

1 large onion, chopped

6 juniper berries, crushed

1 celery stalk, chopped

1 bay leaf

salt and freshly ground black pepper

1½ cups red wine

1 tsp butter

2 slices of white bread, soaked in stock and squeezed dry

1 Preheat the oven to 425°F (220°C). Place 2 bacon strips side by side lenghthwise on a cutting board. Place one duck on top of the strips, wrap the strips around, tying with pieces of butcher's string to secure. Repeat for the other duck. Transfer to a roasting pan and roast in the oven for 15 minutes. Remove and set aside to rest for 15 minutes.

2 Use a sharp knife to remove the breasts from the roasted ducks. Slice the meat on one side of the breast bone and following the contour of the bone, cut down to the back of the bird just below the wing. Place the breast meat on a plate, cover with foil to keep warm, and set aside. Coarsely chop the rest of the bird and keep aside.

3 Pour the fat and juices from the roasting pan into a large, heavy-bottomed pan. Add the chopped meat, the onion, juniper berries, celery, and bay leaf. Season with salt and pepper and pour in the wine. Bring to a boil, then reduce the heat and simmer for 30 minutes until the sauce reduces by half. Remove from the heat and set aside.

4 Melt the butter in a pan. Add the livers and cook for 4–5 minutes, until well-browned. Transfer the livers to a sieve along with the soaked bread slices, mash with the back of a spoon, and strain into a bowl. Strain the sauce into a pan, skim off any impurities, and whisk in the liver mixture. Heat the sauce gently, but do not boil. Cook for 5–6 minutes, or until it takes on a creamy texture. Slice the duck breasts thinly and arrange on a plate. Pour the sauce over and serve.

FASINJAN

A classic Iranian dish, the addition of pomegranate molasses provides an exotic sweetness.

THE CUT Whole wild duck

SERVES 4
PREP 15 mins   **COOK** 1½–2 hrs

3 tbsp vegetable oil

2 wild ducks, cut into 6 pieces each

1 onion, coarsely chopped

2½ cups walnuts, coarsely chopped

3 tbsp pomegranate molasses, plus extra to garnish

juice of 1 lemon

1 tbsp sugar

salt and freshly ground black pepper

chopped flat-leaf parsley and pomegranate seeds, to garnish

1 Heat the oil in a large, lidded, heavy-based pan. Add the duck pieces and cook for 5–7 minutes, until they turn brown on all sides. Remove with a slotted spoon and set aside.

2 Add the onions to the same pan and cook, stirring occasionally, for 3–4 minutes until browned. Then stir in the walnuts and cook over low heat for 2–3 minutes, stirring occasionally. Add the molasses, 2 cups water, lemon juice, and sugar, and bring to a boil.

3 Add the duck pieces to the pan, season with salt and pepper, and reduce the heat to simmer. Cover and cook for 1½ hours, or until the meat is tender. To serve, ladle a spoonful of the meat over boiled rice. Sprinkle with the chopped parsley and pomegranate seeds, and serve hot.

OSTRICH BURGERS

A lean alternative to the beef burger, served with savory ingredients that complement the richness of the meat.

THE CUT Ground ostrich

SERVES 4
PREP 15 mins, plus chilling   **COOK** 10 mins

1¾lb (800g) ground ostrich meat

1 onion, finely chopped

2 tbsp chopped flat-leaf parsley

1 tbsp capers, drained and chopped

4 anchovy fillets, chopped

salt and freshly ground black pepper

1 Place all the ingredients in a large bowl, season well, and mix to combine. Divide the meat mixture into 4 equal-sized balls and gently flatten to make patties. Chill the patties in the fridge for at least 1 hour to help firm them up.

2 Cook the patties on a hot grill or a griddle pan for 2 minutes on each side for medium-rare, or reduce the heat and cook for about 5 minutes, on each side, for well-done. Do not cook the patties for long over high heat as they will dry out fast. Serve with hamburger buns, mustard, and pickles.

VARIATION

Pheasant burgers Use ground pheasant meat in place of ground ostrich. Add a teaspoon of chopped dried cranberries and ¼ teaspoon of ground coriander to the meat mixture in step 1 to prevent the patties from becoming too dry. Cook as above.

OFFAL

OFFAL

IN THE RUSH TO EAT EVER MORE EXPENSIVE OR CONVENIENT CUTS OF EASILY PREPARED MEAT, THE SATISFACTION GIVEN BY TEXTURE IS TOO OFTEN IGNORED, YET IT IS THE TEXTURE OF OFFAL AS MUCH AS ITS TASTE THAT IS SO APPEALING. THE VARIETIES OF TEXTURE RUN FROM CRUNCHY TO CREAMY; THE FLAVORS FROM DELICATE TO POWERFUL. IT IS THESE CONTRASTS THAT DIFFERENTIATE OFFAL FROM ORDINARY MEAT.

OFFAL IS SOMETIMES REFERRED to as "variety meats" or "organ meats," but these delicacies comprise an extraordinarily diverse collection of taste and texture sensations. Some types of offal are indeed organs, such as liver, kidney, and heart; some are extremities, such as head, feet, and tail; others could be described as off-cuts from the main carcass, such as bones, fat, and membranes. This is truly the "nose-to-tail" section of the book.

Although every country has its favorite types of offal and ways of cooking them, the Middle East seems to be the center of the offal world, with the most delicious and inventive ways of using every scrap of an animal; surely the best and most sustainable approach to meat eating. In fact, immigrant communities often retain a fondness for the offal dishes of their home country, where waste is sacrilege. Equally, many offal dishes have now been rediscovered by modern chefs, who are thrilled by the diversity they offer.

BUYING OFFAL

As a general rule, organ meat should be cooked or frozen within 24 hours. Many items spoil quicker than ordinary meat

and do not improve with hanging. Therefore, most offal is removed before the carcass is hung to mature. Some items may need to be specially ordered in advance. Traditional butchers, whether indigenous or those catering to specialty communities' needs, are usually the best source of the less common types of offal. It is a measure of your butcher whether or not he can get them for you.

THESE DELICACIES COMPRISE AN EXTRAORDINARILY DIVERSE COLLECTION OF TASTE AND TEXTURE SENSATIONS

COOKING OFFAL

With only a few exceptions—some liver being one—most offal tends to be cooked thoroughly, whether it is by lengthy, gentle simmering or by slow stewing. Sometimes, this is followed by slicing and frying, or roasting. In recent years, though, some cuts that were traditionally stewed or baked (such as heart) are now also enjoyed when quickly fried and served pink, as one would cook a piece of steak. Other recipes, however, involve both lengthy preparation and prolonged cooking, but the reward is a dish full of complex flavor and texture

that is very inexpensive to prepare. These are not dishes suited to working people with little time or inclination to cook, but perfect for those for whom food preparation is deeply satisfying and an economical way of feeding a family.

HEALTH BENEFITS

Most offal is rich in nutrients and essential fatty acids, and low in harmful fat. However, where organ meats, such as chicken liver, come from intensively farmed animals, it should be thoroughly cooked to avoid salmonella poisoning. Organs that act as filters, such as kidney and liver, can accumulate drug residues that are most likely to be found in intensively farmed animals, although all producers must adhere to drug withdrawal periods.

OFFAL—ORGAN MEAT

AS WELL AS PROVIDING A VARIETY OF INTERESTING flavors and textures, organ offal is rich in nutrients and essential fatty acids, and most is low in fat. Organ offal should be bought very fresh and cooked or frozen quickly as it spoils easily, particularly any that act as filters.

LIVER

Liver is a good source of iron and probably the most popular of all the offal cuts. Poultry, veal, lamb, and venison liver have a delicate, sweet flavor; ox and pig liver taste stronger.

PIG'S LIVER This strongly flavored liver is popularly used in pork terrines and pâtés. It can also be fried or braised.

LAMB'S LIVER A sweet-tasting liver, lamb's liver is also at its best quickly fried until pink and sliced thinly.

POULTRY LIVER All poultry liver (such as chicken liver, above) has a particularly subtle, sweet flavor, with fattened duck and goose liver being highly prized.

KIDNEYS

As well as being a main ingredient, kidneys are added to slow-cooked dishes to enhance flavor. Ox kidneys are large clusters while other species, such as lamb (below) are single and sold whole.

CALF'S LIVER Pale and delicate, calf liver is the most tender of all. It is best lightly cooked so that it is still a little pink.

HEART

This muscle has a texture like fine-grained meat. Poultry hearts are sold as a delicacy, and in Scandinavia deer hearts are smoked and dried. Trim off excess fat.

LAMB'S HEART A meaty muscle that can be sliced and fried or braised, or it can be served whole, stuffed, and baked.

POULTRY HEARTS All poultry hearts are tiny (such as chicken hearts, above), so several are needed for each portion. They are most commonly grilled or quickly fried.

SWEETBREADS

An easily digestible delicacy, sweetbreads can be from several organs, most commonly the pancreas and the thymus, but testicles and the parotid gland are also sometimes sold as sweetbreads.

THYMUS SWEETBREADS The thymus is a gland that lies in the throat or neck. Sweetbreads are usually blanched before their final cooking.

PANCREAS SWEETBREADS Pancreas is only present in young animals such as calf and lamb, so it is in short supply and can be expensive.

BRAIN

Brain has a delicate flavor and creamy texture. Both calf's and lamb's brain are esteemed, but there is very little difference other than size between the brains of animals.

TRIPE

Of a ruminant's four stomachs, tripe is usually made from three: blanket tripe from the omasum, honeycomb tripe (below) from the reticulum, and large sausage casings from the abomasum. Tripe complements both mild and spicy flavors.

INTESTINES

A few recipes exist using the intestines of young milk-fed animals but most are used for sausage casings. Sometimes they are chopped and added to coarse-cut sausages such as andouillette.

LUNGS

An organ traditionally used in peasant dishes. Nowadays, because of its spongy texture, it is generally used only in manufactured products such as sausage, and dishes such as Scottish haggis.

SPLEEN

Spleen, or melt, usually comes from pig, ox, or calf and tastes like kidney. Normally made into manufactured products, it can also be stuffed and stewed or used for sandwiches.

GIZZARD

Used by a bird to grind up its food, this is a tough muscle but its flavor is useful for stocks and soups. When cooked as a confit, gizzards become very tender.

PREPARING ORGAN MEAT

- Many kinds of organ meat can be bought ready prepared but others need a little time spent on them before cooking. See pp266–7 for how to prepare kidneys, liver, sweetbreads, gizzard, and brains—the most common types of offal.

- If any wild game liver still has the bile duct attached (a small sac containing a dark green liquid), this should be carefully removed as the taste is powerfully bitter.

OFFAL—OTHER CUTS

These offal cuts are the external extremities of the animal. Many of them are simply muscles that can be cooked like other cuts, although they may contain more fat or bone than carcass cuts. Others are gelatinous or cartilaginous and their particular textures can be emphasized by simmering or roasting.

HEAD

Most commonly simmered, deboned, and molded in its own jelly as headcheese. Boiled calf's head is served along with the feet. A decorated roast boar's head makes a celebratory dish.

EAR

Calf and pig ears are the most common, although lamb's ears are also enjoyed. The cartilage never completely softens and the crunchy texture forms part of their appeal.

MUZZLE

Used to add texture to dishes, muzzle is also cooked and served in its own jelly or stewed in a spiced broth with other parts of the head.

CHEEK OR JOWL

A choice morsel off any animal (although it can be tough) it is included along with the head in headcheese, and is also cured, cooked, and rolled in bread crumbs to make a type of ham.

TONGUE

A nutritious delicacy with a soft melting texture. Tongues of all animals are used, even tiny rabbit and songbird tongues. Beef and reindeer tongues are smoked after being skinned.

POULTRY NECK

Although there is some meat on the neck, it is not easily accessible so it is used for soup and stock. Duck and goose neck skins are stuffed and cooked.

POULTRY FEET

Chicken, duck, and goose feet are not traditionally used in Western cooking, but their crunchy, gelatinous texture makes them much appreciated in Chinese cuisine. They need lengthy simmering to soften the cartilage.

ANIMAL FEET AND TENDONS

An excellent source of gelatin, used to make clear jellies and aspic and to give a silky texture to stocks. Calf's feet and pig's trotters are made into dishes.

TAIL

Oxtail is strong-flavored and meaty. Deer tails make broth in Chinese medicine. Fat-tailed sheep is highly prized in the Middle East for its distinctive brown fat. Pig's tails make tasty a snack.

SKIN

Skin adds texture. When boiled it adds gelatinous succulence, when fried or roasted it adds a crisp finish. Pork skin can be left on a roast to make "crackling."

FAT

Hard back fat is used as a sheet to lard or baste roasts and the caul fat membrane is used to encase meat patties. Lard cubes are used in salami-style sausages.

BONES

Poultry carcasses are used for soups and stocks. Spinal cord is a prized delicacy in some countries. Knuckle and marrow bones make aspic and jelly, and improve soups and stocks.

BLOOD

Most commonly used for blood sausages, which appear in most countries. Duck and goose blood is also mixed with spices and fat and baked into a little patty.

PRESERVED OFFAL

PRESERVED PRODUCTS MADE OF OFFAL are less common than those made with other meats because most offal is very perishable. For this reason, many offal products are either fresh (such as most blood sausages), or only partly preserved to extend their shelf life (such as headcheese, haggis, and foie gras).

CHOURIÇO DE SANGUE Most countries make blood sausages. Some have pork fat added; others have meat, rice, or other grains as well. This Portuguese blood sausage is smoked and dried to preserve it.

FOIE GRAS Geese and ducks are fattened to produce this sumptuous liver, which is cooked and stored in its own fat to preserve it.

HAGGIS The Scots' national dish, haggis is made of sheep's liver, heart, lungs, and fat, as well as oatmeal. The ingredients are stuffed into a sheep's stomach and cooked. It is only lightly preserved.

ZUNGENWURST Large pieces of pork tongue, skin, fat, and meat are bound with blood, oatmeal, and lard to make this attractive German *kochwurst* ("cooked sausage").

COU FARCIE DE CANARD The neck skin of duck is stuffed with shredded cooked meat and chunks of foie gras, then cooked to lightly preserve it.

ANDOUILLE A large French cutting sausage made of brined pig's tripe and intestines that are coiled into skins, then cooked and sometimes smoked.

BATH CHAPS Pork cheeks are cured in a flavored brine to partly preserve them. These little hams are then cooked, skinned, and rolled in bread crumbs.

FIGATELLU This hard sausage from Corsica is made with pork liver and blood, studded with fat. It is then dried and smoked.

PORK RINDS Thin strips of pork rind (skin) are fried or roasted, which renders any attached fat. Lightly salted, they make a popular crunchy snack.

SALCESON Popular in many countries, headcheese is made from boiled pig's head. Like this Polish version, the meat is lightly preserved in its own jelly. Some versions contain other offal.

DRIED CHICKEN FEET Easily preserved by being cleaned and dried, chicken feet (sometimes called Phoenix claws) are popular in Chinese cuisine.

PREPARING ORGAN MEAT

Most organ meat has some kind of a membrane. This needs to be removed before cooking since it will toughen and can make the meat distort. It is usually very easy to peel off.

PREPARING KIDNEYS FOR FRYING

A whole veal kidney is shown here. Beef and veal kidneys, which have multiple lobes, are very different than lamb, pig, and deer kidneys, which have a simple shape and usually very little fat to remove.

1 Carefully pull away and discard the white fat (suet) that surrounds the whole kidney—it will come away quite easily.

2 Lay the kidney upside down. With the point of a paring knife, cut around the fatty core and pull it away to release the membrane covering the kidney.

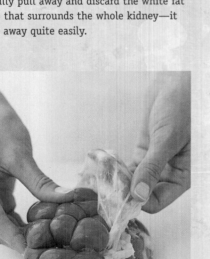

3 Discard the core. Peel the membrane off the whole kidney—it will slip off easily when you tug with your fingers.

4 Cut the kidney into bite-sized pieces following the natural lobes, then cut off the fatty cores from each piece. The kidney is now ready to be pan-fried.

PREPARING LIVER

Liver is at its best if it is cooked pink, or else very gently and slowly—otherwise it can taste bitter.

CALF'S LIVER This is excellent for pan-frying because it cooks very quickly over high heat. Cut away any membranes and arteries with a utility or small slicing knife, then slice the liver thickly.

CHICKEN LIVER Chicken livers are always good value. To clean chicken livers, use a paring knife to cut away any green patches, membrane, and the fibers around the center of each.

PREPARING SWEETBREADS

Soaking sweetbreads whitens them and softens the fine filament that covers them.
If they are not to be used within 24 hours, soak them, then blanch them in salt water.

1 Soak the sweetbreads in cold running water for 1–2 hours, then peel off as much of the filament and patches of blood as possible. The filament is firm enough to peel off easily.

2 Soak them again in a solution of 1 tablespoon of vinegar per 5½ cups (1.5 liters) water for a further 1–2 hours. Then peel off any remaining filament plus any small tubes that are to be found in and around the pieces.

PREPARING GIZZARD

The gizzard is usually already cleaned when bought with domestic poulty giblets, but you will need to clean and prepare the gizzards of game birds.

1 Cut the gizzard almost in half, right through the gritty part in the center; they are tough muscles to cut. Turn them inside out to remove the grit and gizzard contents, then rinse thoroughly under running water.

2 Trim off any soiled pieces around the cut edges and then trim off all the thick silver skin surrounding it. Finally, slice or peel off the thick inner membrane that was next to the grit, trimming off any soiled parts.

PREPARING BRAINS

Remove excess blood by soaking the brains in strong brine for four hours. Then rinse, or leave in a bowl under cold running water. Peel off the membrane. Remove any bone fragments and as much remaining blood as possible. Poach very gently for 5 minutes. Leave to cool. Slice if wished.

MAKING BLOOD SAUSAGE

These French-style blood sausages are soft and creamy. Our recipe uses fresh pig's blood but dried pig's blood can be bought from butchers' suppliers and reconstituted.

1 Mix together 1 tsp allspice, 1 tsp brown sugar, 1/3 cup salt, 4 heaping tbsp finely chopped parsley, and 2 cups bread crumbs. Stir these into 10½ cups fresh pig's blood with 2½ cups heavy cream. Dice 3lb 3oz (1.5kg) pork back fat into ¼–½in (7–10mm) cubes.

2 Cook 3lb 3oz (1.5kg) onions gently in 11 tbsp unsalted butter or ½ cup vegetable oil in a large frying pan until softened but not browned. Cool and then add to the blood mixture. Stir in the diced fat and mix everything together very thoroughly.

3 Knot one end of a 23-ft (7-m) length of ox runner or other casing. Fit the open end on to a funnel's nozzle and pull the remaining skin on to the nozzle. Pour the blood mixture into the nozzle and start to fill the skin.

4 When pouring the blood mixture into the casing, grip the nozzle tightly to keep the skin from slipping off. Fill the skins quite loosely, as the mixture swells when cooked. Knot the end of the skin firmly.

5 Leave the sausage as a coil, or tie it into rings. To do this, divide the sausage into lengths and tie the ends with string. Then fold the skin over the knot and re-tie, then tie both ends together. This prevents the sausages from bursting at the ends, and makes them easier to handle.

6 Half-fill a large boiling pan with water and place a rack on the bottom. Bring the water to a boil, then remove the pan from the heat. Lower the sausages in carefully and return the pan to a very low heat. Do not boil, or the sausages may burst.

7 If the sausages float, prick them with a sterilized needle or toothpick. Cook them very gently for 15 minutes, then prick them again. If the liquid that emerges is bloody, cook for another 5 minutes, or until the liquid comes out brown.

8 Drain off the water carefully because the hot sausages are fragile, or lift them out using the rack. Fill a clean sink with cold water and cool the sausages in it for 15 minutes before handling. Refrigerate the sausages to make them firm, then cut them into slices to cook.

PORK MEATBALLS

The mix of pork and pork offal seasoned with sage and onion makes this a flavorsome and highly nutritious dish.

THE CUT Pig liver and heart

SERVES 6
PREP 1 hr **COOK** 1 hr

2lb (900g) boneless, skinless pork belly, trimmed and sinew removed

2lb (900g) bacon strips

9oz (250g) pig's liver

1 pig's heart

¼ tsp grated nutmeg

¼ tsp ground ginger

1 tsp chopped sage

1 tsp chopped marjoram

1 onion, chopped

¼ tsp salt

5 cups brown bread crumbs

3 large eggs, lightly beaten

½ tsp freshly ground black pepper

1 pig's caul, about 14oz (400g)

1 cup chicken stock

1 Preheat the oven to 375°F (190°C). Roughly chop all the meats and place them together in a large bowl. Add the spices, herbs, onion, and salt, and pass through a meat grinder.

2 Transfer the meat mixture to a large bowl. Add the bread crumbs and eggs, mix to combine, and form into small balls of 2oz (60g) each.

3 Soften the caul in water and spread it out. Cut into squares large enough to cover each meatball. Wrap the caul around the meatballs and place them in a roasting pan. Add in a little stock to prevent them from drying out and cook in the oven for about 1 hour. Remove from the oven and spoon over the pan juices. Serve with mashed potatoes and some green vegetables such as peas.

PORK AND LIVER TERRINE

A classic country-style pâté with layers of ham, it is enriched with both cream and eggs.

 THE CUT Chicken liver and pork fat

SERVES 8
PREP 1 hr **COOK** 1½ hrs

1 tbsp butter

1 onion, finely chopped

4½oz (125g) chicken livers, trimmed

9oz (250g) lean pork leg or shoulder

4oz (115g) pork fat

¼ tsp ground allspice

pinch of ground cloves

pinch of grated nutmeg

2 garlic cloves, crushed

2 tbsp brandy

2 eggs, lightly beaten

⅔ cup heavy cream

salt and freshly ground black pepper

7oz (200g) bacon strips, thinly sliced

7oz (200g) ham, thinly sliced

1 bay leaf

1 Preheat the oven to 350°F (180°C). Heat the butter in a frying pan, add the onions, cook gently until soft and lightly browned. Set aside.

2 Mince the livers, pork, and fat. Place the meat in a large bowl, add the spices, garlic, and brandy. Then add the eggs, cream, and cooked onions. Season and mix well to combine.

3 Line a 1 quart terrine with the bacon, leaving enough of an overhang. Place one-third of the mixture over the bacon, pushing it firmly into the corners so that there are no air pockets. Cover with half the ham slices, and another third of the meat mixture, and press down firmly. Place the remaining ham slices over the top and add the remaining meat mixture. Fold the bacon over to completely cover the mixture. Cut extra pieces of bacon to fill in if there are any gaps. Place a bay leaf on the top and cover with the lid.

4 Place the terrine in a water bath and cook in the oven for 1½ hours or until the juices run clear when pierced in the middle. Leave to cool. Press the terrine down using weights and leave for at least three days. To serve, turn the pâté out of the terrine and cut into slices.

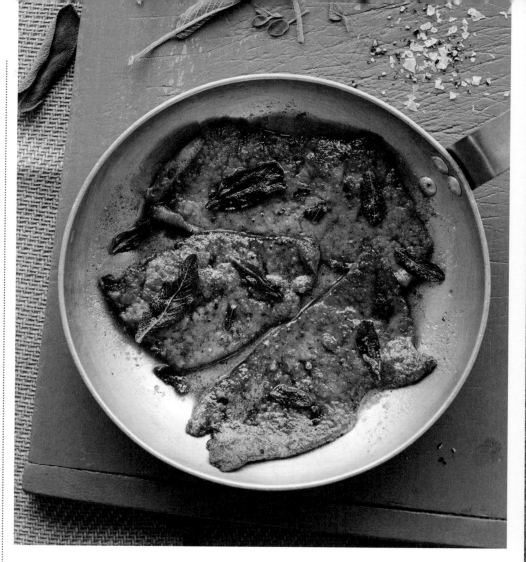

CALF'S LIVER WITH SAGE

The aroma of sage leaves permeates the quickly cooked liver in this classic dish. Replace the lemon juice with balsamic vinegar for a sweet and sour twist.

THE CUT Calf liver

SERVES 4
PREP 15 mins **COOK** 5 mins

2 tbsp all-purpose flour, seasoned with salt and pepper

1lb (450g) calf's liver, trimmed and sliced

1 tsp olive oil

1 tbsp butter, plus a pat of butter extra

handful of sage leaves

juice of 1 lemon

1 Place the flour in a shallow dish. Add the liver, toss to coat lightly, and shake off any excess. Heat the oil and 1 tablespoon of butter in a large frying pan over medium-high heat. As the butter starts to foam, add the liver, making sure the pieces do not touch, and cook for about 2 minutes on each side. Do this in batches to avoid overcrowding the pan. Remove the liver from the pan, place on a serving dish, and keep warm.

2 Reduce the heat and add a pat of butter to the pan. Then add the sage leaves and, as soon as they start to fizzle, add the lemon juice. Place the sage leaves over the liver, pour over the buttery juices, and serve hot.

VARIATION

Calf's liver with bacon Cook a few strips of bacon in the same pan as the liver, until browned. Place the bacon on the liver and add a pat of butter to the pan. Cook the butter and bacon juices, stirring, until they start to foam. Pour the cooking juices over the liver and bacon. Serve hot.

SAUTÉED LIVER AND ONIONS

The sweet, caramelized onions are the star of this delicious dish and can be cooked the night before if you want to get ahead.

THE CUT Calf liver

SERVES 6
PREP 15–20 mins   **COOK** 1 hr

⅓ cup olive oil

2¼lb (1kg) large onions, sliced

salt and freshly ground black pepper

1lb 10oz (750g) calf's liver

FOR THE MASHED POTATOES

1lb 6oz (635g) potatoes, peeled and cut into chunks

¼ cup milk

4 tbsp butter

1 Heat two-thirds of the oil in a frying pan over low heat. Add the onions, season lightly, and cover with foil. Cook the onions for 25–30 minutes, stirring occasionally, until softened.

2 Remove the foil from the pan, increase the heat to medium-high, and cook, stirring constantly, for 5–7 minutes until caramelized and golden, but not browned. Transfer to a bowl with a slotted spoon, leaving any excess oil in the pan.

3 Meanwhile, place the potatoes in a saucepan with salted water, cover, and bring to a boil. Simmer for 15–20 minutes until tender. Drain thoroughly and mash with a fork. Heat the milk in a separate saucepan, add the butter, season, and mix. Gradually, add the hot milk to the potatoes, beating until light and fluffy. Taste and adjust the seasoning and keep warm.

4 Slice the liver about ¼in (5mm) thick and season. Heat the remaining oil in the pan over high heat. Add the liver and cook for 45–60 seconds on each side, until just browned but still pink inside. Transfer to a plate and keep warm. Return the onions to the pan and stir quickly over high heat for 30–60 seconds until very hot. Season and serve at once on warmed plates with the mashed potatoes.

VENISON LIVER WITH ONIONS

A glorious combination of melting liver and sweet, almost caramelized, onions, this classic comfort food takes minutes to prepare.

THE CUT Venison liver

SERVES 4
PREP 15 mins   **COOK** 1 hr

4 tbsp olive oil

4 tbsp butter

1lb (450g) onions, thinly sliced

½ tsp thyme leaves

splash of lemon juice

salt and freshly ground black pepper

1lb 5oz (600g) venison liver, trimmed, sinew removed, and cut into ½in (1cm) slices

all-purpose flour, seasoned with salt and pepper, for dusting

chopped flat-leaf parsley, to garnish (optional)

1 Heat half the oil and half the butter in a large frying pan over high heat. Add the onions and stir to coat in the fat until they start to color. Reduce the heat to low, add the thyme, and cook for 45 minutes, stirring occasionally, until the onions are soft and lightly browned. Add the lemon juice and season, then set aside in the pan to keep warm.

2 Heat the remaining oil and butter in a frying pan. Place the flour in a shallow dish. Add the liver, toss to coat, and shake off any excess. Cook the liver in the pan for 1 minute on each side, until golden brown on the outside but still pink inside. Do this in batches to avoid overcrowding the pan.

3 Spoon the onions onto a warm serving platter and arrange the liver on top. Garnish with some parsley, if you like, and serve with mashed potatoes.

VARIATION

Lamb livers with onions Use lamb livers in place of venison liver and add 1 teaspoon balsamic vinegar to the onion mixture. Cook as above and serve hot.

MOROCCAN SKEWERED LIVERS AND HEARTS

This grilled dish of tender meat is the perfect addition to a summer barbecue and is delicious served rare.

THE CUT Lamb liver and heart

SERVES 4
PREP 15 mins, plus soaking and marinating
COOK 5–6 mins

1lb (450g) lamb livers, trimmed

1lb (450g) lamb hearts, trimmed

2 garlic cloves, crushed

1 tbsp chopped parsley

1 tsp ground cumin

1½ tsp paprika

sea salt

1 tbsp olive oil

1 Soak 12 wooden skewers in cold water for at least 1 hour. Remove the sinew and connective tissue from the livers and hearts. Chop the hearts into cubes suitable for sliding onto a skewer.

2 Place the livers and hearts in a large bowl. Add the remaining ingredients and mix to coat. Let marinate for at least 1 hour at room temperature.

3 Set the broiler at its medium setting. Thread the livers and hearts onto the skewers, alternating between the two. Broil for 3–4 minutes, turning occasionally as they cook, until browned and evenly cooked on the outside, but still pink on the inside. Serve hot with a green salad and tahini.

DO NOT CHOP!

The livers should be left whole to ensure that they do not fall off the skewer during both the cooking and serving process.

QUICK FRY VENISON HEARTS

The easy to prepare marinade adds a depth of flavor to this meltingly tender meat.

THE CUT Venison heart

SERVES 2
PREP 15 mins, plus marinating
COOK 5 mins, plus resting

1 large or 2 small venison hearts, trimmed and gristle removed

½ cup olive oil

2 tbsp red wine vinegar

sprig of rosemary, bruised

1 tsp juniper berries, crushed

salt and freshly ground black pepper

1 tsp butter

2 tsp olive oil

1 Slice the hearts into ½in (1cm) thick pieces and place in a bowl. In a separate bowl, mix the oil, vinegar, and herbs. Season with a pinch of salt and a few grinds of pepper.

2 Pour the oil and herb mixture over the hearts. Mix well to coat and leave to marinate overnight or for about 12 hours.

3 Remove the hearts from the marinade and pat dry with paper towels. Heat the butter and oil in a heavy-bottomed frying pan over high heat.

4 Add the hearts to the pan and brown for 1 minute on each side. Remove from the heat. Remove the hearts from the pan, place on a serving dish, and leave to rest for at least 4 minutes. Serve hot with a green salad and fries.

COOK WITH CARE

It is very important to dry the hearts really well before cooking to ensure that they cook quickly and remain tender.

DIRTY RICE

A classic recipe from the Deep South, this dish gets its name from the color given by the meat.

THE CUT Chicken liver

SERVES 6
PREP 15 mins   **COOK** 1 hr, plus resting

4 tbsp olive oil

1 onion, finely chopped

½ celery stalk, finely chopped

1 green bell pepper, finely chopped

9oz (250g) ground pork

7oz (200g) chicken livers, trimmed and finely chopped

1 green chile, seeded and finely chopped

2 garlic cloves, finely chopped

1 tsp smoked paprika

1 tsp coriander seeds, crushed

10oz (300g) long-grain white rice

salt and freshly ground black pepper

2½ cups hot chicken stock

large sprig of thyme

handful of flat-leaf parsley leaves, finely chopped

1 tbsp finely chopped oregano leaves

1 Preheat the oven to 325°F (160°C). Heat 3 tablespoons of oil in a large heatproof casserole or Dutch oven. Add the onion, celery, and green pepper and cook for about 5 minutes, until soft. Remove from the casserole and set aside.

2 Pour the remaining oil into the casserole and increase the heat to high. Add the pork and the chicken livers, and cook for about 5 minutes, turning occasionally, until the meat is well-browned. Then add the chile, garlic, smoked paprika, and coriander seeds, and cook for an additional 2 minutes.

3 Return the vegetables to the pan, stir in the rice, and season well. Then add the hot stock and thyme, and bring to a boil. Stir the rice well, cover, and transfer to the oven. Cook in the oven for 30–40 minutes, stirring occasionally, until the rice is cooked and the stock absorbed.

4 Remove from the heat and leave to rest for about 5 minutes. Remove and discard the thyme and stir in the parsley and oregano. Taste and adjust seasoning, if needed. Serve hot.

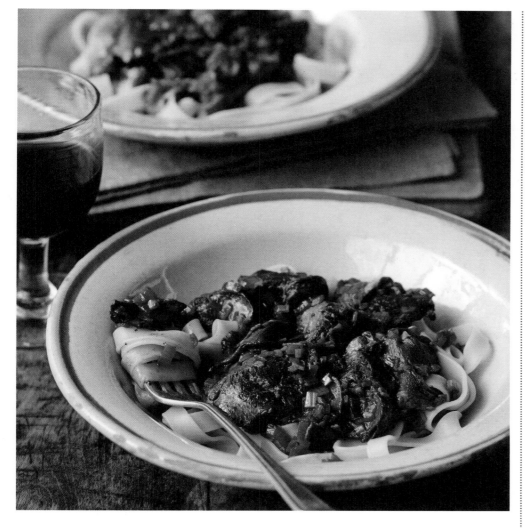

LAMB HEARTS STEWED WITH PRUNES

The natural sweetness of this warm and flavorsome dish is enhanced by the addition of dried prunes.

THE CUT Lamb heart

SERVES 4
PREP 20 mins   **COOK** 1 hr 45 mins

2 tbsp butter

16 baby onions

2 lamb hearts, trimmed and sliced

1 tbsp all-purpose flour

¾ cup red wine

sea salt and freshly ground black pepper

1 clove

1 tsp red currant jelly

12 dried prunes

zest of 1 lemon

1 Melt the butter in a large saucepan over medium heat. Add the onions and cook for about 5 minutes or until lightly browned. Remove from the pan and set aside.

2 Pat the hearts dry with paper towels to remove any excess blood. Place the flour in a shallow dish. Add the hearts, toss lightly to coat, and shake off any excess. Add the hearts to the pan and cook until well-browned.

3 Pour the wine and ¾ cup water into the pan. Season well and add the clove and red currant jelly. Cover the pan and simmer for 1 hour 15 minutes. Check occasionally and add more water if it looks like it is drying out.

4 Then add the prunes and lemon zest, return the onions to the pan, and cook for an additional 20 minutes or until the meat is cooked. Taste and adjust the seasoning. If the sauce looks too thin, remove the meat, onions, and prunes, and reduce a little by rapid boiling. Return the ingredients to the pan and stir through. Serve hot with rice or mashed potatoes.

VARIATION

Rabbit stew with prunes Use rabbit in place of the lamb hearts and all-purpose flour in place of the brown flour. Add 1 teaspoon chopped rosemary and cook as above.

CHICKEN LIVER WITH MARSALA

This delicious dish uses a simple sauce from the Piedmont region of Italy, where wild mushrooms, including truffle, grow in abundance.

THE CUT Chicken liver

SERVES 4
PREP 15 mins, plus soaking
COOK 10 mins

4 tbsp butter

14oz (400g) chicken livers, trimmed

2 shallots, finely chopped

1oz (30g) dried porcini mushrooms, soaked in water for 30 minutes and the water reserved

1 tsp tomato paste

4 tbsp Marsala

1 Heat the butter in a large saucepan over medium heat. Add the livers and cook for about 2 minutes. Remove with a slotted spoon, place on a plate lined with paper towels, and set aside.

2 Add the shallots to the pan and cook until soft. Then add the mushrooms and tomato paste and stir to combine. Stir in the Marsala and shake the pan lightly to mix through.

3 Return the livers to the pan and mix well to coat with the sauce. Taste and adjust seasoning, if needed, and add a little of the reserved soaking water if the sauce seems too thick. Serve hot with tagliatelle mixed with a little truffle oil.

VARIATION

Lamb liver with dry sherry Use lamb livers, cut into small pieces, in place of the chicken livers, 2½oz (75g) crimini mushrooms in place of the porcini, and dry sherry in place of the Marsala. Cook as above and serve hot.

CHICKEN LIVER PÂTÉ

This rich and smooth pâté is flavored with brandy, sage, and garlic. Easy to make, it serves as a delicious appetizer.

SERVES 8–10
PREP 20 mins **COOK** 10 mins

20 tbsp butter, softened

8oz (225g) chicken livers, trimmed

¼ tsp sage

1 garlic clove

2 tbsp brandy

sea salt and freshly ground black pepper

4 tbsp clarified butter, to seal

VARIATION

Chopped liver with boiled eggs Heat 3 tablespoons of chicken fat in the saucepan over medium heat. Add 1 chopped onion, season with a pinch of salt, and cook gently for about 6 minutes until softened. Remove from the pan and set side. Add 3 more tablespoons of chicken fat to the pan. Add the chicken liver, when the fat is hot, and cook until lightly colored but still pink inside. Do not overcook the livers. Transfer the ingredients to a food processor. Add another 3 tablespoons of chicken fat and 1 roughly chopped hard-boiled egg. Pulse briefly until the livers are roughly chopped and still coarse. Season to taste and transfer the mixture to a large bowl. Top with another finely chopped hard-boiled egg and some crispy chicken skin, if you like, and chill. Serve with slices of challah bread and pickles.

CREAMY CONSISTENCY

For a very smooth pâté, at stage 4 press the processed mixture through a sieve using the back of a ladle. Make sure you do this before the butter begins to cool.

1 Trim the livers of any discoloration and pat dry with paper towels to remove any excess blood. Heat 7 tbsp of butter in a saucepan over medium heat. Add the livers and cook for 8 minutes, stirring, until cooked through. Then add the sage and garlic and cook, stirring, for 1–2 minutes.

2 Pour in the brandy and season with half a teaspoon of sea salt and a good grinding of pepper. Pour the mixture into a food processor, scraping up all the bits with a wooden spatula. Pulse the mixture thoroughly, adding the remaining butter a little at a time, to create a smooth paste.

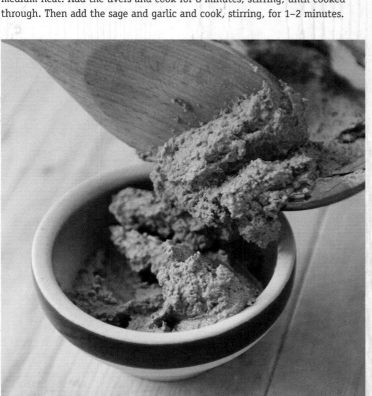

3 Transfer the paste to a ramekin, pressing it down lightly with the back of a spoon to firmly pack it in. Let cool and set.

4 Cover the cooled mixture with a layer of the clarified butter and place in the fridge to chill overnight. Serve cold with toast.

CALF BRAINS IN BLACK BUTTER

The touch of lemon cuts through the creamy texture in this easy-to-cook, melt-in-the-mouth delicacy.

THE CUT Calf brain

SERVES 4
PREP 30 mins, plus soaking and chilling
COOK 25 mins

2 calf brains

2 tbsp flour, seasoned with salt and pepper

2 tbsp olive oil

1 tbsp butter

1 tbsp chopped flat-leaf parsley

juice of 1 lemon

FOR THE COURT BOUILLON

1 small onion, sliced

5 black peppercorns

1 bay leaf

6 flat-leaf parsley stalks

sprig of thyme

1 tbsp white wine vinegar

1 Place the brains in a large saucepan, cover with cold water, and let soak for about 2 hours, changing the water twice to remove the blood.

2 For the court bouillon, place all the ingredients in a large saucepan big enough to hold the brains and add 5½ cups cold water. Bring to a boil and then reduce the heat to a simmer. Add the brains to the pan and poach for 20 minutes, then drain and let cool. Chill the cooled meat in the fridge for at least 3 hours.

3 Peel off the membrane using a pair of scissors and slice the brains. Place the flour in a large shallow dish. Add the brains, toss lightly to coat, and shake off any excess. Heat the oil and 1 tablespoon of butter in a large frying pan over medium heat. When the butter starts to foam, add the brains and cook for 5 minutes, until lightly browned all over. Remove with a slotted spoon and drain on a plate lined with paper towels.

4 Heat the remaining butter in the pan until it begins to turn brown and produces a distinct nutty smell. Pour in the lemon juice and swirl it in the pan. Divide the brains between 4 warm plates, sprinkle with the parsley, and pour over the butter and lemon mix. Serve immediately.

LAMB SWEETBREADS CROSTINI

A delicious first course or light dish, the crunchy toast sets off the creamy texture of the sweetbreads.

THE CUT Lamb sweetbreads

SERVES 4
PREP 10 mins, plus pressing
COOK 10 mins

1lb 10oz (750g) lamb sweetbreads

½ cup flour, seasoned with salt and pepper

7 tbsp butter

1 tbsp capers

1 tbsp chopped flat-leaf parsley

sea salt and freshly ground black pepper

juice of 1 lemon

round toasts cut from a day-old baguette

1 Thoroughly rinse the sweetbreads with water. Blanch them in hot water for 1–2 minutes, then plunge in cold water to cool.

2 Peel off and discard the outer skin using a pair of scissors. Press the sweetbreads between two plates with a weight on top for 1 hour, then slice the sweetbreads into 1in (2.5cm) pieces. Place the flour in a shallow dish. Add the meat, toss to coat, and shake off any excess.

3 Heat the butter in a frying pan over medium heat. When the butter starts to foam, add the sweetbreads and cook for 5–6 minutes until lightly browned all over. Then add the capers and parsley, season well, and squeeze over the lemon juice. Remove from the heat and spoon the sweetbreads onto the toasts. Serve hot.

PERFECT SUBSTITUTE

Lamb sweetbreads can be replaced with veal sweetbreads and prepared in the same way.

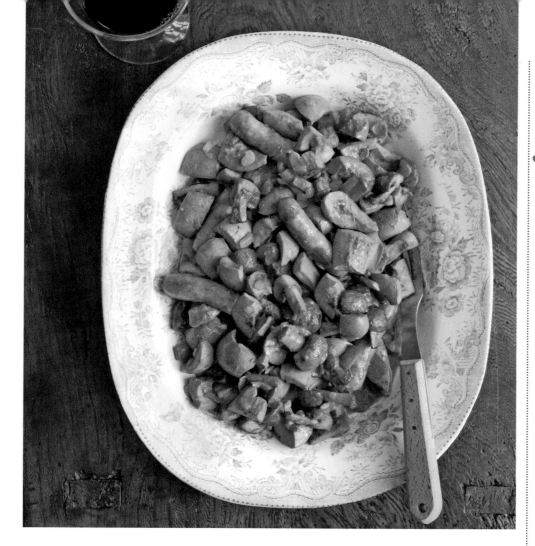

ANDALUCIAN TRIPE

This traditional Spanish stew is flavored with chorizo and made tender with slow cooking.

THE CUT Ox tripe

SERVES 4
PREP 30 mins, plus soaking   **COOK** 3 hrs

4 dried sweet red peppers

2 tbsp extra virgin olive oil

4 tbsp unsalted butter

1 slice of white or brown bread

1 onion, finely chopped

2 garlic cloves, chopped

2½oz (75g) Spanish-style chorizo, sliced

2 tbsp chopped flat-leaf parsley

½ x 14oz (400g) can chopped tomatoes

1 walnut, shelled

¼ tsp ground cloves

¼ tsp ground cumin

sea salt and freshly ground black pepper

¾ cup white wine

1lb 2oz (500g) cooked ox tripe, cut into 1in (2.5cm) pieces

1 x 14oz (400g) can chickpeas, drained

1 Soak the dried peppers in warm water for 1 hour. Heat the oil and butter in a saucepan over medium heat. Add the bread and cook until crisp and golden on both sides. Remove with a slotted spoon and set aside.

2 Add the onion to the pan and cook until softened. Stir in the garlic and cook until soft. Add the chorizo, parsley, and tomatoes. Cook the mixture, stirring, for 1–2 minutes.

3 Meanwhile, place the walnut, bread, cloves, cumin, and a little salt in a mortar and grind with a pestle until quite fine.

4 Drain the peppers, cut them in half, and remove the seeds. Scrape out the flesh, discarding the skins. Add to the pan along with the wine, tripe, and chickpeas. Season and add just enough water to cover. Reduce the heat to a simmer, cover, and cook for 2–3 hours, until the tripe is tender.

5 Stir in the walnut and spice mixture and cook for 1–2 minutes, until the sauce thickens a little. Serve as a tapas or in earthenware bowls sprinkled with a little paprika and some crusty bread.

PIG KIDNEYS TURBIGO

A homely and comforting brunch or supper dish, it is full of spicy, earthy flavors. It is thought to have been named after one of Napoleon III's battle victories.

THE CUT Pig kidney

SERVES 4
PREP 30 mins   **COOK** 20 mins

4 pig kidneys

salt and freshly ground black pepper

1 tsp oil

2 tsp butter

4 chipolata sausages, halved

1 small onion, chopped

5oz (140g) button mushrooms, quartered

2 tsp Dijon mustard

1 tbsp red wine (optional)

splash of Worcester sauce

1 Slice the kidneys in half horizontally and slice each half vertically. Remove as much of the white core as you can, cut into even slices, and season.

2 Heat the oil and 1 teaspoon of butter in a frying pan. When the butter begins to foam, add the kidney pieces, spaced well apart. Cook for about 5 minutes, until well-browned. There should be a little blood still showing. Remove from the pan and set aside.

3 Add the chipolatas to the pan and cook over medium heat for 1–2 minutes, until well-browned. Reduce the heat, add the remaining butter, and stir in the onions. Cook until soft, then add the mushrooms and cook for 1–2 minutes.

4 Stir in the mustard, add the red wine, if using, and simmer for 1–2 minutes. Return the kidneys to the pan along with any juices they may have exuded. Add the sauce, heat through, and check the seasoning. Serve hot with rice pilaf.

TRIPES À LA MODE DE CAEN

A classic French dish using the cider and Calvados of the region to create a satisfying homey dish.

THE CUT Ox tripe and calf foot

SERVES 4
PREP 30 mins   **COOK** 3 hrs

1 onion, cut in quarters

1 leek, trimmed

4 garlic cloves

2 cloves

bunch of flat-leaf parsley

10oz (300g) pork fat

2¼lb (1kg) ox tripe, including all four types, blanched and cut into 2in (5cm) squares

3 large carrots, cut in thin slices

1 calf's foot, blanched and cut in half lengthwise

1 cup hard cider

1 tsp sea salt

freshly ground black pepper

1 tbsp Calvados

1 Wrap the onion, leek, garlic, cloves, and parsley in cheesecloth and tie with butcher's string. Spread the fat over the bottom of a large, heavy-bottomed saucepan. Place half the tripe over it, cover with half the carrots, and then half the calf's foot. Place the cheesecloth bag over, add another layer of the tripe, followed by the remaining carrots and calf's foot.

2 Pour in the cider and just enough water to cover the tripe well, season, and place over low heat. Push the tripe under the liquid to prevent it from blackening. Cover the pan with parchment paper. Bring to a simmer, but do not boil. Then cover and simmer for 2½ hours, or until the tripe and foot are very tender.

3 Remove from heat and discard the cheesecloth. Then remove the calf's foot and separate the meat from the bones. Discard the bones. Stir the meat back into the pan with the Calvados and taste and adjust the seasoning. Serve in large hot soup plates with crusty baguette.

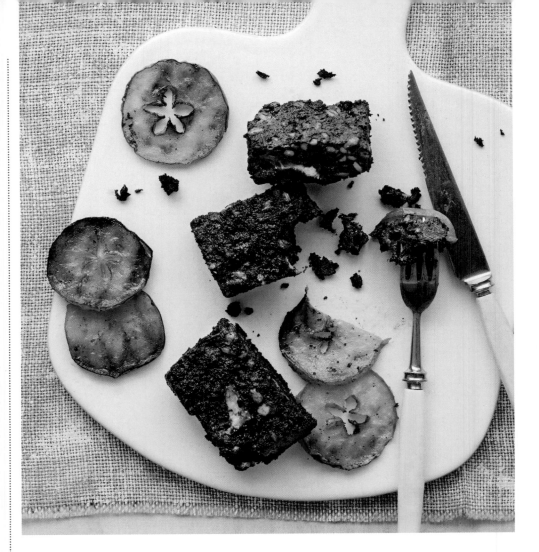

BLOOD SAUSAGE

This northern English version of the traditional European blood sausage is made with barley and oatbran.

THE CUT Pig blood

SERVES 15
PREP 30 mins, plus soaking and cooling
COOK 1½ hrs

oil, for greasing

1lb 2oz (500g) barley or pearl barley

4 cups whole milk

9oz (250g) bread, torn into small pieces

4 cups fresh pig's blood or reconstituted dried pig's blood

1lb 2oz (500g) beef suet or lard, grated

9oz (250g) fine oatbran

2 tsp dried sage

2 tsp each salt and freshly ground black pepper

1–2 tbsp butter, for frying

1 Preheat the oven to 350°F (180°C). Grease 2 large roasting pans. Rinse the barley under cold running water. Transfer to a pot, add enough water to cover, and cook over low heat for 30 minutes. Drain and set aside.

2 Warm the milk until lukewarm, add the bread crumbs, and let soak for 10 minutes. Pour the blood into a large bowl and stir in the milk and bread mixture. Add the barley, suet, oatbran, and sage. Season with salt and pepper and mix thoroughly to combine.

3 Divide the mixture equally between the 2 roasting pans, making sure they are no more than three-quarters full. Press down to get an even finish. Bake for about 1 hour. Remove from the oven and let cool. Then cut into squares and cook in a little butter. Serve with fried apples or alongside mashed potatoes, if you like.

HEADCHEESE

Pig's head has been cooked the world over and this method of extracting all the meat into a firm set mold is classically European.

THE CUT Pig head and trotters

SERVES 10
PREP 1 hrs   **COOK** 4½ hrs, plus setting

1 pig's head, split in two
2 pig trotters, rinsed
bunch of sage or parsley stalks
2 garlic cloves, crushed
2 tsp black peppercorns
3 bay leaves
2 tsp sea salt
skin of 1 onion
2 green chiles (optional)
salt and freshly ground black pepper
2 tbsp chopped flat-leaf parsley
1 tbsp chopped marjoram

1 Place the meats in a large pan. Add all the other ingredients, except the herbs, and cover with water. Bring to a boil, then reduce the heat to a simmer. Skim off any froth and cook for about 4 hours or until the meat falls off the bone. Remove from the heat and let cool.

2 Strain the cooking liquid and return to the pan. Boil rapidly, skimming off any froth, until reduced by half.

3 Meanwhile, remove the trotters. Remove all the meat from the head and discard the bones. Roughly chop the meat and season.

4 Strain the stock through a fine sieve into a bowl. Wipe the pan clean. Pour about 2 cups of the stock back into the pan. Add the meat and herbs, and simmer for about 5 minutes.

5 Pour into a large bowl or terrine mold. Let set in a cool place until the jelly is set solid. Dip the bottom of the terrine in hot water to unmold its contents and then turn it onto a serving platter. Serve with a salad, toast, and mustard or baked potatoes.

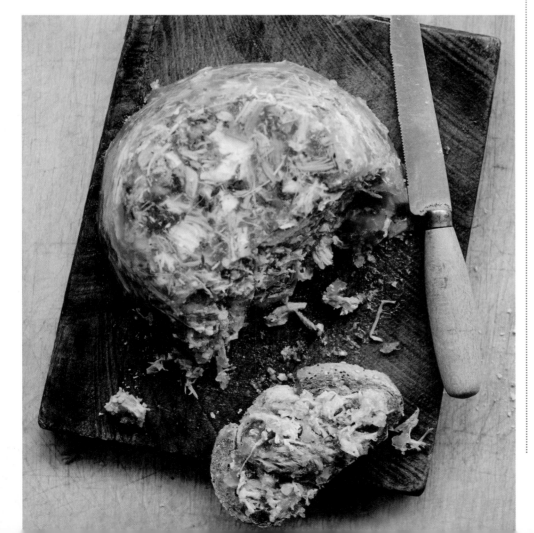

CHITTERLINGS

Often called Chitlins, this lightly spiced dish from the Deep South is made by slow-cooking pig intestines.

THE CUT Pig intestines

SERVES 4
PREP 15 mins, plus washing and soaking
COOK 3½ hrs

4½lb (2kg) Chitterlings (pig intestines)
2 potatoes
2 tbsp malt vinegar
1 onion, sliced
2 red bell peppers, seeded and sliced
1 tsp dried red pepper flakes
2 garlic cloves, finely crushed with a little salt
2 tbsp white wine vinegar
1 cup chicken stock

1 Wash the chitterlings thoroughly under cold running water, removing any discolored membrane. Place them in a large bowl, cover with water, and soak for 2 hours.

2 Remove the chitterlings from the bowl and wash again under cold running water. Place them in a separate bowl, add the potatoes and malt vinegar, and let soak for another 2 hours.

3 Drain and rinse the chitterlings and discard the potatoes. Place the chitterlings in a large saucepan. Add the onions, peppers, red pepper flakes, garlic, and vinegar. Then add the stock and just enough water to cover.

4 Place the pan over high heat and bring to a boil. Then reduce the heat to a simmer and cook for 3½ hours, stirring occasionally, until the chitterlings are tender. Remove from the heat and serve hot with greens.

OX TONGUE WITH BEETS AND CAPERS

Ox tongue needs to be brined and cooked in advance. This tenderizes it and enhances the flavor.

THE CUT Ox tongue

SERVES 6
PREP 15 mins, plus cooling and curing
COOK 3–4 hrs

3¼lb–4½lb (1.5–2kg) ox tongue

2 medium beets, roasted or lightly boiled, peeled, and sliced into thick matchsticks

2 tbsp small capers

FOR THE BRINE

1¼ cups sea salt

1 cup brown sugar

3 bay leaves

5 juniper berries

FOR THE COURT BOUILLON

3 celery stalks

2 onions, halved

2 leeks, trimmed

1 carrot

2 tsp black peppercorns

1 whole garlic bulb, cut in half horizontally

1 cinnamon stick

2 bay leaves

sprig of thyme

sprig of rosemary

FOR THE DRESSING

2 tsp Dijon mustard

2 tbsp olive oil

1 tbsp white wine vinegar

juice from ½ lemon

1 tbsp chopped flat-leaf parsley

salt and freshly ground black pepper

1 For the brine, place all the ingredients in a large saucepan. Add 7 cups cold water and bring to a boil. Remove from the heat and let cool completely. Pour the brine into a large nonreactive container and add the ox tongue. Leave to cure for 2–5 days.

2 Remove the ox tongue from the brine, rinse, and pat dry with paper towels. Discard the brine. For the court bouillon, place all the ingredients in a large, deep saucepan. Pour in 5½ cups water and add the ox tongue. Bring to a boil and skim off any gray scum that rises to the surface.

3 Then reduce the heat to simmer, cover partially, and cook for 3–4 hours, until tender. Remove from the heat and let cool. When cool enough to handle, remove the tongue, take off the skin, and trim any bone and gristle from around the root. Discard the cooking liquid.

4 For the dressing, place all the ingredients in a small bowl, whisk to combine, and season to taste. Mix the beets and the capers in a separate bowl. Slice the tongue thinly and place on 4 plates. Sprinkle over the beets and capers and drizzle over the dressing.

LAMB TONGUE WITH GREENS AND SMOKED BACON

This dish has a remarkable combination of color, flavor, and texture and makes for a perfect first course.

THECUT Lamb tongue

SERVES 6
PREP 15 mins, plus soaking and cooling
COOK 1 hr

6 lamb tongues, about 3½oz (100g) in total, soaked in cold water for at least 2 hours

peel of 1 lemon

2 cinnamon sticks

½ tsp sea salt

1 small green cabbage, such as Savoy or Hispi

3 tbsp olive oil

5oz (140g) smoked bacon, chopped

1 tsp soy sauce

1 Rinse well and drain the lamb tongues. Place them in a large saucepan and cover with about 2½ cups water. Bring to a boil over high heat, and skim off any froth that rises to the surface. Then add the lemon peel, cinnamon, and salt. Reduce the heat to simmer and cook for about 45 minutes until the meat is tender.

2 Meanwhile, remove the tough outer leaves of the cabbage. Cut the cabbage into quarters, and remove the core. Shred finely and wash thoroughly in a colander. Set aside with the leaves still wet.

3 Remove the tongues from the pan and let cool. When cool enough to handle, remove the skin, pat dry with paper towels and keep warm.

4 Heat the oil in a large frying pan over high heat. Add the bacon and cook until well-browned. Then add the cabbage and stir thoroughly to coat in the oil and bacon juices. Cook for a few minutes until it wilts.

5 Add the soy sauce and mix thoroughly. Remove from the heat. Place mounds of the cabbage mixture on 4 warmed plates. Top with the lamb tongues and pour over any cooking juices from the cabbage. Serve hot.

CALF TONGUE

An easy to prepare dish, it is usually served with the cooking liquid poured over the tongue, as its delicate flavor goes well with the tender meat.

THECUT Calf tongue

SERVES 4
PREP 15 mins   **COOK** 3 hrs, plus cooling

1 calf tongue, about 7oz (200g)

1 celery stalk, roughly chopped

6 black peppercorns

small onion, studded with 5 cloves

1 whole garlic bulb

1 Place all the ingredients in a large stock pot. Pour in just enough water to cover the meat. Bring to a boil, then reduce the heat to simmer, and skim off any gray scum that rises to the surface. Cook the tongue for about 3 hours. Remove from the heat and leave the tongue to cool completely in the stock.

2 Remove the tongue from the pot. Peel the skin using a sharp knife. Strain the stock and reserve the liquid. Cut the tongue into thick slices and serve hot with some of the cooking liquid poured over. It can also be served cold, cut into thin slices, along with mustard and pickles.

VARIATION

Calf's head and feet with vinaigrette You can use calf's head and feet in place of the tongue and cook the dish for 4 hours. Remove the meat from the bones, discarding the skin and bones. For the vinaigrette, combine 3 tablespoons of olive oil, 1 tablespoon of lemon juice, and 1 teaspoon whole-grain mustard in a bowl. Season with a pinch of salt, 3 grinds of black pepper, and a of pinch sugar. Mix well to combine. Serve the meat cold with the vinaigrette.

PIED DE COCHON STE. MENEHOULD

In this classic French method of preparing pig's feet, slow-cooking with vinegar helps to soften the bones so that they can be eaten as well.

THE CUT Pig's feet

SERVES 4
PREP 20 mins, plus cooling   **COOK** 8½ hrs

4 front feet, tied in pairs with butcher's string

¾ cup white wine

¾ cup white wine vinegar

6 cloves

2 bay leaves

sprig of marjoram

4 tsp sugar

½ tsp ginger

2 garlic cloves, crushed

salt and freshly ground black pepper

¼ cup fine bread crumbs

1 Place the pig's feet in a large heatproof casserole. Pour the wine and vinegar over them. Then add the cloves, bay leaves, marjoram, sugar, ginger, and garlic. Season with 2 teaspoons of salt and add just enough water to cover the meat. Bring to a boil.

2 Reduce the heat to simmer, cover, and cook for 8 hours, adding water as necessary. You can also cook the pig's feet in a slow cooker or in the oven at 300°F (150°C) for 8 hours.

3 Remove from the heat and leave to cool slightly. Remove the pig's feet from the cooking liquid and place on a large plate. Place another plate on top and press them together, to help them retain their shape while cooling. Let cool completely. Preheat the oven to 375°F (190°C).

4 Remove the butcher's string, carefully, and separate the pig's feet. Sprinkle each foot with the bread crumbs and transfer to the oven. Cook in the oven for 30 minutes. Set the broiler at its highest setting.

5 Remove from the oven and brown quickly under the broiler. Season well. Strain the cooking juices and place in a large bowl. Taste and adjust the seasoning, if needed. Place the pig's feet on a large serving dish and serve with some of the strained cooking juices poured over.

CRACKLINGS

The perfect snack to go with an aperitif, this delicious dish is made by drying and roasting pig skin.

THE CUT Pig skin

SERVES 8
PREP 15 mins, plus overnight drying
COOK 2 hrs

3–4½lb (1.35–2kg) pig skin

1 tbsp fine sea salt

1 Place the pig skin on a clean work surface and cut into ¾in (2cm) strips. Place the strips on a baking sheet and chill in the fridge overnight to help them dry out.

2 Preheat the oven to 300°F (150°C). Remove the baking sheet from the fridge. Sprinkle the salt evenly over the pig skins and transfer the baking sheet to the oven.

3 Roast the skin in the oven for 1 hour. Then remove from the oven, turn them over, and return to the heat for 1 more hour, until crisp all over. Remove and drain on a plate lined with paper towels. Serve hot.

SPICY TWIST

For a variety of flavors, sprinkle with different spices, such as Chinese five-spice powder or paprika, after they come out of the oven.

OX CHEEKS WITH GREMOLATA

The rich flavor and gelatinous texture of this dish contrasts perfectly with the citrusy dressing.

THE CUT Ox cheeks

SERVES 4
PREP 30 mins   **COOK** 4½ hrs, plus resting

2¼lb (1kg) ox cheeks

salt and freshly ground black pepper

1–2 tbsp olive oil

1 tbsp butter

8 shallots

3 carrots, sliced thickly at an angle

2 cups beef stock

1 bay leaf

2–3 sprigs of thyme

FOR THE GREMOLATA

2 tbsp chopped flat-leaf parsley

1 garlic clove, finely chopped

grated zest of 1 lemon

1 Preheat the oven to 300°F (150°C). Season the ox cheeks well. Heat the oil in a heatproof casserole. Add the meat and cook until well-browned. Remove from the pan and set aside. Add the butter to the pan. Then add the shallots and carrots, and cook until browned.

2 Reduce the heat and return the meat to the pan. Pour in the stock and reduce the heat to simmer. Add the herbs and cover with a disk of parchment paper, cut to fit snugly in the pan, to keep the moisture in. Cover and braise in the oven for 3½–4 hours. Check to make sure the liquid does not reduce too much and add more liquid if necessary.

3 Remove the casserole from the oven. Let the meat rest in the liquid for at least 30 minutes. Meanwhile, for the gremolata, mix the parsley, garlic, and lemon zest in a bowl.

4 Remove the meat and vegetables with a slotted spoon. Strain the liquid into a separate pan and discard the herbs. Cook the sauce over low heat to reduce a little. Taste and adjust the seasoning, if needed. Slice the cheeks and add to the sauce along with the vegetables to reheat. Remove from the heat. Sprinkle a spoonful of gremolata over the cheeks and serve with the shallots, carrots, and some of the sauce.

CASTILLIAN PIG TROTTERS

Ground almonds show a Moorish influence in this rich, flavorful, and lightly spiced dish.

 Pig trotters

SERVES 4
PREP 30 mins   **COOK** 2½ hrs

2 onions

4 cloves

4 front trotters, split lengthwise

3 bay leaves

salt and freshly ground black pepper

1 tbsp lard

1 garlic clove, finely chopped

1 tbsp almonds, roughly chopped

1 tbsp all-purpose flour

½ cup white wine

1 tsp hot paprika

2 carrots, diced

1 Stud 1 onion with the cloves. Wash the trotters thoroughly and place them in a large, lidded stock pot. Add the studded onion and bay leaves, and pour in just enough water to cover the meat. Bring to a boil.

2 Reduce the heat to a simmer and season with salt and pepper. Cover and cook for 2 hours, until the meat is almost falling off the bone. Remove from the heat. Use a slotted spoon to lift the trotters out of the pot. Place them on a large plate, cover with foil, and set aside. Strain and reserve the cooking liquid.

3 Heat the lard in a shallow frying pan over medium-low heat. Thinly slice the remaining onion. Add the sliced onions and garlic to the pan and cook until soft. Stir in the almonds and flour and cook until lightly browned.

4 Add 2 cups of the strained cooking liquid to the pan, then pour in the wine, stirring continuously to prevent the formation of lumps. Season with salt, pepper, and paprika.

5 Add the carrots and simmer for 10 minutes. Gently place the trotters in the pan and simmer for another 20 minutes. Remove from the heat. Serve hot with rice. It can also be chilled in the fridge overnight and reheated the next day.

BRAISED OXTAIL WITH CLEMENTINE

Oxtail is rich and robust, and braising it very slowly tenderizes it completely. The fruity sweetness and texture of prunes and clementines complement the meat well.

 Oxtail

SERVES 4–6
PREP 20 mins   **COOK** 3 hrs 15 mins

2 oxtails, about 3lb (1.35kg) each, cut into pieces

salt and freshly ground black pepper

2 tbsp olive oil

2 red onions, sliced

3 garlic cloves, finely chopped

a pinch of dried chile flakes

1½ cups red wine

4 star anise

handful of black peppercorns

1 bay leaf

8 soft prunes, pitted and chopped

3 cups hot beef stock

4 clementines or 2 oranges, peeled and sliced into rings

small bunch of curly parsley leaves, finely chopped

1 Preheat the oven to 300°F (150°C). Season the oxtail with salt and pepper. Heat half the oil in a large heatproof casserole over medium heat, then add the meat in batches and cook for 8–10 minutes until browned on all sides. Remove with a slotted spoon and set aside.

2 Heat the remaining oil in the casserole over medium heat, add the onions, and cook for 3–4 minutes to soften. Stir through the garlic and chile flakes, then pour in the wine and let it simmer for about 5 minutes until slightly reduced. Return the meat to the casserole and add the star anise, peppercorns, bay leaf, and prunes, and pour in just enough stock to cover the meat. Bring to a boil, then reduce to a simmer. Add the remaining stock, cover, and place in the oven for about 2½ hours. Check occasionally that it is not drying out, and add a little more hot water if needed.

3 Add the clementines, return the casserole to the oven, and cook, uncovered, for another 30 minutes, until the liquid has thickened slightly and the meat has fallen off the bones. Stir occasionally to keep the oxtail moist and coated with the gravy. Remove from the heat. Remove and discard the bone, bay leaf, and star anise. Serve on a bed of pasta, sprinkled with some parsley.

VARIATION

Braised oxtail with Jerusalem artichokes Add 9oz (250g) Jerusalem artichokes, scrubbed or peeled and cut into chunks, and 2 sliced carrots to the mixture before cooking. Leave out the star anise, chile flakes, and clementines. Add 1 tablespoon brandy with the red wine and cook as above. Serve over fluffy mashed potatoes.

OSSO BUCO

Winter citrus lends a delicious fragrance to this Italian classic. Ask your butcher for a hind leg of veal as they are meatier than the front legs.

THE CUT Bone-in veal shank

SERVES 4–6
PREP 30–35 mins
COOK 1 hr 45 mins–2 hrs 15 mins

¼ cup flour, seasoned with salt and pepper

4lb (1.8kg) bone-in veal osso buco

2 tbsp vegetable oil, plus extra if required

2 tbsp butter

1 carrot, thinly sliced

2 onions, finely chopped

1 cup white wine

1 x 14oz (400g) can Italian plum tomatoes, drained and coarsely chopped

1 garlic clove, finely chopped

grated zest of 1 orange

salt and freshly ground black pepper

½ cup hot chicken or veal stock

FOR THE GREMOLATA

small bunch of flat-leaf parsley, leaves picked and finely chopped

grated zest of 1 lemon

1 garlic clove, finely chopped

1 Preheat the oven to 350°F (180°C). Place the flour in a shallow bowl. Add the veal pieces, toss to coat lightly, and shake off any excess.

2 Heat the oil and butter in a large heatproof casserole over medium heat, add the meat (in batches and with extra oil, if necessary), and cook until well-browned. Transfer to a plate with a slotted spoon and set aside.

3 Add the carrot and onions to the casserole and cook, stirring occasionally, until soft. Add the wine and boil until reduced by half. Stir in the tomatoes, garlic, orange zest, and season. Place the meat on top and pour in the stock. Cover and put in the oven for 1½–2 hours until very tender. Check occasionally that it is not drying out, adding a little hot water if needed.

4 For the gremolata, mix the parsley, lemon, and garlic in a small bowl. To serve, place the veal on warmed plates, spoon the sauce on top, and sprinkle with the gremolata.

VARIATION

Osso buco with celery, leek, and almonds Prepare in the same way, but substitute 1 sliced leek for 1 onion, and add 2 chopped celery stalks to the mixture at the beginning of step 2. Use an Italian red wine, such as Chianti, instead of the white wine and add a pinch of sugar in step 3. Prepare the gremolata for garnish, but add a small handful of toasted almond slices to the mix.

ROASTED VEAL BONE MARROW

Delicious and simple to prepare, bone marrow is best served with toast or as a side with beef or veal sauces.

THE CUT Veal bone marrow

SERVES 4
PREP 5 mins   **COOK** 30 mins

12 pieces veal bone marrow, 3in (7.5cm) each

green salad, to serve

handful of mixed herbs, finely chopped, to serve

1 Preheat the oven to 450°F (230°C). Place the marrow bones in a large roasting pan, making sure they are spaced well apart. Avoid using smaller pieces of marrow bones as it would be difficult to remove the marrow from these after roasting.

2 Transfer the roasting pan to the center of the preheated oven. Roast the marrow bones for about 20 minutes, enough to loosen the marrow but not to melt it.

3 Remove from the heat and spoon the marrow out of the bones. Spread it on toasts and serve along with a crisp green salad and herbs. You can also add it to beef sauces and gravies to enrich their flavor.

HOME BUTCHERY

HOME BUTCHERY

CUTTING UP YOUR OWN MEAT IS FASCINATING. THE SKILLED ART OF BUTCHERY TAKES MANY YEARS TO ACQUIRE, AND IN EVERY REGION OF EVERY COUNTRY, BUTCHERS WILL TACKLE CARCASSES DIFFERENTLY. THIS IS A STEP-BY-STEP GUIDE TO SOME BUTCHERY BASICS.

OUR STARTER GUIDE shows some simple ways of breaking down carcasses into manageable cuts without the need for specialized large butchery equipment. There are many other cuts that can be produced; the more you trim and divide muscles, the leaner and smaller the pieces become.

USING OUR CUTTING GUIDE

Read through each section before starting, then decide which cuts you want to produce. This determines in which order you cut, or debone, the various parts. Some steps may need to be done in a different order than the sequence in which they are written. These choices are highlighted.

Whatever its size, the muscles are the same on every mammal, so some techniques, such as removing the forequarter, are common to all animals. The larger the animal, the more the muscles are divided, and the more the meat is taken off the bone. Small animals have more cuts left on the bone.

There are many examples online of how to cut meat and some are very helpful. Some demonstrations are aimed at wholesale butchers or chefs, who use different cuts than the home cook. Try to find examples that make retail cuts.

SAFETY

• Be careful when handling and carrying heavy carcasses, so as not to cause injury.
• Make sure the table you plan to work on is solid and stable. Meat carcasses are heavy, and a wobbly table can be dangerous when sawing and chopping.

• Always point knives toward the floor when walking around; never point them outward.
• Always wear a protective metal apron and a stainless steel mesh glove, since some butchery procedures require the knife to be cut toward the body, and butcher's knives—and animal bones—are extremely sharp.
• Fat and scraps dropped onto the floor can make it very slippery.

HYGIENE

• Keep the temperature of the room as low as possible; use an air conditioner if necessary. Keep all meat refrigerated when not cutting it up.
• Use fly coverings over open doors and windows, and an electric fly killer inside. Never leave meat uncovered. If possible, butcher meat during the winter, when there are fewer flies.
• Scrub hands and nails thoroughly before starting.
• Sterilize knives from time to time. Pour boiling water into a large bucket deep enough to hold the knives. Keep them in the hot water for a minimum of 2 minutes.
• When you've finished butchering, clean all surfaces and equipment. First use cool water to remove all blood and meat, then use hot water and detergent to remove fat. Rinse off detergent using sanitizer or a weak solution of bleach and water.

MAKING THE MOST OF YOUR MEAT

Many muscles can be improved and made suitable for flash-frying if they are thoroughly trimmed. Remove excess fat, but leave some to lubricate the meat.

Remove gristle, sinew, cartilage, and membranes from roasts and steaks, but some can be left on for slow-cooking cuts.

Dry-aged meat may have some dried, slippery, or even slightly moldy parts on the edges; this is normal, but trim off these parts before you start.

EQUIPMENT

• **Sturdy table**
• **Large, heavy cutting board**
• **Boning knife** with thin, flexible blade
• **Chef's knife** for cutting large slices
• **Sharpening steel**
• **Butcher's saw and sawblades**
• **Large containers and trays or pans** for meat and trimmings
• **Covers** to prevent fly damage
• **Kitchen twine**
• **Skewers** to secure meat before tying

Protection:
• **Stainless steel mesh glove:** worn on the hand not holding the knife
• **Metal apron:** essential for beginners as some movements require the knife to be moved or pointed toward the body
• **First-aid kit**

WHATEVER ITS SIZE, THE MUSCLES ARE THE SAME ON EVERY MAMMAL, SO SOME TECHNIQUES ARE COMMON TO ALL ANIMALS.

TOP TIPS

• Use the saw as little as possible; bone dust is gritty and it makes meat taste sour. When there is bone dust, brush it off.
• Use your fingers to feel for splinters of bone. The bones of small animals can easily shatter when cut.
• When deboning meat, find the natural seams between the muscles with the tip of the knife and pull them apart by hand, using the knife to ease stubborn parts.
• Make use of gravity. If part of the animal can hang over the table edge, it makes cutting off large pieces easier.
• Put a thick, damp towel under your cutting board to keep it from sliding around.
• When trimming, cut or scrape off all bloody meat, white bone sheath, bone splinters, excess fat, lymph nodes, gristle, and silver sinew.

USING KNIVES

The diagrams show how to hold the knife. For most processes it is held vertically and the wrist is articulated to move the knife. For slicing, the knife is held in the conventional fashion. Tilt the knife edge toward the bone to avoid slashing the meat. Never cut toward your hand.

When cutting a long length of meat, mark the initial cut and then deepen it with a stroking motion. Use this stroking motion to take meat off rib bones, too.

USING SAWS

Before using a saw, cut through as much meat as possible around the bone with a knife. Then open out the meat to expose the bone. As soon as the saw reaches the end of the bone, switch back to a knife to avoid tearing the meat.

TYING A ROAST

Two methods of tying a roast of meat are shown below. It helps to practice on a rolled-up kitchen towel. Butchers' elastic bands can be used instead of twine if necessary, but these are not recommended because, when removed after cooking, they flick fat and meat juices around.

Tying meat the butcher's way

This method produces the neatest roasts, which can be divided into smaller roasts or slices by cutting between the strings. This is the method used in "Roll and tie a roast" on page 299.

1 Slide the string under the meat and tie a slip knot loosely, as shown, in the center of the meat. Leave 2in (5cm) on end A. Now lift up end B (as shown on p299) and gently tighten the knot against the meat. Once it is in the correct place, give it a tug to secure it.

2 Secure the tightened slip knot by making another simple knot: loop end B around end A and tighten. This ensures the knot cannot come undone.

3 The knot looks like this when finished. Trim the ends of the string. Continue tying strings around the meat, spacing them evenly. If the roast looks unstable, tie another string around from end to end.

Tying meat the "parcel" way

This method is easier than above, but it is less tidy and is of no use if the meat needs to be cut between the strings.

Tie these two ends together

1 Slide the string under one end of the roast and tie a slip knot (see step 1, above). Leave at least 4in (10cm) on end C.

2 Loop the string around the meat as shown, distributing the strings evenly as you go. Pass the string under the roast and tie it to the long end of the first knot.

PORK, LAMB, AND SMALL DEER

THE PRINCIPLES FOR BUTCHERING THESE THREE SPECIES ARE VIRTUALLY THE SAME—ANY EXCEPTIONS HAVE BEEN HIGHLIGHTED. THE DIAGRAMS SHOW A PIG BEING BUTCHERED; LAMB AND DEER ARE SLIMMER AND MORE ELONGATED, BUT ALL THE MUSCLES AND BONES ARE IN THE SAME PLACE.

CUT INTO PRIMALS

To make the carcass easier to handle, first divide it into three parts, or "primals": forequarter, middle or saddle, and back leg or haunch. The breastbone will already have been cut open; if not, saw it open before starting.

REMOVE THE FOREQUARTER

PRELIMINARY STEP

For pork only, first cut off the head behind the jawbone and ears. Saw it in half or leave whole, as wished.

1 Open the chest cavity and count 5 ribs from the head end. Insert the knife through the flank at this point, and cut between the 5th and 6th ribs on both sides.

2 Turn the carcass over and continue to cut all the way up to the backbone, cutting through all the meat. Repeat on the opposite side.

3 Saw through the backbone to remove the forequarter. Scrape off the bone sawdust from the cut edges.

NOTE: Cutting between the 5th and 6th ribs leaves 8 ribs on the middle part for making a rack. Pork is sometimes cut between the 4th and 5th ribs, and lamb between the 6th and 7th.

DIVIDE THE MIDDLE FROM THE BACK LEGS

1 Feel for the hip bone and cut, from the flank edge, right through to the backbone. Repeat on the other side.

2 Counting from the leg (tail) end, cut between the 1st and 2nd lumbar vertebrae. Use a knife to cut through the cartilage disc of the backbone, being careful not to cut through the meat on either side. Cut the loin meat to remove the legs

FOREQUARTER MIDDLE OR SADDLE BACK LEG OR HAUNCH

PIG SKELETON

Cut open the chest cavity

5th rib

6th rib

2nd lumbar vertebra

1st lumbar vertebra

Cut here to remove the forequarter

Cut here to remove the back legs

Hip bone

CHOICE!

For pork: if you want the fillet or tenderloin in one whole piece, remove the head of the fillet muscle from the pelvic bone before dividing the middle from the back legs (see p301).

THE FOREQUARTER

THERE ARE MANY WAYS OF PREPARING THE FOREQUARTER, especially with pork, and you can choose a combination of cuts, making bone-in cuts from one half and boneless cuts from the other. Lamb and small deer are cut more simply. Beef is usually entirely deboned.

SPLIT IN HALF

For both boneless and bone-in cuts, the forequarter needs to be halved and prepared. Scrape off any bone sawdust, because it makes the meat deteriorate more quickly.

PRELIMINARY STEPS

For lamb and small deer only, first saw 1–1½in (2–3cm) off the neck end and discard. Saw off the remaining neck ready to debone the meat for stew or grinding, or into bone-in slices. **For pork**, cut off the trotters.

The fat lies between the ribs and the outer skin, at the neck end

The paddywack lies just under the skin above the backbone

1. LAY THE FOREQUARTER ON ITS BACK and mark a line down the center of the backbone with your knife to use as a guide. Saw through the backbone, then cut through the meat on the other side to cut the forequarter in half.

2. REMOVE THE WHITE SPINAL CORDS as shown (this is only mandatory for lamb, but is desirable for other species). Cut out and discard the triangle of fat near the neck, which contains a gland. Remove the paddywack, a tough yellow piece of gristle.

MAKE BONE-IN CUTS

There are many different bone-in cuts. To make a **whole bone-in forequarter**, either with or without the shank, see below; to make **shoulder chops**, a **spare rib roast**, or a **whole bone-in shoulder roast**, see page 294.

1. TO MAKE A WHOLE BONE-IN FOREQUARTER ROAST, simply trim off the breast bone cartilage where it meets the ribs. In lamb, this is sometimes called a whole shoulder.

Breast bone cartilage

2. CUT OFF THE SHANK OR HOCK (optional). This may be cut off (usual for pork) or left on the shoulder. Use the knife and saw to cut through the roast.

Blade half

Halfway point

Shank half

Blade half

Slice a chop from here

TO CUT SHOULDER CHOPS, saw the forequarter just under the lowest curve of the backbone as shown, and use the blade half. Chops can include some bladebone, or be cut after the shoulder is lifted off, as it is for the whole bone-in roast, below. Cut between the foreribs with a knife, and continue the cut through the eye muscle. Saw carefully through the neck bone into chops.

TO MAKE TWO HALF SHOULDER ROASTS, saw through the ribs at the halfway point. Cut through the meat and bone. Remove bone sawdust. The top part is the blade half and the other is the shank half (also called the butt and hock in pork).

TO MAKE FOREQUARTER SPARE RIBS, cut the ribs off the breastbone and slice into spare ribs. The long neck vertebrae can also be cut off the backbone to make "spare ribs."

TO MAKE A SPARE RIB ROAST, divide the shoulder as for chops (above). Cut through the meat until it hits the bladebone, then saw through the bladebone and cut through the remaining meat.

REMOVE THE PIECE OF BLADEBONE from the forerib as shown. Tie if wished.

Lift the shank to see where to insert the knife

TO MAKE A WHOLE BONE-IN SHOULDER ROAST, lift off the whole shoulder blade. Lift up the shank and insert the knife where the meat stretches under the arm. Keep lifting the foreleg to help part the meat and, using the point of the knife, carefully pare away the shoulder from the forequarter (it is not attached by bones). Cut off the shank at the elbow joint if wished. Trim off excess fat if necessary.

Bladebone

Backbone

DEBONE THE FOREQUARTER

To make steaks, rolled roasts, diced stew, and ground meat, the shoulder needs to be deboned. Work from the inside of the carcass so the outside skin is left intact and is neat to roll. Leave the hock or shank bone on so it can be used as a lever.

1. REMOVE THE RIBS AND BACKBONE: Starting at the breast edge, lift off the rib bones. Loosen the meat from the rib bones, then, keeping the knife tilted toward the ribs, scrape off the flank meat with a stroking motion, working down toward the backbone.

2. ONCE YOU HAVE ENOUGH TO HOLD, pull the ribs up with a tugging motion. Gravity will help the knife to part the meat from the bone. Work carefully around the eye muscle meat to remove the backbones, and ribs in one piece.

Eye muscle

Hock or shank

Ball-and-socket joint

Bladebone

Arm bone

3. TAKE OUT THE BLADEBONE: With the hock or shank pointing away from you, insert the point of your knife, at 90°, down through the very center of the shoulder (where the ribs ended) until you hit the ball-and-socket joint where bladebone meets arm bone. Note this mark. Now look for the edge of the bladebone where the forequarter was cut off, and mark a line from here to the ball-and-socket joint. Cut down the inside edge of the bladebone with your knife. Keeping your knife edge tilted to the bone, scrape off the flesh on top of the bladebone until you reach the socket joint.

4. WHEN THE MEAT from on top of the bladebone is freed off, turn the shoulder over skin-side up. Hold the shank or hock and wiggle it until you can feel the joint between shank and arm bone moving. Pull the shank up toward you to pop open the joint.

5. NOW WORK AROUND THE BLADEBONE to remove the meat from either side of the ridge. Pull out the bladebone, using your knife to free it off, if necessary.

Bladebone

6. TAKE OUT THE ARM BONE: Run the knife down either side, and underneath, the arm bone and around the ball joints until the bone can be removed.

Arm bone

NOW YOU CAN...

- Trim off any surplus fat, gristle, and sinew.
- Cut shoulder steaks from the leanest, thickest parts.
- Carefully remove the eye muscle to produce a lamb or deer neck fillet, or a pork rib-eye roast.
- Roll into a shoulder roast (see p299).
- Dice into stew meat and use trimmings for ground meat.
- Saw off the soiled end of the shank or hock to cook it whole.
- Remove the shank meat and dice or grind it.

THE MIDDLE OR SADDLE

THIS SECTION, WHICH IS ALSO KNOWN AS THE LOIN, includes the finest meat on the carcass—the loin and the fillet or tenderloin. There is often a lot of fat on this part, although deer has less.

CUT OFF THE FLANK AND RIBS

The ribs may be cut at different lengths. To make a traditional saddle roast, see right.

TO CUT OFF THE FLANK, mark a straight line on the inside of the ribs with a knife, parallel to the backbone, at the length you wish the chops to be (usually a maximum of twice the width of the eye muscle). Saw through the rib bones. Cut through the meat. Some people prefer to remove the flanks after the middle has been split (see step 1, below).

Forequarter end

Eye, or loin eye, muscle

Leave the ribs long enough to make chops and racks

NOTE: Old animals (mutton, goat, and wild deer) have tough sinews on the back, so a saddle should be trimmed of all the outer fat, skin, and sinew, then barded (see p232) for roasting.

MAKE A SADDLE ROAST

TO MAKE A SADDLE ROAST, cut off the flanks as shown, left, but closer to the eye muscle, as shown here. Leave whole for a long saddle roast, or cut off the carvery saddle end—it has no ribs and includes the fillet. Cut it off where the ribs end, as marked. To make double or sirloin lamb chops, cut slices straight across the carvery end of the saddle.

Cut here to divide the carvery saddle from the ribs

Rump end

The fillet and loin eye muscle are the two most tender cuts

Cut sirloin lamb chops from this end

The flank includes the spare ribs and belly

MAKE BONE-IN CUTS

These include loin and double loin chops, elegant rack roasts, and sirloin lamb chops (see above).

1. SPLIT THE SADDLE OR MIDDLE: Turn the saddle onto its back. Mark down the center of the backbone with a knife to create a guideline. Saw down the center to part the two sides, then cut through the remaining meat and fat with a knife.

2. REMOVE THE CHINE BONE (optional): This removes the sharp edges from chops and racks. Saw off the backbone at a 45° angle, starting at the ribs, until the bone is nearly cut through, then part the meat off the backbone with the knife at the cartilage. Be very careful not to cut into the meat. An alternative method, using a cleaver, is shown on page 193.

MAKE ROASTS, RACKS, AND CHOPS

TO DIVIDE THE BONE-IN LOIN INTO ROASTS, RACKS, CHOPS, OR DOUBLE LOIN CHOPS: Trim off excess skin, fat, and sinew, then cut between the ribs, using the point of a knife to find the gristle between the vertebrae. Cut down firmly with a large knife to break open the joint. Then cut through the meat. Alternatively, saw through the backbone, being careful not to cut the meat. See page 193 for instructions on French trimming chops and racks.

Loin

Rack

Loin chop or cutlet has a rib bone and no fillet

Double loin chop includes fillet

MAKE BONELESS CUTS

Once deboned, this section yields roasts and steaks from the fillet, loin, and loin eye. Loin eye has all the external fat and sinew removed.

1. REMOVE THE FILLET OR TENDERLOIN (if not already removed): With the loin lying skin-side down, scrape the fillet away from the bone. Keep the knife close to the backbone. Trim off any silver sinews and the chain steak (a thin strip of meat that runs along the length of the fillet).

THE RIBS, BELLY, BREAST, AND FLANK

A

B

TO MAKE SPARE RIBS, lift off the flap of flank (A) covering the rib ends and the ribs from the belly at the point where the ribs end. The ribs can be left as a set or cut into individual spare ribs. Alternatively, all the rib meat can be taken off the bone. Slide the knife under the rib bones as shown (B), and scrape off the meat. The belly, breast, and flank can be rolled and tied (see p299), sliced, ground, or made into bacon (see p21).

The wing bones lie under the fillet and are only visible when the fillet is removed

2. BONE OUT THE MIDDLE: Keeping the knife as close to the bone as possible, make a long cut all the way down the inside of the backbone and wing bones. When you reach the backbone at the bottom, turn the knife 90º and cut the meat off the backbone.

NOW YOU CAN...

Trim off excess skin, fat, and sinew, or leave it on if preferred. Then slice the meat into **loin steaks**, trimmed **loin eye steaks**, or **loin roasts** as required.

THE BACK LEG OR HAUNCH

WITH SMALL ANIMALS SUCH AS LAMB AND DEER, the leg or haunch is usually simply divided into bone-in roasts, or even left whole. But it can also be deboned for rolled roasts and steaks. Whole pork legs are used for hams and large roasts, but most are deboned for steaks and boneless roasts. Page 303 shows how to debone and divide a leg.

SPLIT THE LEGS

Because of their shape, the legs can be difficult to hold steady while sawing them apart. If necesssary, wedge something under one side to secure it.

PRELIMINARY STEP

For pork only, cut off the trotters. (This may be done later if wished.)

CUT THE SKIN AND CARTILAGE BETWEEN THE LEGS and through the pelvic bone. Cut or saw through the backbone and tail bones to part the legs.

MAKE BONE-IN ROASTS

With lamb and deer, the leg roast is often left whole with the chump or rump left attached; the pelvic bone can be removed for ease of carving. To do this, see "To remove the entire pelvic bone", below. Pork is more likely to be cut into smaller pieces.

A   B   C

This tough piece of tendon is cut off. Sometimes the end of the bone is scraped clean of meat

THE LEG CAN BE CUT INTO SEVERAL BONE-IN ROASTS. The lines above indicate the usual cutting points. Part A is the chump end (to remove, see "To cut off the chump," opposite). It is not easy to carve because of the pelvic bone so is either deboned (to remove, see "To debone the chump," opposite), or cut into chops. Part B is the leg end. It is also easier to carve with the pelvic bone removed (see "To remove the entire pelvic bone," below). Part C is the shank or hock. It is often included with a leg of lamb or deer. The small, bony end part is usually removed in lamb and deer, and the tendon removed. To make bone-in leg steaks, cut slices of the leg including leg bone, and saw through the bone. Remove any saw dust.

Cut off shank here

Pelvic bone parted from leg bone

TO REMOVE THE ENTIRE PELVIC BONE (aitch bone, hip, and tail bone), remove the head of the fillet from the hip bone to expose it (see "To debone the chump, opposite). Work the tip of the knife around the aitch bone around to the ball-and-socket joint. Part the piece of connective gristle in the ball-and-socket joint. Work around the tail bone to free off the meat. Work around the pelvic bone and lift all the bones out. Trim off excess fat and skin.

TO REMOVE THE SHANK OR HOCK, without using a saw, feel for the halfway point at the hock (knee) joint and make a cut through the cartilage. Using the edge of the table, vigorously bend back the hock to crack open the joint, then cut through the connecting gristle. Cut through the meat to remove the hock.

Slice the shank into osso buco, saw off the soiled end to serve as a whole shank or hock, or debone and dice or grind the meat.

Pelvic bone

Hip bone

TO CUT OFF THE CHUMP, cut halfway between the pubic bone and the 1st lumbar vertebra (count from the tail end) at a 45° angle through the bone, then slice through the meat to remove the chump. Leave whole for a bone-in chump roast or, using the knife and saw, cut into slices for chump chops. Trim off any remaining flank as required.

MAKING BONELESS ROASTS

TO DEBONE THE CHUMP, take the fillet head off to expose the pelvic bone. Keeping the knife close to the bone, cut the bone out of the meat. Slice to make chump steaks, or roll and tie into a chump roast.

TO REMOVE THE LEG BONE, see p303, steps 3–6. The boneless leg is now ready to roll and tie (see below). With the topside and leg bone removed, the deboned leg can be made into a large rolled roast, with or without the shank. Roll the topside into a smaller roast or slice into leg steaks.

TO SLICE STEAKS, hold the piece of meat firmly down on the table, close to the edge where it will be cut, to keep it from moving. Cut even slices across the grain, using a large knife and long, smooth cutting strokes.

ROLL AND TIE A ROAST

Single muscles can be roasted without tying, although tying gives a better shape. Butchers' elastic bands may be used but they are very messy to remove after cooking.

1. TO ROLL MEAT READY TO TIE INTO A ROAST: Make sure the meat is of an even thickness thoughout. Cut out muscles from thick parts and lay them into thin parts. If there is a large flap at one end, this makes it easier to roll (e.g., when rolling loin, leave a flap of flank attached). Roll the meat as tightly as possible; if necessary, hold it in place with skewers.

2. TO TIE A ROAST: Make the first tie in the middle. Slide the string under the meat and tie a slip knot (see "Tying meat the butcher's way," p291, step 1). Pull the knot up over the meat as shown, then tug it down gently onto the meat. Now give another tug to tighten it. Then secure it with a simple knot (see p291, step 2). For a single-muscled roast, tie strings from the center to the ends. For a multi-muscled roast, tie the second and third strings at either end and then fill in. This prevents the meat from slipping out. Slice off any untidy ends of the roast. If the roast looks unstable, tie some strings around from end to end to secure it while cooking.

BEEF AND LARGE DEER

THIS SECTION SHOWS HOW TO BUTCHER BEEF AND LARGE DEER CARCASSES. A FOREQUARTER OF BEEF IS TOO LARGE FOR DOMESTIC BUTCHERY. HOWEVER, THE PRINCIPLES OF CUTTING BEEF (AND LARGE DEER) ARE THE SAME AS FOR PORK, LAMB, AND SMALL DEER—SEE PAGES 293–5.

SIRLOIN OR MIDDLE (WITHOUT FLANK)

LEG, TOP BIT, OR HAUNCH

FORERIB RIB SIRLOIN OR SHORT LOIN RUMP

The fillet runs through the sirloin into the rump

BEEF SKELETON

THE SIRLOIN OR MIDDLE (WITHOUT FLANK)

A SIRLOIN AND RIB OF BEEF is usually bought as a side (one half), without the flank. For deer, see page 296 for splitting the saddle and removing the flank. First, decide whether you want bone-in cuts or boneless cuts, or a combination. This determines in which order you butcher the meat.

Before starting, remove the kidney: turn the sirloin or saddle on its back and remove the large knob of kidney fat. Run the knife under the fat and pull the fat from the bone, making sure not to damage the fillet underneath. The kidney is embedded within the fat. Deer may have little or no fat around the kidney.

BONE-IN CUTS

Bone-in cuts include sirloin, rib, and forerib roasts, as well as T-bone and Porterhouse steaks. To make venison saddle roasts, see page 296.

If the fillet or tenderloin is required as a whole piece, see "To remove the fillet," opposite, and remove the whole fillet first. However, note that you will not then be able to cut a sirloin roast or T-bone steaks, as these cuts include the fillet muscle.

1. REMOVE THE RUMP FROM THE SIRLOIN: Cut off the rump where the curved set of tail bones changes into the larger back bones (lumbar vertebrae). Cut through the meat in a line that just misses the tip of the hip bone.

Hip bone

Cut through here

2. SAW THROUGH THE BACKBONE to part the rump from the loin, being careful not to saw into any meat. See opposite to debone the rump.

Push the meat apart to make it easier to cut

NOW YOU CAN...
PREPARE BONE-IN ROASTS AND STEAKS

SIRLOIN ROASTS
These have a portion of fillet so there is meat on either side of the backbone, which makes it more difficult to cut without damaging the meat. They have short wing bones rather than rib bones. Decide what size of roast is wanted, and use the knife to cut through the fillet and loin meat. Then part the meat and saw carefully between the vertebrae to cut off the meat.

SIRLOIN RIB, STANDING RIB, AND FORERIB ROASTS
These are cut from the front part that has rib bones but no fillet. Choose the number of ribs desired, and cut through the meat between the bones with a knife. Saw through the backbone, then cut through the loin eye muscle with a knife. This picture (see right, top) shows only three ribs, but if the whole sirloin and rib is longer, the forerib end may contain a small piece of bladebone cartilage, which should be removed. Remove the chine bone if wished (see p296, step 2), and also French trim the ends of the roast if wished (see p193).

PORTERHOUSE STEAKS
These steaks (see right, bottom) are cut from the sirloin where the rump was removed. It is cut to the full thickness of the first vertebra. T-bone steaks may be any thickness, but must include some fillet meat. To cut these steaks, slice through the meat on one side of the backbone and then cut on the other side of the bone. Part the meat slightly, then saw through the bone. This avoids having to saw into the meat.

The fillet ends where the ribs start

Forerib end

Porterhouse steak is very thick and includes the fillet muscle

BONELESS CUTS

Boneless cuts include roasts and steaks cut from the boneless sirloin and loin eye, as well as fillet steak and roasts. Forerib cuts, such as rib-eye steak, are fattier.

TO DEBONE THE RUMP: Take out the fillet head that lies on top of the flat aitch bone. Then remove the bone—one of the most awkward bones. Follow the twisting contours, keeping the knife edge tightly against the bone to avoid slashing the meat. Trim the meat thoroughly, since the rump has a lot of fat and gristle.

NOW YOU CAN...
PREPARE RUMP CUTS

The meat can be used as a roast, sliced into rump steaks, or used for stir-fry. The thinner pointed end is point steak. The thin muscle lying over the rump can also be removed and sliced into a cap of rump steak. Depending on how the carcass was cut, there may also be a part of the thick flank attached; this is the tri-tip.

TO REMOVE THE FILLET: Lay the loin on its back and start at the thin tapered end of the fillet. Keeping the edge of the knife close to the ribs, scrape the fillet off the bones with a stroking movement. At the point where the rib bones end, ensure that the knife does not slip into the loin muscle underneath. Once you reach the rump (if not already cut off), the fillet head (called the chateaubriand) divides into 2 muscles. It is partly embedded in the pelvic bone. Just keep scraping the fillet head out of the pelvic bone as cleanly as possible until the whole fillet is removed.

NOW YOU CAN... PREPARE FILLET CUTS

Remove the chain steak—a long, slightly ragged muscle on the backbone edge of the fillet that runs most of its length. Trim off fat, gristle, and any bone shards. The fillet can be cut into pieces for roasting, or sliced into steaks.

Wing bones

1. DEBONE THE LOIN: First free the rib and wing bones. With the loin lying ribs uppermost, slide the knife underneath the cut rib ends and start to cut the meat off the bones using a stroking movement ("stroke" the knife toward you at this point). Lift up the rib bones to make it easier to take the meat off them.

2. REMOVE THE RIBS AND BACKBONE: Once you meet the backbone (vertebrae), turn the knife downward to keep taking the meat off the backbone. Watch out for the knobby sections that stick out from the vertebrae. Remove all the bones from the loin.

NOW YOU CAN... PREPARE LOIN CUTS

First trim the loin. Turn the meat so the skin is uppermost and cut off about 2cm (1in) of the dried-up edge and the strip of gristle that runs along the backbone edge. Angle the knife upward so that there is no danger of the knife making a downward cut into the eye muscle. Trim off excess fat. The boneless loin can be divided into roasts or steaks as wished. The muscle cap over the front part of the rib-eye (from the part where the ribs were) can be taken off and used as a thin deckle steak. If wished, the skin, fat, and all silver skin can be removed to make fully trimmed loin-eye roasts or steaks.

THE LEG, TOP BIT, OR HAUNCH

THESE SPECIES ARE LARGE, so the back leg is rarely cooked whole, or even on the bone. The main butchery task in this section, therefore, is deboning and dividing the muscle blocks into manageable sections to make steaks, roasts, stew meat and ground meat.

DEBONE THE LEG AND DIVIDE INTO 3 MUSCLES

You will need to remove the remaining piece of hip bone and shank first, and then remove the leg bone so that the three main muscles can be divided.

Ball end of leg bone

2. REMOVE THE SHANK: Cut through the white cartilage just after the shank muscle ends, about 2in (5cm) after it curves inward. Insert the knife into the cartilage to find the spot where the bones join and then slice through the cartilage. Cut the meat around the other side of the bone, then saw through the bone.

1. REMOVE THE HIP BONE AND TAIL FROM THE RUMP END: Lay the leg with the hip bone uppermost. Scrape away any fat and the thin layer of meat from above the hip bone. (The diagram shows this fat and meat already removed, the bone exposed, and the large ball end of the leg bone visible.) Cut in behind the sawed bone edge, as shown, and work carefully around it, keeping the knife against the bone. To make it easier to see what you are doing, push the meat away from the bone as you work. When you reach the ball-and-socket joint, pull the hip bone backward to expose the main tendon. You can use the steel to lever it back. Cut through the tendon and continue to cut around the hip bone until it can be removed.

NOW YOU CAN... PREPARE THE SHANK

For osso buco, cut through the meat around the bone in thick slices. Then saw through the bone. Remove the sawdust. Remove the thin, sharp bone next to the leg bone by feeling for it with your fingers, then work around it with your knife and remove. Discard the slices at either end. Alternatively, take all the meat off the bone then slice, dice, or grind. The thick knuckle bone makes good gelatinous stock.

3. START DEBONING THE LEG:
Divide the topside muscle from the thick flank at the natural seam that runs diagonally from one end of the leg bone to the other. It is visible on deer, but in beef it is covered with fat. The seam runs at an angle so tilt the knife to cut between the muscles, right down to the bone. Work around the bone to divide the topside from the thick flank. Use the table edge to help part the muscles. Part the seam carefully all the way down to the leg bone.

Thick flank

5. REMOVE THE BONE:
Keeping the knife edge next to the bone, scrape the topside away until the two bone ends are freed. Then scrape off the silverside muscle from the underside of the leg bone until it can be lifted out.

4. REMOVE THE THICK FLANK: As you scrape the thick flank off the leg bone, allow this muscle to bend over the edge of your cutting block, which makes it easier to see the thick silvery sheet of sinew on the silverside muscle. Part the thick flank from the silverside (located underneath the bone) by cutting it off at the kneecap cartilage, and set aside.

Topside

Silverside

Thick silver sinew

6. PART THE TOPSIDE FROM THE SILVERSIDE:
Look for the division between the topside (the cushion-shaped muscle on top) and the silverside. Using the tip of the knife, carefully part these muscles and peel back the topside, as shown. Once the topside has been peeled back, cut through the outer skin to remove it.

NOW YOU CAN... PREPARE BONELESS CUTS

TOPSIDE
The topside is roughly triangular in shape, with skin and fat on the outer edge and exposed meat on the cut sides. The thin outer cap of topside (or deckle) can be removed and used for frying steak. For boneless roasts, cut the topside lengthwise—with the grain—into several pieces, or slice it across the grain into steaks. Alternatively, it can be divided along the natural seam into a small and large muscle, which can be further divided if wished. Trim off excess fat and silver skin.

SILVERSIDE
The silverside has a thick, tough, silver sinew where it joins the thick flank. This must be removed. The silverside can be split into 2 separate muscles along the natural seam. The larger piece can be left as a roast or sliced into steak. The smaller muscle is called the salmon cut and makes a good roast, or can be cut into steaks. Trim off excess fat and silver skin.

THICK FLANK
Cut off the knee bone and gristle at the knuckle end. Lift off the thin cap of muscle that lies over the top. This is the tri-tip or cap of rump. The rest of the thick flank is made up of several muscles, which can be divided further if wished. It can be sliced thickly for braising steak, thinly for minute steak, or diced for stew. This muscle is very lean so makes extra-lean ground meat.

Thick flank

Silverside

Topside

Salmon cut

PLUCKING GAME BIRDS

WILD GAME VARIES IN THE WAY IT IS SHOT AND, IF IT IS BADLY DAMAGED, IT IS NOT WORTH PLUCKING THE WHOLE BIRD. INSTEAD, JUST REMOVE THE UNDAMAGED BREASTS. THE BIRD BEING PLUCKED IN THESE SEQUENCES IS A PIGEON.

SHOT DAMAGE

Look for signs where shot may have entered the flesh, and then try to locate the shot and remove it with a pair of tweezers. Often, a piece of feather will have been drawn into the hole with the pellet.

FEATHERS, BEAK, AND FEET

Tail and wing feathers are the toughest to remove. Waterfowl (duck and geese) have a layer of down underneath the feathers, which must be plucked after the feathers have been removed.

The bird's age affects how you prepare it. The beak and feet of a young bird are softer than on an old one and the feet can be easily torn

off. Also, the spurs on a male bird are short and stubby on young birds, but long and pointed on older ones.

PREPARATION TIPS

If working inside, make sure there are no drafts that could blow the feathers around. If you prefer to sit, hold the bird on your knee and pluck straight into a box or bag. Ruffle the feathers a bit to make them stand up on end. This makes it easier to grasp a few at a time. Some people prefer to pluck the breast and back before the legs. Either way is suitable, although the breast has the most delicate skin so extra care is needed to avoid damaging the breast while plucking the legs.

EQUIPMENT

- **Poultry shears or other strong shears:** for cutting off the wings and feet.
- **Pair of pliers:** for grasping the tail and wing feathers.
- **Plastic bin bag or large cardboard box:** for plucking into and catching the feathers.
- **Small sharp knife:** for cutting through the skin.

REMOVING THE BREAST MEAT

1. PLUCK A STRIP OF FEATHERS off the breast from vent to neck. This prevents the meat from getting covered in feathers. Insert a small knife just above the vent and, with the knife pointing away from the meat, cut the skin right up to the neck.

Lift the skin as you cut it to avoid slashing the meat

2. PULL THE SKIN BACK AS FAR AS IT WILL GO, right down to the legs and to the very end of the neck or wing end of the breast. Cut the breast down close to the breastbone. Turn it at right angles along the top of the chest cavity. Run the knife down the edge of the wishbone at the neck end and cut off the breast as far down toward the neck and wing as possible. The fillet (aiguillette) lies under the breast and should be removed with it.

The breast meat should be exposed right down to the neck

TIP

There is a sinew attaching the aiguillette to the carcass. To remove the sinew, hold it between finger and thumb and hold the aiguillette in the other. Pull back the sinew to remove it. This is much easier to do while it is still attached to the carcass.

PLUCKING AND DRAWING

1. START WITH A LEG, beginning at the foot end. Hold the foot in one hand and, with the other, pull the feathers away from the direction in which they lie, using short sharp tugs so as not to tear the skin. If it looks as though the skin might tear (or has already torn), very carefully pull individual feathers the other way (in the direction they are lying) and, with your other hand, hold down the skin so it can't lift up and tear.

2. PLUCK THE BACK, then under the wings, the breast, and about 4in (10cm) of the neck. Pluck these feathers in the direction they lie as this skin is more fragile.

3. PLUCK UP TO THE FIRST WING JOINT: Take the rest of the wings off with poultry shears or other strong shears. Pull the wing and tail feathers out, one by one, in the direction of growth. Pliers are helpful. To remove tiny feathers and long hairs, hold them over a candle or gas ring to singe them off. Avoid singeing off too much feather or the bird will taste of burnt feathers.

On smaller birds, you can cut off the whole wing

The crop contains the food the bird was eating

4. MAKE A CUT ALL THE WAY AROUND THE LEG at the foot joint, but only through the skin, not the meat or tendons. Bend the feet backward and forward (to loosen the tendons), then crack the joint until it snaps. Holding the drumstick in one hand, pull off the foot and the tendons from the leg. These may be tough.

5. CUT OFF THE HEAD. Pull the plucked skin toward the body so it is crumpled up. Then cut through the bone as close to the body as possible. You can fold the neck skin underneath for cooking.

6. FIND THE CROP AT THE HEAD END. Loosen it from the neck and body skin with your finger, pulling back the skin. The crop parts quite easily. Pull it out of the cavity and remove the gullet and windpipe as well.

Make the cut above the vent, not in it

The gizzard is tough (see p267 for how to prepare it)

7. LOOK FOR THE VENT and make a shallow cut around it, ensuring that you do not pierce the gut. Make a small slit about 1–2in (2–4cm) long in the skin above the vent up toward the chest to make a small hole.

8. INSERT 2 FINGERS UNDER THE CHEST, right up to the diaphragm, and draw out the entrails. The gizzard will come out with the entrails; the heart and liver afterward. The bird is now drawn. Pat the inside of the bird dry. If there has been any spillage of the gut contents, run water through the cavity to clean it thoroughly.

SKINNING SMALL GAME ANIMALS

THE SAME METHOD CAN BE USED TO SKIN AND CLEAN A RABBIT, HARE, OR SQUIRREL (THE SEQUENCE BELOW SHOWS A RABBIT). FOR INSTRUCTIONS ON DEBONING A RABBIT OR HARE, SEE PAGE 233. SQUIRREL, BEING SO SMALL, IS OFTEN COOKED WHOLE OR SIMPLY DIVIDED INTO LEGS, SADDLE, AND SHOULDERS.

RABBITS AND HARES are easy to skin since the skin comes off readily. Squirrel skin, on the other hand, is tough to remove so more knife work is needed.

If you shoot your own rabbit, hare, or squirrel, make sure you empty its bladder as soon as it is shot. This keeps the carcass cleaner.

Skinning and cleaning can either be done on a table or the draining board of a sink. Alternatively, hang the carcass head down, with the back

legs tied apart. It's a good idea to put some newspaper on the floor or table since there may be drips.

If the animal has already been gutted, follow the procedure below as far as step 5, but take extra care when pulling off the skin so that the meat is not ripped off as well.

Use the tip of your knife to start separating skin from meat. If the skin is very soiled, try to keep it from contaminating the meat. You will

need to trim off some of the edges of the stomach cavity and the cavity itself is more likely to be soiled, so be sure not to contaminate the meat while working.

Keep the blood of a hare to thicken the sauce used during cooking. It collects in the chest cavity. Place a bowl underneath the chest and add a tablespoon of vinegar to the bowl. This will prevent the blood from coagulating as it drains into the bowl.

Point the knife edge away from the meat

1. CUT A RING AROUND EACH BACK LEG ABOVE THE HEEL, being careful to cut the skin only, and not the tendon. Cut around the front paws in the same way. Make a slit down the ouside of one of the hind legs from the heel to the base of the tail. Once you have inserted the tip of the knife under the skin, keep the sharp edge pointing outward and downward (away from you) as you slide it under the skin. Cut the skin only, not the meat. Repeat with the other leg.

Make sure the skin does not rip at the stomach and genitalia

2. EASE THE SKIN AWAY FROM THE LEGS, using the tip of the knife to nick any sinew that is tough or threatens to pull the meat off with the skin. Pull the skin off the leg downward toward the tail and stomach. Repeat with the other leg. Make a slit in the fur at the base of the tail from leg to leg. Snap off the tail with your knife and make sure the skin is fully detached from the meat around the base of the tail. Ease off the skin around the genitalia; you may need to use the knife to sever the skin and avoid tearing the meat.

If the meat starts to tear, use the knife to free it

3. PULL THE SKIN OFF THE ENTIRE TORSO, turning it inside out.

4. EASE THE FRONT LEGS OUT OF THE SKIN, using the elbows to pull them out. Continue to pull off the skin until the head or ears prevent it from going any further.

5. CUT OFF THE HEAD WITH A KNIFE. Then cut off the paws and feet. Bend them backward to break the joint and use a knife to sever them. If the carcass is dirty at this point, wash it clean and pat dry before removing the guts.

Point the knife edge away from the guts

If the guts burst, trim off any contaminated meat

6. REMOVE THE GUTS by inserting the tip of your knife into the bottom of the belly cavity and, lifting it upward to avoid piercing the stomach contents, make a slit about halfway up to the chest.

7. INSERT YOUR FINGERS BETWEEN THE CHEST AND GUTS right up to the diaphragm, and gently pull the stomach contents out of the cavity.

8. CAREFULLY CUT THE GUTS AWAY around the anus. Discard the guts, genitalia, and bladder. Remove the heart, liver, and kidneys if wished. Without bursting it, cut off the bitter green gall bladder, attached to the liver. Pat the cavity dry. For hare only, place a bowl containing 1 tbsp vinegar underneath the chest cavity. Open the cavity and catch the blood in the bowl. Put the liver in the bowl with the vinegar and blood.

PREPARING AND MAKING SAUSAGES

Making your own fresh sausages is immensely satisfying and there are endless possibilities for flavor combinations. Omit the bread crumbs and oatmeal if preferred, and vary the spices and herbs according to taste. If you experiment with new recipes, cook a small sample of the mixture first, taste, and adjust spicing accordingly.

EQUIPMENT

Apart from knives and cutting boards, you'll need one or two special items. Suppliers of ingredients and equipment can be found online, as can second-hand equipment.

- **Grinder.** This can be hand-operated or electric, or you can use the grinder attachment for a food processor or mixer.
- **Large bowls** A plastic bowl, at least 5 quarts (5 liters) capacity. Anything that can chip is dangerous for mixing raw meat.
- **Large, deep plastic tray** For mixing spices into meats, and receiving sausages after filling into skins. The deeper they are, the easier it is to mix well.
- **Large funnel** A funnel must be fairly wide. You'll need a wooden or plastic stick to push the meat down into the skins.
- **Sausage filler**
- **Filling nozzles**

TABLETOP GRINDER
You can buy hand grinders that clamp onto a table, both with coarse and fine plates. Some can be used with nozzle attachments for filling.

FILLING NOZZLE
These are attachments for sausage-filling machines and grinders. Use different widths for the different sizes of skins. Two sizes will normally suffice.

SAUSAGE FILLER
Makes the job quicker and cleaner. Some food mixers have these as attachments.

GRINDING PLATES
A coarse plate chops meat. A fine one produces tiny pieces; grinding twice gives a very smooth texture.

LARGE FUNNEL
A large funnel is useful for filling skins if you don't have a sausage filler.

HYGIENE AND HEALTH

CLEANLINESS It is crucial that everything is kept both clean and cold when making sausages, especially if the sausage is to be eaten uncooked. The more meat is chopped or ground, and other ingredients added, the more high-risk a product it becomes. Wearing food-grade plastic gloves helps to prevent contamination.

STORING AND COOKING TEMPERATURES
Try to work in as cold an environment as possible, and refrigerate your sausages to below 40°F (4°C). Thorough cooking to a minimum internal temperature of 165°F (75°C) will destroy harmful bacteria. Use a meat thermometer to check the temperatures.

INGREDIENTS

Almost any ingredient can be used to make sausages. Using the best-quality ingredients possible will produce the finest sausages, and do make sure that all spices and herbs are as fresh as they can be, because they quickly lose their aromas and flavors as they age.

- **Meat** Shoulder is the preferred cut for sausages; it should be very fresh. Remove excess gristle and sinew, and any blood spots. If you do not have a grinder, buy ground meat and use it immediately.
- **Fat** This lubricates sausages and makes them taste good. Hard back fat is used for texture and in salamis; soft belly fat melts quickly, adding succulence. If no filler is used, the usual ratio is 1:4 fat to lean meat.
- **Spices** and **herbs** Use dried herbs for enhanced flavor and measure them accurately using one-third of the weight of fresh herbs.
- **Fillers** Using fillers makes sausages soft, and they allow the fat content to be reduced. Use dried bread crumbs, oatmeal, bulgur wheat, or rice. They should be as dry as possible.
- **Liquid** Adding some liquid (usually iced water) helps to ease sausage meat into the casings and reduces air bubbles. Wine or fruit juice add different flavors. Wine vinegar helps to ferment sausages.

SAUSAGE SKINS

Also called "casings," sausage skins come in many widths. Natural skins make the best quality sausages, as they are more resilient, easier to form into links, and do not toughen when cooked. They come either dry salted or in brine and need soaking. They are sold in bundles and by length.

HOG CASINGS are the most common kind of all. They are used to make chorizo, kiełbasa, and the thicker types of fresh or scalded sausages.

SHEEP CASINGS are more expensive, but are thin, strong, and make the most tender eating. They are used to make slim fresh sausages and Frankfurters.

COLLAGEN CASINGS Made from reconstituted cow hide, these casings don't need soaking but are harder to make into attractive sausages. They can toughen up a bit on cooking.

PREPARING AND FILLING SKINS

When making sausages for the first time, it is far easier (and more fun) to have two people: one to turn the filler handle; the other to hold the skins while they are being filled. It does become easier with practice! Don't worry if your sausages are misshapen, they will still taste delicious.

1 Soak salted casings overnight, or brined casings for 30 minutes, then drain. Run fresh water through them. Tie a knot in one end. Keep in cold water.

2 Open the unknotted end and slip it over the nozzle, pulling up the rest onto the nozzle. Keep damp. Squeeze out extra air or they could burst when cooking.

3 Holding gently but firmly, push in the meat. If it bursts, break the sausage and re-knot the end. For links or cooked sausages, don't fill too tight or they will burst.

MAKING FRESH SAUSAGES

This sausage is best suited to grilling or pan-frying. Use sheep casings if you would prefer to make thinner sausages. Wrap the sausages in plastic wrap, in convenient one- or two-portion amounts, before freezing.

MAKES

5½lb (2.5kg)

SPECIAL EQUIPMENT

Large 5–6 quart (5–6 liter) unbreakable mixing bowl

meat grinder

sausage filler

food grade plastic gloves

INGREDIENTS

2¾lb (1.25kg) lean pork

1lb 2oz (500g) pork belly

1lb 2oz (500g) pork back fat

3oz (85g) salt

1½ tsp dried sage

1 tsp ground nutmeg

½ tsp ground ginger

6oz (180g) bread crumbs or medium oatmeal

9fl oz (275ml) iced water

20ft (6m) of ¾–1½in (28–35mm) sheep or hog casings, soaked and one end knotted

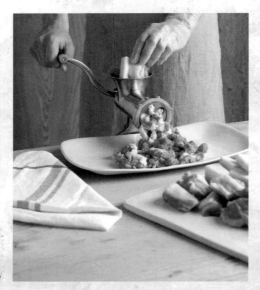

1 Chop the meat and fat into chunks, and chill thoroughly. Grind the meat and fat through a coarse grinding plate on to a deep, wide tray, putting alternate pieces of meat and fat through the grinder.

2 Mix the salt, herbs, and spices with the bread crumbs or oatmeal. Sprinkle this mixture over the ground meat and start to mix. Drizzle with the water and mix thoroughly to distribute the spices.

3 Test the mixture by making a small patty and cooking it in a frying pan, Taste to check if it is to your liking. If more spices are needed, add them and mix well.

4 Grind the mixture through a fine grinding plate. Fit a skin onto the filler nozzle and fill the sausages. Do not fill the skin too tight, or it will burst when making links.

FORMING COILS

5 Twist the end of the sausage to close it. Decide on the length you want each sausage to be and pinch the length at that point, easing the meat away to form a gap in the casing.

6 Twist the casing twice between the sausages. Pinch the meat again to form the next sausage, but twist the casing in the opposite direction so that the sausages do not unravel.

Forming a coil is most easily made with thin sheep casings. Start the coil in the center and wind the sausage around to the desired width, keeping it tightly coiled. Secure with a skewer for cooking.

FORMING RINGS

7 Continue along the length of the sausage skin. If air bubbles remain, pierce the skin at that point with a sterilized needle or toothpick. Check if any sausages are loosely filled. If they are, then push the meat away from the twist, and twist it again to tighten.

Leave 2½in (6cm) of empty skin at the end of each sausage and exclude all air. Make a knot at the end of each piece of skin. Bring the two ends together to form a ring, and tie them together. This shape is a common one for smoked sausages.

INDEX

Entries in **bold** indicate ingredients.

ACKNOWLEDGMENTS

ABOUT THE AUTHOR

Nichola Fletcher MBE is regarded as one of the world's leading authorities on meat. She pioneered the UK's first venison farm with her husband John more than 30 years ago, and is a writer, consultant, speaker, and course leader on all things meat-related. She has co-authored eight books, including *Ultimate Venison Cookery* (2007) and DK's *Sausage* (2012). An award-winning food historian, Nichola lives in Scotland, where she was awarded an MBE for her services to the venison industry in the 2014 New Year Honours list.

ABOUT THE RECIPE WRITERS

Christopher Trotter is a food writer, restaurant inspector, food consultant, and author of several cookbooks including *The Whole Hog* (2010) and *The Whole Cow* (2013). He runs bespoke cooking classes and food tours around his native Scotland, and appears on radio programmes talking about seasonal food. He is currently on the committee of the Guild of Food Writers.
Elena Rosemond-Hoerr is a writer and photographer, and the author of the award-winning blog biscuitsandsuch.com and DK's *The American Cookbook* (2014). A confirmed lover of pie, she lives on the North Carolina coast with her husband and two dogs.
Rachel Green is an award-winning chef, food writer, food campaigner, and TV presenter. She is a farmer's daughter from Lincolnshire and her family have farmed in the county for 14 generations. Rachel has cooked for Her Majesty the Queen and 800 guests at the Savoy Hotel, London, and her TV appearances include *The One Show*, *Countryfile*, *World on a Plate*, *Kill It, Cook It, Eat It!*, *Farm of Fussy Eaters*, and *Flying Dishes*. www.rachel-green.co.uk

NICHOLA FLETCHER WOULD LIKE TO THANK:

Ralf Lautenschlaeger in Germany for his help with European meat cuts; Stephen Rimmer in São Paulo for his help on meat cuts in Brazil; The Q Guild, and Jonathan Crombie from Crombie's of Edinburgh for advice on the naming of meat cuts in Britain; John Fletcher for veterinary and animal welfare advice; David Stewart for providing game; Quality Meat Scotland for their meat cutting guides; The Balgove Larder, St Andrews, for allowing us to invade their butchery and take photographs of their meat being cut. Most of all, Nichola would like to thank Graeme Braid, their master butcher, for going the extra mile to advise us on the home butchery section.

DK WOULD LIKE TO THANK:

Charlotte Tolhurst for new recipe photography; Stuart West and William Reavell for additional photography; Sara Robin, Geoff Fennell, Kat Mead, and Penny Stock for photography art direction; Fern Greene, Nancy McDougall, Rob Morris, Rebecca Rautner, and Isla Mackenzie for food styling; Matthew Ford and Lucy Pedder for food styling assistance; Wei Tang, Linda Berlin, and Tamsin Weston for prop styling; Adam Brackenbury and Tom Morse for image retouching; Sonia Charbonnier for technical support; Juliet Percival for the butchery illustrations and animal artworks; Harriet Yeomans for designing the butchery section; Jane Bamforth, Anna Burges-Lumsden, Jan Fullwood, Chris Gates, Anne Harnan, and Sue Harris for recipe testing; Kathy Woolley, Nidhilekha Mathur, Divya Chandhok, and Charis Bhagianathan for editorial assistance; Vicky Read, Laura Buscemi, Sourabh Challariya, and Aparajita Barai for design assistance; Claire Cross, Dorothy Kikon, Ligi John, and Janashree Singha for proofreading; and Vanessa Bird for the index.